Power Macintosh Programming Starter Kit

Power Macintosh Programming Starter Kit

Tom Thompson

Hayden
Books

Power Macintosh Programming Starter Kit

Library of Congress Catalog Number: 94-75236
ISBN: 1-56830-091-3

96   95   94   4   3   2   1

Interpretation of the printing code: the rightmost double-digit number is the year of the book's printing; the rightmost single-digit number is the number of the book's printing. For example, a printing code of 94-1 shows that the first printing of the book occurred in 1994.

*To my wife, Brenda Jean,
and my children, John and Evelyn*

The Hayden Books Team

Publisher: David Rogelberg

Managing Editor: Karen Whitehouse

Library Editor: Don Crabb

Development Editor: Brad Miser

Copy and Production Editor: Marj Hopper

Technical Reviewers: Richard Hooker,
IBM Microelectronics;
Alan Lillich,
Apple Computer, Inc.;
Mark Anderson, Metrowerks, Inc.

Cover Designer: Jean Bisesi

Interior Designer: Barbara Webster

Production Analysts: Dennis Clay Hager,
Mary Beth Wakefield

Production Team: Gary Adair, Brad Chinn,
Kim Cofer, Mark Enochs,
Stephanie Gregory, Jenny Kucera,
Beth Rago, Bobbi Satterfield,
Marc Shecter, Kris Simmons,
Greg Simsic, Carol Stamile,
Robert Wolf

Indexers: Michael Hughes, C. A. Small

Composed in: FC-Serifa, FC-Imago,
and MCPdigital

About the Author

Tom Thompson has a BSEE degree and bought his first 128K Macintosh in early 1984. He is a Senior Tech Editor at Large for *BYTE* Magazine and has been covering the Mac for over ten years. He is an Associate Apple Developer, and has substantial programming experience including several shareware utilities. He has also researched and written numerous articles on programming and hardware technology.

Overview

Contents

Acknowledgements

A book is a lot like a programming project. It involves a lot of people working in concert to achieve the final outcome—all on budget and on schedule. While publishing doesn't normally involve writing code and using debuggers, in some ways it is more work because you have to explain things in a way that makes the most sense to the most people. People are pretty imprecise beings, unlike computers. Of course, this is a programming book where you *do* have to write code, use debuggers, as well as try to make things sensible. It can be done, but not without the capable assistance of many good people whom I'd like to thank.

To David Rogelberg, Karen Whitehouse, and Brad Miser at Hayden Books for their faith that this book could be done, and for transforming my idea of a Power Mac Toolkit book into a reality. Thanks to Marj Hopper for making my prose sensible.

To Greg Galanos, Jean Bélanger, Dan Podwall, John McEnerney, Berardino Baratta, and the rest of the Metrowerks gang for providing timely support and updates to their excellent CodeWarrior software during the course of writing this book.

To Jordan Mattson at Apple for his support and access to PowerPC material.

To Eric Shapiro of Rock Ridge Enterprises for his valuable code contributions and suggestions. Eric taught me everything about 68K trap patching, and did it again for PowerPC trap patching. A lot of his code appears in the FlipDepth Extension shown in chapter 6, and he made many recommendations that improved the SwitchBank application. Without his efforts and timely support, chapter 6 would not have been possible.

To the technical reviewers, Richard Hooker of IBM, Alan Lillich of Apple, Mark Anderson of Metrowerks, and Don Crabb, for setting me straight on the facts of the PowerPC chip and the Power Mac system software. Special thanks to Randy Thelen for his insights into the Power Mac run-time architecture, which helped shape chapter 5.

Thanks to Steve Jasik for providing a copy of The Debugger, software that will really make a difference in debugging PowerPC programs.

Last but not least, to my wife, Brenda, who gave me her support, even through the many late nights I spent writing code and this book.

To Our Readers

Thank you on behalf of everyone at Hayden Books for choosing *Power Macintosh Programming Starter Kit* to enable you to begin programming for the Power Macintosh (even if you now only have a 68k Mac). We have carefully crafted this book and software to maximize your learning and hopefully, to provide long-term value for you.

What you think of this book is important to our ability to better serve you in the future. If you have any comments, no matter how great or small, we'd appreciate you taking the time to send us E-mail or a note by snail mail. Of course, we'd love to hear your book ideas.

David Rogelberg
Publisher, Hayden Books and Adobe Press

You can reach Hayden Books at the following:

Hayden Books
201 West 103rd Street
Indianapolis, IN 46290
(800) 428-5331 voice
(800) 448-3804 fax

E-mail addresses:

America Online:	Hayden Bks
AppleLink:	hayden.books
CompuServe:	76350,3014
Internet:	hayden@hayden.com

Dear friend,

Why did you buy *Power Macintosh Programming Starter Kit*?

Maybe you want to migrate existing Macintosh programs based on the older 680x0 Macs. Maybe you're considering programming the Mac for the first time now that Apple has made the jump to light speed with the PowerPC-based Power Macintoshes. Or maybe you're simply curious about doing your software development work on a Mac.

All of these are good reasons for buying this book, which was written by my good friend Tom Thompson. Tom, who has been programming and writing about the subject for more years than either of us cares to remember, is a senior technical editor for *Byte* and an unabashed Macintosh fan. Back in our salad days, Tom edited my Macintosh column ("Macinations") for *Byte*, a task that I'm sure shortened his life.

The point of this book is not to shove any single programming doctrine down anyone's throat. The truth is, there are a number of good programming environments and systems that are available (or will become available) that allow you to compile native mode Power Macintosh code on 680x0 Macs and on Power Macintoshes. Apple's own Macintosh Programmers Workshop (MPW) with its Power Macintosh Software Development Kit and other systems will do the job nicely for a number of folks.

Having said that, this book does take a stance—as any expertly written programming book ought to—that using the new CodeWarrior unified programming environment from Metrowerks makes a lot of sense for both migrating 680x0 Mac programs to the Power Macs and for creating new Power Mac software.

In fact, I happen to agree wholeheartedly with that sentiment. While I understand the power of MPW and its many tools and its flexible modular structure, I also love CodeWarrior's unified and lean approach—a love that Tom shares. CodeWarrior does a great job of taking the tedium out of the edit-compile-link-crash cycle of program development. While Tom's book will work well for folks who want to get an introduction to Power Macintosh programming, but who will eventually work with MPW, it really shines as a construction set for CodeWarriorites. That design is conscious and is reflected in the limited version of CodeWarrior included with the book, along with running versions of the sample programs Tom has developed for you.

I can't overrecommend this book. Frankly, I'm a little jealous that Tom could write such a technically excellent book with such smoothness and directness. Tom and I and the Hayden team of technical editors and programming experts have spent many extra hours ensuring that all the code examples are tight and error-free and conform to Apple's programming guidelines. As someone who has taught programming at the University of Chicago for nearly fifteen years, I am proud to have this book as part of the Don Crabb Library. Please feel free to let me know what you think, too.

Don Crabb
May 1994

Introduction

This book is a road trip. In it, you'll find information on Power Macs, RISC technology, and a C development environment by Metrowerks called Metrowerks CodeWarrior. You'll find an assortment of programming hints and tips and insights into how the Mac works, and you'll discover what new features—and pitfalls—await on the Power Mac. Most important, while I'll supply plenty of programming examples, I'll also explain how the Power Mac works. I firmly believe that if you understand how something works, you're in a better position to use it (or in the case of a personal computer, program it).

What You'll Need

My basic assumption is that you know how to use a Macintosh and have some knowledge of the C programming language. If you're not familiar with C, the best reference on this language is Kernighan and Ritchie's *The C Programming Language, Second Edition*, published by Prentice Hall. You should also have Apple's reference works on the Mac Toolbox, *Inside Macintosh*. Of course, you'll have a demonstration version of Metrowerks CodeWarrior because it's on the CD-ROM accompanying this book. If you don't have a Power Mac (yet), that's OK. Much of the material in here works with existing Macs as well, which is perhaps the real beauty of the Power Mac design.

I have structured this book so it offers material useful to both novices and experienced Mac programmers. The novice should begin at the beginning, but more experienced programmers should feel free to browse about and find a subject of interest. Consult the brief summaries at the beginning of each chapter to determine if the material is of interest to you. The following brief road map will help you decide *your* course.

The Road Map

Chapter 1 covers the Power Macs themselves, with a brief peek at the processor—the PowerPC 601—that gives these systems their great horse-power. It also discusses how these systems manage to run existing Mac software, thereby preserving that pile of Mac software you've accumulated over the years.

Chapter 2 provides a tour of Metrowerks CodeWarrior, Metrowerks' high-speed integrated development environment. Here, you'll be shown the environment's editor, compiler, linker, and project manager. When you write a C program, you must pick the version of CodeWarrior to create either 680x0 processor (68K) code or PowerPC (PPC) code. CodeWarrior can also generate a file with both PPC and 68K code types (called a *fat binary*). This feature enables your program to run on any Mac. This process of making a fat binary isn't automatic, but we'll show you how it's done in chapter 6.

Once you're familiar with the Metrowerks CodeWarrior environment, chapter 3 helps you write your first real C program. It won't have a friendly Mac interface, but it will perform a useful job. If you're new to the Mac, bypassing the user interface details for the moment limits the number of unknowns you have to deal with while you gain confidence with the development tools.

In chapter 4, you'll tackle some of those user interface details dodged in chapter 3. You'll add a friendly interface and discover the forked nature of Mac files. If you don't know what a Mac file's data fork and resource fork are, don't worry. This chapter will explain them to you. You'll also learn about resources (which, not surprisingly, reside in resource forks) and how to edit them for use in your program.

Chapter 5 is a rest stop on our journey. We will have reached a point where we must lay aside our tools for the moment and gain some insights into the Power Mac's new system architecture. I'll explain how Apple managed the feat where one set of source code can support two different processors. I go on to describe how the underpinnings of the Power Mac, as much as it resembles the 68K Mac on the surface, are fundamentally a different operating system. I'll explain what code fragments are, and what they mean to future application design. I also describe Apple's Mixed Mode Manager, the part of the operating system that manages to keep two wildly different sets of processor code—the 68K and the PPC—operating in harmony. It will be of general interest to most readers, and required reading for those writing special programs and extensions. Finally, I'll explain how both 68K and PowerPC code can be embedded in a single application file called a "fat binary," that's capable of running on either Mac. You'll use some of these details later when we explore certain Power Mac-specific features.

Chapter 6 is where you put into practice the information you learned in chapter 5. Most of this material will be of interest to advanced programmers. We'll write an application that controls the Mac's File Sharing software. This will require writing a function that works with the Mixed Mode Manager to enable a switch between 68K and PowerPC code. I'll also show how to make this application a fat binary, capable of running on both 68K and Power Macs. Next, we'll write an Extension that changes a Power Mac's screen depth. You'll see how to access code fragments. It also demonstrates how to patch the operating system, both for a 68K Mac and Power Mac.

In chapter 7, it's time to focus on how to fix a program that misbehaves. Information on the types of debuggers, and debugging tools can be found here. A look at CodeWarrior's high-level debugger is provided. Tips on debugging, and defensive coding are discussed.

For those who want a better understanding of the processor, Appendix A provides a look at the PowerPC family.

Appendix B consolidates information on how to port an existing Mac application's C code to the Power Mac. It will be of interest to advanced programmers who just want to dive in and start retooling their programs immediately.

Appendix C provides the complete source listings for the programs discussed in this book.

Appendix D tells you how you can locate more CodeWarrior and Power Mac programming information.

The Limited Verison of Metrowerks CodeWarrior on the CD

The version of Metrowerks CodeWarrior that is on the CD that came with this book is limited in that it can only work with the sample code also provided on the CD. Other than that limitation, it's functionality is the same as a full-fledged version of Metrowerks CodeWarrior.

This text of the book was written using the full version of Metrowerks CodeWarrior. You'll have to use slightly different steps when using the limited version on the CD. Since the limited version can only work with the sample files provided on the CD, the commands Add File... and New Project are not available.

So, if you are following along using the limited version of CodeWarrior that's on the CD, when the text tells you to use the New Project or the Add File... command, you should instead open the related project file and keep it open throughout the exercise. All the associated files will already be in the project and so you won't need the Add File... command. Then, you can follow the same procedures as if you were using the full version of CodeWarrior.

We've provided all the code discussed in the book on the CD, so you don't have to retype it, unless you find it valuable to do so.

You should also note that Metrowerks cannot provide technical support for this limited version. However, there is a way you can get all the CodeWarrior information you could ever want and also meet other Code Warriors. See Appendix D for details. Once you buy a full-up version for your very own, then Metrowerks will be happy to provide full technical support.

Additional Notes

There are probably better ways to write some of the functions presented here and I welcome input from you. However, the purpose of my code is to illustrate Power Mac features while being readable by an audience of C programmers with a wide range of experience. I also bias my code towards readability because, more often than not, six months later I usually have to modify the code for use in other projects.

While I've tried to produce error-free code, and I actually use some of these programs in my day-to-day work, it's possible that some of the code examples have bugs. Please send me bug reports via E-mail or some other means. If you have access to AppleLink, my E-mail address is T.THOMPSON, while on the Internet it is tom_thompson@bix.com. If you prefer a more conventional method, mail your comments and bug reports to me in care of Hayden Books.

Please note these signposts along the road as we travel.

Backround Info

Question mark icons flag sections of the book where additional background information can be found. For those unfamiliar with a topic, this extra information promotes a better understanding of the material. Seasoned Mac programmers can skip these sections.

Important

Exclamation point icons signal important topics. These sections provide information necessary to understand the material in each chapter, or illustrate an essential point on the software or operating system. Even seasoned programmers might want to examine these sections for Power Mac-specific details.

Hazard

Bomb icons signal potential hazards. These sections supply crucial information required to keep your program from crashing and your Power Mac system intact. Do not skip these parts of the book.

User input text appears in a bold monospace font, as in

Type **MyFile** and press Return.

Directives, routines, streams, and functions appear in a monospace font, as in

Before we call `Munge_File()`, we fetch the stopwatch cursor icon using `GetCursor()`.

Filenames appear in quotation marks, as in

For a complete source code listing, check the file "switchBank.c" on the CD-ROM.

This symbol ➡ has been used to represent program lines that have wrapped.

Well, enough preliminaries. Let's hit the road...

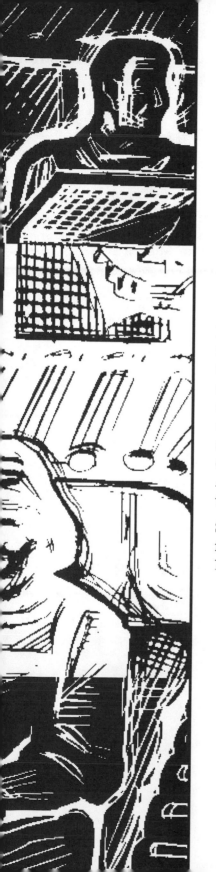

The Power Macs and a Brief History

In early 1994, Apple changed the face of the personal computer industry—again. The company took a powerful processor technology previously available only in expensive workstations and offered it to small businesses and average users through affordable desktop computers. Importantly, these low-cost computers won't run those arcane workstation operating systems. Instead, they offer an interface renowned for its ease of use: the Macintosh operating system, or Mac OS. Put simply, Apple has introduced a new line of high-performance Macintosh computers, the Power Macs.

Since these Power Macs borrow heavily from the Macintosh design, a brief history of the Mac itself is in order.

The Early Mac

Just a decade ago, Apple introduced its newest personal computer during the 1984 Super Bowl. This famous commercial, titled "1984" and directed by Ridley Scott, depicted a bleak, gray, future dystopia where shaven-headed drones shuffled toward the ultimate video conference. A runner—hammer held high and wearing an Apple logo on her shirt— raced onto the scene, hotly pursued by the faceless thought police. The hammer was hurled at the conference screen, shattering it. The implication was that Apple's then-new Macintosh computer would save us from that same gloomy fate. The verdict is still out on whether or not the Mac accomplished that goal, but no one disputes its effect on how we deal with computers and information. Desktop publishing, digital image editing, color printing, and other applications were either invented on the Mac or driven by the demands of its users.

The original Macintosh (now termed "classic Mac" in Apple's technical literature) was a small beige box with a 7.83 MHz 68000 processor. It came equipped with a built-in 9-inch black-and-white monitor, 128K of random-access memory (RAM), a single custom 3 ½-inch Sony floppy drive, two serial ports, and 64K of read-only memory (ROM). The classic Mac was a "closed system" since it offered no slots or easy expansion capabilities.

The Mac ROMs provided a large array of support routines that implemented the graphic user interface (GUI) and system services such as memory management and file I/O. These routines are known collectively as the Mac Toolbox. Since it is easier to use the Toolbox services than write code from scratch, the Mac has always encouraged a consistency in application design. Much of the Mac's "personality," or behavior, comes from these Toolbox routines.

Important

Because Toolbox routines are relied on heavily when writing a Mac application, expect to become familiar with them as you progress through this book. Keep *Inside Macintosh* nearby; those manuals provide important details on Toolbox routines. As you become comfortable with programming the Mac, you'll frequently consult them when writing new applications and adding features to existing applications.

Since well-behaved applications only access the system through the Toolbox interface, Apple has retained the option of significantly revising the hardware and software behind the interface without requiring modifications to existing applications. For example, a new Mac might use a new stereo sound chip, but your application would still use the same sound generation routines and be able to play music or sound effects on it. The Toolbox sound routines still present the same interface to the programmer, but the code underneath this interface layer converts your program's commands into a format the new hardware understands. This design eliminated many compatibility problems as Apple enhanced both the Toolbox routines and the hardware. Of course, not all compatibility problems were avoided, but Apple was able to limit them by using the Toolbox to define a "virtual machine."

Just as important, the Mac GUI helped enforce a consistency in the application's user interface, making Mac applications easier to use than those on other computers. Once you mastered one application, you knew the basics of using other Mac applications as well. To be sure, there were application-specific features you had to learn (text formatting in a word processor, or how to use a pen tool in a drawing package), but users didn't start over each time with the basics. They could always count on finding file manipulation commands under an application's File menu, and locating the editing commands in the Edit menu.

Faster and Better

Over the years, Apple improved the original Mac and introduced new models. First the company added more memory and a SCSI port. With the Mac II, Apple used the faster 68020 processor and opened the computer's closed design by adding NuBus slots. It introduced newer Macs with faster processors and a larger array of features. These machines went by such arcane names as the Mac IIcx, IIci, IIsi, IIvi, and IIvx. Apple minimized the confusion temporarily by giving certain product lines unique group names. The Mac notebook computers were labeled PowerBooks, and the first 68040 processor-based Macs were dubbed Quadras. Numbers were tacked onto the end of the names to help identify the characteristics of each computer. Still, things got out of hand. A mid-range line of Macs, labeled Centris, appeared and disappeared, being integrated into the Quadra product line. Apple introduced a Performa line of Macs, which were identical computers but repackaged for the home market. Mac system taxonomy and nomenclature began to require a scorecard—a very large one at that.

The Modern Mac

This brings us nearly to the present. Apple was feeling competitive market pressures to lower costs and improve performance. To reduce hardware design costs, Apple standardized most of its computers on three basic models.

- The first model uses a low, compact chassis with minimalist expansion capabilities to reduce costs. This design debuted with the Centris 610, followed later by the Quadra 610. It has a single Processor Direct Slot (PDS) that's connected directly to the processor bus. By use of an adapter, the PDS can accept one NuBus board.

- The second model is a desktop configuration that offers three NuBus expansion slots and more capacity for internal peripherals. This chassis was first introduced with the Mac IIvx and was subsequently used in the Centris 650 and Quadra 650 systems.

- The third model is a mini-tower chassis introduced with the Quadra 800 and followed by the Quadra 840AV. Like the second model, this tower system offers three NuBus slots. However, there's ample space for three to four large SCSI hard drives internally, plus a beefy power supply to support them.

All three models have a bay for adding an optional CD-ROM, other removable media drive, or a high-capacity hard drive.

In the area of performance, Apple had been investigating the use of RISC processors in future system designs. This research was evident in products such as Apple's 8·24 GC display board, which uses an AMD 29000 RISC processor to accelerate screen drawing. Also, the company demonstrated System 7, which was written for the 680x0 processor (henceforth known as the 68K processor), running in an emulator on a Motorola 88000 RISC processor.

Background Information

RISC is the acronym for Reduced Instruction Set Computing. This processor design achieves its high processing speed by implementing many simple instructions. These instructions are usually of a fixed length and execute very rapidly, usually one instruction for every tick of the system clock. This speed is accomplished by limiting what each instruction can do. For example, there is a handful of instructions that load data from memory to a register, or store data from a register to memory. All other instructions perform fast operations on the contents of the processor's many registers.

Also, these instructions are carefully tailored to minimize overlap between the operations of other instructions. This lets processor designers add execution units—subsections of the processor dedicated to a specific function, such as an integer math unit and a floating-point math unit—that can run in parallel and boost performance by executing two or more instructions simultaneously. As you might expect, simpler instructions require you to use more of them to implement a specific task, so RISC programs are typically larger than Complex Instruction Set Computing (CISC) programs.

We can contrast RISC processors with CISC processors like the Motorola 68K and the Intel x86 family. CISC uses variable length instructions to achieve high code density (that is, lots of instructions can be packed into a small amount of memory). These instructions, as their name implies, can perform a sophisticated set of operations and use a wide variety of addressing schemes. One instruction might perform an operation on a location in memory, then step to the next memory location. Another might retrieve a value from memory and then perform a math operation on it. While some of the simpler CISC instructions can be completed in one clock tick, many cannot. There are several reasons for this. First, because of the variable-sized instructions, the processor is forced to decode the incoming bytes to determine an instruction's length. This takes a clock cycle to perform the initial decode, and then the processor spends additional clock cycles reading in the rest of the instruction. Second, a complex instruction that modifies a memory location requires extra clock cycles to perform the bus operations necessary for the memory access.

Finally, the very complexity of CISC instructions often requires the implementation of a small internal processor—a processor within a processor, so to speak—dedicated to instruction decoding and processor control. This internal processor uses programs called *microcode* that perform the decode operations. Again, this additional layer of complexity requires extra clock cycles to shuffle instructions through the decoder and operate the microcode that translates the instruction bits into processor actions. Because of RISC's simple instructions, a sophisticated decoder isn't required: You won't find microcode inside a RISC processor. The RISC instruction decoder is implemented completely in hardware and runs at hardware speeds. It takes only several clock cycles at most to translate a RISC instruction into its corresponding actions. A RISC processor's performance is better than a CISC processor's because it can execute more instructions for a given set of clock cycles than the CISC processor.

If RISC technology is so much better than CISC, why is the latter so pervasive on desktop computers? RISC came onto the computing scene much later than CISC. RISC came out of research at IBM, Stanford, and Berkeley in the early 1980s, and wasn't commercialized until the middle of that decade. In contrast, Apple Computer sold its first microcomputer, the Apple I, in 1976. By the time RISC processor architecture appeared in the computing industry, CISC processor architecture had been in use for practically a decade.

While CISC has a big advantage in terms of an existing software base, RISC's performance edge should entice users to make the switch. RISC not only allows personal computers to run today's tasks such as spreadsheets, image editing, engineering simulations, and 3-D image rendering significantly faster, it also provides sufficient horsepower to enable a host of new system services and applications. Some of the new system services might include a robust, preemptive, multitasking operating system, integrated telephony and fax functions, voice and handwriting recognition, and speech synthesis. New applications would be real-time data processing, effortless 3-D image generation and manipulation, and all sorts of multimedia work.

Apple and IBM, Who Could Have Imagined It?

In 1991, Apple teamed up with Motorola and IBM to form an alliance to define the next-generation processor for future desktop computers. Despite the huge legacy of applications composed of CISC code on their respective platforms (Intel x86 code on IBM PCs and Motorola 68K code on Macintoshes), they decided that only RISC offered the necessary performance. Cost was an important factor here too: What hindered the acceptance of other RISC systems was the high cost of the RISC processor's fabrication, which in turn resulted in expensive computers.

The alliance is designing and producing a family of RISC processors to be introduced in stages. Each family member is targeted at a specific segment of the computer market. The first family member, the PowerPC 601, was introduced in April 1993. It's targeted at the low-end desktop market, but offers better performance than today's most advanced CISC processor, Intel's Pentium. In October 1993, the alliance introduced the PowerPC 603, a low-power sibling to the PowerPC 601. It is geared toward the notebook market. In April 1994, the PowerPC 604 was announced. Its high-performance design with multiple execution units addresses the mid- to high-range desktop market. Even faster PowerPC processors will be introduced over time.

The PowerPC 601 processor is a 32-bit implementation of the 64-bit PowerPC architecture around which these chips are designed. It has a high-speed 32-bit address bus and 64-bit data bus. Three independent execution units—an integer unit, a floating-point unit, and a branch unit—work in parallel to process as many as three instructions at once. A flexible 32K on-chip cache helps minimize execution stalls by keeping frequently used code and data in the cache rather than fetching it from slower main memory. To learn more about the PowerPC family of processors, read appendix A.

The PowerPC 601 (from now on, I'll just call it the 601) is the heart of Apple's new line of RISC-based Macintoshes. These systems, mentioned earlier, are called Power Macs to emphasize their performance. There are three systems, and each targets a specific user (see table 1.1). Each system is built around one of the three standard model designs discussed earlier. Each Power Mac comes equipped with a base 8M of 80 nanosecond RAM, a hard drive, built-in Ethernet, and 16-bit stereo sound hardware. Also bundled with these computers is AppleScript, a batch control language for automating certain tasks, and QuickTime Extension for multimedia support. An optional AV Technologies expansion board that provides video I/O and digital video capture can be plugged into the PDS slot on these systems. Bundled with the AV boards is the PlainTalk voice recognition software and the text-to-speech engine.

Table 1.1   An Overview of the Power Macintoshes

Power Macintosh	6100/60	7100/66	8100/80
Processor	PowerPC 601	PowerPC 601	PowerPC 601
Speed	60 MHz	66 MHz	80 MHz
Cache	optional	optional	256K standard
Performance		≈25% faster than 6100/60	Nearly 2x faster than 6100/60
Native apps	2 to 4x 68040 @ 33 MHz		
Emulated apps	fast 68030 to 68040		

Power Macintosh	6100/60	7100/66	8100/80
RAM	8M standard	8M standard	8M standard
DRAM expansion	72M	136M	264M
SIMM slots	2	4	8
Expansion Slots	One 7" NuBus	3 full-size NuBus	3 full-size NuBus
Storage			
Standard HD configs	160M to 250M	250M to 500M	250M to 1G
Floppy	1.4M with DMA	1.4M with DMA	1.4M with DMA
CD-ROM	Optional	Optional	Optional
Video			
DRAM video	Standard	Standard	Standard
VRAM video		1M standard	2M standard
VRAM expansion		2M	4M
Standard support	1 monitor	2 monitors	2 monitors
SCSI	High-speed asynch	High-speed asynch	High-speed asynch Dual SCSI channels
Networking			
	Ethernet on-board with DMA channel, AAUI connector		
Other built-ins			
	16-bit audio stereo in/out with DMA		
	2 Serial ports—LocalTalk with GeoPort compatible with DMA channel		
	Apple Desktop Bus (ADB for input devices)		

The Power Mac 6100/60 takes aim at the low-end user by providing a RISC-based Mac at a low price. It uses the Centris 610/Quadra 610 chassis and the 601 processor is clocked at 60 MHz. The Power Mac 7100/66 uses the Centris 650/Quadra 650 chassis. With the 601 clocked at 66 MHz and three NuBus expansion slots, this system should meet the mid-range computer user's needs. The Power Mac 8100/80 stakes out high-end users, with its processor clocked at 80 MHz for best performance. Its Quadra 800/840AV chassis contains ample room for several high-speed SCSI hard drives, and memory can be expanded up to 264M, which should satisfy the needs of the most demanding power user. Both the Power Mac 7100/66 and the 8100/80 provide a second monitor port, which you can use to expand the screen work area or to run a different operating system on the second monitor.

The number after the slash in each Power Mac's name denotes the speed of its processor clock. This naming scheme enables faster versions of these Power Macintosh systems to be shipped with the same name because only the trailing digits change. This arrangement eliminates a lot of the confusion created by the previous method in which minor changes to existing Macs begat whole new model names. It also explicitly states the processor speed, which is handy when comparing systems.

As nice as these systems are, you might suspect that there's a catch, especially regarding software compatibility. After all, didn't Apple and the others sacrifice the existing software base on the altar of performance? Apple tries to let you have your cake and eat it too by placing a 68LC040 emulator in the ROMs of these systems. This emulator is a sort of "virtual" 68040 processor that can execute the 68K code in existing Mac applications without modification, but this emulator doesn't support the 68040's floating-point unit (FPU) and memory management unit (MMU) instructions. (Only very eclectic utility applications would ever try programming a processor's MMU, and such code won't work anyway with the Power Mac's vastly different memory architecture.) The emulator is complete in every other detail so it can run the bulk of the existing 68K-based Mac applications and utilities. Lack of an FPU in the emulator may or may not be a problem, depending upon how smart the application software is in dealing with the machine environment. If the application simply expects an FPU, it will crash. Some applications detect the absence of an FPU, and either refuse to run, or will do their own computations in software. This slows down the application significantly, because such software computations run in the emulator. Those applications that use Apple's math routines will run somewhat faster, because portions of these routines were rewritten as PowerPC code.

One reason the emulator works is because of the virtual machine defined by the Mac Toolbox routines. Recall that Mac applications obtain system services (such as reading a file and drawing to the screen) through the Toolbox, and these Toolbox calls act as well-defined entry points into the operating system. What Apple accomplished with the Power Macs was to literally slide a RISC processor into the system and then use "native" (that is, PowerPC) Toolbox code to handle the application's requests. For example, the Mac OS provides a set of screen drawing primitives known collectively as QuickDraw. An application's drawing functions that use QuickDraw on a 68K Mac continue to work on a Power Mac without recompiling the application. That's because the Power Macintosh ROMs present an identical QuickDraw interface to the application, even though this QuickDraw is written in PowerPC code. Whatever application code isn't using the Toolbox gets executed by the emulator.

This is a simplified explanation of the situation, of course. The Power Mac's operating system has to know at any given moment whether it's emulating a 68K processor or running native PowerPC code. This is a serious problem because not only is the instruction set different, but the system environment for each processor is different. There are all sorts of system variables, arguments pushed on the stack, and other elements that have to be accounted for when execution switches from the emulated 68K processor environment to the PowerPC processor environment and back. A Mixed Mode Manager built into the ROMs along with the emulator manages this context switch. It keeps track of what processor environment the application is currently in, switches the context to the different environment when required, and makes any required adjustments between the two. Such adjustments might pass a drawing request to the native Toolbox code, while another adjustment might communicate the result of the request back to the calling program. For the most part, Mac programmers won't have to concern themselves with how the Mixed Mode Manager works, but there are exceptions. I'll cover them when we get into Power Mac-specific features in chapters 5 and 6.

For those of you still waiting to hear about a catch in this setup, here it is: The emulator—not surprisingly—musters only the performance of a fast 68030 or slow 68040 processor. Performance varies, depending upon how often the 68K application calls the Toolbox routines written in PowerPC code. Since Apple estimates that Mac applications spend 60 to 80 percent of their time in Toolbox code, it's possible that a 68K application runs faster than emulated speeds because it spends most of its time actually running native Toolbox code rather than running as emulated 68K code. The performance question is complicated by the fact that, for compatibility reasons and time to market issues, Apple hasn't yet ported all several thousand of the Toolbox calls to PowerPC code. 68K Toolbox routines that weren't ported get handled by the emulator. In some cases a call to the Toolbox might execute native code, resulting in a brief performance boost, while another Toolbox call might continue through the 68K emulator, for a performance hit. It's also important to note that the overhead of the Mixed Mode Manager handling numerous context switches can degrade performance.

So are these Power Macs faster or not? Yes, they're faster. The emulator and Mixed Mode Manager provide compatibility for existing software. They serve as a bridge that allows 68K applications to run until the real solution arrives: these same applications written in native code. For such native applications, the overhead of the emulator and Mixed Mode Manager practically disappears, with the exception of those Toolbox routines still implemented as 68K code. Over time, applications will run even faster as more of the Mac Toolbox is rewritten as PowerPC code. You can expect future releases of the Mac OS to replace more of the 68K portions of the Mac OS with native code, yielding better performance. However, early reports indicate that despite the mixture of 68K and PowerPC Toolbox code, Mac applications recompiled into native code run very fast on the Power Macs. On the low-end Power Mac 6100/60, such native applications run at Intel Pentium speeds. These same programs run nearly twice as fast on the Power Mac 8100/80.

Time for a Change (to Power Mac)

To make the switch to native Power Macintosh applications, programmers need development tools that can compile their existing application code into PowerPC code. While there are many different development tools available, the best possible situation would be tools that run on both 68K Macs and Power Macs. Source code that you wrote and tested on a 68K Mac could be copied to a Power Mac and easily recompiled, making the initial application port to the PowerPC a snap. (Note: those applications that are fine-tuned to the 68K run-time environment will require some adjustments or even a major redesign.) The result is a pair of applications, each of which runs on 68K Mac or a Power Mac. With some additional work, you could combine the code in these two applications to make a fat binary application, one that could run on both types of Macs. Or, if the target audience is just Power Mac users, you'd simply write your source code on the Power Mac to begin with. Application testing and maintenance would be further simplified if these tools also provided a source code level debugger.

Such development tools exist. It's time for you to meet Metrowerks CodeWarrior.

CodeWarrior:
A Guided Tour

This chapter provides a brief overview of software development, and introduces the CodeWarrior development tools. Intermediate and expert users can browse this chapter for specific features of the CodeWarrior compiler.

One of the most aggravating aspects of programming is the wretched edit-compile-link-crash cycle. You know how it goes: write the program source code, compile the source code, link any libraries to the resulting object code, run the linked program...and watch it crash. Next, you use the debugger to determine what caused the crash. Finally, you restart the computer and the cycle begins anew as you start editing the source code again. There's no escaping this development cycle for the moment, unless there's a huge breakthrough in software technology soon. (I'm not

holding my breath while I wait for that to happen.) The realistic solution is to make the development environment faster. A faster turnaround time on this cycle means the programmer, rather than waiting on a slow compiler or linker to run its course, spends the recovered time writing more code.

The code writing situation has improved dramatically with the introduction of integrated development environments (IDEs). An IDE combines all the development tools—editor, compiler, and linker—within a single application. With a keystroke or a menu choice, a built-in editor creates a new file window where you can enter a program's source code. Another keystroke runs the compiler on the source code, and yet another keystroke links the code and libraries. If you're feeling really brave, you can even launch the resulting application and test it. When you quit the application (assuming you don't crash), you land back in the development environment. These IDEs greatly accelerate the turnaround time in writing software, and such development tools have been wildly successful in the personal computer industry. The first IDE was Lightspeed C, pioneered by THINK Technologies, and introduced in 1985. (This was before the company was acquired by Symantec and the compiler was renamed THINK C. To minimize confusion, I'll call it THINK C from now on.) The PC has similar development IDEs.

Metrowerks CodeWarrior offers such an integrated environment. Metrowerks CodeWarrior is a software tool kit that features several utilities and a compiler that contains the IDE. If you've used an IDE before, especially THINK C's, then you'll feel right at home in CodeWarrior. For this book we're using the C compiler, but the CodeWarrior CD contains a Pascal compiler as well. For fans of Object Oriented Programming (OOP), CodeWarrior's C++ compiler is part of the C compiler. The Metrowerks CodeWarrior toolkit comes in several configurations. A Bronze package offers a 68K version of the compiler and produces 68K applications only. The Silver package has a fat binary version of the compiler. It generates PowerPC code. This compiler thus runs on either 68K Macs or Power Macs, but makes only PowerPC programs. The Gold package supplies both the 68K and PowerPC compilers.

CodeWarrior Requirements

One big advantage to CodeWarrior is its small memory and disk footprint. On a 68K Mac, the compiler requires System 7, a 68020 processor, 1.5M of RAM, and 7M of hard disk space, although Metrowerks recommends a 68030-based Mac and 5M of RAM for best performance. On a Power Macintosh, the CodeWarrior compiler requires 2M of RAM and 7M on hard disk. The compiler application, which hosts the integrated environment, weighs in at just under 1M. The usual army of header files, libraries, and the source code debugger application comprise the rest of the space. There's also an OOP application framework called PowerPlant and a Pane editor called PowerPlant Constructor. The latter lets you rapidly design parts of an application's interface.

Now that you know what CodeWarrior is, find out what it does. Take the CD out of the book and insert it into your Mac's CD-ROM drive. If you have plenty of room to spare, you can drag the entire contents of the CD-ROM to your hard drive. (If you're using a 68K Mac, you can follow along too. With a few exceptions, CodeWarrior looks and operates the same way on both computers.) Try to preserve the organization of the folders when you make the copy, because certain programs such as the Toolserver rely on this arrangement. The book also directs you to certain files based on this setup. If you don't have sufficient room, double-click on the Software Installer alias icon. After the Installer application launches, click on the Continue button to get past the trademark screen and read the notice for late-breaking information. Click on the Continue button again and choose the software you wish to install on your hard drive. Click on the Install button and pick a destination drive and folder in the window that appears. When the Installer finishes, click on the Quit button. Open the Metrowerks Tools folder for your type of Mac (68K or PowerPC), followed by the Metrowerks C/C++ folder. Now double-click on the Metrowerks C/C++ application icon to launch it and start touring the development environment.

Important

This text was written using the full version of Metrowerks CodeWarrior. You'll have to use slightly different steps when using the limited version on the CD; the limited version can only work with the sample files provided on the CD so the commands Add File... and New Project are not available.

So, if you are following along using the limited version of CodeWarrior that's on the CD, when the text tells you to use the New Project or the Add File... command, you should instead open the related project file and keep it open throughout the exercise. All the associated files will already be in the project and so you won't need the Add File... command. Then, you can follow the same procedures as if you were using the full version of CodeWarrior.

The Toolbar

After the compiler launches, the first thing you'll notice is the Toolbar, as shown in figure 2.1. This Toolbar serves double-duty as a command center and status indicator. The upper half of the bar has an array of buttons, each with its own icon. These buttons represent frequently used commands; clicking on a button with the mouse executes the corresponding command. It's pretty obvious as to what some of the icons do. For example, the printer icon represents the Print command, the scissors icon depicts the Cut command, and the paste jar icon signifies the Paste command. But what on earth does that cracked egg icon mean? It's easy to find out: just move the pointer to the icon and text explaining the command it represents—Disassemble, in this case—appears in the bottom half of the Toolbar. With this built-in self-reference, it shouldn't take you long to learn what each button does. If the text for the command appears italicized, it means that the command is disabled. Using the Disassemble command shown here as an example, the command isn't active because there's no file open; it has nothing to work with.

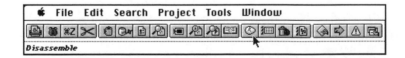

Figure 2.1   *The Toolbar*

The bottom half of the Toolbar is the status display. This is the area where either the command name for a button appears, as described above, or the current status of a development tool is indicated, such as searching, compiling, and linking.

Don't worry if clicking on buttons isn't your style. CodeWarrior uses good interface design and lets you work with it the way that suits you best. Those who prefer to point-and-shoot menu items can find all the Toolbar commands in the menus. If you'd rather keep your hands on the keyboard, there are keyboard equivalents for these commands. As always, you find these keyboard equivalents cross-referenced in the menus. If necessary, the Tools menu even lets you hide the Toolbar. Just think of the Toolbar as a container of frequently used commands that you have ready access to onscreen.

What if you don't like the commands in the Toolbar or the arrangement of the commands already there? No problem. You can customize the Toolbar to suit your needs. To rearrange the buttons, press Control and click on the desired button. A dashed outline appears around that button. Next, drag this outline to the desired spot on the Toolbar and release the mouse button. Your button appears in this new spot. The other buttons shuffle about to accommodate the button's new position.

If you don't like a certain command on the Toolbar, you can delete it by pressing Control-Command and clicking on the offending button. To add a command, press Control-Command while selecting it from a menu. Up to fifty-two buttons can be added to the Toolbar, although the limit actually depends upon the size of your monitor. The Tools menu has several commands that deal with the Toolbar. The Hide Toolbar command hides the Toolbar. The Anchor Toolbar command "anchors" (makes immovable) the Toolbar at the screen's upper left corner. Or you can unanchor the Toolbar so that you can drag it to a different location onscreen. The Reset Toolbar command restores the factory-default buttons in the Toolbar.

The Project

CodeWarrior manages software development through the use of a project. This is a special file that consolidates all the source, header, and library files used by your program. When you write a program in CodeWarrior, you first create a project file and name it. Once created, you can add source files and libraries to the project file.

Metrowerks CodeWarrior uses the project information to control the development environment so that it provides version tracking for the source files. Let's say you edit two out of many previously compiled source files in the project, and now want to create a new version of your application. The project knows to compile only the two altered files, while linking in the object code for the rest of the files. If you change a header file, the environment recompiles all of the source files which rely on that particular header file. This version tracking keeps all of the project's object code up to date, yet it does so efficiently by compiling only those files that require it.

With that in mind, give the Toolbar some company by creating a project. Select New Project... from the File menu. A Standard File dialog box appears. Type in a name, such as **foobar**, and press Return. A Project window appears, as shown in figure 2.2

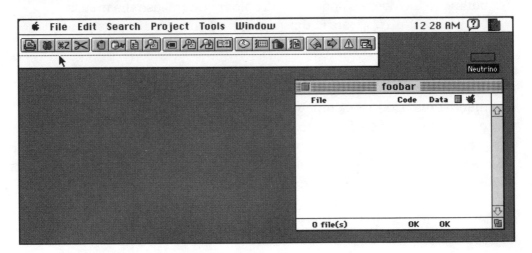

Figure 2.2 *The foobar Project window*

Looks pretty dull, doesn't it? That's because the Project window serves as a snapshot of a program's makeup. It normally displays a program's relevant source code files and any libraries used to make the program. Along with each source file and library filename is the size of the object code and data created by these files and information about whether each file contains segment and debug data. Because you've just created the project and there's nothing in it, the Project window is empty.

Liven up project foobar a bit. Go back to the File menu and select New. A window opens. This window belongs to the built-in editor and is called the Program window. To keep it simple, type in the C source to the well known "Hello world" program (see figure 2.3). Now select Save from the File menu to save this window as a file named **hello.c**.

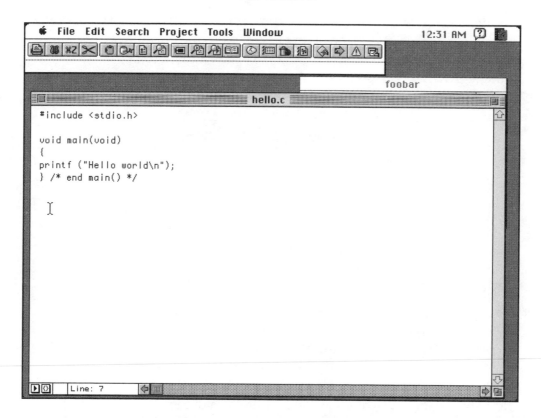

Figure 2.3   *A Program window with source code*

Now you'll add "hello.c" to the project. As you might expect, the Project menu has all sorts of commands that deal with projects. The Add Window and Add File... commands add files to the project and the Remove command takes them out of the project. The Compile command compiles source code files and adds the resulting object code to the project, and the Disassemble command disassembles object code files in the project. There are also some version control commands to either remove all object files (Remove Binaries) or make the object code of all modified source files current by compiling them (Bring Up To Date). There's a Make command that does a full-blown compile of all the source code files if required, and links the resulting object code and library files to create a Mac application. A Build Library command gives you the option of linking your code to generate a library file if you are distributing your own utilities or development tools. Finally, the Run command performs a make operation on your application and then launches it so that you can test it.

Back to adding "hello.c" to project foobar. Choose Add Window from the Project menu. This places the open file in the Program window—in this case, "hello.c"—into the project. Now take a look at the Project window (see figure 2.4).

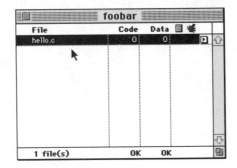

Figure 2.4 *The Project window with "hello.c" added*

The file "hello.c" appears in a slot (the dotted lines) in the Project window. Since the file has yet to be compiled, the sizes of the object code and data are zero. Now pick Compile from the same menu (or from the Toolbar). The built-in C compiler compiles the file. The Toolbar's status window will briefly flash a message telling you it's compiling "hello.c" and the object and data numbers will change. Select Run from the Project menu. The linker links the code again (CodeWarrior takes no chances) and a Message window appears (see figure 2.5).

The Message window shows errors and warnings detected by the compiler and linker. It looks like we forgot a library, doesn't it? Go back to the Project menu and add some libraries to the project. Use the Add File... command, which presents a Standard File dialog box that you use to maneuver into the ANSI folder and then into the Libraries folder. Choose the library file "ANSI C.PPC.Lib." (For a 68K Mac the path is the same, but choose

"ANSI (2i) C.68.Lib.") Now the Project window shows two filenames. For a 68K Mac, you're done, but for a Power Mac you need to add several support libraries. Two of these are located in the MacOS folder and then in the Libraries folder. They are called "InterfaceLib," and "MathLib." In the C++ Runtime folder is a small bit of code called "MWCRuntime.Lib." Again, use the Add File... command to put these files into your project. The object code for these files obviously hasn't been loaded into project foobar, because like "hello.c" previously, the size of each file's code and data are zero. Select Bring Up To Date from the Project menu and you'll see these numbers change as the libraries load (see figure 2.6).

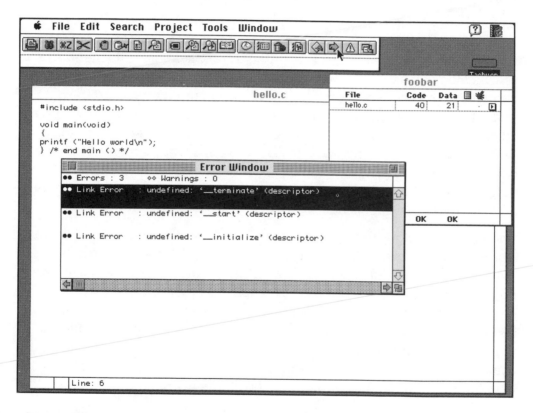

Figure 2.5   *The Message window displaying an error*

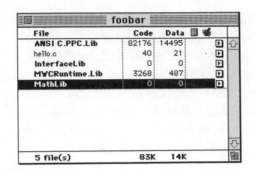

Figure 2.6 *The Project window with the source file compiled and libraries added*

Finally, you can choose Run from the Project menu and watch the program run. To exit the program, select Quit from the application's File menu. You'll see a dialog box asking if you want to save foobar.A.out (which is the contents of the screen). Click on the Don't Save button to discard the data and return to CodeWarrior. You'll notice that the default name of the application file just created was "foobar.A." Later, in the preferences section of CodeWarrior, you'll learn how to change the application's name. This was obviously a simple programming example, but it should give you a feel for maneuvering about in the CodeWarrior environment, setting up projects, and creating a Mac application.

The Project window helps you manage the project's files in various ways. Double-clicking on a file's slot in the window makes the editor open that particular file. If you click on the file's slot under the icon that looks like a bug, a dot appears. This informs the compiler that you want the file compiled with debugging information. Next to the debug icon is a small rectangle with lines, called the segment icon. It indicates whether the file has multiple segments. (You'll learn more about segments in a moment.) If you click on the small boxed arrowhead (or triangle) icon for the hello.c slot and hold down the mouse button, a small pop-up menu appears (see figure 2.7).

This pop-up menu shows what header files the compiler used while processing this file's source code. Picking a filename from this menu opens the header file for your inspection. At the top of this menu, a single menu item appears that states either "Has to be compiled" or Touch. The "Has to be compiled" item is just informative: you haven't compiled the file yet, or you've just made a change to the file that requires it be compiled again. As a Touch item, you can choose it to inform CodeWarrior that you want the file recompiled the next time the project is brought up-to-date, whether you've changed the file or not. Note that once you've "touched" a file, you can't unmark the file. For libraries, this pop-up menu will either state "Has to be compiled" if the library isn't loaded, or Touch if it is loaded.

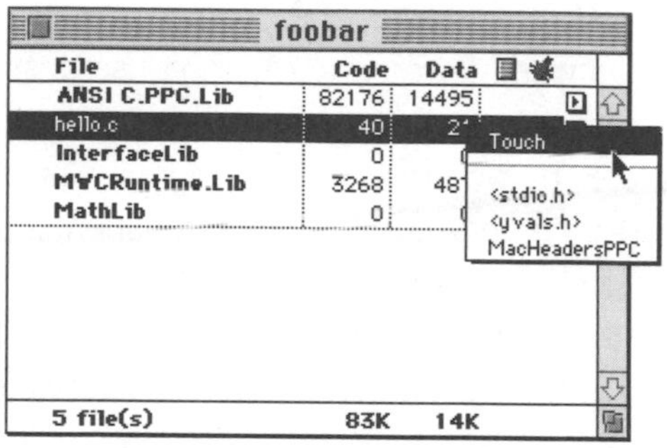

Figure 2.7   *The pop-up menu for "hello.c" shows the header files used*

On 68K Macs, you can click on the file slot in the Project window and drag it about. If you drag the slot beyond the dashed line of the bottom-most filename, you create a new segment (see figure 2.8). This allows you to visually arrange your source files into the code segments you want; the linker will handle the details of building the code segments when it creates the application. You can also use the #pragma segment directive to define segments in your 68K source code. If you do this, in the Project window a dot appears under the segment icon in the file's slot, which indicates that the source file has multiple segments.

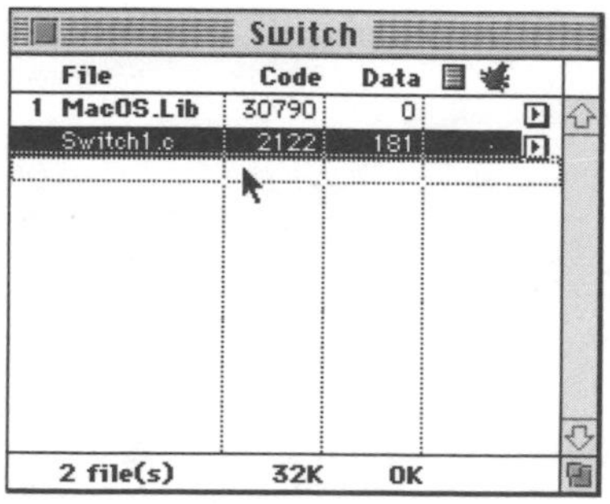

Figure 2.8   *Segmenting a 68K Mac program by dragging a filename*

Background Info

On 68K Macs, object code can be combined into chunks called segments. Segments came about because early Macs required program code to be in small pieces that could be brought into or removed from memory as required. With 128K of RAM, the operating system had to shoehorn code into any spare opening it could find in memory. These openings might appear at different memory addresses as code was loaded and purged while the Mac application ran. For this technique to work, program code can't use absolute addressing schemes, but instead uses PC-relative addressing. PC-relative addresses are calculated by using the current address in the Program Counter (PC), plus an offset value. This enables the code to be position independent and loaded into any part of memory. The size of these offsets for PC addressing was limited by the classic Mac's 68000 processor to only 16 bits. (Actually, the processor used a signed two's complement value. The sign of the value pointed to the next address's direction, relative to the PC. A positive value pointed forward to higher addresses, while a negative sign pointed backward to lower addresses. Because it was a signed value, only 15 bits were actually used for the offset value.) This limited code segments to 32K in size. Later Macs used the 68020 and successive processors that had a 32-bit offset value, effectively removing the 32K size limitation on segments. Nevertheless, for compatibility with 68000-based Macs, and to operate efficiently within limited memory, most programmers still segment 68K Mac code. This isn't an issue for Power Macs, because pieces of 601 code, called *code fragments*, can be any size. A Power Mac application is usually a single code fragment, although it might obtain code or data from other code fragments.

Figure 2.9 summarizes the Project window's functions.

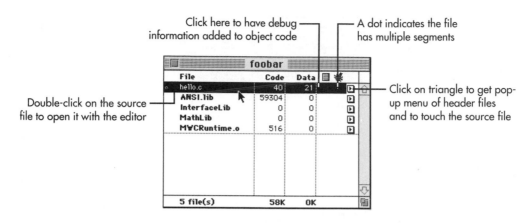

Figure 2.9 *How to use the Project window to manage project information*

The Editor

Since you'll spend most of your time entering and modifying source code in the built-in editor, Metrowerks has added a number of features to make your stay a pleasant one. Let's check out the editor by opening one of the sample project files on the CD-ROM. Go to the FlipDepth folder and open the file "Klepto.π." After the Project window opens, double-click on a source file slot Klepto.c to open the file with the editor. (Such filenames end with a .c extension. You can't open a library or object file with the editor.) A Program window appears, displaying the file's source code (see figure 2.10).

Two icons are in the bottom left corner of this Program window. The first icon is a triangle, and looks similar to the one in the Project window. Sure enough, if you click on it and hold down the mouse button, a pop-up menu appears, containing the names of all the header files used by the file (see figure 2.11).

You can scroll through the names and open the desired header file by selecting a filename from the menu. The item at the very top of this Triangle menu is either Touch or "Has to be compiled." These items operate the same way as in the Project window. The Triangle menu thus provides a convenient way to access certain project management functions when a Program window hides the Project window.

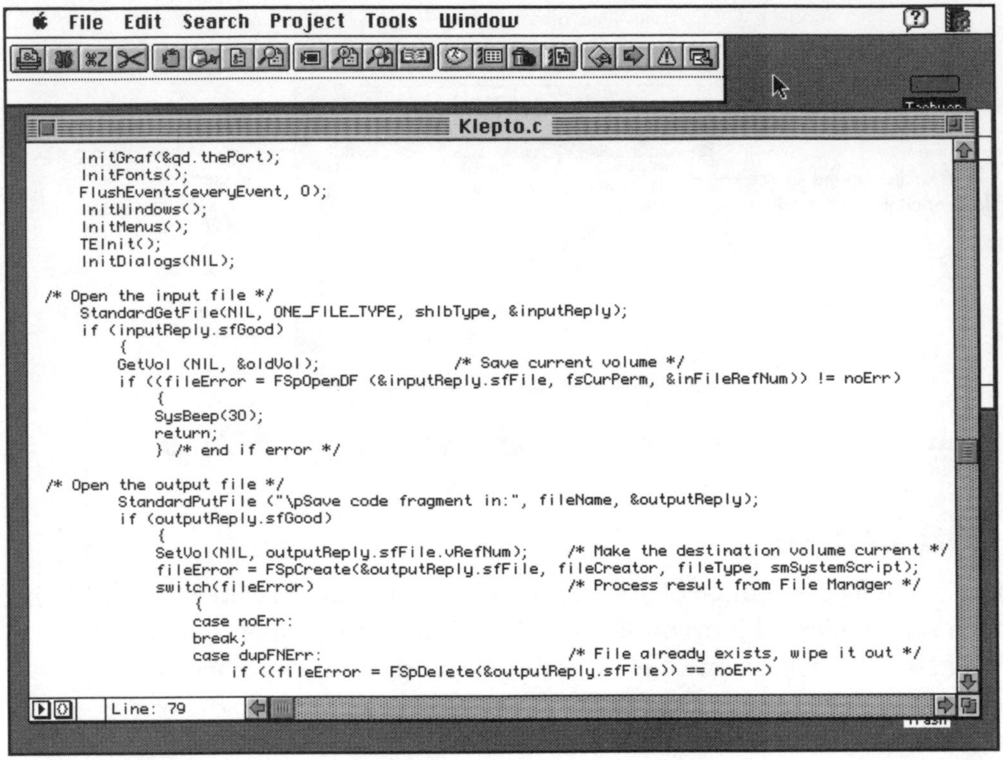

```
 File  Edit  Search  Project  Tools  Window                    ?

 ═══════════════════════════ Klepto.c ═══════════════════════════

      InitGraf(&qd.thePort);
      InitFonts();
      FlushEvents(everyEvent, 0);
      InitWindows();
      InitMenus();
      TEInit();
      InitDialogs(NIL);

  /* Open the input file */
      StandardGetFile(NIL, ONE_FILE_TYPE, shlbType, &inputReply);
      if (inputReply.sfGood)
          {
          GetVol (NIL, &oldVol);               /* Save current volume */
          if ((fileError = FSpOpenDF (&inputReply.sfFile, fsCurPerm, &inFileRefNum)) != noErr)
              {
              SysBeep(30);
              return;
              } /* end if error */

  /* Open the output file */
          StandardPutFile ("\pSave code fragment in:", fileName, &outputReply);
          if (outputReply.sfGood)
              {
              SetVol(NIL, outputReply.sfFile.vRefNum);    /* Make the destination volume current */
              fileError = FSpCreate(&outputReply.sfFile, fileCreator, fileType, smSystemScript);
              switch(fileError)                          /* Process result from File Manager */
                  {
                  case noErr:
                  break;
                  case dupFNErr:                         /* File already exists, wipe it out */
                      if ((fileError = FSpDelete(&outputReply.sfFile)) == noErr)

  Line: 79
```

Figure 2.10   *The Program window*

The Braces icon next to the Triangle icon is another pop-up menu, called
the Function menu. When you click on the Braces icon and hold down the
mouse button, a pop-up menu appears and displays all of the C functions
the file uses (see figure 2.12). If you Option-click on this icon, the function
names appear in alphabetical order. A checkmark by the function's name
indicates that this function has the editor's insertion point located in it. If
you pick a function name from this menu, the editor takes you to that
function, with the first line of its source code appearing at the top of the
Program window. This is very handy when you're tracking down a Toolbox
routine and happen to know the name of the function that uses it. Note that
the editor's insertion point doesn't move when you jump around the file this
way. To avoid editing mishaps, be sure to click on a source line when you
land in the desired function.

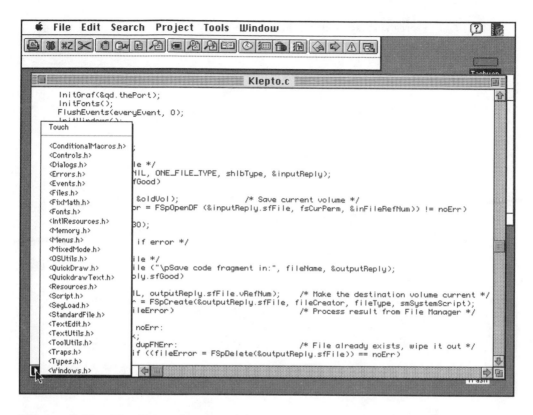

Figure 2.11 *The Triangle pop-up menu presents a list of header files used by the file*

The editor also has a comprehensive set of search functions that let you locate something by name. For example, if you know only the routine name, pick Find... from the Search menu. A Find window appears, where you can type in the routine name (see figure 2.13). You can search multiple files, such as the header files or the source files in your project. You can perform a search on a name and replace it with another name, an action called search and replace. It's valuable when you want to replace all occurrences of, say, the Toolbox routine `NewWindow()` with `NewCWindow()` in your program.

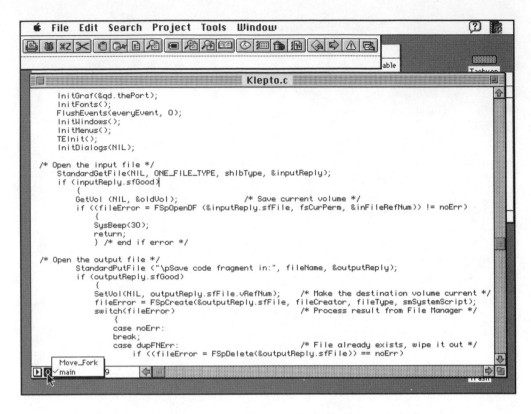

Figure 2.12 *The Function pop-up menu lists all of the file's functions*

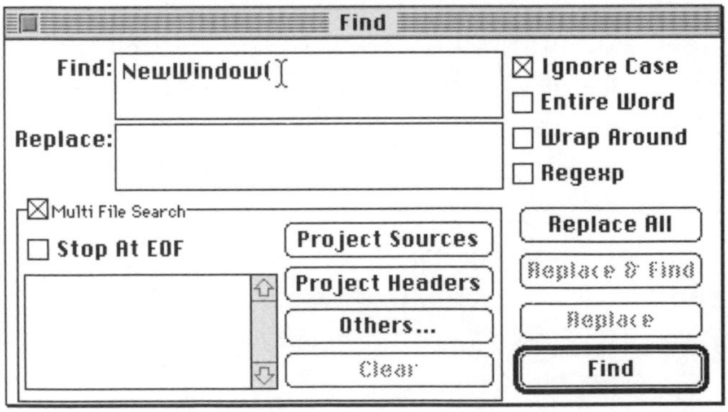

Figure 2.13 *The Find window*

Further along the bottom of the Program window, past the Triangle and Function pop-up menus, is an area that indicates the editor insertion point's location by displaying the appropriate source code line number. If you click on this area, the Go To Line Number dialog box appears (see figure 2.14). When you enter a new line number here and click on the OK button, the editor insertion point and the Program window display are moved to the desired line. This go to capability is helpful when the Message window gives you an error message with a line number. A useful shortcut that jumps you to the problem source line is to double-click on the error message in the Message window.

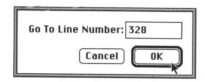

Figure 2.14   *The Go To Line Number dialog box*

Keyboard mavens can maneuver through the source code using the arrow keys. Move the editor insertion point one character left or right using the Left and Right Arrow keys and one line up or down using the Up and Down Arrow keys. Using the Option key with the Left and Right Arrow keys moves the insertion point left or right by a word. If you use the Command key with these arrow keys, the insertion point is placed at the start or end of a line. When you use the Option key with the Up and Down Arrow keys, you move the insertion point up or down one "page," or screen, of text. The Command key, when used with these keys, moves the insertion point to the beginning or end of the file.

If you have a color monitor, you can set the colors of the C language key words (the default is blue) and of the comments (the default is red) in the source code. Coloring the key words helps you quickly spot a particular key word as you scroll through the code. Coloring the comments helps you identify chunks of source code peppered among lengthy comments in the file. (You are going to comment your code a lot, right?) It also helps you spot those early morning coding gaffes where you accidentally forget to close a comment and thus inadvertently comment out dozens of lines of source code.

The editor automatically scans your code as you enter it, watching to see if you balance your bracket characters. Bracket characters consist of the parentheses ( ), the square brackets [ ], and the braces { }. If you add a surplus right bracket character, the editor triggers an alert sound. You should note that this scan function operates only after the source code is saved to a file and that surplus left brackets are not detected. If you don't like the editor beeping at you, this feature can be disabled with the Preferences... command. Finally, if you need to know where the file you're editing is located on the Mac's hard drive, press the Command key and click on the Program window's title bar. A pop-up menu shows the complete pathname of the open file.

Figure 2.15 summarizes the features of the Program window.

Command-click here to display this file's pathname

```
                          Switch1.c
    MoreMasters();
    MoreMasters();
    MoreMasters();
    MoreMasters();

    InitGraf(&qd.thePort);
    InitFonts();
    FlushEvents(everyEvent, 0);
    InitWindows();
    InitMenus();
    TEInit();
    InitDialogs(0L);
    InitCursor();

    initStatus = TRUE;   /* Assume successful setup (for now) */
    for (i = APPLE_MENU; i <= LAST_MENU; i++)
        {
        myMenus[i] = GetMenu(i);
        if (myMenus[i] == NIL)
            return FALSE;
        }; /* end for */

    AddResMenu(myMenus[APPLE_MENU], 'DRVR');   /* get DA */

    for (i = APPLE_MENU; i <= LAST_MENU; i++)
        InsertMenu(myMenus[i], 0);
    DrawMenuBar();

    if(!Init_AE_Events())   /* Set up our high-level event handlers */
        return FALSE;
    Get_Depth();            /* Get machine's video info, load variables, and setup */
                            /*   Periscope menu */

    return initStatus;
```

Line: 624

Click here to jump to a new line

The Function menu displays the functions in the file

The Triangle menu displays the header files used by this file

Figure 2.15 *Features of the Program window*

The Compiler and Linker

The built-in C compiler is unobtrusive. It doesn't have windows like the built-in editor, yet at the click of a button or keystroke, you summon it to compile your source code. On large projects, you'll see status messages in the Toolbar that indicate it's busily processing header and source code files. If your code passes muster, values change in the Project window. If not, the compiler opens the Message window and drops error and warning messages into it. Ditto for the linker: It quietly does its job and either an application file pops into existence or warnings appear in the Message window. This isn't to say these two tools in the IDE aren't important. They're absolutely crucial to generating the end result, the finished Mac application. Because the project file keeps track of all the relevant information—source files, header files, libraries, and whether these files are current—all the compiler and linker really have to do is the follow-up work of translating source code into object code and linking the object code into an application file.

Nevertheless, there are situations when you want to exercise control over what the compiler and linker do. For example, you might want to generate code for a shared library instead of an application, or have the linker add debug symbols into the resulting application. But if the compiler and linker have such low profiles, how do you get at them to change their behavior? You do this through the Preferences settings. Since these Preferences also touch on the operation of other parts of the IDE we'll briefly review all the preference settings.

Preferences

Start by selecting the Preferences... command from the Edit menu. The Preferences dialog box appears (see figure 2.16). In the left side of the window is a scrolling list of icons. Each icon represents a certain portion, or group, of the environment. Select the group whose settings you want to change by scrolling through this icon list with the mouse and clicking on the group's icon. Each group has a unique panel in the Preferences window that controls a number of adjustable settings. Figure 2.16 shows the panel for the Font group.

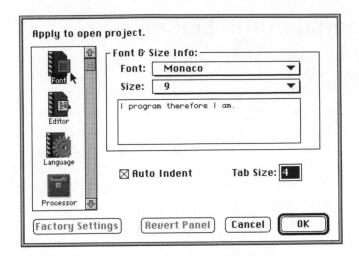

Figure 2.16 *The Preferences window, showing the Font group panel settings*

At the window's bottom are four buttons: Factory Settings, Revert Panel, Cancel, and OK. They operate as follows:

■ The Factory Settings button takes all the settings of the chosen group and restores them to the default values suggested by Metrowerks. You'd use this button if you suspected that one of the group settings you changed might be causing a problem.

■ The Revert Panel button undoes any changes you made to a group's panel. Unlike the Factory Settings button, Revert lets you preserve the current group settings. For example, say you've already got your custom Linker group preferences set up properly. You happen to be examining the Linker group panel and accidentally click on a checkbox. Revert discards the last change, without wiping out the rest of the settings.

■ The Cancel button closes the Preferences window without saving any changes you made to a group's settings.

■ The OK button saves the changes you made to the group settings and closes the Preferences window. You can make changes to one group and scroll to another group panel to make changes before clicking on the OK button. For certain groups, you get an alert window warning you that to use these new settings, you have to recompile or relink the project's files. The Factory Settings and Revert buttons dim or undim depending upon whether the current group preferences match that button's settings.

Let's complete our tour by examining each group's preference settings. In figure 2.16, the Preferences window displays the Font group's current settings. This adjusts the font used in the Program window. One pop-up menu selects the font while the other pop-up menu selects the size.

The Editor preferences, as its name implies, adjusts the built-in editor (see figure 2.17). Change the color of comments or keywords by clicking on their respective color bar in the panel. This action opens the Color Picker window, where you select another color. The Dynamic Scroll checkbox determines how text scrolls when you move the scroller (or thumb) on a Program window. Save All before "Run" determines whether all modified source files are automatically saved before CodeWarrior builds and launches your application. It's a good idea to check this setting since the application might cause a crash severe enough to force you to restart the Mac—you'd like to have the last file changes saved to disk in this situation. The Remember settings tell the editor how to precisely reproduce the Program window when you open a file. The Projector Aware setting is for use with Apple's Projector, a version control application.

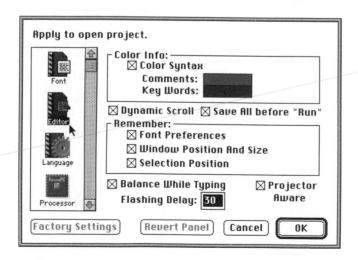

Figure 2.17   *The Editor preferences group*

The Language preferences group determines how the compiler handles your source code (see figure 2.18). The Source Model pop-up menu lets you select Custom, ANSI C, ANSI C++, Apple C, or Apple C++ (the latter two settings allow for language extensions added by Apple to support the Mac Toolbox). The appropriate Language Info options are checked automatically when you make a choice from this pop-up menu. The Custom setting is selected when you pick Language Info settings that don't provide compatibility with the ANSI standard. The Prefix File option lets you select or deselect a file that contains a precompiled set of header files. The default is MacHeadersPPC (or MacHeaders68K), which is a Metrowerks-supplied file with a subset of precompiled System 7 header files.

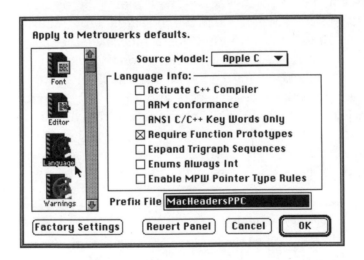

Figure 2.18   *The Language preferences group*

The Warnings Info group lets you set how strict or lax the compiler is with the language (see figure 2.19). Depending upon the settings you make, the compiler can ignore the vagrancies of code written at 2 AM, or notify you of "dead code" (that is, code that's not used by the function). I prefer to check the Extended Error Checking item, as it provides a modest amount of sanity checks on my program code.

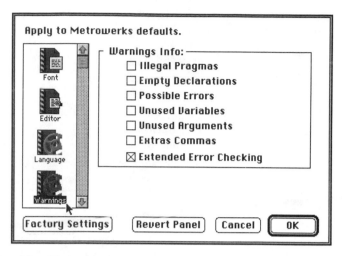

Figure 2.19   *The Warnings preferences group*

The Processor preferences group is shown in figure 2.20. The Power Macintosh settings are displayed. The Struct Alignment pop-up menu lets you pick 68K, 68K 4-byte, or PowerPC memory alignment for the data structures used in your program. Use the first two settings if you plan to make an application to run on both Power Macs and 68K Macs. Make String Literals ReadOnly determines whether character strings are stored in the program code (which are marked read-only in code fragments). The Generate Profiler Calls has the compiler generate code that supports code tracing for the purpose of measuring a program's performance. The other options adjust optimization settings. The Optimize pop-up menu tells the compiler to optimize for size or speed. On a 68K Mac, you'll have a different Preferences panel where you can set optimizations and designate what type of processor code is generated (68000, 68020, and 68881 floating-point instructions).

The Linker preferences group determines how Power Mac code is linked (see figure 2.21). The Link Options settings determine whether symbol table and address map files are created (which are useful for debugging), supress warning messages (necessary for certain types of code), and whether the linker operates out of memory. The Entry Points settings are for the code fragment's initialization function, its main() function, and a completion function. You'll typically leave these settings alone. The 68K Mac linker group panel lets you add debug information to the executable code, generate symbol table files, and indicate whether or not you want to create multi-segmented code.

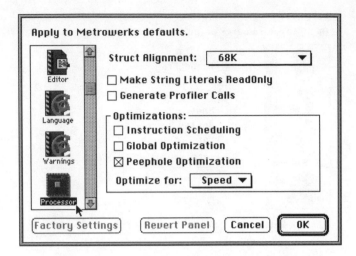

Figure 2.20   *The Processor preferences for a Power Mac*

The PEF (Preferred Executable Format) preferences group panel (see figure 2.22) determines whether or not the code fragment that makes up your application exports symbols and shares code or data. The default settings in the pop-up menus are for a typical Mac application, and like the PEF group, just leave them alone for now. The 68K Mac version of CodeWarrior doesn't have a PEF group at this time.

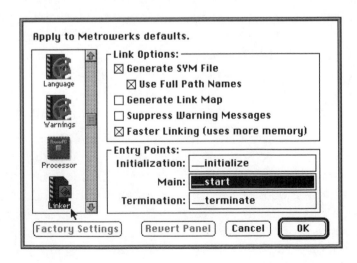

Figure 2.21   *The Linker group preferences for a Power Mac*

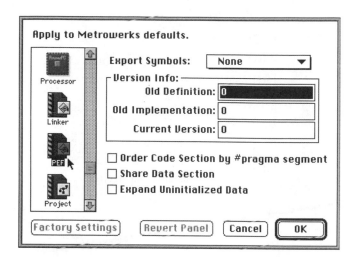

Figure 2.22 *The PEF group preferences for a Power Mac*

The Project preferences group panel (see figure 2.23) is where you'll spend most of your time. Here's where you set the type of code you generate (Application, Shared Library, Code Resource, or Library) in the Project Type pop-up menu. This is also where you set the creator and type of the resulting file produced by the project and choose its name. Finally, you indicate the amount of memory the application requires and its SIZE flags using the SIZE Flags pop-up menu. The operating system uses the SIZE flags to determine what sorts of events the application responds to and whether it can operate in the background. Some special-purpose applications, such as File Sharing, can only operate in the background and there's a special flag for that here as well.

Finally, the Access Paths group settings, as shown in figure 2.24, let you select additional folders for the compiler and linker to search. They normally only search the Metrowerks folder and your project folder for any header, source, and library files. Access Paths lets you redirect the search path of these tools to other folders when looking for project files. This is handy in situations where certain project files might be located on a server for version control. To do this, click on the Add button and use the Standard File dialog box to navigate and select other folders. The Change button lets you alter existing search paths and the Remove button deletes folders from the search path.

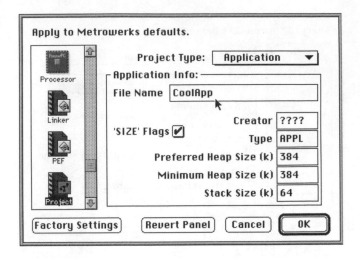

Figure 2.23   *The Project preferences group for a Power Mac*

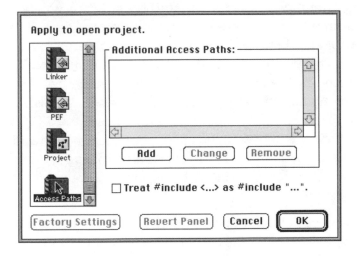

Figure 2.24   *The Access Paths group preferences*

The Tour's Over

In this chapter we've looked at some of the features of CodeWarrior's IDE. We've even run the "Hello world" program, to see how you build a project, and ultimately an application, in CodeWarrior. This tour has not covered all of the features Metrowerks CodeWarrior has, but it has touched on the significant ones. We'll use this knowledge to build a practical C application on the Power Macintosh—starting in the next chapter.

Beginning Programs

This chapter is for the novice programmer. It shows you how to use the ANSI C Standard Libraries supported by the Metrowerks C compiler to do simple tasks on the Mac. The interface for these programs won't be pretty, given that the ANSI Libraries stem from UNIX's character-based heritage. The goal here is not appearance, however, but function. These libraries provide a safety net that you can rely on as you explore the Mac's Toolbox and operating system.

As an aspiring Mac programmer, you've no doubt heard this often-quoted maxim about the Mac: "Easy to use, hard to program." Why is this? If you've already leafed through the half-dozen or so volumes of *Inside Macintosh*, you may even know the answer to that question.

Out of this wealth of information, where do you start? Put another way, how do you determine which Toolbox calls to use when starting an application and which ones to call in order to access services provided by the operating system?

About the Toolbox

The Mac Toolbox and operating system provide over four thousand routines at your disposal, of which about several hundred are commonly used. The Mac is a complex gestalt of these routines and data structures that you must understand fairly well in order to write a program. How do you know which routines to use? After all, you must understand how to initialize the application's environment so that these routines function, how to plug the application into the operating system so that it coexists and cooperates with fellow applications, and last, but not least, how an event-driven interface works. This seems like a rather dismal attitude to take for a book on Mac programming, but I'd rather you appreciate that there's a lot to learn just to get started in Mac programming, than get frustrated and give up entirely.

> **Background Info**
> So that we won't get confused later when I start talking about calling functions, we'll make a distinction between those functions our program uses, versus those belonging to the Mac Toolbox/OS. Following *Inside Macintosh* conventions, I'll use the term *routine* to indicate Toolbox functions.

Having said that, now I can say it's not impossible to learn how to program the Mac. The trick is to limit the unknowns you're dealing with so you can break the job into smaller, manageable portions. Fortunately, Metrowerks CodeWarrior itself provides a way to limit the problems you face, as you'll see in a moment. Another way to deal with some of the unknowns is to have plenty of source code examples handy. This way you can learn how particular routines operate and when to use them. I'll help you here by supplying some working code examples.

Munge It

I firmly believe in learning by doing, so let's start by solving a problem. One of my jobs as a technical editor is to take manuscripts and edit them. I clarify certain points in the manuscript, reorganize the flow of thought, request missing material, and perform other editorial tasks. I receive these manuscripts as ASCII text files sent via electronic mail (E-mail) on the Internet or other online services. Ideally, I get a manuscript file and simply start editing it in a word processor. In reality, sometimes there are problems.

Most word processors, both Mac and PC, use a carriage-return (CR) character to end a paragraph of text. This allows the word processor to neatly "wrap" or fit the text on the screen as you add or eliminate words inside the paragraph. However, some word processors save the text with CRs at the end of each line. The text looks fine—until you have to change the manuscript using a different word processor. Because of the extra CRs, the word processor can't wrap the words, and you wind up with a mass of jumbled text. The author probably meant well, but the editor now has to laboriously prune those spare CRs from the text, line by line. This type of file is a headache for me to edit.

After hacking away at one long manuscript for over an hour, I decided that this chore was a great job for the Mac to handle. I'd write a Mac program to munge, or hack out, those extra CRs for me. Basically, the program would read an input file, filter out most of the CRs, and write the rest of the data to an output file. Thinking more along the lines of how the computer has to do it, the program reads a byte—or character, actually—from the input file, examines the byte, and if it passes muster (it's not a CR), writes the byte to an output file. If the byte is a CR, it's tossed into the bit bucket instead. If the program detects the end of a paragraph (a double CR, or a blank line), then the end of paragraph (the double CR) is written to the output file. This makes the resulting output ASCII text organized the way a word processor expects it. Stated this way, the problem seems easy enough.

Now here's where CodeWarrior helps. Metrowerks CodeWarrior supports the ANSI C Standard Library, which is based on the UNIX C function libraries. These libraries supply functions that handle file I/O and provide an interactive console where you enter commands and get screen output. Since these functions were originally implemented on old UNIX systems, they typically deal with character-based I/O. This doesn't make for a nice Mac interface, but it lets you concentrate on the problem without having to learn lots of Toolbox routines all at once.

> **Important**
> CodeWarrior's console I/O provides support for the C Standard Library's **stdin**,
> **stdout**, and **stderr** streams. It opens a virtual console window where all these
> streams are directed. The console window is set up and managed by
> CodeWarrior's SIOUX (Simple Input/Output User eXchange) library, which is
> automatically linked to an application when you add the ANSI C library (ANSI.lib)
> to the project.

Getting Started

Let's get started by launching the CodeWarrior C compiler. The easiest way
to do this is go inside CodeWarrior folder, open the Code Examples ƒ folder,
followed by the Munger ƒ folder, and double-click on the file "munger.c."
CodeWarrior launches, and you should see the following code:

```c
#include <stdio.h>

#define CR 0x0D
#define LF 0x0A

FILE *istream, *ostream;

void main (void)
{
short   crflag;
long    icount, ocount;
char    ifile[64], ofile[64];                    /* Path names must be 64 chars or less */
int     nextbyte;

printf ("Enter input file: ");
gets (ifile);
if ((istream = fopen(ifile, "rb")) == NULL)      /* Open the file OK? */
    {
    printf ("\nError opening input\n");          /* NO, say so */
    return;                                      /* Bail out */
    } /* end if */
```

```
printf ("Enter output file: ");
gets (ofile);
if ((ostream = fopen (ofile, "wb")) == NULL)          /* Can we write an output file? */
    {
    fclose (istream);                                 /* NO. First close input file */
    printf ("\nError opening output\n");              /*   then warn, and bail out */
    return;
    } /* end if */


icount = 0L;          /* Set counters */
ocount = 0L;
crflag = 0;

/* Read char.s until end of file */
while ((nextbyte = fgetc (istream)) != EOF)
    {
    icount++;                                         /* Bump input char counter */
    switch (nextbyte)                                 /* What char was read? */
        {
        case CR:
        if (crflag >= 1)                              /* Two in a row, end of paragraph */
            {
            fputc(nextbyte, ostream);                 /* Write two CRs to the output */
            fputc(nextbyte, ostream);
            crflag = 0;                               /* Reset the flag */
            ocount++;
            } /* end if */
        else
            crflag++;                                 /* Bump the flag, and toss the CR */
        break; /* end case CR */
        case LF:                                      /* Toss LF, but don't touch crflag */
        break; /* end case LF */
        default:
            fputc (nextbyte, ostream);                /* All other char.s get written */
            ocount++;
            crflag = 0;                               /* Clear the flag */
        } /* end switch */
    } /* end while */
fclose (istream);                                     /* Clean up */
fclose (ostream);
printf ("Bytes read:    %ld\n", icount);
printf ("Bytes written: %ld\n", ocount);
} /* end main () */
```

Let's take a closer look at this code.

The Code Tour

The munger program first prompts for an input file name, using the printf() function to put a message in a console window made by the C Standard Library. It uses gets() to read the keyboard when you type in a filename and press Return. Your input is placed in the array ifile. Note that ifile and ofile are sixty-four characters long. If you're opening files with either long names, or the file is in a folder with a long name, you need to increase these array sizes so that the pathname fits.

Background Info

A *pathname* is the complete description of the directory path used to locate a file. For example, if the Mac's hard drive is named Tachyon, and a file "Read Me" is in the folder New Info *f*, the pathname for the file is Tachyon:New Info *f*:Read Me. This convention is similar to DOS/Windows pathnames, but instead of a backslash (\), the Mac OS uses colons as separator between the drive, folder, and filenames. This is also why you can't use a colon in a filename.

Next, the program uses `fopen()` to open the file:

```
if ((istream = fopen(ifile, "rb")) == NULL)      /* Open the file OK? */
    {
    printf ("\nError opening input\n");          /* NO, say so */
    return;                                       /* Bail out */
    } /* end if */
```

Note that we check to see if this open operation fails. If it does fail, the program halts. With the minimalist input provided by the C Standard Library, it's quite possible for you to mistype the filename, which creates an error condition when `fopen()` fails to open the file. The program then uses similar code to set up the output file and checks for trouble as it does so. This is a good time to emphasize that no matter how simple or complex your program is, always, ALWAYS, *ALWAYS*, check for errors. You can eliminate a lot of crashes, trashed hard disks, and needless debugging by having your program determine if the routines it calls complete successfully.

The heart of the program is the `while` loop, which reads a stream of bytes from the input file and processes them. The `switch` statement inside the loop determines the fate of the byte under scrutiny. Any character other than a CR or linefeed (LF) falls through to the default `case`, which writes the character to the output file. Since I get lots of files from PCs, and DOS ASCII text files use a LF-CR combination to end each line, the program also filters out any LF characters it happens to find in the character stream. The program handles this filtering operation with the LF `case` statement, which simply does nothing, and as a consequence the LF never gets written to the output file.

Now to those CRs, which are handled by the `case` statement:

```
case CR:
if (crflag >= 1)                          /* Two in a row, end of paragraph */
    {
    fputc(nextbyte, ostream);             /* Write two CRs to the output */
    fputc(nextbyte, ostream);
    crflag = 0;                           /* Reset the flag */
    ocount++;
    } /* end if */
else
    crflag++;                             /* Bump the flag, and toss the CR */
break; /* end case CR */
```

The program logic works on the assumption that most folks separate paragraphs with a blank line. This means that the last line of the paragraph ends with a CR, which is followed immediately by a blank line composed of a second CR. So when the program encounters the first CR character, it gets tossed into the bit bucket and the flag `crflag` is incremented. If a character other than CR is read next, the program clears `crflag`. This handles situations where the CR just terminates a line of text. Notice the exception here: A LF character doesn't reset `crflag`, since it occurs jointly with the CR in DOS files. When a second CR in a row occurs because of a blank line, the `if` statement detects that `crflag` is set. The code now writes two CRs to the output file to ensure the line break between paragraphs. Of course, we clear `crflag` to begin the search for the next paragraph ending.

Finally, the program closes both files and writes a summary to the console window of the bytes read and written, as tallied by the counters `icount` and `ocount`. Since the program's function is to throw away bytes, fewer bytes should have been written than read. It's not necessary to do this, but the summary serves as a sanity check on the program's operation, which is reassuring to me. It's possible to defeat the paragraph detection logic by submitting an ASCII text file with no blank lines between each paragraph, but I can add thirty to seventy blank lines to a manuscript within minutes, while manually stripping CRs from over several hundred lines takes up to an hour.

Important

This text was written using the full version of Metrowerks CodeWarrior. You'll have to use slightly different steps when using the limited version on the CD; the limited version can only work with the sample files provided on the CD so the commands Add File... and New Project are not available.

So, if you are following along using the limited version of CodeWarrior that's on the CD, when the text tells you to use the New Project or the Add File... command, you should instead open the related project file and keep it open throughout the exercise. All the associated files will already be in the project so you won't need the Add File... command. Then, you can follow the same procedures as if you were using the full version of CodeWarrior.

Making Munger

Let's make this file munging program. We've opened the file "munger.c," so the next step is to make a project for it. From the File menu, select New Project..., type **Munge.π** (you get the π character by typing Option-P) for the project name into the Standard File dialog box that appears, and press Return. There's an informal convention where you denote a project file by attaching either a .π or .prj extension to the name. This naming convention isn't required, but if you're working with other programmers or plan to share code with other users, it helps identify the project file for them. Now choose Add File... from the Project menu. In the Standard File dialog box that appears, locate the file "munger.c" and click on the Add button (see figure 3.1).

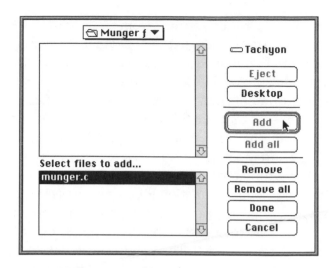

Figure 3.1 *Adding "munger.c" to a project*

The Add button dims, and next you click on the Done button. The source
file "munger.c" is added to project Munger.π. Since we're adding files to the
project, let's finish up by adding the library files. Again, using Add File...,
select the files "InterfaceLib," and "MathLib," from the path
CodeWarrior:MW C/C++ PPC *f*:MacOS *f*:Libraries *f*, "MWCRuntime.Lib"
from the path CodeWarrior:MW C/C++ PPC *f*:C++ Runtime *f*, and "ANSI
C.PPC.Lib" from the path CodeWarrior:MW C/C++ PPC *f*:ANSI *f*:Libraries *f*.
Once you've collected all these files, click on the Done button and these
files appear in the Project window (see figure 3.2).

File	Code	Data		
InterfaceLib	0	0	▣	
MathLib	0	0	▣	
munger.c	0	0	▣	
MWCRuntime.Lib	0	0	▣	
ANSI C.PPC.Lib	0	0	▣	
5 file(s)	OK	OK		

Figure 3.2 *Adding the library files to project Munger.π*

We're not done yet. Select Preferences... from the Edit menu. Scroll to and click on the Language group icon. In the panel that appears, click on the checkbox for Require Function Prototypes (see figure 3.3). This setting demands that you declare each function, specifying the function's number and type of input arguments and the type of the result (if any). This can catch potential problems that can occur when you call the function with a set of arguments different from what it expects. This might happen because you're modifying the function, or inadvertently passed the function an argument of the wrong type, as when you call a Toolbox routine. In either case, checking Require Function Prototypes nails this error at compile time. Otherwise, when the program runs, such improper function calls might cause a crash. I also delete the MacHeadersPPC precompiled header filename from the Prefix File Item. This is because my work often involves parts of the Mac OS that aren't normally in the precompiled header file.

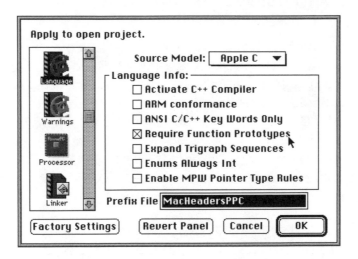

Figure 3.3 *Setting the Language preferences for project Munger.*π

Next, go the the Warnings group and click on Extended Error Checking. Like Require Function Prototypes, we actually don't need this setting for this project, but since both enforce good programming practices, you ought to get into the habit of setting them now. Extended Error Checking uses stricter rules when compiling the C code, flagging code goofs such as unused variables.

Now scroll to the Linker group icon and click on it. In this group's panel, go to the Entry Points section. We're just going to check the default functions that get called when our program initializes, starts, and exits. These functions, which are part of the Power Mac run-time architecture, get called when a native program launches and quits. For the Initialization item in this panel, you should see the __initialize function name. The Main item has a function name of __start. This function is responsible for calling our program's main() function. The Termination item (see figure 3.4) has the function name __terminate. For typical C programs, __initialize and __terminate do nothing. For C++ programs, __initialize sets up any static C++ program's objects, while __terminate destroys these static C++ objects.

Finally, go to the Project panel and type **Munger** for the application name into the File Name text box (see figure 3.5) and click on the OK button. Click on the Toolbar's Make button or select Make from the Project menu, and let CodeWarrior go to work on the project. If there are no problems, processing statements from the compiler and linker briefly appear in the Toolbar's status area. An application named Munger is created.

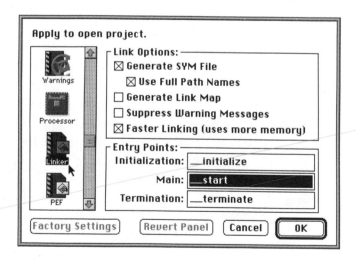

Figure 3.4 *Setting the Termination entry point for the project*

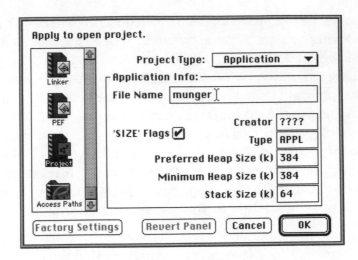

Figure 3.5 *Setting the name of the application file that the project makes*

Running Munger

Suppose that on a Mac hard drive named Tachyon, in the CodeWarrior tools folder called CodeWarrior *f*, that there's a folder named Code Examples *f*, followed by a folder named Munger *f*. Inside it is a text file called "PowerPC.txt." Suppose "PowerPC.txt" is loaded with surplus CRs. First, open the file in MacWrite Pro and examine the file with the Show Invisibles set in the View menu. Show Invisibles displays all the characters in the file—including invisible control characters such as CR—instead of just text characters. In figure 3.6, you can see that each line ends with a small bent arrow symbol; they represent CRs. If you don't have MacWrite Pro, don't worry: other word processors can also display such "invisible" characters. Check the documentation for your word processor for details how to do this.

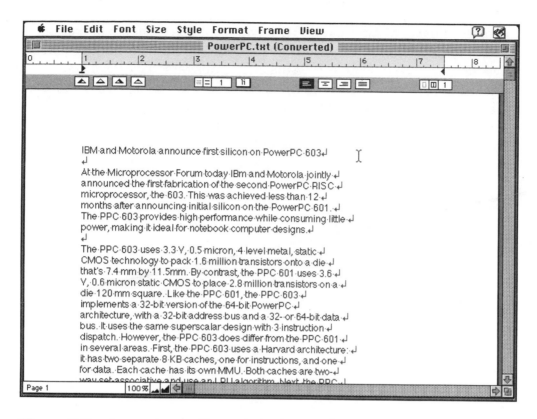

Figure 3.6 *A sample text file, with CRs at the end of every line*

It's time to set "munger" to work on this file and see what happens. Launch "munger" from Metrowerks CodeWarrior by clicking on the Run button in the Toolbar. A console window called munger.out appears. Type in the pathname to the sample text file we examined earlier as follows:

Tachyon:CodeWarrior ƒ:Code Examples ƒ:Munger ƒ:PowerPC.txt. Of course, if your hard drive name and CodeWarrior tools folder are named differently, you'll type in the appropriate names into the pathname. If you goof on the filename, "munger" complains and the program stops. If the filename is OK, "munger" asks for an output filename. Type in a filename that uses the same file path, such as **Tachyon:CodeWarrior ƒ:Code Examples ƒ:Munger ƒ:PowerPC.out.** Press Return and "munger" processes the file. You'll get a summary of the operation, as shown in figure 3.7. The munger.out console window remains present, and you have to pick Quit from the File menu to leave "munger." When you do so, a dialog box appears that asks if you want to save munger.out's contents. Click on the Save button if the console window's output is important to you. Otherwise, click on Don't Save to discard the console window's output. This feature enables you to capture the output of a job as required. For lengthy pathnames, as in our example, the SIOUX console window lets you copy and paste characters. You only have to type the pathname in once for the input file prompt, select this text with the mouse, copy, and then paste the bulk of the pathname into the prompt for the output file pathname. Now all you have to type is the output filename.

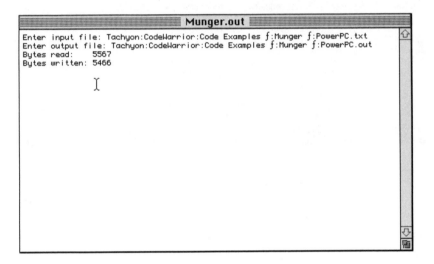

Figure 3.7 *The console window of program "munger" after it processes a file*

Now if you open the resulting file "PowerPC.out" with your favorite word processor, you'll see that "munger" did handle the surplus CRs (see figure 3.8).

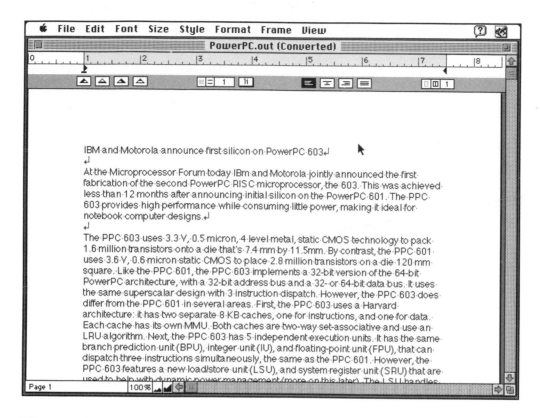

Figure 3.8   *The munged output file*

Where's the Mac?

OK, so we got some C code to run on the Mac, but where is that easy-to-use Mac interface? The point is that we got code running quickly without getting mired in too many details. We let the C Standard Library handle the job of initialization. It also provided I/O through a Mac window masquer-ading as a console window. The important thing to carry away from this exercise is that you can use the C Standard Library to act as a scaffolding while you test various algorithms and Toolbox calls. The programs you make this way aren't meant to be friendly, just useful enough to test code. We will start adding our own Mac interface to our "munge" program in the next chapter.

Here's another example where the C Standard Library pitches in while we investigate some Toolbox routines. Under System 7, active applications are called processes. Certain system services such as File Sharing, PlainTalk voice recognition, and the Express Modem are actually processes themselves. These system services don't show up on the application menu, but they do operate quietly in the background. As the Mac migrates to a preemptive multitasking OS, processes will become even more important to the overall operating system design. With that in mind, let's take a closer look at processes.

Processes Revealed

The Mac OS allocates each process a partition in memory where it runs and assigns it a unique ID number. This ID number is called the process serial number (PSN) and it is used by the operating system to reference the process and control it. *Inside Macintosh: Processes* documents a group of Toolbox routines, known collectively as the Process Manager, that manage these processes and supply information on them. To find out more about processes, let's examine another quick program. Go the the Code Examples ƒ folder, and open the Process ƒ folder. Double-click on the "process.c" file.

```c
#include <processes.h>
#include <stdio.h>

void main (void)
{
register int           i;
ProcessInfoRec         thisProcess;
ProcessSerialNumber    process;
FSSpec                 thisFileSpec;
unsigned char          typeBuffer[5] = {0};
unsigned char          signatureBuffer[5] = {0};

thisProcess.processAppSpec = &thisFileSpec;             /* Aim pointer at our storage */
thisProcess.processInfoLength = sizeof(ProcessInfoRec); /* Store record size */
thisProcess.processName = (unsigned char *) NewPtr(32); /* Allocate room for the name */
process.highLongOfPSN = kNoProcess;                     /* Clear out process serial number */
process.lowLongOfPSN = kNoProcess;

while (GetNextProcess(&process) == noErr)               /* Loop until all processes found */
    {
```

```
     if (GetProcessInformation(&process, &thisProcess) == noErr)  /* Obtain detailed info
*/
        {
        for (i = 0; i <= 3; i++)          /* Copy type & sig info into string buffers */
           {
           typeBuffer[i] = ((char *) &thisProcess.processType)[i];
           signatureBuffer[i] = ((char *) &thisProcess.processSignature)[i];
           } /*end for */
        printf ("Process SN: %ld, %ld, Type: %s, Signature: %s, Name: ",
           thisProcess.processNumber.highLongOfPSN,
           thisProcess.processNumber.lowLongOfPSN,
           typeBuffer,
           signatureBuffer);
        printf (" %s \n", P2CStr(thisProcess.processName));  /* Now print the name */
        } /* end if */
     } /* end while */
} /* end main() */
```

This program uses the Process Manager to obtain information about all of
the processes running on the system. Notice that we include one more
header file, `<processes.h>`, to the source. This header file defines the Process Manager routines and a data structure called `ProcessInfoRec` that acts
as a container for all of the process's relevant information. The lines:

```
thisProcess.processAppSpec = &thisFileSpec;              /* Aim pointer at our storage */
thisProcess.processInfoLength = sizeof(ProcessInfoRec);  /* Store record size */
thisProcess.processName = (unsigned char *) NewPtr(32);  /* Allocate room for the name */
process.highLongOfPSN = kNoProcess;                      /* Clear out process serial number */
process.lowLongOfPSN = kNoProcess;
```

are used to set up our local copy of `ProcessInfoRec`, called `thisProcess`. Then
we direct pointers in `thisProcess` to the appropriate storage locations. For
example, `processAppSpec`, which contains the location of the file that created
the process, is aimed at `thisFileSpec`. And `processName`, which holds the
process's name, is directed to a chunk of memory allocated by `NewPtr()`, a
Toolbox memory allocation routine. Last, we clean out the PSN variables by
assigning `kNoProcess`, which equals zero, to it.

Now we use a `while` loop that calls the Process Manager routine
`GetNextProcess()` repeatedly. `GetNextProcess()`, when called with a PSN of 0,
starts at the beginning of an internal list of PSNs maintained by the Process
Manager and returns the first PSN on the list. By passing each returned PSN

back to `GetNextProcess()` on subsequent tours of the loop, we walk this list and use another routine, `GetProcessInformation()`, to grab information on every process in the system. When `GetNextProcess()` finally reaches the end of the PSN list, it returns an error value and the loop completes.

While the loop cycles, `GetProcessInformation()` extracts in-depth information on the current process and stuffs it into `thisProcess`. As usual, notice that we check for errors. If `GetProcessInformation()` reports no errors after it completes, we dump some of the information it gathered to the console window.

Gathering Processes

It's time to compile the "process.c" program and see what it gathers. There are seven steps, and they are nearly identical to the first program, "munger."

1. Save the code (if you typed it in) into a file called "process.c."

2. Create a new project called process.π, and add "process.c" to the project. Then round up the usual suspects, "InterfaceLib," "MathLib," "MWCRuntime.Lib", " and "ANSI C.PPC.Lib" and add them as well. The Project window should resemble figure 3.9.

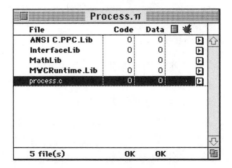

Figure 3.9 *The Project window for the process program*

3. Set the Language and Warning preferences the same way you did for the Munger.π project.

4. In the Linker preferences panel, check the entry point settings. As mentioned previously, the defaults for this program are fine, but you should get into the habit of visiting this panel when we start writing more capable Mac applications.

5. Name the output file **Process** in the Project preferences panel.

6. With all the preferences set, make the program.

7. Finally, pick Run from the Project window. The console window appears and displays information on each process's PSN, type, signature, and name (see figure 3.10). Note the presence of our own program, "Process," as well as the CodeWarrior compiler, the Finder, the File Sharing Extension, and other applications.

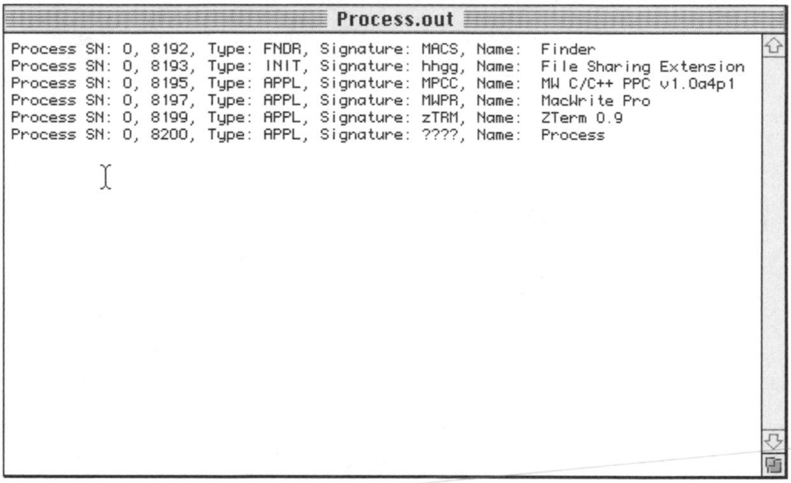

```
Process.out
Process SN: 0, 8192, Type: FNDR, Signature: MACS, Name:    Finder
Process SN: 0, 8193, Type: INIT, Signature: hhgg, Name:    File Sharing Extension
Process SN: 0, 8195, Type: APPL, Signature: MPCC, Name:    MW C/C++ PPC v1.0a4p1
Process SN: 0, 8197, Type: APPL, Signature: MWPR, Name:    MacWrite Pro
Process SN: 0, 8199, Type: APPL, Signature: zTRM, Name:    ZTerm 0.9
Process SN: 0, 8200, Type: APPL, Signature: ????, Name:    Process
```

Figure 3.10 *The process program displaying all processes on the system*

A Word of Caution

As you can see, with the assistance of the I/O functions provided by the C Standard Library, you easily can delve into the Mac's inner workings. Even with all the Mac code I've written over the years, I still frequently use the C Standard Library I/O functions to quickly test code that uses unfamiliar Toolbox routines.

Hazard

Since the C Library does its own application initialization, you need to exercise caution when mixing this library with certain Toolbox routines. For example, the `printf()` function has the C Library create a Mac window that mimics a console window. If your program happens to use a Window Toolbox routine, this creates a situation where your code butts heads with the window data structures created by the C Library, and causes a crash.

To avoid this pitfall, never match the I/O functions you use with the Mac Toolbox with those of the C Library in the program. If you use QuickDraw or Window Toolbox routines in your code, don't use the C Library functions that require a console window. Or, if your program uses the C Library's file I/O functions, don't use Mac Toolbox's file I/O routines. Also be aware that not all of the C Library functions are implemented. Check the CodeWarrior's C Library Reference manual for any discrepancies.

Just the Beginning...

In this chapter we've seen how to build a practical application, leveraging off the I/O functions in the C Standard I/O Library. We outlined seven steps required to build and run the application in Metrowerks CodeWarrior. We also examined how to use the C Library to help us experiment with various Toolbox routines in isolation. Now we can apply this knowledge to learn how the Mac works, which ultimately assists us in writing Mac applications. Try some experiments of your own, and then proceed to the next chapter where you'll write a full-blown Mac application.

Using the Toolbox

At this point you should be comfortable with the Metrowerks CodeWarrior integrated development environment and how to create and manage a project. In a jam, you can rely on CodeWarrior's C Standard Library to help you learn how to use new and unfamiliar Mac Toolbox and OS routines. Does this mean you're ready to write a full-fledged Macintosh application? Not quite. For novice Macintosh programmers, there are a number of basic concepts to learn. These include program initialization, resources, event handling, and the structure of files. These concepts cover a lot of ground, but I'll keep the information doses manageable by introducing them in stages, along with programs that demonstrate these aspects of the Mac OS. Readers with intermediate Mac expertise may wish to jump to the back of the chapter and study the code on Apple Events. The rest of us will catch up with you later.

In chapter 3, I mentioned a Process Manager. As we learned, it is a collection of routines that deals with processes,

which are running applications. It should come as no surprise that many of the Toolbox routines are organized into groups of related functions, or Managers. There's the Event Manager, which deals with low-level events such as mouse clicks and keystrokes. A Memory Manager has routines that allocate memory, release memory, and adjust the size of the stack. A Window Manager provides routines necessary for the care and feeding of windows, while a Font Manager deals with the various fonts you see on the screen or use to print. The list goes on and on. One of the few exceptions to this naming scheme is QuickDraw—the routines that handle drawing on the screen or onto a page image bound for the printer. These various Managers serve as libraries of routines available for your use.

Important

For 68K Macs, a routine's entry point is handled by a 680x0 processor exception. With the Power Macs, the various routines now actually exist in code libraries.

What's nice about this scheme is that it helps organize all of those thousands of Toolbox routines. For example, if you need a function that reads a file, look at the File Manager routines. As a novice, you should spend some time just browsing through *Inside Macintosh*. The new editions organize the technical content by category, such as files, memory, text, and so forth, rather than by volume number as they did in the past. This arrangement helps you locate the various Managers by function. Along with the usual reference information, the new editions of *Inside Macintosh* also include some tutorial material. You might not understand all of the information presented there (for now), but it will give you a good idea of what Managers exist, and what they do. When necessary, I'll make reference to the appropriate *Inside Macintosh* edition.

Meet Some Managers

To get you used to the idea of Managers, let's start by rewriting that "Hello world" program that we wrote in chapter 2. This will also demonstrate how to initialize a Mac application. Start by opening the Code Examples *f* folder.

Now open the MacHello *f* folder and double-click on "hello1.c." Now let's take a close look at the code:

```c
#include <Types.h>
#include <QuickDraw.h>
#include <Fonts.h>
#include <Windows.h>
#include <Memory.h>
#include <Events.h>
#include <OSUtils.h>

#define NIL             0L
#define IN_FRONT        (-1)
#define IS_VISIBLE      TRUE
#define NO_CLOSE_BOX    FALSE
```

Already you'll notice that there are a lot more header files involved than just using the Standard C Library's `<stdio.h>`. That's because the Standard C Library includes every I/O function possible plus the kitchen sink. In contrast, each Toolbox Manager has a separate header file. This keeps both your workload and the compiler's at a manageable level. It means that you have to be more aware of what routines you plan to use (yet another reason to browse through Inside Macintosh).

Background Info

Like Symantec's THINK C, the Metrowerks CodeWarrior compiler uses a special header file called "MacHeaders68K" or "MacHeadersPPC," depending upon the type of code you're generating (68K or PowerPC, respectively). These files incorporate the most frequently used header files, such as "QuickDraw.h," "Fonts.h," "Windows.h," "Files.h," and others. The "MacHeaders68K" and "MacHeadersPPC" files are precompiled, which helps boost the compiler's processing speed when it searches for routine definitions. It also means that if you stick with the most frequently used Manager routines, you needn't worry at all about typing in include statements. However, not all of the header files are incorporated into MacHeaders. If you're using some of the more sophisticated Toolbox routines to, say, play sounds or do special printing, you'll need to include those files. Or you can edit and recompile the appropriate "MacHeaders.c" source code file supplied with the CodeWarrior compiler.

Personally, I prefer to enter all of the header files anyway. You keep better track of what Managers you're using, which helps with your program design. It doesn't hurt having the header files declared in your program, because even if you use the "MacHeaders" file, the Metrowerks CodeWarrior compiler is smart enough to sort things out and prevent redundant declaration errors from cropping up.

The definitions `NIL`, `IN_FRONT`, `IS_VISIBLE`, and `NO_CLOSE_BOX` are for use later in the program. As you'll see, they'll make a Window Manager routine that we use a lot easier to understand. Now enter:

```
void main(void)
{
WindowPtr    thisWindow;
Rect         windowRect;

/* Lunge after all the memory we can get */
    MaxApplZone();
    MoreMasters();
    MoreMasters();

/* Initialize the various Managers */
    InitGraf(&qd.thePort);
    InitFonts();
    FlushEvents(everyEvent, 0);
    InitWindows();
    InitCursor();
```

Now we're getting somewhere. The variable `WindowPtr` holds a pointer to a data structure that the Window Manager creates for us. The data helps manage the window that will display the phrase "Hello world." `Rect` is a data structure that describes a rectangle object to QuickDraw. If you use the Metrowerks editor to examine the "Types.h" file, you'll find `Rect`, which looks like this:

```
struct Rect {
    short    top;
    short    left;
    short    bottom;
    short    right;
};

typedef struct Rect Rect;
```

Top and left correspond to the x and y coordinates of a point that QuickDraw uses in its drawing space. The bottom and right variables define a second point's coordinates. QuickDraw uses these two points to draw the rectangle. How does it make a rectangle made up of four points (or eight x and y coordinates) with just two points? QuickDraw relies on the fact that a rectangle can be drawn with this amount of data. First, QuickDraw draws a line from point (top, left) to point (top, right) to draw the top of the rectangle. Next, QuickDraw draws a line from point (top, right) to point (bottom, right), which draws the right side of the rectangle. Then QuickDraw follows with a line from point (bottom, right) to point (bottom, left) to draw the bottom of the rectangle. The line drawn from point (bottom, left) to point (top, left) closes the rectangle.

MaxApplZone() is a Memory Manager routine that ensures the application has sufficient memory. It does this by expanding the application's heap (also called a zone) as much as possible within the memory partition built for it by the Process Manager. This is followed by calls to MoreMasters(), a routine that allocates what are called *master pointer blocks*. These blocks contain pointers that help implement the handles that are frequently used to access Toolbox data structures. If you run out of master pointers, the Memory Manager will create more for you automatically. However, since the master blocks can't move about in memory, you run the risk of fragmenting the application's heap as memory becomes littered with these immovable memory blocks. The application will also run more slowly as it struggles to organize the fragmented memory. If you provide sufficient master blocks now, it eliminates potential memory and performance problems in the future. Obviously, it's better to call MoreMasters() too much at initialization time, rather than too little.

Initializing Managers

Now we initialize the various Managers that we plan to use:

```
InitGraf(&qd.thePort);
InitFonts();
FlushEvents(everyEvent, 0);
InitWindows();
```

InitGraf() initializes QuickDraw. QuickDraw in turn sets up some global variables it uses to manage the application's graphic environment. The storage for these variables is set up by the development system, which QuickDraw accesses via the global pointer **thePort** that you provide. Next, the Font Manager is initialized, so that text can be displayed within the window. **FlushEvents()** clears the event queues of any stray events when the application launched. **InitWindows()**, of course, readies the Window Manager.

Now it's time to get into the actual mechanics of displaying the phrase "Hello world." Add to the program:

```
/* Set up the window */
   windowRect.top = windowRect.left = 40;
   windowRect.bottom = 200;
   windowRect.right = 300;
   if ((thisWindow = NewWindow(NIL, &windowRect,
      "\pHello world", IS_VISIBLE, documentProc,
      (WindowPtr) IN_FRONT, NO_CLOSE_BOX, NIL)) != NIL)
      {
      SetPort(thisWindow); /* Make window the current port */
      MoveTo (20, 20);
      DrawString("\pHello world");
      InitCursor();

      while (!Button()) /* Wait until mouse button clicked */
         ;

   DisposeWindow(thisWindow); /* Clean up */
      } /* end if */
   else
      SysBeep(30);


} /* end main() */
```

The first two lines of code plug coordinate data into the rectangle **windowRect** that are used to make the window. If you're puzzled over the point data's positive values, that's because in QuickDraw's coordinate system, the upper left corner of the screen is the origin, and larger positive numbers move a point toward the right and downwards. The values in **windowRect** have QuickDraw create a window located forty pixels down and forty pixels to the right of the screen's origin. The window's upper left corner starts at this position, and the window is two hundred pixels tall and three hundred pixels wide.

The NewWindow() routine actually makes the window. The #defines we created at the top of the program are put to use here. From them we can surmise that the new window is visible on the screen, is supposed to appear in front of all other windows, has no close box (the small square in the window's upper left corner that, when clicked on, removes the window), and its title will be Hello World. NewWindow()'s first argument allows you to place a pointer to a data buffer for the window's use. If this argument is NIL, as it is in our example, the Window Manager allocates the window's data storage on the heap, which is fine for simple operations. However, if you display lots of text or large color images in the window, you can severely fragment the heap. For these jobs, it's best to pass the address of a memory block to NewWindow(). Consult *Inside Macintosh: Macintosh Toolbox Essentials* and *Inside Macintosh: Memory* for more information on these issues.

Notice that we do some error checking here. If NewWindow() successfully creates the window, it will return a pointer to the window's data structure. If NewWindow() has a problem making the window (possibly there's not enough memory), the routine returns a value of NIL. The if statement determines if we received a valid pointer from the Window Manager. If not, the application beeps and exits. Admittedly, a beep doesn't offer much diagnostic aid to the user, but it's preferable to signal a problem this way and quit cleanly, rather than have the Mac crash.

If we have a valid window pointer, the program next sets the window to be the current drawing port by using SetPort(). QuickDraw always draws to the screen through a graphics port or *grafport*, which is another data structure that describes to QuickDraw an area to draw on the screen, the size and shape of this area, its coordinate system (which can be different from the screen's), what type of text to use, and other information. The Window Manager creates a grafport for every window it makes, and your application can create and manage many windows—and thus grafports—at once. Through the SetPort() routine, we inform QuickDraw what grafport to draw in, which in this case is our shiny new window. The following MoveTo routine nudges the current drawing point within the window down and right twenty pixels. These values use the window's own coordinate system, whose origin is located at the window's upper left corner. Finally, we use the DrawString() routine to write the phrase "Hello world" in the window.

When the Process Manager starts the application, it changes the mouse pointer, or cursor, to a stopwatch to indicate the Mac is busy. Now that our initialization code has completed and the program displays the greeting, we call `InitCursor()`, which changes the cursor back to an arrow. This indicates that our application is ready to deal with the user.

If we simply let the program proceed, the window would appear briefly and be gone. To let the window linger so that we can admire our handiwork, we insert a `while` loop. This loop cycles until the routine `Button()` returns `TRUE`, which occurs when you press the mouse button. Once the loop completes, we clean up after ourselves by calling `DisposeWindow()`, which removes the window and purges the data structure made by `NewWindow()`. The final shape of the program looks like so:

```c
#include <Types.h>
#include <QuickDraw.h>
#include <Fonts.h>
#include <Windows.h>
#include <Memory.h>
#include <Events.h>
#include <OSUtils.h>

#define NIL          0L
#define IN_FRONT     (-1)
#define IS_VISIBLE   TRUE
#define NO_CLOSE_BOX FALSE

void main(void)
{
WindowPtr    thisWindow;
Rect         windowRect;

/* Lunge after all the memory we can get */
   MaxApplZone();
   MoreMasters();
   MoreMasters();

/* Initialize the various Managers */
   InitGraf(&qd.thePort);
   InitFonts();
```

```
    FlushEvents(everyEvent, 0);
    InitWindows();

/* Set up the window */
    windowRect.top = windowRect.left = 40;
    windowRect.bottom = 200;
    windowRect.right = 300;
    if ((thisWindow = NewWindow(NIL, &windowRect,
        "\pHello world", IS_VISIBLE, documentProc,
        (WindowPtr) IN_FRONT, NO_CLOSE_BOX, NIL)) != NIL)
        {
        SetPort(thisWindow); /* Make window current drawing port */
        MoveTo (20, 20);
        DrawString("\pHello world");
        InitCursor();

        while (!Button())     /* Wait until mouse button clicked */
            ;

        DisposeWindow(thisWindow);
        } /* end if */
    else
        SysBeep(30);

} /* end main() */
```

Run the Code

Let's compile and run this code. Using the seven-step procedure outlined in chapter 3, we first save the code (if we typed it) into a file called **Hello1.c**. Next, create a project called **Hello.π**. Add "Hello1.c," "InterfaceLib," and "MWCRuntime.Lib" to it. (Remember that you don't need to do this with the limited version. The project is already made.)

Set the preferences in this project for the Language, and Project groups. For the Language preferences panel, ensure that the Require Function Prototypes item is checkboxed, and in the Warnings panel that the Extended Error Checking item is checkboxed. For the Project preferences panel, name the output file **Hello**. Now make the project and run it. You'll get a window that resembles that shown in figure 4.1.

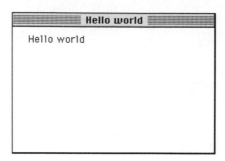

Figure 4.1   *The result of the "Hello world" program*

Click on the mouse button to quit the application. The font used in the window was the default application font Geneva. One of Mac OS's finer features is that it has a smart set of defaults, which simplifies programming.

It took fifty lines of code to implement the "Hello world" program. Our resulting application doesn't do much—but then neither did the UNIX-style version of the program that we wrote in chapter 2. It does illustrate that the Mac OS is a complex environment that requires attention to a lot of details before you can write code.

This very simple application required that we have a grasp of the Memory Manager, the Window Manager, and QuickDraw. I've only provided superficial descriptions of some of the Toolbox routines used in the setup code. For additional information, consult *Inside Macintosh: Macintosh Toolbox Essentials*, *Inside Macintosh: Memory*, and *Inside Macintosh: Imaging*.

"Hello1.c" demonstrates the general initialization setup for a Mac application. Later programs will require the setup of more Managers, but these will be just additions to the code you've written here. Like the understanding of the Mac itself, Mac programming is just a matter of continually adding components to a basic structure.

The Fork in the File

Now that we've covered program initialization, let's delve into a Mac file's structure. A Macintosh file is composed of two sections, a *data fork* and a *resource fork*. Physically, there's nothing different about these forks; each is simply a stream of bytes located somewhere on the hard disk. However, the Mac OS treats each file fork differently. The data fork typically contains data created by an application, such as text from a word processor, numbers from a spreadsheet, or PostScript commands from a drawing application.

The resource fork is a container for objects called—you guessed it—resources. Resources contain data that's organized into predefined formats. This data typically describes graphic elements such as icons, windows, and color tables. Resources also contain non-graphic yet essential elements such as drivers or program code. A resource type defines the resource to the Mac OS, so that it can properly interpret the data packaged within the resource. A resource type is a four-character code, such as 'CODE', 'MENU', 'WIND', 'cicn', 'cdev', and so on. As examples of how the resource type indicates what's inside a resource, consider that CODE resources contain processor code, MENU resources contain the items that appear on a menu, and cicn resources hold data that displays a color icon. In summary, the resource fork of a 68K application contains such elements as program code, menu lists, windows, and icons. The structure of a Power Mac application is somewhat different: It still keeps the graphical elements in its resource fork, but the program code is stored as a single block inside the file's data fork. More on this later. For more details on a file's data and resource forks, consult Inside Macintosh: Files, and for more on resources, check Inside Macintosh: Macintosh Toolbox Essentials.

Besides the two forks, each file also has a type and creator. Like resource types, file type information is a four-character code that describes a file's contents to the application that opens it. For example, a file type of 'TEXT' indicates that the file contains ASCII text, 'TIFF' indicates the file has Tagged Image File Format bit-mapped data (typically a scanned image), and 'APPL' means the file contains program code and is thus an application. The creator information is a four-character code signature that's unique to the application that created the file. Each file's type and creator information is maintained in a desktop database file by the Mac OS. Where does the desktop database get the type and creator information from? From resources in your program, of course. The Finder, the shell application that displays and manages the so-called virtual desktop on your Mac's screen, uses the database file to display each file's icon at the appropriate screen location.

To see how all this fits together, consider what happens when you double-click on an document icon (say, a CodeWarrior project file). The Finder detects this action, and obtains the file's creator information from the desktop database. Next, it searches for a file of type 'APPL' (an application) with the same creator signature. If the Finder finds this application file (the CodeWarrior compiler), it has the Process Manager launch that application. If the Finder can't locate the application file, you get a warning onscreen that states: "The document 'Foobar' could not be opened, because the application program that created it could not be found."

Obviously, the Metrowerks CodeWarrior compiler manages the CODE resources in the application that we make. However, to build a complete Mac application with menus, windows, its own custom icon, and signature information, it's probably dawning on you that you're going to have become familiar with resources in greater detail. This assessment is correct, so let us begin.

Making Resources

As usual, the best way to learn about resources is to do something with them. A great place to start would be to put a friendly interface on that user-hostile file munger program we wrote in chapter 3. First, consider what we want the munger program's interface to do. It should basically behave as before and let you pick a file to open, ask you to name an output file, and then process the chosen file. When munger finishes the job, you want a status report. Once you've finished processing one or more files, you quit munger. With some thought, we conclude that all the munger application really needs is an Apple menu, a File menu, and an Edit menu. The Apple menu is just a placeholder for an application's About Box, the window where the program's description hangs out. The File menu needs an Open command to open the desired files and a Quit command to exit the program. The Edit menu won't be of much use to our application; it's there to assist passing events to other applications under System 7's cooperative multitasking environment. We also need to design dialog boxes, which are the windows that display processing statistics and warn of problems.

Finally, we want to display a cool About Box dialog box that describes munger when the About command is chosen from the Apple menu.

Locate ResEdit, the resource editor, in the Apple Tools folder on the CodeWarrior CD-ROM and copy it to your hard disk, if you haven't done so already. As its name implies, ResEdit is a resource editor. It lets you create resources, modify them, and save them to a file's resource fork, much like a text editor does with text data in a file's data fork. Launch ResEdit. Click on the splash screen to dismiss it. Click on the New button. When the Standard File dialog box appears, type in **munger.π.rsrc**.

Hazard

It's very important that you type the filename exactly as it appears. That's because when you test drive an application in the CodeWarrior IDE, it does some important housekeeping for you. CodeWarrior searches for resources (except for the CODE resources that it made) in a file whose name begins with the project name and ends with the string ".rsrc." For example, for project munger.π, we'll keep our resources in a file called "munger.π.rsrc." This setup allows you to rapidly modify graphical resources without having to attach the them to the program's resource fork every time you want to test changes to the interface.

A window called munger.π.rsrc appears. This window serves as a view of the file's resource fork. It's empty because there are no resources in it—yet. Thinking back to our interface design meeting a little while ago, we decided that munger needed several menus. Go to the Resource menu and choose the Create New Resource command, as shown in figure 4.2.

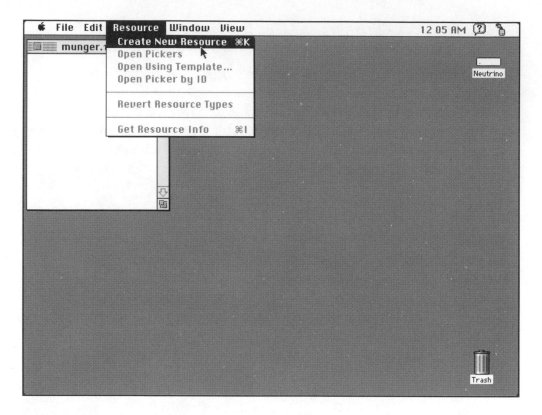

Figure 4.2   *Preparing to make a new resource in ResEdit*

Making Menus

A dialog box appears, asking for a resource type. You can either scroll through the list of defined resource types or type in one if you know it. Type in **MENU** (as shown in figure 4.3) and press Return.

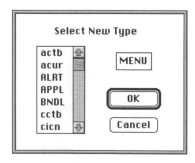

Figure 4.3   *Making a MENU resource*

Two new windows appear (see figure 4.4). The frontmost belongs to the menu resource editor, used to create and modify MENU resources. Say, this looks promising. But what's that MENU ID = 128 in the window title? To distinguish among resources of the same type (MENU, in this case), each resource has its own ID number. To uniquely identify and use a single resource, you specify its type and this ID number. The resource ID number is a 16-bit signed value. ID numbers from -32768 through 127 are reserved for use by the Mac OS, while you're free to use ID numbers from 128 to 32767. What ResEdit's menu resource editor did when it created the resource was conveniently pick the first available ID number.

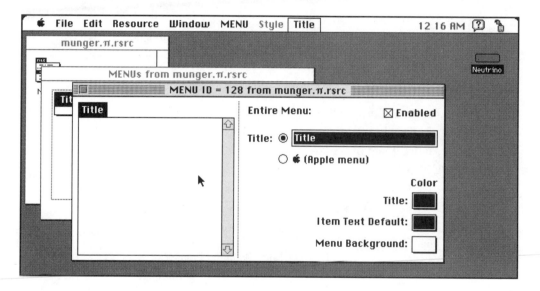

Figure 4.4   *The MENU resource editor*

Since the first menu is the Apple menu, click on the Apple menu radio button in this window. The word Title changes to the Apple symbol, as shown in figure 4.5. Note also that the outlined menu formerly named Title in the menu bar changed to the Apple symbol as well. This menu is a clone of the menu you're constructing and it's used for examining a menu's arrangement and appearance.

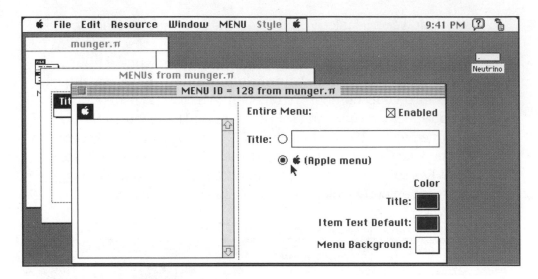

Figure 4.5   *Making the Apple menu*

Now, press Return. You'll get a highlighted (darkened) area under the Apple symbol. This is where you begin to add menu items. For the Apple menu, type **About Munger...** (see figure 4.6) and press Return. This is the program's About Box menu item.

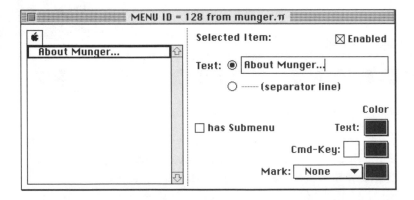

Figure 4.6   *Making the About Box menu item for the Apple menu*

For the Apple menu, the next menu item is simply a separator or divider line, used to indicate where the application's menu ends and the rest of the Apple menu begins. To add a separator line, click on the separator line radio button, as shown in figure 4.7.

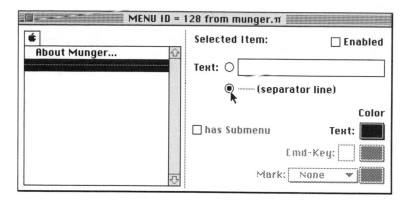

Figure 4.7 *Adding a separator line to the Apple menu*

Now click on the window's close box and you'll see MENU resource 128 (see figure 4.8).

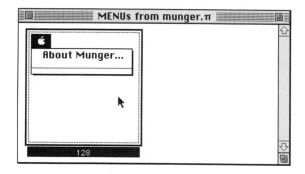

Figure 4.8 *MENU ID 128, as it will appear in the application*

We still have two more menus to go. Once again select Create New Resource from the Resource menu, or type Command-K. A new MENU ID = 129 window appears. Enter **File** for the menu's title, press Return, and type **Open...** for the first menu item. Before you press Return, click on the box to the right of the item labeled Cmd-Key in the Editor window, or press Tab to select it. Type **O** in this box (see figure 4.9). The O character is the keyboard equivalent for the Open menu selection. That is, typing Command-O initiates an Open action, as if it were selected from the menu. Because keyboard equivalents rely on the Command key, they are also called Command-Key equivalents. This also explains the name of this Cmd-Key item in the Editor window.

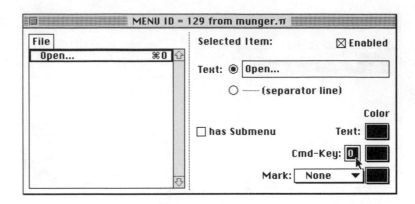

Figure 4.9 *Entering the keyboard equivalent for the Open menu item*

Press Return and then add a separator line by clicking on the separator radio button. Press Return again and type **Quit**. Then, type a **Q** in the Cmd-Key item box. That completes the File menu. You can then pull down the test menu to examine it (see figure 4.10). Click on the window's close box and save the file.

Now to add the last menu, the Edit menu. Type Command-K to create a new menu resource. The window MENU ID = 130 appears. Type **Edit** for the menu title, press Return, type **Undo**, press Tab, type **Z**, and press Return, which makes the Undo item in the menu. It has the keyboard equivalent of Command-Z. Add a separator line and press Return, type **Cut**, press Tab, type **X**, then press Return to add the Cut item to the Edit menu. Add the Copy item by typing **Copy**, Tab, **C**, and pressing Return, then type in **Paste**, Tab, and **V** to create the Paste item. Click on the window's close box, and you should see all three menus, ready to go, as shown in figure 4.11. Save the file, and close the window by clicking on the close box, or typing Command-W.

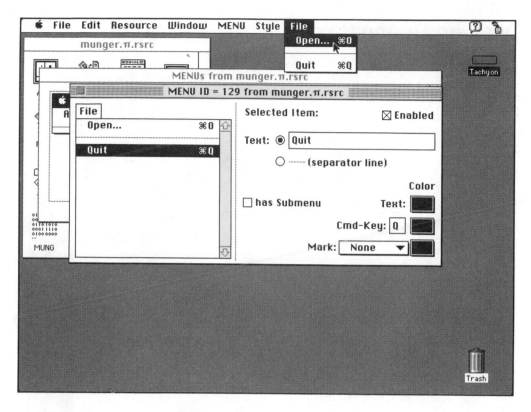

Figure 4.10 *Testing the completed File menu in ResEdit*

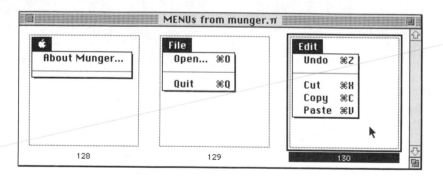

Figure 4.11 *The complete MENU IDs for the munger application*

Making Dialog Boxes

Now, let's make the dialog boxes for munger. Choose Create New Re-source again, and this time type **DLOG** and press Return. A dialog editor window opens, with the title DLOG ID = 128 (see figure 4.12).

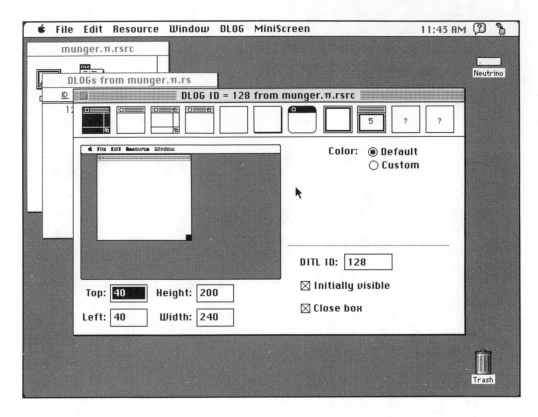

Figure 4.12 *The dialog editor window*

About Boxes are typically dialog windows, because this type of window requires little program code to support it. By default, the editor has selected a standard document window, complete with a drag region, a close box, and a grow icon (the small box at the window's bottom right corner). In short, a window with all the bells and whistles. Go over to the sixth window icon from the left and click on it, as shown in figure 4.13. Notice that the window's appearance has changed. This is the alternate dialog window, which is just a variation of the dialog window. This window type has no drag bar, no close box, and no grow icon. It's pretty simple as windows go, which is what we want.

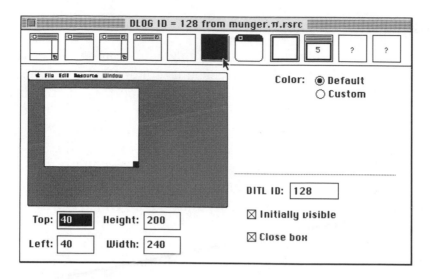

Figure 4.13 *Picking the alternate dialog window*

Click on this window's upper left corner and drag it near the top of the screen. Next, click on the dark square at bottom right of the window, and drag it. The window's size will change depending upon how you drag this square. Size the window according to what suits you, and release the mouse button (see figure 4.14).

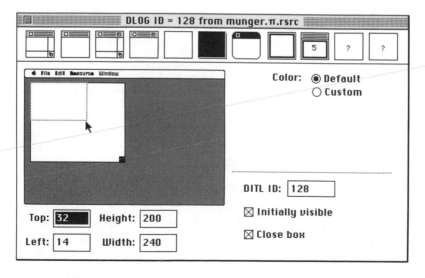

Figure 4.14 *Resizing the dialog window*

Editing Dialog Boxes

Now, double-click on this window. A pair of windows appears (see figure 4.15). This is the dialog item, or DITL, resource editor. While the menu editor lets you add and delete items from a MENU resource, the situation is more complicated with dialog windows. The dialog editor manages DLOG resources, which determine a dialog window's type and size. However, objects that appear in the window, such as buttons, icons, and text, belong to another resource, of type 'DITL'. DITL resources contain lists of dialog items, just as MENU resources contain lists of menu items. Naturally, changing DITL resources requires a separate editor, which is why that dialog item editor just appeared.

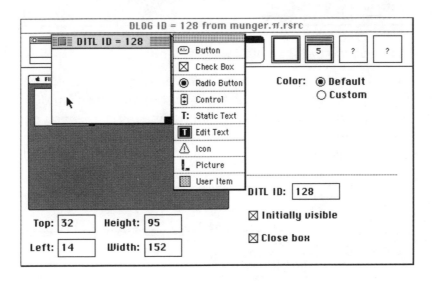

Figure 4.15 *The DITL editor, for modifying dialog items*

Although the DLOG and DITL editors operate so seamlessly that they appear to function as a single editor, it's very important that you remember that you're working with two different resources here. Notice that the DITL ID number is 128. It's not required that a dialog's items (DITL resources) have the same ID number as the dialog window (DLOG) that they appear in, but it does keep tracking the relationships between the two resources simple. If you need to use a different DITL ID number, you can change the linkage by typing a different ID number in the DITL ID item on the DLOG Editor window in the background.

Go to the floating window with the dialog items on it (the window at the right), and drag the static text object to the dialog window, as shown in figure 4.16. Static text can't be changed by the user during the life of the dialog window, so it's useful for handling the titles of buttons and controls.

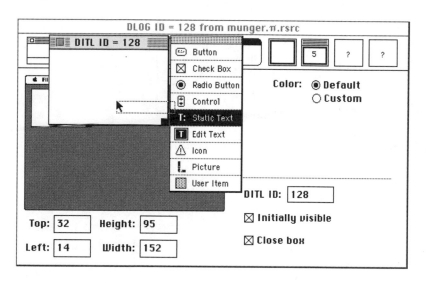

Figure 4.16   *Adding a static text item to the About Box*

Release the mouse button when you've positioned the text object where you want it. In this example, let's drop it near the top of the window. Now double-click on this object, and a window titled Edit DITL item #1 appears. Replace the highlighted text by typing **Munger 1.0**, pressing Return, typing **Written in**, pressing Return, and typing **Metrowerks C** (see figure 4.17). This is our About Box information.

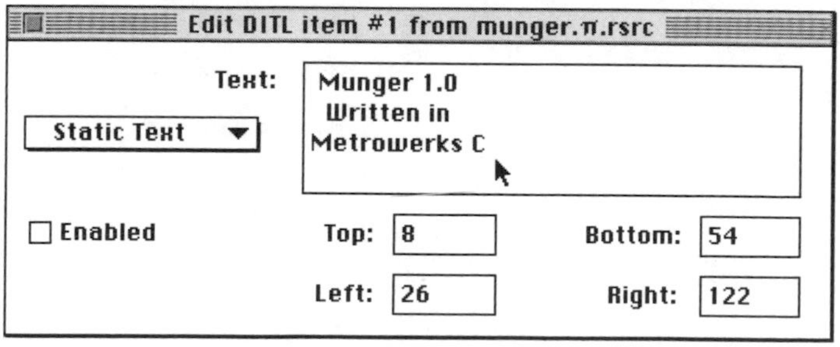

Figure 4.17   *Changing the text of DITL item #1*

Click on this window's close box, and resize the static text box by clicking
and dragging with the mouse (see figure 4.18). You'll have to tinker with the
box and text somewhat until you get it to look neat. Use ResEdit's Alignment menu to center this text box in the window.

Figure 4.18   *Modifying the size of the dialog item*

Adding Buttons

Now, go back to the dialog items window, and drag a button item to the
dialog window, and position it under the text, as shown in figure 4.19.

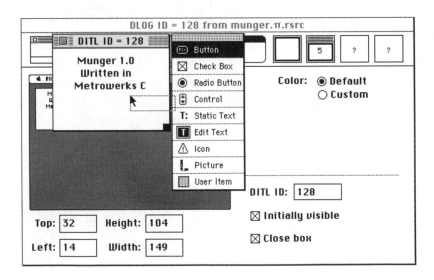

Figure 4.19   *Adding a button to the dialog window*

Release the mouse button and a button item appears. Double-click on it to open an Editor window so that you can change the button's text. Type **OK** (see figure 4.20). Close the window and use the Alignment menu to center the button.

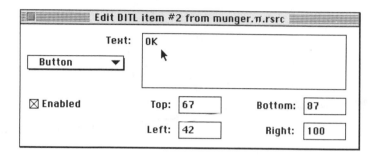

Figure 4.20   *Changing the button's title*

Numbering Dialog Items

There's one more crucial step we have to do here: renumber the dialog items. The reason is that certain dialog Toolbox routines that manage the dialog items look for Return keystrokes. They pass this action onto the first item in the dialog list, just as if you had clicked on that item. What we want to happen is that when the user presses Return, it activates the OK button, which then dismisses the About Box window.

Go to ResEdit's DITL menu, and select Renumber Items.... A new window appears, with instructions on how to renumber the items. Hold down the Shift key, then click first on the OK button, and then the About Box information (see figure 4.21). Click on the renumber button, and you're done. You could have avoided renumbering these items by putting the OK button in the window first, then adding the About Box static text. Occasionally you have to renumber items after the fact, so it's worth pointing out this feature in ResEdit now.

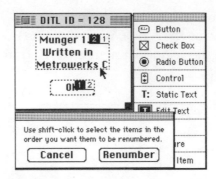

Figure 4.21   *Changing the dialog item numbers*

Close the DITL editor by clicking on the close box, which lands you back in the DLOG editor. If you want to preview how the About Box looks, pick Preview at Full Size from the DLOG menu. Close the DLOG window and save the file.

Status Display

We also decided that we wanted a status display when munger finishes processing a file. Let's start by typing Command-K to create a new DITL resource. As the title to the DITL Editor window indicates, this resource has an ID of 129. Click on the eighth window from the left to select the dialog window type. The window changes from a document window type to a dialog window, as shown in figure 4.22.

Double-click on the window to bring up the DITL resource editor. Go to the floating dialog item window and drag a static text item to the new window. Adjust the item's width by dragging with the mouse until the item spans most of the window. Now Copy and Paste this item. Nothing appears to have happened, but if you click and drag on the static text item, you'll see an identical item beneath it. Copy and Paste again to clone the item one more time, then arrange the three items above one another in the dialog window. This gives you three static text items of the same size. Use the Alignment menu to center the items in this window, as shown in figure 4.23.

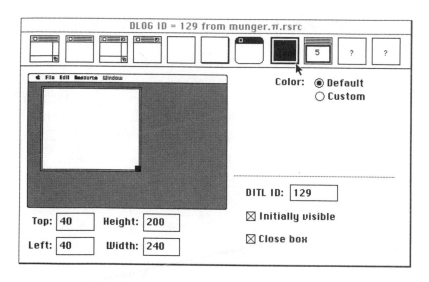

Figure 4.22 *Changing the window type to a dialog window*

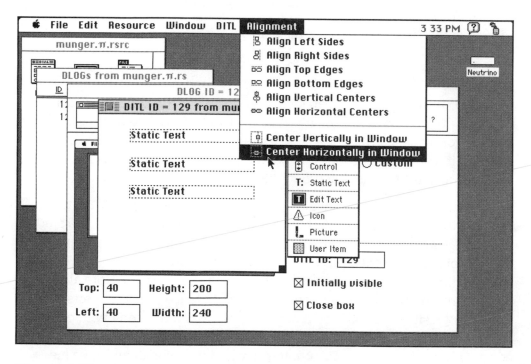

Figure 4.23 *Centering the three cloned dialog items*

Click on the top static text item to select it and edit its contents by double-clicking on it. Type **File: ^0**. The caret and number operate as a special placeholder where the dialog Toolbox call will substitute a text string, in this case a filename. We'll see how this works a little later. Go to the second item, open the item, and type **Bytes read: ^1**. Open the last item and type **Bytes written: ^2**. Resize the window and align the items again. The dialog window should appear similar to the one in figure 4.24. This completes the status window.

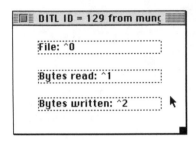

Figure 4.24   *The completed status dialog*

Adding Alerts

Now for one last window. In an ideal world, our code is bug-free and a user will never try to add one more munged file to a jam-packed hard disk. Since such a world doesn't exist, we need to report errors when they occur, whether it's problem with the code or a user mistake. For this window, we'll use an alert resource of type 'ALRT'.

What is an alert? It's a special dialog window that beeps the Mac and requires that you click on a button to dismiss the alert. This way, the alert grabs the user's attention and ensures that he responds to the error message. There are several types of alerts—note, caution, and stop—and each has a distinctive icon to indicate the severity of the problem. Note alerts provide information, usually to offer the user a choice. Caution alerts warn the user of a situation that could result in data loss if not dealt with carefully. For example, caution alerts warn of insufficient disk space to save a certain file, or that memory is running low and the user should save his work, or that proceeding with an operation will delete a file. Stop alerts flag a problem so serious that the application can't complete the operation. An example of a stop alert is when the program detects an error while writing a file to disk.

For the munger program, we can anticipate that disk I/O is where most problems will occur. Since most disk I/O problems—such as running out of disk space—are difficult to recover from without lots of intervention on the user's part, munger will just quit the operation and post a stop alert.

Let's make a stop alert for munger. Get out of ResEdit's DLOG editor by closing the Editor window. Type Command-K to make a new resource, and type **ALRT** in the Select New Type dialog. The alert resource Editor window appears, with a default of ALRT resource ID 128. Notice that the alert window already has dialog items in it (see figure 4.25). Remember that the objects displayed in the dialog box actually belonged to a different resource? What's happening is that the alert editor is, by default, using DITL resource ID 128, whose items already belong to the About Box dialog.

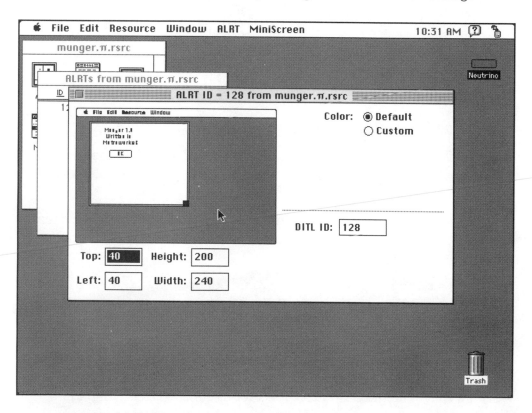

Figure 4.25 *The alert resource editor*

You have two options here. You can change the ID number that links the DITL resource to the ALRT resource, or change the ALRT resource ID. I keep the organization of these linked resource ID numbers simple by using an ascending list of ID numbers that's divvied up among the DLOG and ALRT resources. That is, an ALRT resource might get an ID of 128, a dialog a resource ID of 129, another ALRT gets ID 130, and so on. So, let's change the ALRT resource ID. Start by selecting Get Resource Info from the Resource menu, or typing Command-I. An Info box appears (see figure 4.26). Type **130** to change the ALRT ID, and then close the window.

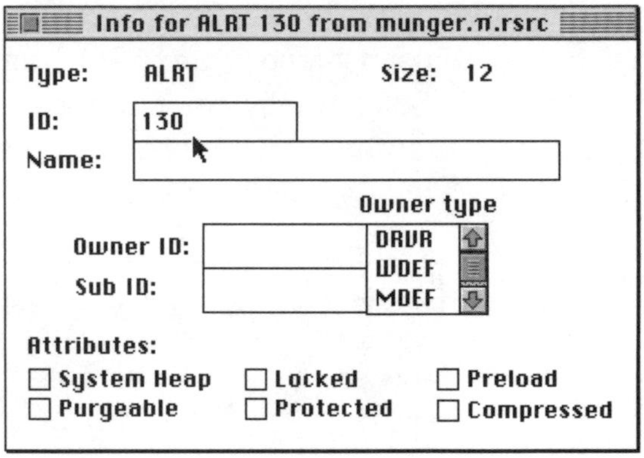

Figure 4.26 *Changing the ID of the alert resource*

You'll notice that the dialog items haven't changed yet. Go to the DITL ID item in the alert Editor window and type **130**. Now you have a blank window, as appears in figure 4.27.

Double-click on the window to summon the DITL editor. Drag a static text item to the window, and edit it to say **I/O error, ID = ^0**, as shown in figure 4.28.

Now drag a button item to the window and edit it to say **OK**. Align the two items and resize the window to fit. Be sure to leave room at the window's top left corner so that the Dialog Manager can drop a 32- by 32-pixel stop alert icon into the window when it's drawn. Renumber the dialog items so that the OK button is item number 1. Again, we do this because the Dialog Manager passes Return key events to the window's first dialog item, and we want that to be the OK button. Also, for alerts, the Dialog Manager draws a bold outline around DITL item 1, on the assumption that it's the default button (an OK button in this instance). The alert window should appear as shown in figure 4.29.

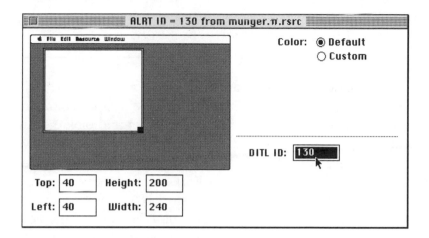

Figure 4.27 *Changing the ID of the alert's DITL resource*

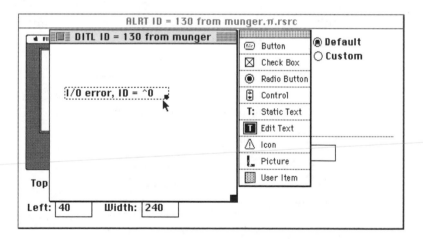

Figure 4.28 *Adding the alert's static text message*

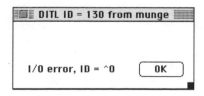

Figure 4.29 *The completed alert dialog*

> **Important**
>
> As discussed earlier, the default button—the item that the program assumes the user will pick most of the time—is always DITL item 1. For alert boxes with more than one button, DITL item 2 should always be the Cancel button.

There are two last details to take care of. First, we want the alert window to appear centered on the screen. This turns out to be a simple job. Close the DITL Editor window to get back into the alert editor and pick the Auto Position... from the ALRT menu. A dialog window appears that allows you to set the window's characteristics so that System 7 will automatically center the window for you (see figure 4.30). Go to the active pop-up menu (the one on the left), and select the alert position. (Alert windows are required to appear on certain areas of the screen.) The right pop-up menu becomes active, but since the Main Screen default setting is fine for now, just click on the OK button to make the changes. Save the file. If you want, you can also enable the auto-centering settings of the other dialog boxes. Before you do, consult *Inside Macintosh: Macintosh Toolbox Essentials* for important guidelines on these settings.

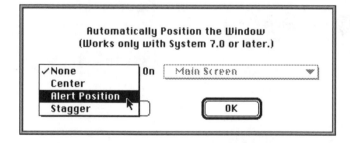

Figure 4.30   *Setting the alert window's screen position*

> **Background Info**
>
> In pre-System 7 days, dialog boxes would appear on-screen where they were drawn in the resource editor. Since monitors of any size and shape could be attached to the Mac, the default location of these windows weren't always in the best position for visibility, especially on a large monitor. You could always write

code to determine the Mac's screen size and then position the dialog window appropriately before showing it. This code could get extremely complicated if the system had multiple monitors in use. While such code isn't impossible to write, it was an imposition on the programmer's resources, which were better spent writing the application, not managing the interface. As you saw with the alert editor, System 7 now handles this job. This is one of the many improvements in System 7 that both relieves the programmer of an interface detail, and makes applications more visually consistent to the user.

The other detail is that the dialog item lists aren't cleared from memory automatically when the alert or dialog box is closed. To help the Memory Manager reclaim the memory used by these item lists, we mark the DITL resources as purgeable. To do this, first close the alert resource editor window and then the ALRT resource window. The resource fork of "munger.π.rsrc" should contain four resources, as shown in figure 4.31.

Figure 4.31   *The resources the munger application uses*

Next, double-click on the DITL icon to get a view of the DITL resources, from 128 to 130. Hold down on the Shift key and click on each DITL resource to select it. Choose Get Resource Info from the Resource menu and three Info windows should appear, as shown in figure 4.32. Click on the Purgeable checkbox for each DITL resource to select Purgeable. Close the windows. Save the file and quit ResEdit.

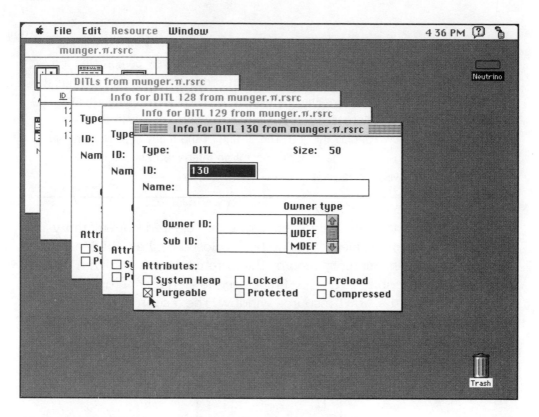

Figure 4.32   *Setting the DITL resources as purgeable*

Saving Resource Data as Text

This excursion with ResEdit covered a lot on resources. You might be wondering if there is a way to save the information they represent in a text format. This would allow a resource's contents to be distributed on paper, or as 7-bit ASCII over the Internet. For huge programs with dozens of menus, windows, dialogs, and alerts, it's easier to search for an item to modify using a text editor rather than poking around in a resource fork with ResEdit. And yes, you can save the information in a text format. Along with ResEdit, CodeWarrior supplies two Macintosh Programmer's Workshop (MPW) tools, called DeRez and Rez. The DeRez tool takes an existing .rsrc file and translates its resources into text descriptions. The text description uses a C-style programming language that accurately describes a resource's data. The Rez tool takes these text files and converts them back into binary resources. You can access these tools from the Metrowerks CodeWarrior IDE by selecting Start Toolserver from the Tools menu.

Some Words on Events

Now that we've got the new and improved munger interface constructed, we're almost ready to start writing code. First, a brief description of how a Mac application operates is in order. As you work with the Mac, you generate *events*. There are two types of events: low-level and high-level. Low-level events are actions such as keystrokes, mouse clicks, and the insertion of the occasional floppy disk. The Mac OS uses the Event Manager to detect these actions and place them in an event queue for the application. High-level events are used to establish communications among applications. Such communications might request data from another application, or command an application to print a file. We'll deal with high-level events later in this chapter.

Your application takes these events from the queue and responds to each type as required. It does this using what's called an *event loop*. In the event loop, the application circles endlessly, obtaining events from the OS by calling the routine `WaitNextEvent()`. If an event is forthcoming from `WaitNextEvent()`, the event loop next calls the appropriate function to handle the event. For example, if your application receives a keystroke (actually a key down event to the Mac), the action is passed to a function that might drop the character into a document window. Note that if certain windows are active (such as a Desk Accessory) or certain key combinations are pressed, different sets of handler code might be called to process the event. Continuing with our key down example, if you hold down the Command key while typing a character, the application instead calls functions that ultimately have a Menu Manager routine field the event. (Recall that a Command-key combination can be the keyboard equivalent for a menu choice.) A Mac application, in some instances, can be programmed to ignore certain events.

The basic structure of a Mac application is shown in figure 4.33. A Mac application goes through its initialization phase and then runs in an event loop. As events trickle in, the event loop code checks to see what type of event occurred, and calls the corresponding function to handle the event. It keeps doing this until the user signals the application to quit. At this point the application exits the event loop and performs any required clean up operations, such as saving files or discarding memory buffers.

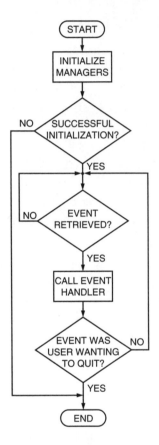

Figure 4.33   *Structure of a Mac application*

An important distinction to make here is that events might occur in any order, and your program must be structured to deal with such disordered input. It shouldn't force the user through a gauntlet of dialog boxes that prompt for information. Also, because users aren't likely to explore every menu choice or dialog box setting, applications should provide reasonable defaults that help them get started. As an example of this, a word processor should default to a specific font (such as Times) and point size (say 12 for example) when displaying text. Along these same lines, any setting that the user might change frequently (such as the baud rate in a terminal emulator application) should be easy to find and change. If you're not familiar with this sort of user interface design, be sure to check out Apple's Human Interface Guidelines.

Code at Last

With the interface in place and a firm understanding of events, we can rewrite the munger program. Fire up CodeWarrior's compiler and create a new project. For a project name, type **munger.π**. (Remember that the project name must correspond to the resource filename "munger.π.rsrc" we made with ResEdit.) Now pick Add File... from CodeWarrior's Project menu, and along the path CodeWarrior:Example Code ƒ:MacMunger, open the file "Macmunger.c." Inside the Project window, double-click on the "Macmunger.c" file to open it with the built-in editor. In the Editor window, examine the following code:

```c
#include <Types.h>
#include <QuickDraw.h>
#include <Windows.h>
#include <Fonts.h>
#include <Controls.h>
#include <Dialogs.h>
#include <Menus.h>
#include <Devices.h>
#include <Memory.h>
#include <Events.h>
#include <Desk.h>
#include <OSEvents.h>
#include <OSUtils.h>
#include <ToolUtils.h>
#include <TextUtils.h>
#include <StandardFile.h>
#include <Errors.h>
#include <Resources.h>
#include <DiskInit.h>

/* Resource ID numbers */
#define LAST_MENU       3    /* Number of menus */
#define APPLE_MENU      128  /* Menu ID for Apple menu */
#define FILE_MENU       129  /* Menu ID for File menu */
#define EDIT_MENU       130  /* Menu ID for Edit menu */
#define RESOURCE_ID     127  /* Starting index into the menu array */
```

```
#define ABOUT_BOX        1     /* About box menu item # in Apple menu */

#define OPEN_FILE        1     /* Open item # in File menu */
/*---------------------*/      /* Separator line is item # 2 */
#define I_QUIT           3     /* Quit item # in File menu */

#define ABOUT_BOX_ID     128   /* Resource IDs for our windows & dialogs */
#define STATUS_BOX_ID    129
#define ERROR_BOX_ID     130

/* Various constants */
#define NIL              0L
#define FALSE            false
#define TRUE             true

#define INIT_X           112   /* Coords for disk init dialog box */
#define INIT_Y           80

#define APPEND_MENU      0
#define CHAR_CODE_MASK   255
#define IN_FRONT         -1
#define NO_CURSOR        0L
#define ONE_FILE_TYPE    1
#define LONG_NAP         60L

#define CR               0x0D
#define LF               0x0A
```

As you can see, we intend to use a lot more Managers this time, and consequently have a lot more header files to include.

Next, we define the resource ID numbers of our menus and dialog boxes. These values come straight from our work in ResEdit. Look carefully at the menu item numbers in this section. These are values that the Menu Manager returns to the program when the user makes a menu choice. Notice that the menu item numbers start at 1, and that each separator line also counts as a menu item. If you add or remove items from a menu resource, the item numbers returned by the Menu Manager will change. You'll have to edit the definitions here to match the new menu resource. To help keep this arrangement straight, notice how the **#define**s for the File menu are written so that they resemble the File menu layout. The rest of the section defines constants that we'll use elsewhere in the program, including Return and Line Feed.

Here are some function prototypes:

```
/* Function prototypes */
Boolean Do_Command (long mResult);
Boolean Init_Mac(void);
void Main_Event_Loop(void);
void Report_Error(OSErr errorCode);

/* Application-specific functions */
void Ask_File(void);
void Munge_File(short input, short output, unsigned char *fileName);

/* Globals */
MenuHandle  gmyMenus[LAST_MENU+1];   /* Handle to our menus */
EventRecord gmyEvent;                /* Holds event returned by OS */
WindowPtr   geventWindow;            /* Our private window */
Boolean     guserDone;               /* Indicates user wants to quit */
CursHandle  gtheCursor;              /* Current pointer icon */
short       gwindowCode;
WindowPtr   gwhichWindow;            /* The window that got an event */

OSType      gfileCreator = {'MUNG'}; /* Output file's creator */
OSType      gfileType = {'TEXT'};    /* Output file's type */
```

You'll recognize some basic functions here, such as Init_Mac(), Do_Command(), and Main_Event_Loop(), whose purpose is obvious. Also, we have a function that asks for a file, and—of course—a function to munge the file's contents. We also declare some globals here. The global gmyMenus[] is an array of handles that will point to menu records. Menu records are data structures that the Menu Manager builds to manage menus, somewhat like the data structures the Window Manager uses for windows. The gmyEvent global contains an event record, which is a data structure that describes the type of event passed to the application. The globals gfileType and gfileCreator contain the type and creator information for munger's output file.

> **Background Info**
> Everyone has his or her own style for writing code. I'll explain my style here, not because it's superior, but so that you'll quickly understand what the code is doing. To prevent confusion between the Mac Toolbox routine names and the program's function names, I use underscores in the program function names. So, `StandardGetFile()` is a Toolbox routine, while `Ask_File()` is a function that I wrote. Variable names begin with a lowercase letter, such as `fileName`, unless it's a global variable. Global variable names begin with a lowercase g, such as `gmyEvent`. Program constants are all upper case, such as `LAST_MENU`, unless it's a well-publicized constant defined by Apple, such as `everyEvent` or `watchCursor`. Lately, Apple has been preceding their constants with a lowercase k, such as `kCoreEventClass`, which helps identify them. Feel free to use a style that works for you. Just be consistent, and always comment your code.

The First Function

Now it's time to look closely at the first function in "Macmunger.c":

```
void Report_Error(OSErr errorCode)
{
unsigned char errNumString[8];

    NumToString((long) errorCode, errNumString);
    ParamText(errNumString, NIL, NIL, NIL);
    StopAlert(ERROR_BOX_ID, NIL);
} /* end Report_Error() */
```

This is our minimalist error reporting function. When a Toolbox routine returns an error code, we pass it to `Report_Error()`. Inside `Report_Error()`, we use the Toolbox routine `NumToString()` to convert the error code to a displayable text string. The resulting Pascal string is then passed to `ParamText()`, whose job is to insert up to four strings inside a window. Since we have only one string to display, `ParamText()`'s other three arguments are `NIL`. How does `ParamText()` know where to place each text string? Recall that when we made the alert resource's DITL item for munger, we typed in "I/O error, ID = ^0." The ^0 is the placeholder for this string. `ParamText()` substitutes the placeholder text with the string in errNumString, staying within the rectangle defined by DITL item. After ParamText() does the insertion, we call StopAlert() to create the stop alert window. An example of how the alert box appears is shown in figure 4.34.

Figure 4.34 *The Report_Error() alert box*

As error functions go, this is adequate for our work. If you get the stop alert, you can open the "errors.h" file from within the Metrowerks CodeWarrior compiler and search for the error code to get an idea as to what went wrong. If you plan to unleash this program upon unsuspecting users, be nice to them and write an error reporting function that provides an explanation of the problem and suggests remedies. Don't dump a cryptic error ID number on the screen when trouble strikes.

Munger Code, Revisited

Let's examine the file munging code next:

```
void Munge_File(short input, short output, unsigned char *fileName)
{
long          amount;
unsigned char buffer;
short         crflag;
long          icount, ocount;
unsigned char inNumString[12], outNumString[12];
DialogPtr     statusDialog;

   amount = 1L;
   crflag = 0;
   icount = 0;
   ocount = 0;
   while (FSRead(input, &amount, &buffer) == noErr)
     {
     icount++;                    /* Bump input char counter */
     switch (buffer)              /* What char was read? */
       {
```

```
        case CR:
           if (crflag >= 1)          /* Two in a row, end of paragraph */
              {
              FSWrite(output, &amount, &buffer);  /* Write two CRs */
              FSWrite(output, &amount, &buffer);
              crflag = 0;                        /* Reset the flag */
              ocount++;
              } /* end if */
           else
              crflag++;                          /* Bump the flag, and toss the CR */
        break;  /* end case CR */
        case LF:                                 /* Toss LF, but don't touch crflag */
        break;  /* end case LF */
        default:
           FSWrite(output, &amount, &buffer);
           ocount++;
           crflag = 0;                           /* Clear the flag */
        } /* end switch */
     } /* end while */

/* Display processing statistics */
   if ((statusDialog = GetNewDialog(STATUS_BOX_ID, NIL,
                             (WindowPtr) IN_FRONT)) != NIL)
     {
     NumToString(icount, inNumString);           /* Convert bytes read to string */
     NumToString(ocount, outNumString);
     ParamText (fileName, inNumString, outNumString, NIL);
     DrawDialog(statusDialog);
     Delay (120L, NIL);
     DisposDialog(statusDialog);
     } /* end if != NIL */
   else
     SysBeep(30);


} /* end Munge_file() */
```

Munge_File() accepts several arguments: an input file reference number, an output file reference number, and a pointer to a string containing the input filename. Since computers prefer to handle things as numbers, the File Manager provides reference numbers for files that you open for reading or writing. These reference numbers remain valid as long as the files are open and you pass them to File Manager routines that perform the actual I/O. As you probably suspect, the function Ask_File() obtains these file reference numbers and then calls Munge_File().

We use a `while` loop to read bytes with `FSRead()`, and then write bytes using `FSWrite()`, two other File Manager routines. If you compare this loop to the original munger.c code in chapter 3, you'll see that the two are very similar, with `FSRead()` replacing `getc()` and `FSWrite()` replacing `fputc()`.

Once the loop completes, we briefly display the processing statistics in a dialog box. To display these numbers, we fetch the `STATUS_BOX_ID` dialog resource using the routine `GetNewDialog()`. Like creating a window, we check to see if `GetNewDialog()` was successful at this. If it was, we convert the values in `icount` and `ocount` to strings. We pass these strings, plus the input filename, to `ParamText()` for inclusion in the dialog box. These strings will be substituted for the placeholders in the status box's DITL items, the same way it occurs in `Report_Error()`'s alert box. With the dialog box's contents set up, we call `DrawDialog()` to display the window. Next, we use `Delay()` to wait for two seconds. (`Delay()` waits for intervals of time called *ticks*, which are sixtieths of a second; 120 ticks is therefore two seconds.) Finally, we remove the dialog box and we're done.

Background Info

Seasoned Mac programmers will notice that we test for a failure by examining the pointer returned by `GetNewDialog()` to see if it is `NIL`. This type of check didn't work with earlier versions of the Mac OS. That's because these versions of `GetNewDialog()` would return a trash value if it failed. The workaround was to use a Resource Manager routine to see if the dialog resource existed before calling `GetNewDialog()`, like so:

```
if (GetResource('DLOG', ABOUT_BOX_ID) != NIL)
    {
    theDialog = GetNewDialog(ABOUT_BOX_ID, NIL,
                             (WindowPtr) IN_FRONT);
    ModalDialog(NIL, &itemHit);
    DisposDialog(theDialog);
    } /* end if != NIL */
else
    SysBeep(30);
```

Thanks to improvements to the Dialog Manager in System 7, we can use one consistent algorithm to test the results of Window and Dialog Manager routines.

There are a couple of things to note here. First, we don't do much error checking on the file I/O. This is so that you can examine the code easily. Don't worry about this; we'll add this error-checking when we add high-level events to munger later. The other thing is that this code isn't very efficient, reading and writing only one byte at a time. FSWrite() automatically buffers some of the data during output, which improves performance somewhat. However, for faster I/O you'd set amount to a large value so that FSRead() would read lots of data into a big buffer, process that buffer's contents, and then have FSWrite() write out large sections of the buffer. However, for my needs, the performance was adequate so that it wasn't worth the extra effort to improve the application's speed.

Input and Output Filenames

The next function to write is one that queries the user for input and output filenames, opens them, and supplies Munge_File() with the file reference numbers. This function is Ask_File(), whose code follows.

```
void Ask_File(void)
{
unsigned char     fileName[14] = {"\pMunge.out"};
short             inFileRefNum, outFileRefNum;
OSErr             fileError;
short             oldVol;
SFTypeList        textType = {'TEXT'};

StandardFileReply inputReply, outputReply;

/* Open the input file */
   StandardGetFile(NIL, ONE_FILE_TYPE, textType, &inputReply);
   if (inputReply.sfGood)
      {
      GetVol (NIL, &oldVol);              /* Save current volume */
      if ((fileError = FSpOpenDF (&inputReply.sfFile, fsCurPerm,
                                 &inFileRefNum)) != noErr)
         {
         Report_Error(fileError);
         return;
         } /* end if error */
```

```c
/* Open the output file */
    StandardPutFile ("\pSave text in:", fileName, &outputReply);
    if (outputReply.sfGood)
        {
        SetVol(NIL, outputReply.sfFile.vRefNum);
        fileError = FSpCreate(&outputReply.sfFile, gfileCreator, gfileType,
                              smSystemScript);
        switch(fileError)              /* Process result from File Manager */
            {
            case noErr:
            break;
            case dupFNErr:             /* File already exists, wipe it out */
                if ((fileError = FSpDelete(&outputReply.sfFile)) == noErr)
                    {
                    if ((fileError = FSpCreate(&outputReply.sfFile,
                                               gfileCreator, gfileType,
                                               smSystemScript)) != noErr)
                        {
                        Report_Error(fileError);
                        FSClose (inFileRefNum);
                        SetVol(NIL, oldVol);
                        return;
                        } /* end != noErr */
                    } /* end if == noErr */
                else
                    {
                    Report_Error(fileError);
                    FSClose (inFileRefNum);
                    SetVol(NIL, oldVol);
                    return;
                    } /* end else */
            break;   /* end case dupFNErr */
            default:                       /* Unknown error, try to abort cleanly */
                Report_Error(fileError);
                FSClose (inFileRefNum); /* Close the input file */
                SetVol(NIL, oldVol);    /* Restore original volume */
                return;
            } /* end switch */

/* Open data fork */
        if (!(FSpOpenDF (&outputReply.sfFile, fsCurPerm, &outFileRefNum)))
            {
            gtheCursor = GetCursor(watchCursor);   /* Change the cursor */
```

```
            SetCursor(&**gtheCursor);
            Munge_File (inFileRefNum, outFileRefNum, (unsigned char *)
                        inputReply.sfFile.name);
            FSClose (outFileRefNum);
            SetCursor(&qd.arrow);                /* Restore the cursor */
            } /* end if !fileError */
        FlushVol (NIL, outputReply.sfFile.vRefNum);
        } /* end if outputReply.sfGood */
    FSClose (inFileRefNum);
    SetVol(NIL, oldVol);
    } /* end if inputReply.sfGood */

} /* end Ask_File() */
```

This code looks pretty scary, but it's not. We do a lot of error checking in this function, because this is where the goofs that wipe out entire files can happen. First, `Ask_File()` uses the Toolbox routine `StandardGetFile()` to query the user for an input filename. The arguments `ONE_FILE_TYPE` and `textType` presented to `StandardGetFile()` have this routine filter out all file types but one, the 'TEXT' type. This averts potential fireworks by eliminating the possibility of accidentally opening a file loaded with binary data. When the routine returns, the file information is packaged in a `StandardFileReply` data structure. A part of this structure, the Boolean `sfGood`, indicates whether the contents of `StandardFileReply` are valid—that is, whether the user actually picked a file. We stop processing if `sfGood` is `FALSE`, because this occurs only when the user clicks on Cancel, which means they decided against munging a file.

If `sfGood` is `TRUE`, the program proceeds to open the file. First, we save the current default volume number using `GetVol()`. We do this because we will make the volume where the output is directed the current default volume temporarily. This way the actions of all File Manager routines apply to this specific volume, which might be another hard drive on the system or a shared Mac on the network. Then we use `FSpOpenDF()` to open the file's data fork. If there are no problems, `FSpOpenDF()` supplies a file reference number to be used with subsequent File Manager calls. Next, the program prompts the user for an output filename, using `StandardPutFile()`. The variable `fileName` provides a default name of "Munge.out" that `StandardPutFile()` offers when it displays the Standard File dialog. Again, we check `sfGood` to ensure that the user typed a filename (or used the default name) and clicked OK. If that's the case, then we set the output file's volume as the default volume.

While the tests for opening a file for input are simple, opening a file for output is anything but. For example, it's possible that the filename the user typed matches the name of a file that already exists in the folder. Fortunately, `StandardPutFile()` does this check for us and even tosses a dialog box on the screen, as shown in figure 4.35, that warns of the conflict. However, if the user clicks on Replace, it's up to us to delete the existing file. We use a `switch` statement to deal with this situation and other errors.

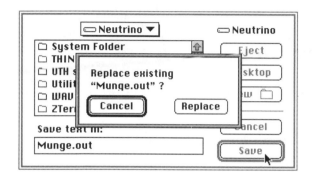

Figure 4.35 *The name conflict dialog box*

First we attempt to create the file using `FSpCreate()`. If a duplicate filename error (-48) occurs, we delete the file with `FSpDelete()`, then try `FSpCreate()` again. If there are problems with these actions, or the first call to `FSpCreate()` happens to return an unexpected error code, we simply stop the operation. This is accomplished by calling `Report_Error()`, closing the input file (which we had opened), restoring the default volume number, and exiting `Ask_File()`. This might seem like a drastic response, but when there's a disk full of files at risk, it's better to play it safe.

Assuming everything has worked flawlessly so far, `FSpCreate()` makes an output file of the requested creator and type, and the data fork is opened using `FSpOpenDF()`. If there are no errors, `FSpOpenDF()` returns a file reference number for the output file. Now we have all the information required by `Munge_File()`, since we can obtain the input filename string from `sfFile.name`, which is part of `StandardFileReply`.

Before we call `Munge_File()`, we fetch the stopwatch cursor icon using `GetCursor()`. The program places it onscreen by calling `SetCursor()`, to indicate that it is busy processing a file. Then, the program calls

Munge_File(). When the function returns, the program sets the cursor back to an arrow. Now all that's left is the clean up. The output and input files are closed, and FlushVol() is called to update the volume information for the new file. Finally, the original default volume number is restored.

Background Info

Old timers will recognize that System 7's StandardGetFile() and StandardPutFile() are similar to the old Standard File Manager calls, SFGetFile() and SFPutFile(). The differences between the two sets of routines are minor, except for the type of reference number returned. These old routines are still supported.

Basic Application Functions

Now it's time to look at some of the basic application functions that implement the user interface. Let's start with the code that handles menu commands:

```
Boolean Do_Command (long mResult)
{
unsigned char   accName[255];
short           itemHit;
Boolean         quitApp;
short           refNum;
DialogPtr       theDialog;
short           theItem, theMenu;
GrafPtr         savePort;       /* place to stow current GrafPort when */
                                /*    Desk Accessory (DA) is activated */

    quitApp = FALSE;           /* Assume Quit not chosen */
    theMenu = HiWord(mResult); /* Extract the menu selected */
    theItem = LoWord(mResult); /* Get the item on the menu  */

    switch (theMenu)
      {
      case APPLE_MENU:
         if (theItem == ABOUT_BOX)            /* Describe ourself */
            {
```

```
            if ((theDialog = GetNewDialog(ABOUT_BOX_ID, NIL,
                                (WindowPtr) IN_FRONT)) != NIL)
              {
              ModalDialog(NIL, &itemHit);
              DisposDialog(theDialog);
              } /* end if != NIL */
            else
              SysBeep(30);
            } /* end if theItem == ABOUT_BOX */
          else                             /* It's a DA */
            {
            GetPort(&savePort);            /* Save port (if DA doesn't) */
            GetMenuItemText(gmyMenus[(APPLE_MENU - MENU_RESOURCE)],
                    theItem, accName);
            refNum = OpenDeskAcc(accName);  /* Start it */
            SetPort(savePort);             /* Done, restore the port */
            }
        break; /* end APPLE_MENU case */

      case FILE_MENU:
        switch(theItem)
          {
          case OPEN_FILE:
            Ask_File();                    /* Obtain file info & process */
            break;
          case I_QUIT:                     /* User wants to stop */
            quitApp = TRUE;
          break;
          } /* end switch */
        break; /* end FILE_MENU case */

      case EDIT_MENU:                      /* Pass events to OS */
        SystemEdit(theItem - 1);
      break;
      default:
        break;
      } /* end switch */

  HiliteMenu(0);        /* Switch off highlighting on the menu just used */
  return quitApp;
} /* end Do_Command() */
```

The **Do_Command()** basically takes a menu choice passed to it by the main event loop, and uses `switch` statements to route program execution to the appropriate handler code. This is accomplished by reducing the menu choice value in `mResult` into components using the `HiWord()` and `LoWord()` Toolbox routines. These components consist of the menu chosen, which is stored in `theMenu`, and the item on that menu, which is stored in `theItem`. For example, if someone using munger selected Quit from its File menu, `theMenu` would be 129 and `theItem` would be 3.

The first `switch` statement uses `theMenu`'s value to branch to a code section corresponding to that particular menu. Here a second `switch` statement uses `theItem`'s value to pick the function responsible for that specific menu item. Depending upon the number and structure of an application's menus, these `switch` statements can be sparse or complex.

For the Apple menu, if the About Box item is selected, then munger displays the dialog box we constructed in ResEdit. As usual, we check to see if `GetNewDialog()` encountered difficulties making the window. If not, `ModalDialog()` fields all events, keeping the About Box on the screen until the OK button is clicked or Return is pressed. If another item is picked on the Apple menu, its name is extracted using `GetMenuItemText()`. This name is passed to `OpenDeskAcc()`, which opens the Desk Accessory, application, document, or alias file in the Apple Menu Items folder. Note that we do some grafport housekeeping, just in case.

Background Info

In pre-System 7 versions of the Mac OS, the only items in the Apple menu were small utility programs called Desk Accessories that were embedded in the System file. They were actually a special type of driver, so that they could run concurrently with the application in the original single-tasking environment. With the advent of cooperative multitasking under MultiFinder in System 6.0.x, the Mac OS treated Desk Accessories as miniature applications, or "applets," although the code and location of Desk Accessories didn't change. System 7 altered this arrangement further by creating an Apple Menu Items folder where the Desk Accessories appear as separate files. Not only that, but applications, documents, and the aliases to remote volumes can be placed in this folder, and can be picked from the Apple menu. `OpenDeskAcc()`'s role, which was formerly limited to starting drivers in the System file, has thus expanded to deal with a variety of objects located in a special folder.

Munger's File menu is pretty simple. If the Open item was picked, we just call `Ask_File()`, and let it handle the job. If Quit was chosen, we set the variable `quitApp` to `TRUE`, to signal the main event loop that it's time to stop. The Edit menu is even simpler. As mentioned earlier, it's mostly a place-holder used to trickle certain events to other applications. The program calls `SystemEdit()`, which checks to see if the Edit menu selection (such as a Paste command) should be passed to a Desk Accessory or handled by the program itself. This is a holdover from the single-tasking days when only one application could run at a time, yet could support one or more Desk Accessories running symbiotically within it.

Just before `Do_Command()` exits, it performs some screen maintenance. When you make a menu selection, the Menu Manager highlights the menu's title. This serves as a visual cue that the application is doing something, especially if the chosen operation happens to be a lengthy one. (Ideally, the programmer also changes the cursor to a stopwatch, or some other busy indicator.) Once the operation completes, we call `HiliteMenu(0)` to restore the menu title's appearance. Finally, `Do_Command()` returns the value of `quitApp` to the main event loop.

Main Event Loops

Speaking of main event loops, it's time to check it out:

```
void Main_Event_Loop(void)
{
Point     where;

   FlushEvents(everyEvent, 0);        /* Clear out left over events */
   guserDone = FALSE;

   do
      {
      if (WaitNextEvent(everyEvent, &gmyEvent, LONG_NAP, NO_CURSOR))
         {                            /* We have an event... */
         switch(gmyEvent.what)        /* Field each type of event */
            {
            case mouseDown:           /* In what window, and where?? */
               gwindowCode = FindWindow(gmyEvent.where, &gwhichWindow);
                  switch(gwindowCode)
```

```
                            {
                            case inSysWindow: /* It's a Desk Accessory (DA) */
                                SystemClick(&gmyEvent, gwhichWindow);
                            break;
                            case inDrag:       /* Drag the window */
                            break;
                            case inGrow:       /* Change the window's size */
                            break;
                            case inContent:    /* Bring window to front if it's not */
                            break;
                            case inMenuBar:    /* In a menu, handle the command */
                                guserDone = Do_Command(MenuSelect(gmyEvent.where));
                            break;
                            } /* end switch gwindowCode */
                        break; /* end mouseDown */
                    case keyDown:
                    case autoKey:              /* Command key hit, pass to MenuKey */
                        if((gmyEvent.modifiers & cmdKey) != 0)
                            guserDone = Do_Command(MenuKey((char) (gmyEvent.message
                                            & CHAR_CODE_MASK)));
                        break; /* end key events */
                    case updateEvt:            /* Update the window */
                        gwhichWindow = (WindowPtr) gmyEvent.message;
                        break;
                    case diskEvt:              /* Handle disk insertion event */
                        if (HiWord(gmyEvent.message) != noErr)
                            {
                            DILoad();
                            where.h = INIT_X;
                            where.v = INIT_Y;
                            DIBadMount(where, gmyEvent.message);
                            DIUnload();
                            } /* end if != noErr */
                    break; /* end disk event */
                    case activateEvt:          /* Activate event */
                        gwhichWindow = (WindowPtr) gmyEvent.message;
                    break;
                    default:
                    break;
                    } /* end switch gmyEvent.what */
                } /* end if on next event */
            } /* end do */

    while (guserDone == FALSE);      /* Loop until told to stop */
} /* end Main_Event_Loop() */
```

`Main_Event_Loop()` is the heart of the application. The program tours the loop in this function for the life of the application, retrieving events from the operating system queue and responding to them. The loop stops only when the user selects Quit from the File menu.

This function starts by clearing out any leftover events using `FlushEvents()`, and then sets `guserDone` to FALSE so that the `do` loop cycles permanently. Inside the `do` loop, the program calls `WaitNextEvent()` periodically, looking for events to handle. The first argument to this Toolbox routine is the event mask, which determines the types of events you want returned to the application. The munger program allows all of them. This mask can be modified in eclectic applications to filter out certain events. The second argument is a pointer to an event record, the data structure containing information on the type of event received, the pointer's screen location (necessary if the event was a mouse down), and any modifier information. *Modifiers* are the Command, Option, Shift, and Control keys. When these keys are pressed, typically during a key down or mouse down event, they modify the meaning of the event, hence their name. You're already familiar with one modifier key: pressing Command and another key transforms a key down event into a menu selection.

The `LONG_NAP` constant informs `WaitNextEvent()` that munger should sleep for one second intervals, thereby yielding processor time to other applications. Like `Delay()`, this value is in tick intervals. This might seem like a lot of time to offer to the rest of the system, but munger isn't doing a time-critical background task such as a ZMODEM download, or copying a file across a network. Since munger does no background processing, the `if` statement around `WaitNextEvent()` locks out any null events. In this case, `LONG_NAP` simply serves as a placeholder in the routine. The constant `NO_CURSOR` tells the Mac OS that no special pointer handling is required.

Important

It's very important that your application periodically surrender the processor to other applications. (That is, `LONG_NAP` should never equal 0.) System 7 currently uses cooperative multitasking, where applications agree to share processing time amongst themselves. If your application fails to share time with other applications, background processing ceases because those applications can't get processor time to run.

The context switch to another application is handled through the `WaitNextEvent()` routine, so it must be called periodically to ensure that these switches occur. This isn't a problem when program execution is in the main event loop. However, functions called by the main event loop in response to a user command might keep program execution out of the loop long enough so that these application switches fail to happen regularly. For example, if `Munge_File()` performs disk I/O to a floppy—a slow peripheral device—other background applications get starved for processor time until the slow file I/O completes, and execution returns to munger's main event loop. The solution is to have the function periodically call `WaitNextEvent()` itself as it runs. Cooperative multitasking dictates that this type of program design must be used, since it's up to the application to relinquish control to other applications frequently. Hopefully, these sorts of issues will disappear when the microkernel-based Mac OS arrives.

Historically, applications used the original event dispatching routine `GetNextEvent()`, and it's still supported for compatibility. However, it's preferable to use `WaitNextEvent()`, since this routine is better suited for System 7's multitasking environment. For example, `WaitNextEvent()` provides the sleep argument, while `GetNextEvent()` doesn't.

The event loop code has an arrangement similar to `Do_Command()`, where `switch` statements zero in on the function that deals with a specific event. The first switch statement uses the information in `gmyEvent.what` to jump to the code section for that event type.

Background Info
The types of event types defined by the Mac OS are: mouse down, mouse up, key down, key up, auto key, update, disk insertion, activate, high-level, null events, and OS events. Most of these events are self-explanatory, but a brief description of the others is in order. The auto key event occurs when a key is held down long enough to begin repeating the character. The disk insertion event indicates a floppy or other removable media has been placed in a drive. The update event signals an application to redraw the contents of a specific window. Update events occur when other windows cover the application's

window(s) temporarily, perhaps because of an application context switch or because of a dialog box. The activate event informs the application that a certain window has been clicked on with the mouse, and if it isn't the current active window, it must be made so. Null events indicate that the user has done nothing; there are no other events to report. The application can either discard this type of event, or perform some background processing, such as blinking an I-beam cursor in a window with text. OS events are used for window maintenance and Clipboard data conversion when your application switches into the background or foreground. Since munger has no windows, and doesn't use the Clipboard, we ignore this event type.

Depending upon the event type, yet another `switch` statement might be used to further refine what code should respond to the event. For example, the mouse down event section uses a second `switch` statement to determine if the mouse was clicked on a window, the desktop, a Desk Accessory, or in the menu bar. Conversely, dealing with disk insertion events is a straightforward procedure, and so its section just has the code that handles the event.

Let's look closely at how events are dealt with. For a mouse down event, the code has `FindWindow()` evaluate where the mouse click occured. We provide `FindWindow()` with this point from `gmyEvent.where`, which is part of the event record that contains the mouse position. `FindWindow()` returns a code that describes the part of the window clicked on, such as the title bar section of a window, the content region (where the application-specific information appears in the window), its size box (the box at a window's lower right, used to resize the window), or elsewhere. Elsewhere can be the onscreen desktop or the menu bar. If the code corresponds to a window element, `FindWindow()`'s second argument returns a pointer to that window. We use `FindWindow()`'s results in a `switch` statement to hop to the appropriate handler code. Since munger doesn't use a window, most of the handlers in this `switch` statement are stubs.

If the mouse click occurred in a system window (a Desk Accessory), we call `SystemClick()` to forward the event to it. This is one of those vestigial routines used for compatibility with older software. If the click happened in the menu bar, we hand the event off to `Do_Command()` for processing.

Key down and auto key events are treated the same way. Again, since munger doesn't use a document window, processing keystrokes is fairly simple. We peek at the modifier field (`gmyEvent.modifiers`) for each key event record. If the Command key wasn't pressed, then we toss the event in the bit bucket. If it was, the key event might be a menu's keyboard equivalent. First, we extract the character out of the `message` field of the event record. We use `CHAR_CODE_MASK` to do this, because this field is an amalgam of the key's character code, a virtual key code (a special code used to identify a physical key on the keyboard), and the address of the keyboard on the Apple Desktop Bus (ADB). We pass the character to `MenuKey()`, which maps it to the menu and menu item with the corresponding keyboard equivalent. `MenuKey()` returns a match in a format that we can simply pass along to `Do_Command()` to complete.

Like the mouse down window handlers, since the activate and update events pertain only to windows, we only put code stubs in the event loop for them. If your application uses windows, you'll have to flesh out this code.

The disk insertion event actually turns out to be a critical one for munger. Suppose someone decides to save the munged output to a blank floppy? When such a disk insertion event occurs, munger's handler code springs into action.

It checks the event's `message` field for an error code the Mac OS might return when it attempts to mount the volume (floppy). If a formatted floppy was inserted, the Mac OS mounts it so that a floppy disk icon appears on the desktop, and no error is reported. If there was a mount error, we retrieve the event and call `DILoad()` to load the Disk Initialization Manager. We pass the event's `message` field to `DIBadMount()`, a routine used to initialize (or format) volumes. `Message` supplies `DIBadMount()` with the error code and the drive number. `DIBadMount()` places a dialog box on the screen, asking the user to initialize or eject the floppy. The user presumably initializes the floppy and `DIBadMount()` exits. `DIUnload()` then removes the Disk Initialization Manager from memory and the user has a fresh floppy on which to save munged files.

If munger didn't field this event, when the user poked a blank floppy into the drive, nothing would happen. The disk insertion event would remain queued until the user switched to another application (probably a database to look up my Internet address and rightfully complain). This application would handle the event, and the disk initialization dialog would appear unexpectedly, further confusing the unhappy user. Although munger uses `DIBadMount()` to initialize a floppy disk, this routine can also initialize hard disks. See *Inside Macintosh: Files* for more information.

As the event loop completes its course, the variable `guserDone` is checked. If `Do_Command()` returns `TRUE` in response to a Quit command, this changes the state of `guserDone`. In this case the event loop quits, as does the application.

The Initialization Function

Now all that's left to do is examine munger's initialization function:

```
Boolean Init_Mac(void)
{
short i;

/* Lunge after all the memory we can get */
   MaxApplZone();

/* Make sure we've got some master pointers */
   MoreMasters();
   MoreMasters();
   MoreMasters();
   MoreMasters();

/* Initialize managers */
   InitGraf(&qd.thePort);
   InitFonts();
   FlushEvents(everyEvent, 0);
   InitWindows();
   InitMenus();
   TEInit();
   InitDialogs(NIL);

/* Loop to setup menus */
   for (i = APPLE_MENU; i < (APPLE_MENU + LAST_MENU); i++)
     {
     gmyMenus[(i - RESOURCE_ID)] = GetMenu(i); /* Get menu resource */
     if (gmyMenus[(i - RESOURCE_ID)] == NIL)   /* Didn't get resource? */
```

```
        return FALSE;                          /* No, bail out */
    }; /* end for */


/* Build Apple menu */
   AppendResMenu(gmyMenus[(APPLE_MENU - RESOURCE_ID)], 'DRVR');


/* Add the menus */
   for (i = APPLE_MENU; i < (APPLE_MENU + LAST_MENU); i++)
       InsertMenu(gmyMenus[(i - RESOURCE_ID)], APPEND_MENU);


   DrawMenuBar();
   InitCursor();                               /* Tell user app is ready */
   return TRUE;
} /* end Init_Mac() */
```

If you think this function looks similar to the "Hello world" example at the start of this chapter, you are correct. Notice that we've added code to initialize the Menu Manager, Dialog Manager, and TextEdit, a Manager that deals with simple text entry and editing. TextEdit is required to handle characters typed into the Standard File dialog box when `StandardPutFile()` asks for a filename.

We also have to set up the menus. First, we use a `for` loop to load the menu resources, using `GetMenu()`. This routine returns a handle to menu record, which we immediately stow in our `gmyMenus` array. We do some math to convert the menu resource ID into an array index. Since the initialization code runs only once, we can afford to do some extra calculations here. We also perform a fail-safe check to see that `GetMenu()` successfully locates the menu resources and returns valid handles to menu records. If there is a problem, `GetMenu()` returns `NIL`. In this case we simply abort the initialization process and have the function return `FALSE`.

Next, we use `AppendResMenu()` to construct the Apple menu. The `AppendResMenu()` routine searches any resource files open to the application for the requested resource type. It then adds the names of these resources to the specified menu. We specify the DRVR resource to collect the Apple menu items. Like the operation of `OpenDeskAcc()` routine, this resource type selection is a remnant of the pre-System 7 days when Desk Accessories were driver resources in the System file. However, `AppendResMenu()` now fetches the names of all the files in the Apple Menu Items folder, as well as the Desk Accessories.

With the Apple menu built, we use another `for` loop to add munger's own menus using `InsertMenu()`. Finally, we display the new menus using `DrawMenuBar()`, followed by `InitCursor()`, which sets the mouse pointer to an arrow to show the munger is ready.

The last thing left to do is type in `main()`, and here it is:

```
void main(void)
{
   if (Init_Mac())
      Main_Event_Loop();
   else
      SysBeep(30);
} /* end main */
```

When the application launches, it calls the initialization function. If the function reports no problem (by returning `TRUE`), then execution proceeds to the main event loop. This is where munger runs until the user asks it to quit.

Build Munger

Now it's time to build munger. Add "Macmunger.c," "InterfaceLib," and "MWCRuntime.Lib" to the project. Go to the Project preferences panel and type in **munger** for the application filename. Build the application and an application file, sporting the generic application icon and the name `munger`, should appear in the folder. Launch munger, and try it out.

Important

If munger beeps and quits immediately, there's a problem with its menu resources. First, check to see that the .rsrc filename matches the project filename. (That is, the project munger.π should have a resource file named "munger.π.rsrc.") Next, open the .rsrc file with ResEdit and make sure the ID numbers of the MENU resources match those defined in munger's source code. If not, correct the problem by changing the ID numbers in ResEdit, or editing "Macmunger.c." Note that Macmunger.c's initialization code relies on the MENU ID numbers to be in ascending order.

Choose Open... from the File menu, and search for a file to munge. You'll see that the only files that appear in the Standard File dialog are folders or text files. Select a text file, such as the example file in CodeWarrior:Code Examples ƒ:Munger ƒ:PowerPC.txt and let munger have at it. When munger is done, you'll get the status dialog box (see figure 4.36) that reports on the results of the filtering operation.

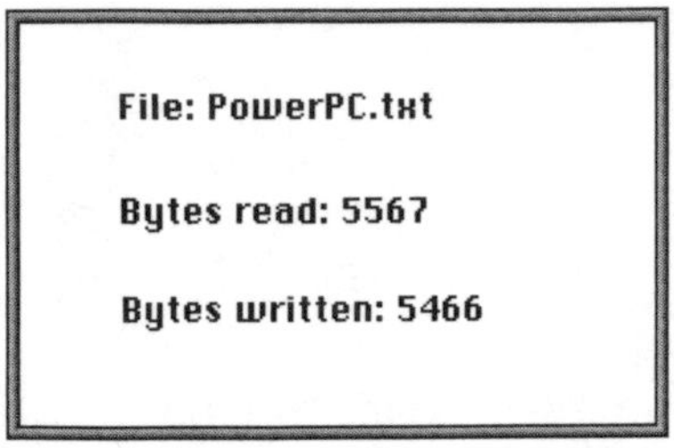

```
File: PowerPC.txt

Bytes read: 5567

Bytes written: 5466
```

Figure 4.36   *Munger's status report dialog box*

High-Level Events

We've seen how an application's event loop retrieves and responds to low-level events posted by the operating system. Under System 7, a second event mechanism enables applications to communicate with one another. Called high-level events, these events can be used as messages to request data from or provide data to other applications. High-level events that follow the Apple Event Interprocess Messaging Protocol (AEIMP) are called Apple events. The message format is defined by suites of published commands. For the sake of simplicity, we will consider Apple events and high-level events one and the same. For more information on Apple events, consult *Inside Macintosh: Interapplication Communication*.

Why should you care about Apple events? Because if your application responds to them, it can be controlled by an AV Power Mac's voice recognition software, or the AppleScript programming language, both which communicate through Apple events. At the very least, an application should respond to the four required Apple events, which are: Open Application, Open Documents, Print Documents, and Quit Application. Although this quartet of required events seem rather limited, a creative script can do a lot with them.

For example, you can write a program in AppleScript that searches a folder for the E-mail you just downloaded, launches a word processor application, instructs it to print your E-mail files (Print Documents event), and then stops the word processor (Quit Application event). The Finder, where possible, uses the required events to open documents and handle print requests. Of course, the applications have to be "savvy" (or understand) Apple events for the Finder to do this. A special resource in the application tells the Finder whether it's Apple event savvy or not. If not, the Finder uses older, pre-System 7 methods to start the application and handle the request.

One compelling reason to add high-level event support to munger is that it allows us to use System 7's neat "drag and drop" mechanism. That is, someone selects a text file icon with the mouse, drags it across the desktop, and drops it onto the munger icon. Munger launches, and through high-level event communications, opens the desired file and processes it. Let's add this capability to munger, since we only need one of the four required Apple events to implement it. While we're at it, we'll give munger a distinctive icon, and beef up the error checking in the `Munge_File()` function, as promised earlier.

Make Munger Handle High-Level Events

There are four key sections in munger that we have to change so that it handles high-level events. First, we've got to make our event loop code aware of this new type of event. Second, we need a mechanism that delivers these high-level events to the appropriate handler functions. Third, we need the handler code itself. Last but not least, we have to make the operating system aware that our application can deal with high-level events.

Begin by making a copy of "Macmunger.c." Select the "Macmunger.c" file and pick Duplicate from the Finder's File menu, or type Command-D. Rename the file copy "SonOMunger.c" and add it to the munger.π project, while removing the original "Macmunger.c" from the project. Open "SonOMunger.c" with the editor to add a few more header files to the program. Beneath the other header files, type:

```
#include <AppleTalk.h>
#include <AppleEvents.h>
#include <EPPC.h>
```

```
#include <PPCToolBox.h>
#include <Processes.h>

struct AEinstalls
   {
    AEEventClass theClass;
    AEEventID theEvent;
    AEEventHandlerProcPtr theProc;
   };
typedef struct AEinstalls AEinstalls;

#define LAST_HANDLER     3    /* Number of Apple Event handlers - 1 */
```

Most of these header files define Apple event data structures and routines.
"AppleTalk.h" is required because high-level events can be sent across the
network to other computers. To communicate to other applications, Apple
events also use certain Process Manager routines and so that header file
appears. The structure **AEInstalls** organizes certain Apple event data
structures and the addresses of handler functions for installation in a
dispatch table. **LAST_HANDLER** indicates how many of these handlers must
be installed in the dispatch table. There a few more function prototypes to
define, too:

```
/* High-level Apple Event functions */
Boolean Init_AE_Events(void);          /* Install the handlers */

/* Post high-level event to the dispatch table */
void Do_High_Level(EventRecord *AERecord);

/* The four required handlers */
pascal OSErr Core_AE_Open_Handler(AppleEvent *messagein,
                                  AppleEvent *reply, long refIn);
pascal OSErr Core_AE_OpenDoc_Handler(AppleEvent *messagein,
                                     AppleEvent *reply, long refIn);
pascal OSErr Core_AE_Print_Handler(AppleEvent *messagein,
                                   AppleEvent *reply, long refIn);
pascal OSErr Core_AE_Quit_Handler(AppleEvent *messagein,
                                  AppleEvent *reply, long refIn);

/* Note change! */
OSErr Munge_File(short input, short output, unsigned char *fileName);
```

There's the usual initialization function to install the handlers, a function to route the high-level events to the handlers, and the four handlers themselves. As part of its improved I/O checks, `Munge_File()` returns an error value now.

Modifying the Event Loop Code

Now let's start with the first item on the list, which is modifying the event loop code. Go to `Main_Event_Loop()`, and in the first `switch` statement (the one that deals with the event type), add:

```
case activateEvt:              /* Activate event */
    gwhichWindow = (WindowPtr) gmyEvent.message;
break;
case kHighLevelEvent:          /* Handle Apple Event */
    Do_High_Level(&gmyEvent);
break;
default:
break;
} /* end switch gmyEvent.what */
```

I've included a few of the surrounding source code statements so that you can recognize where to place the code. From this code you can see that high-level events are just another event passed to the application via the Event Manager. The operation of this new code is simple: When `WaitNextEvent()` retrieves a high-level event for us, we just call `Do_High_Level()` to handle it.

Delivering High-Level Events

Let's write `Do_High_Level()` next, since it's a portion of item two, the delivery mechanism. Type:

```
void Do_High_Level(EventRecord *AERecord)
{
   AEProcessAppleEvent(AERecord);
} /* end Do_High_Level() */
```

Was that tough, or what? The event record gets forwarded directly to
`AEProcessAppleEvent()`. This routine uses information in the event record to
determine what handler routine to call in the dispatch table. The
application's dispatch table is searched first, followed by the system's
dispatch table. A match is based on the event's class and event ID. If there
is a match, `AEProcessAppleEvent()` calls the handler associated with that
dispatch table entry. This brings up the question of what builds the dispatch table. For the answer, type:

```
Boolean Init_AE_Events(void)
{
OSErr err;
short i;
static AEinstalls HandlersToInstall[] =  /* The 4 required Apple Events */
    {
       {kCoreEventClass, kAEOpenApplication, Core_AE_Open_Handler},
       {kCoreEventClass, kAEOpenDocuments, Core_AE_OpenDoc_Handler},
       {kCoreEventClass, kAEQuitApplication, Core_AE_Quit_Handler},
       {kCoreEventClass, kAEPrintDocuments, Core_AE_Print_Handler}
    };

   for (i = 0; i < LAST_HANDLER; i++)
     {
     err = AEInstallEventHandler(HandlersToInstall[i].theClass,
                                 HandlersToInstall[i].theEvent,
          NewAEEventHandlerProc(HandlersToInstall[i].theProc),
                                              0, FALSE);
     if (err)    /* If there was a problem, bail out */
        return FALSE;
     } /* end for */

   return TRUE;
} /* end Init_AE_Events() */
```

It's the responsibility of `Init_AE_Events()` to construct the table. The objects in the array `HandlersToInstall[]` correspond to the dispatch table
elements of an event class, an event ID, and a pointer to a handler function.
A simple `for` loop calls `AEInstallEventHandler()`, a routine that plugs these
items into the table. If the routine reports an error, we pass a failure indicator (`FALSE`) back to `Init_Mac()` to halt the application.

Hazard

Don't overlook the `NewAEEventHandlerProc()` routine that's buried innocuously as an argument in the call to `AEInstallEventHandler()`! This routine is critical for the proper setup of the handler functions. Since the Power Mac's system software is a mixture of 680x0 and PowerPC code, it gets tricky for the operating system to know what type of code it will be running next when the thread of execution hops to another function. To combat this problem, Apple devised Universal Procedure Pointers, or UPPs. The UPPs describe to the Mixed Mode Manager what type of processor code (PowerPC or 680x0) the function uses, the number of arguments the function uses, and the programming language used to implement the function. The programming language distinction is necessary since C programs pass their arguments to a function in an order that's different from Pascal.

The C header files incorporate this UPP information for every Toolbox routine, so that the programmer is normally unaware which routines are PowerPC code, and which are 680x0 code. For certain functions that you write, it's up to you to explain their nature to the Mixed Mode Manager by providing UPPs for them. Functions that fall in this category are external functions (such as plug-in modules that might be a mixture of 68K or PowerPC code), or internal functions called by the operating system (such as our high-level handler routines). If you fail to provide a UPP for these functions, the Mac OS can get terribly confused when it jumps to them. This is because the operating system doesn't know what processor code the function is written in, nor can it determine the size of the arguments used. If the Mac OS guesses wrong, the result is a spectacular crash.

The rule of thumb is: If a mode switch is involved, you need a UPP. Native PowerPC plug-in modules that add capabilities to a PowerPC application don't require UPPs because there is no mode switch involved.

If you're worried about getting bogged down in the details of writing a UPP, relax. The header files supply routines that do this work for you, especially when it's known that the operating system will be calling back into your application. `NewAEEventHandlerProc()` is such routine; it constructs a UPP for those high-level event handlers whose addresses you supply. Don't forget to use this routine when setting up your handlers!

We call `Init_AE_Events()` as the SonOMunger initializes, so that it is prepared to respond to Apple Events immediately once it is running. Go to the `Init_Mac()` function and type:

```
DrawMenuBar();

if (!Init_AE_Events())          /* Set up our high-level event handlers */
   return FALSE;

InitCursor();                   /* Tell user app is ready */
```

Again, I have included a few neighboring lines of code so that you get the idea of where to locate the function call. This completes item two.

Writing the Handlers

Item three on our list is writing the handlers themselves. Enter the following code:

```
/* High-level open application event.  */
pascal OSErr Core_AE_Open_Handler(AppleEvent *messagein,
                                  AppleEvent *reply, long refIn)
{
   return noErr;
} /* end Core_AE_Open_Handler() */


/* High-level print event */
pascal OSErr Core_AE_Print_Handler(AppleEvent *messagein,
                                   AppleEvent *reply, long refIn)
{
   return errAEEventNotHandled;   /* No printing done here, so */
                                  /* no print handler. */
} /* end Core_AE_Print_Handler() */


/* High-level quit event  */
pascal OSErr Core_AE_Quit_Handler(AppleEvent *messagein,
                                  AppleEvent *reply, long refIn)
{
   guserDone = TRUE;   /* Tell main event loop we want to stop */
   return noErr;
} /* Core_AE_Quit_Handler() */
```

The three handlers you see here are fairly simple. Notice that arguments passed to them are simply ignored. The Open Application Apple Event notifies the application to perform any start-up tasks required of it. For example, the application might create an untitled document window, or establish a connection to a database. Since SonOMunger's design of pipelining of data between two files is very focused, it doesn't need any start up tasks. Therefore, when munger receives an Open Application event, the function `Core_AE_Open_Handler()` reports a "no error" message back to the caller while doing nothing. Since SonOMunger doesn't do any printing, `Core_AE_Print_Handler()` responds with an error message that indicates SonOMunger can't field the Print Documents event. Upon the receipt of a Quit Application event, `Core_AE_Quit_Handler()` simply sets `guserDone` so that SonOMunger halts on the next tour of the event loop, and returns a "no error" message.

SonOMunger uses the Open Document Apple event to implement the drag and drop feature. When you drop a text file icon onto the SonOMunger icon, the Finder sends it an Open Document event that also contains the dropped filename. Drag and drop applications are generally expected to complete the job without further input from the user. That is, you drop a file on SonOMunger, and you expect a processed output file to appear. With that in mind, let's write the `Core_AE_OpenDoc_Handler()` function. Type:

```
/* High-level open document event */
pascal OSErr Core_AE_OpenDoc_Handler(AppleEvent *messagein, AppleEvent *reply, long
refIn)
{
short          i, j;
AEDesc         fileDesc;
OSErr          highLevelErr;
AEKeyword      ignoredKeyWord;
DescType       ignoredType;
Size           ignoredSize;
long           numberOFiles;
unsigned char  outFileName[64];
FSSpec         inFSS, outFSS;
short          inFileRefNum, outFileRefNum;
OSErr          fInErr, fOutErr, mungeResult;
```

```
        gtheCursor = GetCursor(watchCursor);   /* Indicate we're busy */
        SetCursor(&**gtheCursor);
        mungeResult = 0;                        /* Clear so FOR loop operates */
/* Get parameter info (a list of filenames) out of Apple Event*/
        if (!(highLevelErr = AEGetParamDesc(messagein, keyDirectObject,
                                            typeAEList, &fileDesc)))
            {
            if ((highLevelErr = AECountItems(&fileDesc, &numberOFiles)) == noErr)
/* Count files */
                {
                for (i = 1; ((i <= numberOFiles) && (!highLevelErr) &&
                                            (!mungeResult)); ++i)
                    {
                    if (!(highLevelErr = AEGetNthPtr(&fileDesc, i, typeFSS,
                                            &ignoredKeyWord, &ignoredType,
                                            (char *)&inFSS, sizeof(inFSS),
                                            &ignoredSize))) /* Get name */
                        {
                        for (j = 1; (j <= inFSS.name[0]); j++) /* Copy filename */
                            {
                            outFileName[j] = inFSS.name[j];
                            } /* end for */
                        outFileName[j] = '.';             /* Tack '.out' on end */
                        outFileName[j + 1] = 'o';
                        outFileName[j + 2] = 'u';
                        outFileName[j + 3] = 't';
                        outFileName[0] = (j + 3);         /* Update string's length */
                        if (!(fInErr = FSpOpenDF(&inFSS, fsCurPerm, &inFileRefNum)))
                            {
                            if ((fOutErr = FSMakeFSSpec(DEFAULT_VOL, NIL,
                                            outFileName, &outFSS)) == fnfErr)
                                {
                                if (!(fOutErr = FSpCreate(&outFSS, gfileCreator,
                                            gfileType, smSystemScript)))
                                    {
                                    if (!(fOutErr = FSpOpenDF(&outFSS, fsCurPerm,
                                                    &outFileRefNum)))
                                        {
                                        mungeResult = Munge_File(inFileRefNum,
                                                        outFileRefNum,
                                                            inFSS.name);
                                        FlushVol(NIL, outFileRefNum);
```

```
                              FSClose(outFileRefNum);
                            } /* end if !fOutErr */
                    else
                        Report_Err_Message("\pError opening output file");
                      } /* end if !fOutErr */
                  else
                      {
                      Report_Err_Message("\pError creating output file");
                      } /* end else */
                    } /* end if == fnfErr */
                else
                    {
                    if (fOutErr == noErr)  /* No error means a file */
                                          /*    already has that name */
                        Report_Err_Message("\pCan't write, file already
                                            exists");
                      } /* end else */
                    FSClose(inFileRefNum);
                      } /* end if !fInErr */
                else
                    Report_Err_Message("\pError opening input file");
                  } /* end if !highlevelErr */
              } /* end for */
          } /* end if == noErr */
      AEDisposeDesc(&fileDesc);                  /* Dispose of the copy made */
                                                 /*    by AEGetParamDesc() */

      } /* end if !highLevelErr */

SetCursor(&qd.arrow);              /* Restore the cursor */
guserDone = TRUE;                  /* We're done, stop the application */
return (highLevelEvent);
} /* end Core_AE_OpenDoc_Handler() */
```

The Open Document event definitely triggers some activity here. Starting
at the top, **Core_AE_OpenDoc_Handler()** first slaps a stopwatch on the
pointer to show that the application is busy. Next, the Apple event gets
passed to **AEGetParamDesc()**, a routine whose arguments tell it to retrieve
the data parameters from the Apple event record. These parameters are to
be coerced (or massaged) into an data array termed a *descriptor list*, as
specified by the **typeAEList** argument. This list is placed in a buffer created
by **AEGetParamDesc()** and pointed to by **fileDesc**.

Now `AECountItems()` determines how many objects make up the descriptor list, which is the number of files dragged and dropped on SonOMunger. We use the value returned by this routine to set up a `for` loop that extracts each filename out of the descriptor list.

Two things to note here are: First, if an error occurs while extracting filenames out of the descriptor list using `AEGetNthPtr()`, the loop terminates. Second, if there's an error during file processing, `mungeResult` goes non-zero, and the loop terminates. We do have to initially zero `mungeResult` so that the loop doesn't quit prematurely.

The `AEGetNthPtr()` routine actually obtains the filenames from the descriptor list. The routine's arguments instruct it to retrieve the descriptor list items as file system specification records (`typeFSS`), a format that's used by most System 7 File Manager routines. Any Apple event keyword and descriptor type information associated with the item is ignored (`ignoredKeyWord` and `ignoredType`). The largest data item returned from the descriptor list must be no larger than a file system specification record (`sizeof(inFSS)`), and the size of the data returned is ignored.

Once an input filename is obtained from the list, we tack an '.out' extension on it, creating our output filename. This eliminates the dilemma of what to name the output file without querying the user. Note that we should add a safety check here, to see that the filename is no larger than twenty-seven characters. The reason is that Mac OS typically limits filenames to thirty-one characters in length. I should (but don't) perform a sanity check to ensure that the user hasn't passed a filename to SonOMunger that will be longer than this 31-character limit when we append the '.out' extension of the file.

To review, munger got the input filename from an Open Document Apple event that was the result of the user's drag and drop, and the output filename is derived from the input name. We use the `FSMakeFSSpec()` routine to make a file system specification record out of the derived output filename. The program then does the usual safety checks to ensure that the input and output files can be opened and written to properly, and gathers the file reference numbers. Finally, `Munge_File()` gets called.

If things proceed smoothly in `Munge_File()`, then the input and output files are closed, and the loop cycles to the next file. If for some reason

`Munge_File()` encounters trouble, the error value it returns stops the loop so that the user can fix the problem. Note that we're trying to help the user do just that by improving the error reporting. The function `Report_Err_Message()` accepts a Pascal string that gets displayed in an alert window. Finally, we call **AEDisposeDesc()** to release the memory allocated by **AEGetParamDesc()** when it made a copy of the descriptor list for our use.

The code for `Report_Err_Message()` is:

```
void Report_Err_Message(unsigned char *errMess)
{

    ParamText(errMess, NIL, NIL, NIL);
    CautionAlert(ERROR_MESS_ID, NIL);
} /* end Report_Err_Message() */
```

This is a simple routine; it just takes a pointer to a Pascal string and passes this to **ParamText()**. **CautionAlert()** then places the message onscreen. The value here is in the descriptive messages that you can provide. This is because we know where the problem occurs in the handler code, so we've got a good idea as to what caused the error.

Last but not least, here's the improved `Munge_File()` function:

```
OSErr Munge_File(short input, short output, unsigned char *fileName)
{
long           amount;
unsigned char  buffer;
short          crflag;
long           icount, ocount;
OSErr          fInOutErr;
unsigned char  inNumString[12], outNumString[12];
DialogPtr      statusDialog;

    amount = 1L;
    crflag = 0;
    icount = 0;
    ocount = 0;
    while (FSRead(input, &amount, &buffer) == noErr)
      {
      icount++;                        /* Bump input char counter */
      switch (buffer)                  /* What char was read? */
        {
```

```
        case CR:
          if (crflag >= 1)          /* Two in a row, end of paragraph */
            {
            if (!(fInOutErr = FSWrite(output, &amount, &buffer)))
              {
              if ((fInOutErr = FSWrite(output, &amount, &buffer)) != noErr)
                {
                Report_Error(fInOutErr);
                return fInOutErr;
                } /* end if != */
              } /* end if ! */
            else
              {
              Report_Error(fInOutErr);
              return fInOutErr;
              } /* end else */
            crflag = 0;            /* Reset the flag */
            ocount++;
            } /* end if */
          else
            crflag++;              /* Bump the flag, and toss the CR */
        break; /* end case CR */
        case LF:                   /* Toss LF, but don't touch crflag */
        break;   /* end case LF */
        default:                   /* Write a character out */
          if ((fInOutErr = FSWrite(output, &amount, &buffer)) != noErr)
            {
            Report_Error(fInOutErr);
            return fInOutErr;
            } /* end if */
          ocount++;
          crflag = 0;              /* Clear the flag */
        break;
        } /* end switch */
      } /* end while */

/* Display processing statistics */
    if ((statusDialog = GetNewDialog(STATUS_BOX_ID, NIL,
                                (WindowPtr) IN_FRONT)) != NIL)
    {
    NumToString(icount, inNumString);   /* Convert bytes read to string */
    NumToString(ocount, outNumString);
    ParamText (fileName, inNumString, outNumString, NIL);
```

```
    DrawDialog(statusDialog);
    Delay (120L, NIL);
    DisposDialog(statusDialog);
    } /* end if != NIL */
else
    SysBeep(30);


    return fInOutErr;
} /* end Munge_file() */
```

This function is nearly identical to the original **Munge_File**, except that the I/O routines are checked for errors. If a problem is detected, we simply call the original **Report_Error()** function, because it's hard to predict the types of problems that can occur at this level. We also pass back the error code to the caller so that action can be taken, as you saw in the Open Document handler code. This completes "SonOMunger.c." If you're confused about where the new functions went, examine "SonOMunger.c" on the CD-ROM. (The pathname is CodeWarrior:Code Examples ƒ:SonOMunger ƒ.) Or, check the complete source listing in appendix C.

However, we're still not finished. All that remains is to add some resources to SonOMunger that provide an alert box for the new error message function, and to inform the operating system that the new and improved SonOMunger is Apple Event-aware. Making SonOMunger appear high-level event savvy to the Mac OS will complete point number four, for those of you keeping score.

Making SonOMunger High-Level Event Savvy

In the CodeWarrior compiler, select Preferences from the Edit menu, and go to the Project panel. Type in **MUNG** for the Creator item. This assigns the application's Creator type, which must match the signature resource you'll make with ResEdit's bundle editor in a moment. Next, click on the checkmark icon next to the Size Flags item to activate the pop-up menu. Pick the isHighLevelEventAware item, and confirm that it is checked (see figure 4.37). Recall that earlier I mentioned that the Macintosh OS used a resource to determine if an application is high-level event savvy or not. The resource used for this determination is the SIZE resource, and we're setting

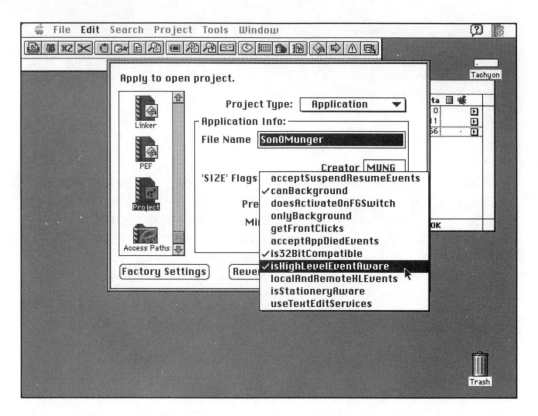

Figure 4.37   *Setting a high-level savvy flag in the application's SIZE resource*

the appropriate flag bit in it to indicate that SonOMunger can handle high-level events. If you fail to do this, the Mac OS assumes that SonOMunger can't handle high-level events and so none are ever sent to SonOMunger.

New Alerts

Now let's add the new resources SonOMunger requires. Start by double-clicking on the "munger.π.rsrc" file, which launches ResEdit. The window that displays the resource fork's contents appears. We'll make the alert box for the `Report_Err_Message()` function first.

Double-click on the ALRT resource icon. After the ALRT resource window opens, select Create New Resource from the Resource menu or type Command-K. When the alert editor window appears, change the DITL ID number to **131**. Next, pick Get Resource Info from the Resource menu or type Command-I. When the Info box opens, change the ID number to **131**. Click on this window's close box, and you have an alert resource with an ID number of 131, ready to edit.

Double-click on the window to bring up the dialog item (DITL) editor. Resize the window, add an OK button, and follow that with a static text box in the window's lower left. (Remember that the OK button needs to be DITL item 1, and that we need to allow space for the alert icon, which appears in the upper left window corner.) Simply type ^**0** for the static text item in this box. You should have an alert window that resembles the one in figure 4.38. Close all of the Editor windows, leaving only the one showing the view of the resource fork.

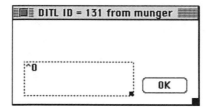

Figure 4.38   *The Report_Err_Message() alert box*

Bundle Resource

To implement the drag and drop filtering, we must provide SonOMunger with a BNDL, or bundle resource. This resource gets its name because it describes the linkages among a so-called "bundle" of resources that are used to supply certain application characteristics to the Finder, and to display the application's icon on the desktop. Let's begin by building some of these bundled resources, beginning with an application icon for SonOMunger, and an icon for its output files.

In ResEdit, create a new resource. Select 'ICN#' for the resource type. The ICON resource contains a single black-and-white icon bitmap, while the ICN# resource contains a list of information on black-and-white and color icons. The ICN# Editor window opens, with a default resource ID of 128. Click on the ICN# item and draw a black and white icon design using the editor's drawing tools (see figure 4.39).

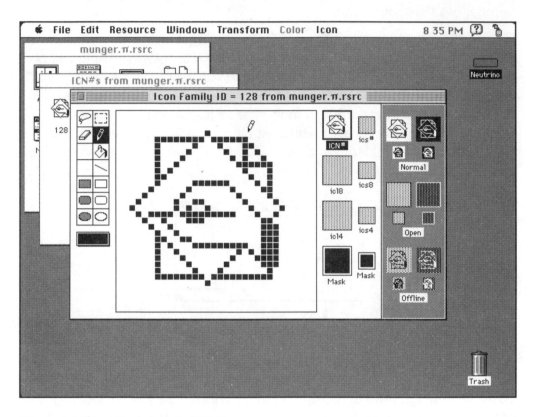

Figure 4.39   *Drawing the ICN# resource*

If you look at the icons at the far right, you'll get an idea of how they'll appear on the desktop. They look OK, except for that square outline surroundng it. So the next thing to do is create the icon mask, which is a black silhouette of the icon. The Finder uses the mask data to punch the icon's outline, cookie-cutter fashion, into the desktop background pattern. The Finder then draws the icon into this opening, fitting the icon's image seamlessly onto the screen. Making the mask is easy: Go to the ICN# item at the Editor window's upper right and drag the black-and-white icon down to the mask item window (see figure 4.40). A silhouette of the icon appears. The appearance of the test display icons should improve dramatically.

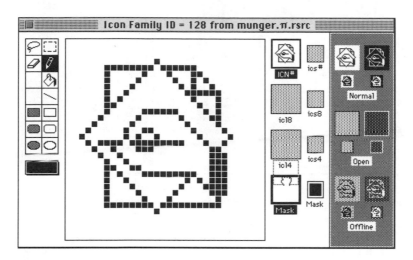

Figure 4.40   *Making the application icon's mask*

Next, drag the ICN# to the icl8 item window and click to select it. Now you can add color to the icon, making an icl8 8-bit color icon resource (see figure 4.41). Similar to how the dialog editor and dialog item editor work in tandem to produce interrelated resources, the ICN# editor lets you create several types of icon resources. When you're done with the icl8 resource, you can make the icl4 (the four-bit color icon) resource, although it's not necessary. Close the ICN# Editor window and save the file.

Select Create New Resource again and the ICN# editor reappears, this time with an ID of 129. Draw a document icon, similar to the one shown in figure 4.42. When you're done, close the ICN# Editor window and save the file. The ICN# Resource window shows the icons, along with their ID numbers. Close this window and you'll see the various resources associated with the icon list resource.

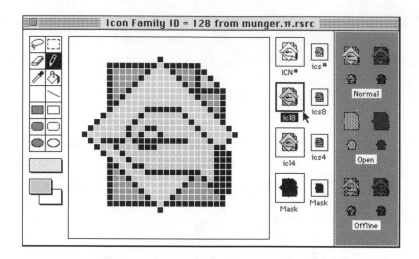

Figure 4.41   *Editing an icl8 resource for the application icon*

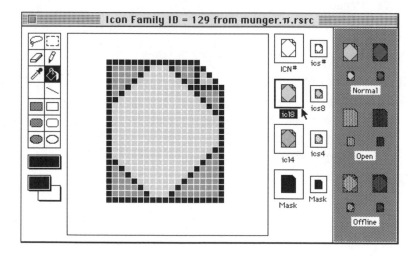

Figure 4.42   *Editing an icl8 resource for the document icon*

Select Create New Resource again and this time type in **BNDL** in the resource type selection window. The BNDL resource window opens, followed by the bundle Editor window. Go to the BNDL menu and choose Extended View. Type in **MUNG** for the signature, to match what you entered in the Project preferences panel in CodeWarrior. Now go to the Resource menu and pick Create New File Type. You'll get a new, highlighted entry in the bundle Editor window, as shown in figure 4.43.

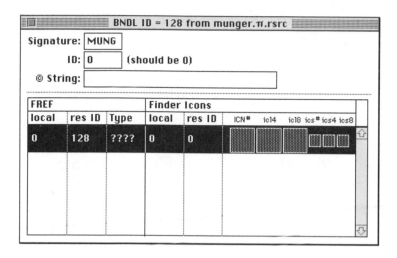

Figure 4.43   *Entering a new file type in the BNDL Editor window*

Move the pointer to the Type item, and notice how it changes to an I-beam symbol, for text entry. Type in **APPL** to replace the four question marks. Next, go over to the icon section and double-click on it. You'll get a dialog box asking you for the icon to use (see figure 4.44). Click on icon resource 128 and click OK. The empty boxes in this section of the Editor window are filled with icons. Select Create New File Type again and type in **TEXT** for the Type item.

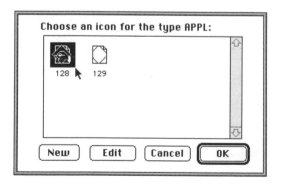

Figure 4.44   *Picking the icon for the application file type*

Pick icon ID 129 for the TEXT file type icons. The BNDL Editor window should appear as shown in figure 4.45.

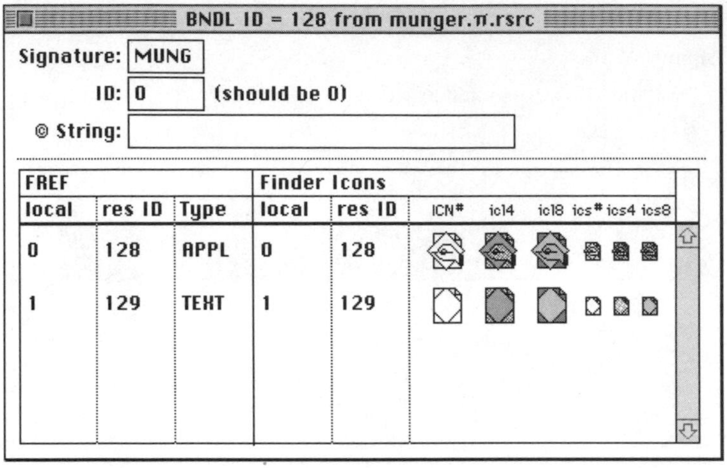

Figure 4.45   *The BNDL resource for SonOMunger, with icons for two file types*

Close this Editor window. You'll notice that beside the new BNDL resource is a resource type of 'MUNG'. This is the application's signature resource, made when you typed in those four characters in the signature item of the bundle editor. There's also a FREF, or file reference resource. This resource is used by the Finder to determine what file types (if any) your application recognizes. When you drag and drop a document on SonOMunger, the Finder compares the document's file type to the file types in SonOMunger's FREF resource. If there's a match (say, a ClarisWorks text file was dropped onto SonOMunger), the Finder launches SonOMunger and sends it an Open Documents Apple Event with the filename. Save the file and quit ResEdit.

At long last, go ahead and make the application.

Finishing Up

The SonOMunger application might still be showing the generic application icon after it is created. To ensure that the Finder brings the desktop database up to date on SonOMunger's capabilities, you have to force the database to be rebuilt. Do this by restarting the Power Mac and holding down the Command and Option keys as the computer boots. Just before the desktop appears, you should get a dialog box asking if you want to rebuild the desktop file. Click on OK. If all went well, SonOMunger's icon should resemble the one we drew in ResEdit. Now drag a text file document onto SonOMunger. It will start automatically and grind away quietly for a few seconds. The status report dialog box appears briefly and then SonOMunger quits. You're not limited to working with one file at a time, either. You can drag several or more files to SonOMunger for processing.

This is why we don't use a modal dialog or alert for the status report, because SonOMunger would stop until you clicked on the OK button for every report displayed. Note SonOMunger lets the user have it both ways for choosing files. The person familiar with the Standard File dialogs can use those to select files, while another person might like the drag and drop approach. As you design Mac applications, always remember, give the user as many ways as possible to operate it.

The Fork in the Road

In this chapter we learned about the forked nature of Mac files. We also learned about resources, the building blocks of Mac applications, and how to edit them in ResEdit. We've learned about both low- and high-level events and how to write a Mac application to respond to them. So far, the Power Macintosh looks pretty much like a 68K Mac, even when programming it. However, although things look the same, the run-time architecture of the Power Mac is fundamentally different. We'll find out about that in the next chapter.

The PowerPC Software Architecture

The material in this chapter will be of interest to all Macintosh programmers, no matter what their level of expertise. It explains how fundamentally different Power Macs are under the hood, even though they look and behave like 68K Macs.

Our road trip has covered quite a bit of ground. We've become acquainted with CodeWarrior's array of development tools and learned about the structure of Mac files and applications. We've made an application that provides a friendly interface and performs useful file I/O. Importantly, this code compiles and runs whether we use the 68K CodeWarrior compiler or the PowerPC (PPC) CodeWarrior compiler. While this appears to trivialize the differences between a Mac and Power Mac, make

no mistake: The computers use very different processors. Given that fact, the ability to use the same code to make processor-specific versions of an application is actually a tremendous technical achievement. Apple has put a lot of effort into making the switch to the Power Macintosh as painless as possible. This effort will pay off for users and developers in the following ways: Users' current 68K application software is still usable and runs with decent performance. Developers can rapidly port code to the Power Mac without a major effort to produce a native application. An added plus for both users and developers is a significantly faster application. This improved performance, combined with the low investment in cost and resources to support two different computers, is a win-win situation. It means that you should see lots of native applications appear early on.

While providing compatibility with the past, Apple also engineered the future into the Power Macs. Behind the consistent application interface, the run-time application architecture of the Power Mac has fundamentally changed. It eliminates some of the limitations inherent in the existing operating system design; limitations that arose out of hardware constraints imposed by the 68K processor.

This chapter will serve as a rest stop on our journey. While we're recuperating, I'll describe the new run-time architecture in some detail. To understand the new, however, we must first understand the old. Let's begin with a description of the existing 68K application architecture. After all, we can anticipate that this type of application will be around for a while longer, thanks to the Power Mac's 68LC040 emulator, and the millions of 68K-based Macs in the industry. Finally, remember that everything you learned about the Mac application's program structure still applies: The code will load resources, have an event loop, and call handlers no matter what processor you write for.

The 68K Application Run-Time Architecture

As we discovered in the last chapter, Macintosh files are composed of a data and resource fork. For a 68K application, the program's code resides in the file's resource fork, as resources of type 'CODE'. Accompanying these CODE resources are other resources, such as DLOG, ALRT, WIND, and

MENU, which supply graphical information (such as icons) or data lists (dialog or menu items) that define the application's user interface. A SIZE resource provides operating system information, such as the amount of memory the application needs, whether or not it can run in the background, and if the application is high-level event aware. The data fork of the application is usually empty (see figure 5.1).

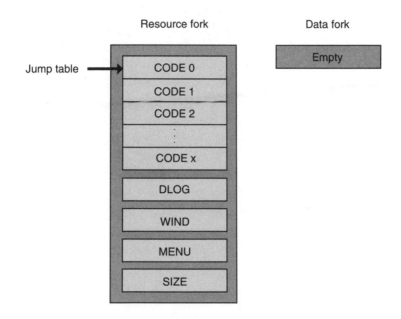

Figure 5.1 *The structure of a 68K application file*

The application's code section is composed of individual CODE resources, or *code segments.* Code segments can be a maximum of 32K in size. This value came about due to a limit imposed by the 68000 processor used in the original Mac. In order to shoehorn code into the confines of that first system's 128K of RAM, the engineers designed the program code to be position-independent. That is, the code uses no absolute addresses. Due to the shifting memory demands of a running application, code segments could be unloaded and subsequently reloaded into memory in different physical addresses at different times, which is possible only if the code is position-independent. This allowed those early Mac applications to run within the cramped memory space by purging unused code segments and then loading only those segments that had to execute at the moment. Naturally, in the scheme of the Mac OS design, a Segment Manager deals with these code segments.

The code references (such as a branch to a different part of the program) of such position-independent code are based on the program counter's current address, plus an offset. This scheme is commonly known as PC-relative addressing, the term coming from the abbreviated name of the program counter (PC). The 68000 processor implements PC-relative addressing with a 16-bit signed value, which allows an address range of plus or minus 32K. The offset's sign indicates if the reference is before or after the current PC address. The tradeoff was that while this scheme made the best use of tight memory, it also constrained the code segment's size. To guarantee that any function within the segment was accesssible to another function, a segment could be no larger than the largest offset possible, or 32K. Remember that this limit only applies to individual CODE resources. The application's actual code section can be rather large, packed with tens or hundreds of 32K CODE resouces, each with its own unique ID number.

Background Info

Later generations of the 680x0 processor expanded the PC-relative offset to a signed 32-bit value. However, while the hardware changed, the software—the 68K application architecture—still uses only 16-bit signed offsets, for reasons of compatibility. Thus, most developer tools don't take advantage of this hardware feature.

This brings up a question. Given the 32K PC-relative addressing limit, how does one function call another, especially if the target function is positioned in physical memory beyond this addressing limit? Or, what if that particular CODE resource isn't in memory at all? This problem is dealt with by using a data structure called a *jump table*. By way of explanation, let's start by reviewing how an application launches.

When you double-click on an application icon, the Finder obtains the filename, which it then passes to the Process Manager. The Process Manager examines the application's SIZE resource to determine the size of the memory *partition*—a contiguous section of physical memory—it must build for the application.

The memory partition subsequently gets divided into three sections. They are referred to as heap, stack, and A5 world (see figure 5.2). The *heap* contains a data pool that the program draws from as necessary to load more resources, or to process data. This could be more code segments, any needed graphical resources (such as a window or a menu), data structures used by the Toolbox routines, and the program's data. The heap starts at the lowest memory addresses in the partition and expands upwards. The *stack* holds temporary variables and starts near the highest addresses in the memory partition. It grows downward, toward the heap. Ideally, the top of the heap and top of the stack never collide. Practically, if an application crashes with a bomb ID of 28, it means the two have met, with disastrous results. The *A5 world* holds the application's global variables, QuickDraw global variables, and the jump table. The name A5 world comes from the fact that all of these objects are accessed as offsets from an address stored in the 68K processor's A5 register. This A5 world is a fixed size and is situated just above the base of the stack. Once these three sections of the application are set up, the Process Manager transfers control to the application's `main()` function.

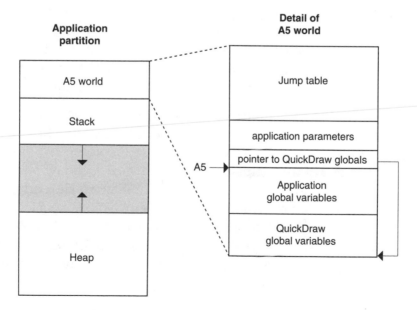

Figure 5.2   *The structure of a 68K application in memory*

An application's code segment 0 (that is, a CODE resource of ID 0) contains information that the Process Manager uses to set up the A5 world, such as the size of the application's globals and the jump table's initial contents. This segment is built by the development software's linker. When the linker stitches all of the program's object code into an application, it keeps track of external function references, that is, calls made to functions outside of a code segment. The linker sorts these references by segment number and then writes this data into the CODE 0 resource. The linker also sizes the global variables used by the application and writes this value into this segment. The Process Manager loads segment 0 into the heap just long enough to establish the A5 world and discards it. It uses a Segment Manager routine, `LoadSeg()`, to do this.

The final application code produced by the linker has two types of function calls. A function call within a code segment becomes a subroutine jump instruction that uses a PC-relative offset. A call to a function outside of the segment becomes a subroutine jump to a jump table entry. Since the jump table is referenced through register A5, this is a subroutine jump instruction that uses the address stored in register A5, plus an offset to a jump table entry. Since application globals must be accessible to every function within the program, they too must be situated in the A5 world. The application and QuickDraw globals thus are referenced as offsets from register A5. As you can surmise, tampering with A5's contents is not a good idea, as the application relies on it to both operate and locate global variables.

Now let's see how the jump table completes the connection to the external function. The jump table is made up of an array of 8-byte entries, as shown in figure 5.3, where each entry represents a function reference. These entries can have one of two formats. The first format is used when a particular function's segment is already loaded into memory. The corresponding jump table entry contains a segment number (2 bytes) and a jump instruction (2 bytes) with a 32-bit absolute address (4 bytes). Therefore, when an external function gets called, the A5-relative subroutine jump hops to a corresponding entry in the jump table, which in turn becomes a jump instruction to the actual function.

Format of a jump table entry when code segment is loaded in memory

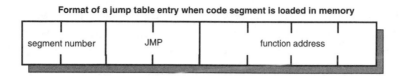

| segment number | JMP | function address |

Format of a jump table entry when code segment isn't in memory

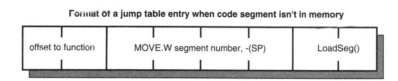

| offset to function | MOVE.W segment number, -(SP) | LoadSeg() |

Figure 5.3   *The two formats of a jump table entry*

If the segment isn't in memory, then the jump table entry uses the second format. The entry contains the target function's offset into the missing segment (2 bytes), followed by an instruction that pushes the segment number onto the stack (2 bytes), and finally a call to the LoadSeg() routine (2 bytes). Now the subroutine jump into the jump table executes the push instruction, and then calls LoadSeg(). LoadSeg() finds the target segment number on the stack, loads the CODE resource with that ID into memory, and locks it there. Next, it takes the offset value in the jump table entry, and adds it to the segment's *current* address in memory to obtain an absolute address for the function's entry point. Remember that the segment might get loaded into different sections of memory, so this absolute address changes each time the segment is loaded. LoadSeg() then converts the jump table entry into the first format so that it now holds the segment number and a jump instruction. It also updates the jump table entries for every function contained in this segment. LoadSeg() finally executes the jump instruction it built in the jump table entry, transferring control to the target function. If a segment happens to get purged from memory (via another Segment Manager routine called UnloadSeg()), the appropriate jump table entries are revised to the second format to reflect this fact.

As you can see, these operations are transparent to the programmer. The jump table mechanism quietly ensures that when a function is called, if its code segment isn't in memory, then it gets loaded automatically. Releasing memory isn't as automatic: the programmer has to call `UnloadSeg()` to indicate to the Mac OS which segments aren't in use.

This carefully choreographed sequence of events enabled graphics-intensive Macintosh applications to run in small amounts of memory. MultiFinder, Apple's first implementation of cooperative multitasking, was possible because each application's position-independent code and jump table allowed them to be loaded and executed anywhere in memory.

However, there's still a problem: How does an application access Toolbox routines? Most of these routines are in the ROMs, which are located in the Mac's memory space, well over a PC-relative jump away. We didn't see anything in the application's jump table to deal with Toolbox routines.

For the answer, we again turn to the 68K processor. Normally a processor trundles along, fetching program instructions and executing them. Occasionally, the processor might detect a trap or exception condition. This is an abnormal state that might be caused by the instruction itself (such as a divide by 0, an invalid instruction, or a code reference to an odd address), a bus error (a memory SIMM or other hardware component failed to respond to a bus access), or a peripheral device requesting service through an interrupt. The processor responds to an exception by first pushing the address of the next program instruction onto the stack, followed by some information—called an exception frame—that's a snapshot of the processor's internal state. The processor then fetches an address from a preprogrammed location in memory whose location is determined by the type of exception that occurred. The processor jumps to this address, which is the entry point to a function that handles the exception. The handler code remedies the problem (if possible), or services the device request. When the handler code completes, the processor retrieves the exception frame from the stack, thus restoring its internal state. Finally, the saved program address is popped from the stack into the PC, which places the processor at the next instruction in the program, no worse for wear.

Motorola defined two special unimplemented instructions for the purpose of extending the capabilities of the 68K processor. When the processor traps on one of these instructions, it executes handler code that emulates new instructions. One of these unimplemented instructions is called the A trap word, so called because it's 16 bits in length and the first four bits in the word are the bit pattern for the hexadecimal A.

Important

In most of the Apple literature, a word is 16 bits in length. This follows a convention where the size of 68K processor's instructions were this length. The current PowerPC processor literature from IBM and Motorola define a word as being 32 bits long. Needless to say, this can cause some confusion. For this discussion, we'll stick with the 16-bit word length and keep the use of the term *word* to a minimum.

Apple used the A trap as an entry point into its Toolbox routines. In its header files, each routine is assigned a word that starts with hexadecimal A, followed by bits that indicate the routine type, some flag bits, and an 8- or 9-bit value. For example, if we peek at the "Dialogs.h" header file, and search for the `StopAlert()` routine, we find the macro:

```
extern pascal short StopAlert(short alertID, ModalFilterUPP modalFilter)
  ONEWORDINLINE(0xA986);
```

The macro ONEWORDINLINE reduces the declaration to:

```
extern pascal short StopAlert(short alertID, ModalFilterUPP modalFilter)\
  = {0xA986};
```

Here we see that the two arguments, `alertID` and `modalFilter`, will be pushed onto the stack, using the Pascal language calling convention. This is followed by the trap word for the StopAlert routine, `0xA986`. Every Toolbox routine uses similar macros that place arguments on the stack or in certain registers, and then hands the job off to the exception handler. If you disassemble your program code using the Disassemble command in CodeWarrior's Project menu, you'll notice the program's 68K machine code is peppered with these A trap words.

Background Info
The last two bytes of jump table entries for code segments not loaded in memory (the second format) are a call to the `LoadSeg()` routine. These bytes contain the trap word 0xA9F0, which is the `LoadSeg()` trap.

Let's put this all together. A Mac is running an application with the 68K processor dutifully fetching and executing instructions. Suppose the program now calls a Toolbox routine. When the processor hits the A trap word that represents this routine, it causes an exception. The processor fetches the address for the location of an A trap exception handler written by Apple and executes it. This handler—appropriately called the Trap Dispatcher—examines the trap word and uses the type bit to select one of two dispatch tables. One table is for the low-level routines, the other is for operating system routines. The Trap Dispatcher then uses the trap word's lower 8 or 9 bits to calculate an offset into the particular dispatch table. The entry at this offset in the dispatch table contains the address of the Toolbox routine. Typically this is an address in ROM, but some routines can be found in RAM. The processor hops to this address and executes the Toolbox routine. When the routine completes, the processor returns from the exception, back to the next instruction in the application. Where do the addresses in the dispatch table come from? They're stored in the Macintosh's ROM and are loaded into the dispatch table when the Mac starts.

Using the exception mechanism as an access point into the Toolbox seems a tad complicated, but the design has some important advantages. First, it allows a code segment anywhere in memory to readily access the Toolbox routines. Second, this mechanism provides flexibility to fix bugs or add new services. For example, assume that it's discovered that the Toolbox routine `ReallySuperbService()`, located in ROM, has a bug. We know that you can't easily change ROM—but you can change the offending routine's address in the dispatch table. Built into the Mac's boot process is a procedure for installing patch code. After the dispatch table is built, but before initialization completes, the System file (early Macs) and System Enabler files (current Macs) are searched for patch code resources. These resources are loaded in memory, locked, and executed. This code modifies the address for `ReallySuperbService()` in the dispatch table so that it points to the improved version of the routine located in RAM, rather than the one in ROM.

Apple uses the same method to add enhancements or new services to the Mac OS. The code implementing new features is loaded and locked in memory. Empty entries in the dispatch table are directed toward routines in the feature code. Apple is thus able to fix bugs or add features to the operating system of existing Macs with just a new release of the system software.

Third party vendors can also supply enhancements through the use of Extension files and Control Panel files. These files have INIT resources that contain the enhancement code, plus code to patch the dispatch table. At boot time, the operating system first installs any patch code; then it searches the Extensions folder and Control Panels folder for files, installs their INIT code, and modifies the dispatch table. Apple's own CD-ROM driver, QuickTime software, and File Sharing software are installed this way.

The PowerPC Application Run–Time Architecture

On the surface, a PowerPC Mac application seems identical to its 68K counterpart. As mentioned earlier, the code you wrote in chapter 4 compiles and runs on a Mac with either processor. However, the run-time architecture behind the API is fundamentally different.

We can see a difference immediately when we examine the structure of a PowerPC Mac application. Looking at figure 5.4, you see that application's resource fork still has the graphical resources and the SIZE resource. However, the program code is located in the file's data fork, as a block of PowerPC code known as a *code fragment*. This code fragment isn't segmented, nor is there a size limit. Thus, all of a PowerPC application's code is stored in a single code fragment. An application with 3M of PowerPC code has a code fragment 3M in size in the data fork, plus whatever resources are required in the resource fork to implement the user interface. After viewing the gymnastics required to support 32K segments in a 68K Mac application, the PowerPC application design appears starkly simple.

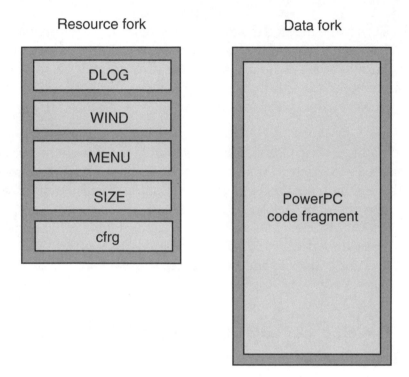

Figure 5.4   *The structure of a PowerPC application file*

Background Info

Lest you think the original Mac design team came up with an unnecessarily complex design, remember that they were working in an era when 256K to 512K of RAM was considered adequate, and that the 68000 processor could only address a maximum of 4M. The simplicity of the PowerPC software architecture stems from the capabilities of today's hardware. The basic Power Macintosh configuration has 8M of RAM and supports virtual memory. The PowerPC 601 processor in these first Power Macs can address 32 bits of physical memory (4G) and 52 bits of virtual memory (4T).

Finally, the Power Mac's System Software engineers had the advantage of a decade's worth of improvements in operating system technology.

Launching a PowerPC Mac application is similar to that of a 68K Mac application, up to a certain point. When you double-click on the application icon, the Finder gets the filename and passes it to the Process Manager as before. However, now the Process Manager calls a *Code Fragment Manager*, whose job is to load code fragments into memory, lock them there, and prepare them for execution. After the code fragment is readied, the Process Manager transfers control to it. The Code Fragment Manager can be considered the PowerPC counterpart to the Segment Manager.

The Power Mac application's memory structure is similar to a 68K application. There's still a heap and a stack, but there's little need for an A5 world. However, for those Toolbox routines that still exist as 68K code and need to access QuickDraw's globals, the Process Manager constructs a pointer to these globals in the application's heap, and your program allocates storage for these globals here as well. The heap also contains any executing code fragments (when virtual memory is off), the application's globals, the globals of any library code fragment the program uses, and any library code fragments not located in ROM (see figure 5.5).

Since a Power Mac has both 68K-based and PowerPC-based Mac applications on it, how does the Process Manager know which Manager to use when you launch an application? Each PowerPC application gives the Process Manager a hint: They have a resource of type 'cfrg' in the file's resource fork. This resource tells the Process Manager that this application contains PowerPC code, so it uses the Code Fragment Manager to load the application. If the cfrg resource is absent, the Process Manager assumes the application is a 68K binary and calls the Segment Manager instead. The cfrg resource is placed in the file by the development software.

What about the Toolbox routines in ROM? They too, are code fragments. After the Code Fragment Manager loads the application's code fragment into memory, it goes about resolving any external references, which are usually the Toolbox calls. The Code Fragment Manager loads any additional code fragments into memory (recall that not all Toolbox or operating system routines are in ROM), and then it replaces each external routine reference with its actual address.

**Application
partition**

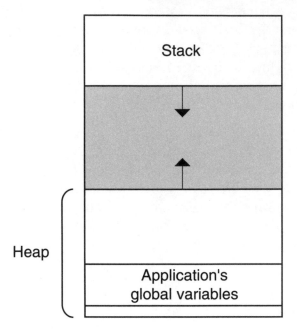

Figure 5.5 *The structure of a PowerPC application in memory*

To see how this is done, let's examine code fragments in more detail. Code fragments come in two executable formats, XCOFF and PEF. XCOFF is the acronym for IBM's Extended Common Object File Format, while PEF stands for Apple's Preferred Executable Format. As its name implies, the preferred format for code fragments for the Power Macintosh is the PEF format. XCOFF is partially supported because the original IBM development tools used this format.

Important

The Code Fragment Manager uses a set of routines known as the Code Fragment Loader to load code fragments from a file into memory. The Code Fragment Loader's function is analogous to **LoadSeg()**'s. The Code Fragment Loader is responsible for recognizing and loading either XCOFF or PEF files. If new file formats are introduced later, the loader will be updated to handle them. You, the programmer, needn't concern yourself with file formats. Just let the Code Fragment Manager handle the job of loading your code fragments.

A PEF consists of a container of code, data, and loader information block. A container is a chunk of contiguous storage, typically a file, although it can be any object that the Mac OS accesses, such as the libraries that house the Toolbox routines in the Power Mac's ROMs. The code and data make up the code fragment itself, and the loader information block enables the Code Fragment Manager to prepare the fragment for execution. The loader information describes the fragment's initialization, start, and termination functions, its imported functions and data, its exported functions and data, and its version number.

The import/export information is crucial to the operation of the PowerPC run-time architecture. It's how the connections between an application and the Toolbox routines are established. Code fragments can export certain entry points or import the entry points of data objects or functions in other code fragments. For example, the Mac Toolbox is a *shared library* in the Power Mac's ROMs. This type of code fragment exports the entry points of its global data and routines. A Mac application, on the other hand, requires Toolbox routines to operate and so it imports the required entry points from the shared library in the ROMs. The development software's linker is responsible for matching up the import names in the application to export names in a shared library. The linker places the exporting library's name and any import names into the code fragment's loader information block. It's important to note that this information is stored as actual name strings. These names get resolved to addresses by the Code Fragment Manager at run time.

Background Info

It's easy to see what libraries and routine names a code fragment requires. To do this, make a copy of the SonOMunger application. Now launch ResEdit. In ResEdit's File menu, select Get File/Folder Info and open the copy of SonOMunger. In the Info box that appears, change the Type item from APPL to

TEXT, close the window, and save the file when ResEdit asks you to. Quit ResEdit. Now, open this file with any word processor. You'll see some gobbledy-gook—that's binary machine code, but there's also a block of text that you can easily read. This block begins with the library name "InterfaceLib," followed by the name of every Toolbox routine used by the application.

When Code Fragment Manager loads the application's code fragment, it first allocates memory for the global variables and static data in the heap space of the partition built by the Process Manager. The Code Fragment Manager then performs any load time relocations for the import symbol information and places this information in critical data structure called the *table of contents*, or TOC. The TOC was built by the development tool's compiler and linker, and it contains the fragment's import symbols (that is, the names of the externally referenced data or functions). The Code Fragment Manager resolves these import symbols and plugs addresses in the appropriate slots in the TOC. The TOC contains lists of three type of pointers. These pointers reference the code fragment's own functions, its own data, and the import names it uses. These import name references are the global data variables or the entry points of functions in other code fragments.

To set up the addresses in the application fragment's TOC, the Code Fragment Manager uses the library names in the loader information block to locate the required shared libraries. It loads these libraries into memory if required, and loads any other libraries that these libraries depend on. The Code Fragment Manager also runs each library's initialization function code, if present. The shared libraries build any data structures they use within the application's heap, and some of the TOC pointers are arranged to point at this data. The Code Fragment Manager then searches for the application code fragment's import names and replaces them with the corresponding export addresses in the shared library, in a process called *binding*. This binding operation sets up the remaining TOC pointers (see figure 5.6). Once the TOC is initialized, the code fragment's preparation is complete and it is ready to execute.

Note that some of these TOC pointers address objects called *transition vectors*. A transition vector is a data structure used by one code fragment to access an import function in another code fragment. The structure consists of one pointer to the target fragment's TOC, and a second pointer to a function within the target code fragment. Therefore, a shared library doesn't actually export the addresses of its routines. It instead exports transition vectors, whose job is to point to the routines. The transition vectors are built by the development software.

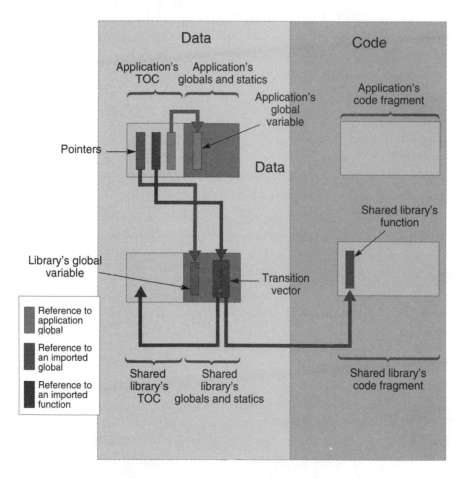

Figure 5.6   *The run-time binding of the application code fragment to its libraries*

Since the TOC is the linchpin of the code fragment's operation, one of the PowerPC processor's general-purpose registers (GPR2) points to the start of the TOC at all times and is called the TOC Register (RTOC). The RTOC serves a function similar to register A5. However, only 68K applications could have an A5 world, while any PowerPC code fragment (a plug-in module, extension code, or a driver) can have a TOC.

The dynamic linking strategy used by the Code Fragment Manager minimizes the copies of shared libraries in memory, especially in a multitasking environment. As you've just seen, each application that uses a library has its own instance of the library's data built for it, unless the library implements a special shared memory strategy. Because the library's code is separate from its data, each application can thus execute the same library code while using its private copy of the data. The shared libraries remain in memory as long as any application uses them. If the library isn't being used, its termination code (if any) is executed, and it's unloaded from memory.

Background Info

Since each application can have its own data copy while using a shared library routine, this capability is said to be reentrant (that is, usable by multiple processes simultaneously, without conflicts). Thus, the Power Macintosh's Toolbox routines are a major step toward the day when Apple releases a microkernal-based operating system that uses preemptive multitasking.

Whereas a 68K application's global variables are intimately tied to its A5 world, a PowerPC code fragment's global variables are readily accessible to other code fragments through its TOC. This makes it easier to access and share global data than was possible with the 68K run-time architecture. Previously, periodic tasks, extension code, or plug-in modules had to use assembly language code to gain access to the global variables inside an application or the operating system. With the PowerPC run-time architecture, no special programming is necessary to obtain access to information within another code fragment.

We've covered how data can be accessed by different code fragments. To complete our understanding of the run-time architecture, let's consider how one code fragment function calls a function in another code fragment. Suppose a code fragment, our Power Mac application, makes a Toolbox call. The imported function address is fetched from the appropriate transition vector and execution hops to the Toolbox code fragment. However, an executing code fragment assumes that the RTOC points to its own TOC, which contains its globals, and addresses of any import functions in another code fragment. How is the RTOC set to this new code fragment's TOC?

The run-time architecture assigns this job to the caller. In other words, before execution passes another code fragment, the program must set the RTOC to point to the target code fragment's TOC. This information is stored in the transition vector.

Getting back to our example, the following three events occur when our application makes a Toolbox call. First, glue code in the application uses the transition vector to set the RTOC to the TOC of the Toolbox's shared library. The glue code then uses the other half of the transition vector to jump to the Toolbox routine. Finally, when the routine completes, execution returns to the application code fragment, and the RTOC is restored to the application's TOC.

Background Info

Following the RISC principle of a simple instruction set, the PowerPC processor has no subroutine call instruction. Subroutine "calls" are implemented as branches, surrounded by additional instructions to set up registers for function arguments, and to preserve critical registers. As an example of this, let's look at the machine code for calling a Toolbox trap, `WaitNextEvent()`. In 68K machine code this is:

```
WaitNextEvent(everyEvent, &gmyEvent, LONG_NAP, NO_CURSOR)


MOVE.W    #$FFFF, -(A7)    /* Load the everyEvent mask onto stack */
PEA       $FFA8(A5)        /* Push address of global gmyEvent onto stack */
PEA       $00C3            /* Lush LONG_NAP (decimal 60) */
```

```
CLR.L     -(A7)              /* Push NO_CURSOR */
WaitNextEvent                /* Trap word A860, go directly to the */
                             /* Trap Dispatcher */
```

Notice that the arguments are pushed on the stack (register A7), and that a trap word takes the processor to the exception handler, the Trap Dispatcher. For the PowerPC, this same function call becomes:

```
addi r31, RTOC, 648  /* Put address of global gmyEvent into r31 */
        .
        .            /* Other program code */
        .
li   r3, -1          /* Load the everyEvent mask */
mr   r4, r31         /* Get the address of gmyEvent */
li   r5, 60          /* Load LONG_NAP */
li   r6, 0           /* Load NO_CURSOR */
bl   .WaitNextEvent  /* Branch to WaitNextEvent(), save return
                            address in link register */
lwz  RTOC, 20(SP)    /* Fix up RTOC to point back to app's TOC */
```

Here the arguments get placed into registers and then a branch is taken into the glue code responsible for managing the jump to the Toolbox shared library. This branch instruction also saves the program's next instruction address into the 601's link register, providing a way home when WaitNextEvent() returns. The glue code, meanwhile, loads the pointer to WaitNextEvent()'s transition vector from your application's TOC. As discussed previously, this glue code uses the transition vector information to adjust RTOC to the TOC of the Toolbox's shared library and then the jump to the shared library is made. When the routine returns, the RTOC is set back to our code fragment. Where does this glue code that accomplishes this magic come from? It's in Interface.Lib.

Unfortunately, this elegant scheme is complicated by the fact that not all of the Toolbox code in the Power Macs is PowerPC code. Rewriting the Mac Toolbox, which consists of nearly 2M of tight CISC processor code (based on the size of the Quadra 840AV's ROMs) into RISC code was a formidable process at best. Not only was the job a large one, but replacing time-proven routines with new ones opens the door to introducing bugs. To achieve high compatibility with 68K applications and still get the Power Macs into the hands of users as soon as possible, Apple elected to rewrite only a portion of the Toolbox. The remaining routines were left as 68K code and the 68LC040 emulator executes them.

Again, if we use our example of an application calling a Toolbox routine, the real question becomes: Is the Toolbox routine about to be called implemented as 68K code or PowerPC code? Put another way, before the processor hops to that routine, how does it determine whether it should simply start fetching PowerPC instructions or call the 68LC040 emulator instead?

The solution is the Mixed Mode Manager. This is a set of routines that enables a PowerPC function to call a 68K function or a 68K function to call a PowerPC function. Basically, the Mixed Mode Manager operates as a stack transformation engine. Its job is to massage the stack so that the function parameters get passed to the target routine in the proper order. The problem is complicated by the fact that the calling conventions used by a 68K environment vary depending upon the programming language used (C, Pascal, and assembler each use a different method), while the PowerPC uses a single, register-based mechanism for all programming languages.

Apple solved this thorny problem by designing a Universal Procedure Pointer (UPP) for all exported functions. A 68K procedure pointer is normally the address of a function's entry point. A UPP has either the usual 68K procedure pointer (the routine's address) or the address of a *routine descriptor*. A routine descriptor is a data structure that contains information enabling the Mixed Mode Manager to make the context switch from one instruction set architecture (ISA) to another. The routine descriptor contains the address of the target routine, the number and size of the parameters passed to the routine, the language calling convention used, and what ISA the routine is implemented in. If the UPP references a PowerPC routine, the routine address inside of the routine descriptor actually points to a transition vector. If you want to study the routine descriptor's structure in more detail, examine the "MixedMode.h" file with the CodeWarrior editor.

When a 68K application calls a Toolbox routine, the following sequence of events occurs. First, execution passes through the UPP for the Toolbox call. This in turn goes to either the routine directly (if it's a 68K application calling a 68K routine) or to a routine descriptor. The head of the routine descriptor has a 68K trap word (that's right, a trap word) that invokes the

Mixed Mode Manager. The Mixed Mode Manager uses the routine descriptor information to build a switch frame on the stack. This switch frame contains the information necessary to transfer the passed arguments in the proper order to the target routine, plus the state of various registers in both the 68K and PowerPC environments (see figure 5.7). The routine descriptor then points to the routine's transition vector, which in turn points to the TOC and entry point of the routine in the Toolbox shared library. The Mixed Mode Manager uses the transition vector to adjust the RTOC and pass control to the Toolbox code (see figure 5.8).

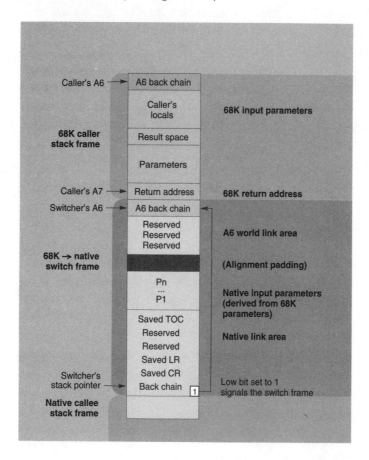

Figure 5.7 *The PowerPC stack during a call from 68K application to a PowerPC routine*

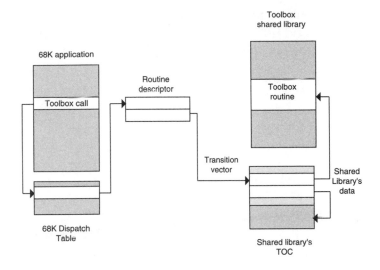

Figure 5.8 *How a 68K application accesses a PowerPC Toolbox routine*

Important

Apple rewrote the most heavily used Toolbox calls in PowerPC code so that 68K applications could benefit from the native performance of the PowerPC processor. The Toolbox calls ported for the first Power Macs include portions of QuickDraw, the Font Manager, TrueType, QuickTime, the Resource Manager, the Memory Manager, fixed-point math, SANE, and the Script Manager (for foreign language support). This will change as Apple releases new versions of the Mac OS. The Code Fragment Manager can use a code fragment's version information to allow updates to the Toolbox shared library located in ROM. Just as important, because some of the Macintosh OS is still 68K, the Trap Dispatcher and dispatch table is supported. This allows existing Extensions and Control Panels to patch the operating system as before.

Please note that the revised SANE is available only to support 68K applications. Native PowerPC applications should use the new industry standard C math libraries to access to PowerPC's floating-point hardware. See appendix B for more information.

The header files for the Toolbox calls contain UPPs for those routines written in PowerPC code. Thus, calls to these native routines bring in the Mixed Mode Manager to handle a context switch, when necessary. Because a UPP points either to a 68K routine address or to a transition vector, the same header files can be used by development tools on either 68K- or PowerPC-based Macs. Normally, you won't be aware of the sleight of hand going on here, except in certain situations.

Hazard

If you're writing custom handlers that the operating system calls back to within your application, you need to write your own UPP so that the Mixed Mode Manager can manage a context switch when that handler is called. The UPP is required because the operating system has no idea of what type of ISA your handler is written in or the arguments it uses. Examples of such handlers are: custom controls for windows or dialogs that use a control definition function, event filters for dialogs or alerts, high-level event handlers, and plug-in modules. Anything in your program that uses a procedure pointer (`ProcPtr`) *requires* a UPP. Otherwise, the Power Mac crashes and burns.

Fortunately, Apple provides special functions in the header files for those routines likely to need a UPP. These functions take the procedure pointer you pass to it and tack a routine descriptor on your custom function. For example, in chapter 4 we saw that `NewAEEventHandlerProc()` helped install our high-level Apple Event functions. For a custom event filter for alerts and dialogs, there's `NewModalFilterProc()`, and so on. These functions help immensely in hiding the gory details of building a UPP from scratch.

Of course, making these context switches has a price. The Mixed Mode Manager has an overhead of fifty to one hundred 68K instructions when handling a context switch between the 68K and PowerPC environment. For certain heavily-called small Toolbox routines, this context switch overhead becomes considerable, and can impact performance. For these routines, Apple actually implemented them as "fat traps." That is, these routines were written in both ISAs (68K and PowerPC code). This way, no matter what ISA calls the routine, it can be used without requiring a context switch. As more of the Mac Toolbox is replaced by native PowerPC code, these Mixed Mode Manager context switches will become more infrequent and the applications will run faster.

A Tale of Two Processors

In this chapter we learned about the Mac's application architecture for both 68K-based and PowerPC-based Macs. While these architectures are quite different, the Power Macintosh's OS manages to support both. The PowerPC's run-time architecture provides a simplified structure that can run faster, as more applications and more of the Mac Toolbox gets written as PowerPC code. It also has separated the data such that the operating system can become a full-blown preemptive multitasking OS in the future. At the same time, the Power Mac OS can support existing 68K code and traps. This capability is provided by the use of special declarations in the Toolbox header files, and in your code for custom functions. We'll see how this is done in the next chapter, "Putting It All Together."

Putting It All Together

This chapter is aimed at intermediate and advanced programmers. Here's where we apply the knowledge gained in chapter 5 to utilize parts of the Power Macintosh run-time architecture. The task might require rolling your own UPP for a custom function or calling the Code Fragment Manager itself.

In the last chapter, we saw that the Power Mac is quite different under the hood, from its PowerPC processor to the run-time architecture used by its native applications. However, by use of unique data structures such as routine descriptors and UPPs, plus special-purpose functions in the Toolbox header files, many of these differences are hidden from you.

Almost.

In this chapter we're going to explore situations that don't quite fall into a category that the header files can conveniently handle.

You'll stray into this gray area while writing something exotic. Such exotic fare includes plug-in modules that expand the capabilities of an application, and extensions that enhance the operating system by adding patch code. Since the Power Mac's run-time architecture makes writing these types of objects easier, it's well worth knowing how to do this. These types of jobs require that you have a firm grasp of the fundamentals that you learned in the last chapter. We'll see how this is accomplished with actual working code.

Let's take an example of writing a custom function first. We'll use a real case example here, where I wrote a custom function that supplied a crucial feature in a utility program called SwitchBank. I wrote SwitchBank out of my frustration in dealing with "captive" CD-ROMs. A captive CD-ROM is where the Mac's File Sharing software mistakenly assumes that you're sharing it with other networked users. When you try to eject the CD-ROM, you get the message "The disk 'Your Favorite CD' could not be put away, because it's being shared," and the disc stays put. This is because the Mac OS tries to protect the networked users' access to the CD-ROM by refusing to eject it.

There are two ways File Sharing comes to this erroneous conclusion. First, in your eagerness to try out that new CD-ROM game, you insert the disc into the drive before the Macintosh completes booting. Or, the Mac crashes with the disc already in the drive. In either case, a feature of the Mac OS is that when it boots with File Sharing active and detects a CD-ROM in the drive, it assumes that you want to share its contents. Thus the Mac OS mounts the disc as a shared volume. This enables a Macintosh file server to resume sharing a CD-ROM such as the Oxford Dictionary after a power glitch. However, for you, the solution is to go to the Control Panels folder, open the File Sharing Setup Control Panel, and turn File Sharing off. Now you can eject the disc.

Later in the day, you're at the other end of the building. While talking with a coworker, you realize there's a file on your Mac you need to give her. Because of File Sharing, it's easy to use her Mac to log onto your Mac, and copy the file to her system, right? Wrong. To your dismay, you discover that you left File Sharing turned off, and so you have to walk back to your office anyway. Since I look at lots of beta software, this scenario happens more often that I care to admit. I finally decided to do something about it.

> **Important**
>
> This text was written using the full version of Metrowerks CodeWarrior. You'll have to use slightly different steps when using the limited version on the CD; the limited version can only work with the sample files provided on the CD so the commands Add File... and New Project are not available.
>
> So, if you are following along using the limited version of CodeWarrior that's on the CD, when the text tells you to use the New Project or the Add File... command, you should instead open the related project file and keep it open throughout the exercise. All the associated files will already be in the project so you won't need the Add File... command. Then, you can follow the same procedures as if you were using the full version of CodeWarrior.

SwitchBank: Initial Investigation and Design

Ideally, I wanted something that would switch off File Sharing long enough to eject the CD-ROM, and restart it. To control File Sharing, though, I first had to know something about it. Simply put, it's an Extension file that, when installed, makes each Mac look like a file server. This leads us to a question: What exactly does the File Sharing Extension do? The answer to that question is an interesting one. Even better, the answer was already available.

Remember the small program "process.c" from chapter 3 that listed all of the running processes on the system? One of the processes it lists is called the File Sharing Extension. This implies that an application actually implements File Sharing, since processes are running applications. To confirm this, I made a copy of the File Sharing Extension file, and opened it with ResEdit. There was the usual INIT resource, but sure enough, tucked in with the ICN#, BNDL, and other resources was a CODE resource. Opening the CODE resource, I saw a CODE resource 0. Could that be a jump table? When I examined that resource closely, I saw an array of numbers, where the value 0xA9F0 appeared frequently (see figure 6.1). Since this value is the **LoadSeg()** trap, this confirmed that this was indeed a jump table. The presence of a jump table in the Extension file meant that there was actually an application embedded in it. This was good news indeed, because we can easily control applications with high-level Apple Events.

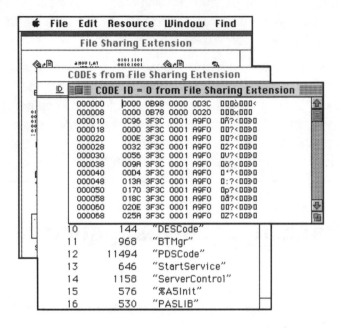

Figure 6.1 *The CODE 0 jump table in the File Sharing Extension file*

Background Info

Why isn't File Sharing written in native code? Remember, not all of the Macintosh Toolbox, which by our loose definition includes operating system software, got ported to PowerPC RISC code. This happens to include some of Apple's own Extensions, including portions of QuickTime, the Apple CD-ROM driver, and others. This will change over time as Apple completes the porting process.

On a related matter, the Express Modem and voice recognition software also use processes to implement their services. If you're curious, turn on these services and use the process program again to see what appears in memory.

SwitchBank's design is simple. It orders the File Sharing process to stop and ejects the CD-ROM. Once that's done, the program restarts the File Sharing application. Like the program, the user interface should be simple as well. The drag and drop feature we implemented in SonOMunger can be used here. We let the user drag the CD-ROM icon to the SwitchBank icon to eject it. To encourage the program's use so that folks will readily drag the CD-ROM onto SwitchBank's icon, it should eject any volume dropped on it.

Building Resources with Rez

We'll use the same approach in building SwitchBank that we applied to Munger and SonOMunger. That is, we'll start by creating the interface resources first. However, we'll use a program called Rez to generate the resources this time around.

Rez is an MPW tool that accepts text statements which use a C-style syntax to describe a resource. It generates the appropriate resources from these descriptions. While this method of resource building doesn't have the point-and-click flexibility of drawing your dialogs, alerts, and windows that ResEdit offers, it does have its advantages. For example, with an appropriately written Rez source file, you could modify the resource ID numbers of all your dialog boxes and dialog items by editing a few definition statements and "recompiling" the file. That's a job that would require lots of pointing and clicking to fix in ResEdit. Also, large applications require sophisticated user interfaces, which in turn means complex resources. These sets of resources are easier to maintain as a Rez source file. Typically, you'll write most of your resources with Rez statements, and draw your icons in ResEdit. You then use the DeRez tool, which is a resource disassembler, to reduce the binary icon resources into text Rez statements.

To begin, launch the CodeWarrior IDE and open a new editor window. Type:

```
#include "SysTypes.r"
#include "Types.r"

#define AllItems      0b1111111111111111111111111111111    /* 31 flags */
#define NoItems       0b0000000000000000000000000000000
#define MenuItem1     0b0000000000000000000000000000001
#define MenuItem2     0b0000000000000000000000000000010
```

```
#define MenuItem3    0b00000000000000000000000000000100
#define MenuItem4    0b00000000000000000000000000001000


#define MENU_BAR_ID  128      /* Menu bar resource for our menus */
#define APPLE_MENU   128      /* Menu ID for Apple menu */
#define FILE_MENU    129      /* Menu ID for File menu */
#define EDIT_MENU    130      /* Menu ID for Edit menu */
#define SWITCH_MENU  131      /* Menu ID for File Share control */


#define ABOUT_BOX_ID 128      /* Resource IDs for our windows & dialogs */
#define ERROR_BOX_ID 130
#define ERROR_MESS_ID    131


#define APPL_FREF    128      /* Resource IDs for file refs & icons */
#define DISK_FREF    129
#define SWITCH_ICON  128
```

Notice the header files "SysTypes.r" and "Types.r." They supply declarations and structures that define the resource statements written here. Observe also that our definitions for the menu and dialog resource IDs are similar to those we used in SonOMunger. That shouldn't come as a surprise, since those definitions tell the program what resource, by its type and ID number, to use. We're using those exact same numbers here to generate the corresponding resources. In fact, some programmers take the definitions in this section and move them into a separate header file that both the program code and Rez source draw on for resource information. The other reason the definitions appear the same is that we're going to reuse a lot of SonOMunger's code.

Now it's time to write some resource descriptions. Type:

```
/* Version info for the Finder's Get Info box
resource 'vers' (1, purgeable)
{
    0x01,
    0x10,
    beta,
    0x00,
    verUs,
    "1.1ß",
    "1.1ß, by Tom Thompson"
};
```

```
/* Menu resources */
resource 'MBAR' (MENU_BAR_ID, preload)
{
    { APPLE_MENU, FILE_MENU, EDIT_MENU, SWITCH_MENU };
};


resource 'MENU' (APPLE_MENU, preload)
{
    APPLE_MENU, textMenuProc,
    AllItems & ~MenuItem2,  /* Disable separator line, enable About Box */
    enabled, apple,
    {
        "About SwitchBank 1.1…",   noicon, nokey, nomark, plain;
        "-",                noicon, nokey, nomark, plain
    }
};


resource 'MENU' (FILE_MENU, preload)
{
    FILE_MENU, textMenuProc,
    AllItems,
    enabled, "File",
    {
        "Quit",             noicon, "Q", nomark, plain
    }
};


resource 'MENU' (EDIT_MENU, preload)
{
    EDIT_MENU, textMenuProc,
    AllItems & ~MenuItem2,     /* Disable separator line */
    enabled, "Edit",
    {
        "Undo",             noicon, "Z", nomark, plain;
        "-",                noicon, nokey, nomark, plain;
        "Cut",              noicon, "X", nomark, plain;
        "Copy",             noicon, "C", nomark, plain;
        "Paste",            noicon, "V", nomark, plain
    }
};
```

```
resource 'MENU' (SWITCH_MENU, preload)
{
   SWITCH_MENU, textMenuProc,
   AllItems,
   enabled, "Controls",
   {
      "Toggle File Sharing",                    noicon, "T", nomark, plain
   }
};
```

To get the ß symbol in the 'vers' resource, type Option-S.

The previous statements describe our menu resources. They define a resource type ('MENU' and 'MBAR'), its ID number, and certain attributes. They also describe the menu's title, and its item list. The item list contains the text of each menu item, and a description of how it appears in the menu. For instance, the Controls menu has a single item called Toggle File Sharing that's displayed with no accompanying icon, no checkmark, and in plain text. It has a Command key equivalent which is the character "T." The 'vers' resource provides the version number information that appears in a file's Info box.

```
/* Our error messages */
resource 'STR#'(128, purgeable)
{
   {
   /* [1] */   "A problem occurred stopping File Sharing.";
   /* [2] */   "A problem occurred starting File Sharing.";
   /* [3] */   "A problem occurred while ejecting the volume.";
   /* [4] */   "You can't eject the startup volume.";
   /* [5] */   "Couldn't find the startup volume.";
   /* [6] */   "Couldn't get valid system information.";
   /* [7] */   "Couldn't locate the File Sharing Extension file.";
   /* [8] */   "A problem occurred while loading the Apple Event
         handlers.";
   /* [9] */   "Sorry, SwitchBank requires System 7 or later to run.";
   }
};
```

These are our error messages stored as Pascal strings in a STR# resource. We place them here, rather than hard-coding them as we did in SonOMunger, for a good reason. As a list in a resource, these strings can be easily modified with ResEdit without having to recompile the program code. This opens the possibility of your program being translated into foreign languages. You can have someone use ResEdit to edit the menu lists, dialog boxes, and error messages so that they appear in another language (say, French) without changing the executable code.

```
/* This ALRT and DITL are used as an About Box */
resource 'DLOG' (ABOUT_BOX_ID, purgeable)
{
   {31, 6, 224, 265},
   altDBoxProc,
   visible,
   noGoAway,
   0x0,                  /* No refCon */
   ABOUT_BOX_ID,
   ""                    /* No window title */
};

resource 'DITL' (ABOUT_BOX_ID, purgeable)
{
   {
      /* Item 1 */
      {154, 80, 175, 180},
      Button { enabled, "OK" },
      /* Item 2 */
      {4, 68, 38, 193},
      StaticText { disabled, " SwitchBank 1.1\nby Tom Thompson" },
      /* Item 3 */
      {86, 11, 102, 250},
      StaticText { disabled, " Copyright © 1994 Tom Thompson." },
      /* Item 4 */
      {44, 114, 76, 146},
      Icon { disabled, SWITCH_ICON },
      /* Item 5 */
      {107, 43, 133, 217},
      StaticText { disabled, "Written in Metrowerks C " }
   }
};

/* The ALRT and DITL for the basic error screen */
resource 'ALRT' (ERROR_BOX_ID, purgeable)
{
   {40, 40, 127, 273},
   ERROR_BOX_ID,
   {
```

```
         OK, visible, silent,
         OK, visible, silent,
         OK, visible, silent,
         OK, visible, silent
      }
};


resource 'DITL' (ERROR_BOX_ID, purgeable)
{
   {
      { 52, 162, 72, 220 },
      Button { enabled, "OK" },
      { 54, 17, 70, 151 },
      StaticText { disabled, "I/O error, ID = ^0" }
   }
};


/* Alert and DITL for error message screen */
resource 'ALRT' (ERROR_MESS_ID, purgeable)
{
   { 40, 40, 147, 280 },
   ERROR_MESS_ID,
   {
      OK, visible, silent,
      OK, visible, silent,
      OK, visible, silent,
      OK, visible, silent
   }
};


resource 'DITL' (ERROR_MESS_ID, purgeable)
{
   {
      { 73, 168, 93, 226 },      Button { enabled, "OK" },
      { 53, 14, 97, 157 },       StaticText { disabled, "^0" }
   }
};


/* File reference resources */
resource 'FREF' (DISK_FREF)
{
```

```
      'disk',
      1,
      ""
};


resource 'FREF' (APPL_FREF)
{
   'APPL',
   0,
   ""
};

/* Bundle resource */
resource 'BNDL' (128)
{
   'SWCH', 0,
   {
   'ICN#', { 0, SWITCH_ICON },          /* Only 1 icon */
   'FREF', { 0, APPL_FREF, 1, DISK_FREF } /* Two types of files */
   }
};

/* Signature resource - all 'STR ' resources must be declared before this! */
type 'SWCH' as 'STR ';

resource 'SWCH' (0) {
   "SwitchBank 1.1B"
};
```

These statements describe our alerts, dialog boxes, and their dialog item
lists. There's also the bundle resource, BNDL, and its satellite definitions in
the FREF resources that describe the application's file type, and a disk
type. This latter type allows file type filtering similar to what's used for
SonOMunger. That is, you can only drag and drop icons representing TEXT
file types onto the SonOMunger's icon, and for SwitchBank you can only
drag and drop an icon representing a disk (or volume) onto its icon. This
filtering action performed by System 7 is very convenient. An application
won't see a high-level Open Document Apple Event unless the Mac OS
deems that the dropped file type matches what the application can handle.

```
/* Our icon data */
data 'ICON' (SWITCH_ICON)
{
    $"7FFF FFFE 4000 0002 5C00 003A 55F8 1FAA"
    $"5D08 10BA 4108 1082 4108 1082 4108 1082"
    $"41B8 1D82 4110 0882 4110 0882 4110 0882"
    $"471C 38E2 4514 28A2 4514 28A2 4514 28A2"
    $"471C 38E2 4110 0882 411F F882 4110 0882"
    $"4110 0882 4110 0882 41FF FF82 4004 2002"
    $"4004 2002 4004 2002 4004 2002 5C04 203A"
    $"5404 202A 5C07 E03A 4000 0002 7FFF FFFE"
};


data 'ICN#' (SWITCH_ICON)
{
    $"7FFF FFFE 4000 0002 5C00 003A 55F8 1FAA"
    $"5D08 10BA 4108 1082 4108 1082 4108 1082"
    $"41B8 1D82 4110 0882 4110 0882 4110 0882"
    $"471C 38E2 4514 28A2 4514 28A2 4514 28A2"
    $"471C 38E2 4110 0882 411F F882 4110 0882"
    $"4110 0882 4110 0882 41FF FF82 4004 2002"
    $"4004 2002 4004 2002 4004 2002 5C04 203A"
    $"5404 202A 5C07 E03A 4000 0002 7FFF FFFE"
    $"7FFF FFFE 7FFF FFFE 7FFF FFFE 7FFF FFFE"
    $"7FFF FFFE 7FFF FFFE 7FFF FFFE 7FFF FFFE"
    $"7FFF FFFE 7FFF FFFE 7FFF FFFE 7FFF FFFE"
    $"7FFF FFFE 7FFF FFFE 7FFF FFFE 7FFF FFFE"
    $"7FFF FFFE 7FFF FFFE 7FFF FFFE 7FFF FFFE"
    $"7FFF FFFE 7FFF FFFE 7FFF FFFE 7FFF FFFE"
    $"7FFF FFFE 7FFF FFFE 7FFF FFFE 7FFF FFFE"
    $"7FFF FFFE 7FFF FFFE 7FFF FFFE 7FFF FFFE"
};


/* SwitchBank's color icon in icl8 format */
data 'icl8' (SWITCH_ICON)
{
    $"00FF FFFF FFFF FFFF FFFF FFFF FFFF FFFF"
    $"FFFF FFFF FFFF FFFF FFFF FFFF FFFF FF00"
    $"00FF 2A2A 2A2A 2A2A 2A2A 2A2A 2A2A 2A2A"
    $"2A2A 2A2A 2A2A 2A2A 2A2A 2A2A 2A2A FF00"
    $"00FF 2AFF FFFF 2A2A 2A2A 2A2A 2A2A 2A2A"
```

```
$"2A2A 2A2A 2A2A 2A2A 2A2A FFFF FF2A FF00"
$"00FF 2AFF 2AFF 2AFF FFFF FFFF FF2A 2A2A"
$"2A2A 2AFF FFFF FFFF FF2A FF2A FF2A FF00"
$"00FF 2AFF FFFF 2AFF F52A F52A FF2A 2A2A"
$"2A2A 2AFF F52A F52A FF2A FFFF FF2A FF00"
$"00FF 2A2A 2A2A 2AFF 2A2A 2A2A FF2A 2A2A"
$"2A2A 2AFF 2A2A 2A2A FF2A 2A2A 2A2A FF00"
$"00FF 2A2A 2A2A 2AFF 5454 5454 FF2A 2A2A"
$"2A2A 2AFF 5454 5454 FF2A 2A2A 2A2A FF00"
$"00FF 2A2A 2A2A 2AFF 7F7F 7F7F FF2A 2A2A"
$"2A2A 2AFF 7F7F 7F7F FF2A 2A2A 2A2A FF00"
$"00FF 2A2A 2A2A 2AFF FF7F FFFF FF2A 2A2A"
$"2A2A 2AFF FFFF 7FFF FF2A 2A2A 2A2A FF00"
$"00FF 2A2A 2A2A 2AFF 7F7F 7FFF 2A2A 2A2A"
$"2A2A 2A2A FF7F 7F7F FF2A 2A2A 2A2A FF00"
$"00FF 2A2A 2A2A 2AFF 5454 7FFF 2A2A 2A2A"
$"2A2A 2A2A FF54 547F FF2A 2A2A 2A2A FF00"
$"00FF 2A2A 2A2A 2AFF 2A54 7FFF 2A2A 2A2A"
$"2A2A 2A2A FF2A 547F FF2A 2A2A 2A2A FF00"
$"00FF 2A2A 2AFF FFFF 2A54 7FFF FFFF 2A2A"
$"2A2A FFFF FF2A 547F FFFF FF2A 2A2A FF00"
$"00FF 2A2A 2AFF F5FF 2A54 7FFF F5FF 2A2A"
$"2A2A FFF5 FF2A 547F FFF5 FF2A 2A2A FF00"
$"00FF 2A2A 2AFF 54FF 2A54 7FFF 54FF 2A2A"
$"2A2A FF54 FF2A 547F FF54 FF2A 2A2A FF00"
$"00FF 2A2A 2AFF 54FF 2A54 7FFF 54FF 2A2A"
$"2A2A FF54 FF2A 547F FF54 FF2A 2A2A FF00"
$"00FF 2A2A 2AFF FFFF 2A54 7FFF FFFF 2A2A"
$"2A2A FFFF FF2A 547F FFFF FF2A 2A2A FF00"
$"00FF 2A2A 2A2A 2AFF 2A54 7FFF 2A2A 2A2A"
$"2A2A 2A2A FF2A 547F FF2A 2A2A 2A2A FF00"
$"00FF 2A2A 2A2A 2AFF 2A54 7FFF FFFF FFFF"
$"FFFF FFFF FF2A 547F FF2A 2A2A 2A2A FF00"
$"00FF 2A2A 2A2A 2AFF 2A54 7FFF F52A F52A"
$"F52A F52A FF2A 547F FF2A 2A2A 2A2A FF00"
$"00FF 2A2A 2A2A 2AFF 2A54 7FFF 5454 5454"
$"5454 5454 FF2A 547F FF2A 2A2A 2A2A FF00"
$"00FF 2A2A 2A2A 2AFF 2A54 7FFF 7F7F 7F7F"
$"7F7F 7F7F FF2A 547F FF2A 2A2A 2A2A FF00"
$"00FF 2A2A 2A2A 2AFF FFFF FFFF FFFF FFFF"
$"FFFF FFFF FFFF FFFF FF2A 2A2A 2A2A FF00"
```

```
        $"00FF 2A2A 2A2A 2A2A 2A2A 2A2A 2AFF 54F5"
        $"2A7F FF2A 2A2A 2A2A 2A2A 2A2A 2A2A FF00"
        $"00FF 2A2A 2A2A 2A2A 2A2A 2A2A 2AFF 542A"
        $"2A7F FF2A 2A2A 2A2A 2A2A 2A2A 2A2A FF00"
        $"00FF 2A2A 2A2A 2A2A 2A2A 2A2A 2AFF 54F5"
        $"2A7F FF2A 2A2A 2A2A 2A2A 2A2A 2A2A FF00"
        $"00FF 2A2A 2A2A 2A2A 2A2A 2A2A 2AFF 542A"
        $"2A7F FF2A 2A2A 2A2A 2A2A 2A2A 2A2A FF00"
        $"00FF 2AFF FFFF 2A2A 2A2A 2A2A 2AFF 54F5"
        $"2A7F FF2A 2A2A 2A2A 2A2A FFFF FF2A FF00"
        $"00FF 2AFF 2AFF 2A2A 2A2A 2A2A 2AFF 542A"
        $"2A7F FF2A 2A2A 2A2A 2A2A FF2A FF2A FF00"
        $"00FF 2AFF FFFF 2A2A 2A2A 2A2A 2AFF FFFF"
        $"FFFF FF2A 2A2A 2A2A 2A2A FFFF FF2A FF00"
        $"00FF 2A2A 2A2A 2A2A 2A2A 2A2A 2A2A"
        $"2A2A 2A2A 2A2A 2A2A 2A2A 2A2A 2A2A FF00"
        $"00FF FFFF FFFF FFFF FFFF FFFF FFFF FFFF"
        $"FFFF FFFF FFFF FFFF FFFF FFFF FFFF FF00"
    };


    /* SwitchBank's color icon, in cicn format */
    data 'cicn' (SWITCH_ICON)
    {
        $"0000 0000 8010 0000 0000 0020 0020 0000"
        $"0000 0000 0000 0048 0000 0048 0000 0000"
        $"0004 0001 0004 0000 0000 0000 0000 0000"
        $"0000 0000 0000 0004 0000 0000 0020 0020"
        $"0000 0000 0004 0000 0000 0020 0020 0000"
        $"0000 7FFF FFFE 7FFF FFFE 7FFF FFFE 7FFF"
        $"FFFE 7FFF FFFE 7FFF FFFE 7FFF FFFE 7FFF"
        $"FFFE 7FFF FFFE 7FFF FFFE 7FFF FFFE 7FFF"
        $"FFFE 7FFF FFFE 7FFF FFFE 7FFF FFFE 7FFF"
        $"FFFE 7FFF FFFE 7FFF FFFE 7FFF FFFE 7FFF"
        $"FFFE 7FFF FFFE 7FFF FFFE 7FFF FFFE 7FFF"
        $"FFFE 7FFF FFFE 7FFF FFFE 7FFF FFFE 7FFF"
        $"FFFE 7FFF FFFE 7FFF FFFE 7FFF FFFE 7FFF"
        $"FFFE 7FFF FFFE 4000 0002 5C00 003A 55F8"
        $"1FAA 5D08 10BA 4108 1082 4108 1082 4108"
        $"1082 41B8 1D82 4110 0882 4110 0882 4110"
        $"0882 471C 38E2 4514 28A2 4514 28A2 4514"
        $"28A2 471C 38E2 4110 0882 411F F882 4110"
        $"0882 4110 0882 4110 0882 41FF FF82 4004"
```

```
        $"2002 4004 2002 4004 2002 4004 2002 5C04"
        $"203A 5404 202A 5C07 E03A 4000 0002 7FFF"
        $"FFFE 0000 0000 0000 0005 0000 FFFF FFFF"
        $"FFFF 0001 CCCC CCCC FFFF 0002 9999 9999"
        $"FFFF 0003 6666 6666 CCCC 0004 EEEE EEEE"
        $"EEEE 000F 0000 0000 0000 0FFF FFFF FFFF"
        $"FFFF FFFF FFFF FFFF FFF0 0F11 1111 1111"
        $"1111 1111 1111 1111 11F0 0F1F FF11 1111"
        $"1111 1111 1111 11FF F1F0 0F1F 1F1F FFFF"
        $"F111 111F FFFF F1F1 F1F0 0F1F FF1F 4141"
        $"F111 111F 4141 F1FF F1F0 0F11 111F 1111"
        $"F111 111F 1111 F111 11F0 0F11 111F 2222"
        $"F111 111F 2222 F111 11F0 0F11 111F 3333"
        $"F111 111F 3333 F111 11F0 0F11 111F F3FF"
        $"F111 111F FF3F F111 11F0 0F11 111F 333F"
        $"1111 1111 F333 F111 11F0 0F11 111F 223F"
        $"1111 1111 F223 F111 11F0 0F11 111F 123F"
        $"1111 1111 F123 F111 11F0 0F11 1FFF 123F"
        $"FF11 11FF F123 FFF1 11F0 0F11 1F4F 123F"
        $"4F11 11F4 F123 F4F1 11F0 0F11 1F2F 123F"
        $"2F11 11F2 F123 F2F1 11F0 0F11 1F2F 123F"
        $"2F11 11F2 F123 F2F1 11F0 0F11 1FFF 123F"
        $"FF11 11FF F123 FFF1 11F0 0F11 111F 123F"
        $"1111 1111 F123 F111 11F0 0F11 111F 123F"
        $"FFFF FFFF F123 F111 11F0 0F11 111F 123F"
        $"4141 4141 F123 F111 11F0 0F11 111F 123F"
        $"2222 2222 F123 F111 11F0 0F11 111F 123F"
        $"3333 3333 F123 F111 11F0 0F11 111F FFFF"
        $"FFFF FFFF FFFF F111 11F0 0F11 1111 1111"
        $"1F24 13F1 1111 1111 11F0 0F11 1111 1111"
        $"1F21 13F1 1111 1111 11F0 0F11 1111 1111"
        $"1F24 13F1 1111 1111 11F0 0F11 1111 1111"
        $"1F21 13F1 1111 1111 11F0 0F1F FF11 1111"
        $"1F24 13F1 1111 11FF F1F0 0F1F 1F11 1111"
        $"1F21 13F1 1111 11F1 F1F0 0F1F FF11 1111"
        $"1FFF FFF1 1111 11FF F1F0 0F11 1111 1111"
        $"1111 1111 1111 1111 11F0 0FFF FFFF FFFF"
        $"FFFF FFFF FFFF FFFF FFF0"
};

/* The system's color caution alert icon */
data 'cicn' (2)
```

```
{
    $"0000 0000 8010 0000 0000 0020 0020 0000"
    $"0000 0000 0000 0048 0000 0048 0000 0000"
    $"0004 0001 0004 0000 0000 0000 0000 0000"
    $"0000 0000 0000 0004 0000 0000 0020 0020"
    $"0000 0000 0004 0000 0000 0020 0020 0000"
    $"0000 0001 8000 0003 C000 0007 E000 0007"
    $"E000 000F F000 000F F000 001F F800 001F"
    $"F800 003F FC00 003F FC00 007F FE00 007F"
    $"FE00 00FF FF00 00FF FF00 01FF FF80 01FF"
    $"FF80 03FF FFC0 03FF FFC0 07FF FFE0 07FF"
    $"FFE0 0FFF FFF0 0FFF FFF0 1FFF FFF8 1FFF"
    $"FFF8 3FFF FFFC 3FFF FFFC 7FFF FFFE 7FFF"
    $"FFFE FFFF FFFF FFFF FFFF FFFF FFFF FFFF"
    $"FFFF 0001 8000 0003 C000 0003 C000 0006"
    $"6000 0006 6000 000C 3000 000C 3000 0018"
    $"1800 0019 9800 0033 CC00 0033 CC00 0063"
    $"C600 0063 C600 00C3 C300 00C3 C300 0183"
    $"C180 0183 C180 0303 C0C0 0303 C0C0 0603"
    $"C060 0601 8060 0C01 8030 0C00 0030 1800"
    $"0018 1801 8018 3003 C00C 3003 C00C 6001"
    $"8006 6000 0006 C000 0003 FFFF FFFF 7FFF"
    $"FFFE 0000 0000 0000 0006 0000 FFFF FFFF"
    $"FFFF 0001 FFFF CCCC 3333 0002 CCCC 9999"
    $"0000 0003 9999 6666 0000 0004 3333 3333"
    $"3333 0005 BBBB BBBB BBBB 000F 0000 0000"
    $"0000 0000 0000 0000 000F F000 0000 0000"
    $"0000 0000 0000 0000 004F F400 0000 0000"
    $"0000 0000 0000 0000 05FF FF50 0000 0000"
    $"0000 0000 0000 0000 04F3 3F40 0000 0000"
    $"0000 0000 0000 0000 5FF1 1FF5 0000 0000"
    $"0000 0000 0000 0000 4F31 13F4 0000 0000"
    $"0000 0000 0000 0005 FF11 11FF 5000 0000"
    $"0000 0000 0000 0004 F311 113F 4000 0000"
    $"0000 0000 0000 005F F12F F21F F500 0000"
    $"0000 0000 0000 004F 314F F413 F400 0000"
    $"0000 0000 0000 05FF 11FF FF11 FF50 0000"
    $"0000 0000 0000 04F3 11FF FF11 3F40 0000"
    $"0000 0000 0000 5FF1 11FF FF11 1FF5 0000"
    $"0000 0000 0000 4F31 11FF FF11 13F4 0000"
    $"0000 0000 0005 FF11 11FF FF11 11FF 5000"
```

```
        $"0000 0000 0004 F311 11FF FF11 113F 4000"
        $"0000 0000 005F F111 11FF FF11 111F F500"
        $"0000 0000 004F 3111 11FF FF11 1113 F400"
        $"0000 0000 05FF 1111 11FF FF11 1111 FF50"
        $"0000 0000 04F3 1111 114F F411 1111 3F40"
        $"0000 0000 5FF1 1111 112F F211 1111 1FF5"
        $"0000 0000 4F31 1111 111F F111 1111 13F4"
        $"0000 0005 FF11 1111 1112 2111 1111 11FF"
        $"5000 0004 F311 1111 1111 1111 1111 113F"
        $"4000 005F F111 1111 112F F211 1111 111F"
        $"F500 004F 3111 1111 11FF FF11 1111 1113"
        $"F400 05FF 1111 1111 11FF FF11 1111 1111"
        $"FF50 04F3 1111 1111 112F F211 1111 1111"
        $"3F40 5FF1 1111 1111 1111 1111 1111 1111"
        $"1FF5 FF31 1111 1111 1111 1111 1111 1111"
        $"13FF FFFF FFFF FFFF FFFF FFFF FFFF FFFF"
        $"FFFF 5FFF FFFF FFFF FFFF FFFF FFFF FFFF"
        $"FFF5"
};
```

Well, you probably won't type all of the hexadecimal codes here that define the color data of SwitchBank's icons, but you get the idea. The ICON resource defines a black-and-white icon, 32 pixels to a side. ICON is the great-granddaddy of the icon formats, starting on the original Mac in 1984. The cicn resource is a color icon format first introduced on the Mac II in 1987. It defines both a black-and-white icon, and an 8-bit color icon. It's not commonly used these days, because its complex format impairs fast data access. We supply it here because the Dialog Manager has a special feature that it uses when a dialog item is an icon. If the icon's cicn resource is available, the Dialog Manager substitutes the color icon for the dialog box's item icon, instead of using the black-and-white one. No special programming is required for this to occur. Our About Box uses an icon and it appears in color when we provide this cicn resource. This is also why we supply the cicn for the system's caution alert icon: When an alert appears, the icon appears in color on a color Mac.

The more prevalent color icon format is the icl8 format, which represents a large (32 pixels per side) 8-bit color icon. There's also a small (16 pixels per side) 8-bit color icon format called ics8, that's used to display file icons in the Apple menu and the Application menu. These formats define color data only, so access to the icon data is fast. If you've used ResEdit to spelunk around in other application resources, you can see that the Macintosh OS uses the icl8 and ics8 format to display file icons. For simplicity, I've omitted the ics8 icon data.

Save this editor window as the file "SwitchBank.r," or copy the file from the CD-ROM from CodeWarrior:Code Examples:SwitchBank ƒ: folder. Like the convention of ending project file names with a .π or .prj extension, Rez source files typically end with a .r extension. Now it's time to compile the Rez source code into resources.

To do that, we'll need the Rez tool, which in turn requires the use of the ToolServer application. A brief explanation is in order here. Apple's MPW software uses an application called the MPW Shell, which serves as an IDE for Apple's development tools. Where MPW differs from Metrowerks CodeWarrior is that many of its development operations—such as compiling, linking, and building resources—are controlled by command lines typed into a Worksheet window managed by the MPW Shell. An MPW tool (such as Rez) is an application that has specialized or little interface code, and thus relies upon the environment set up by the MPW Shell to function. ToolServer is an application that mimics this environment adequately so that these tools can operate outside of the MPW Shell. This makes them available to third-party vendors, which in turn lets CodeWarrior programmers tap into the large suite of MPW tools written over the years.

The first step in generating our resource, then, is to start the ToolServer. Go to the Tools menu in CodeWarrior's IDE and select Start ToolServer. A ToolServer Worksheet window appears, as does a new menu labeled ToolServer in the menu bar (see figure 6.2).

The status pane within the Worksheet's bottom scroll bar shows what tool or script is active. If you're familiar with the MPW enviroment, you can type in the name of a tool and any arguments, then press Enter to start it. (Note: you must press the Enter key on the Extended keyboard, or Command-Return on the Standard keyboard. Pressing the Return key won't have any effect.) While we won't be working with ToolServer this way, we will rely on the output that appears in the Worksheet window to tell us if something's gone wrong. From the ToolServer menu, select ToolServer Tools and a hierarchial menu appears, as shown in figure 6.3.

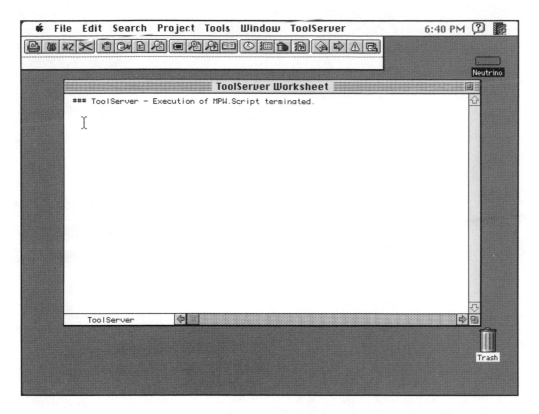

Figure 6.2 *The ToolServer Worksheet window; the status pane in the lower left scroll bar shows the active tool.*

Choose Rez from this menu. The Rez options window appears, as shown in figure 6.4.

Notice that the Type item is highlighted in this dialog box. This and the next item, Creator, are used to specify the type and creator of the file that Rez generates. Type **rsrc** in the Type item, press Tab to select the Creator item, and type **RSED**. RSED is ResEdit's creator signature, so once the output file is made, we can double-click on it to launch ResEdit and examine it immediately.

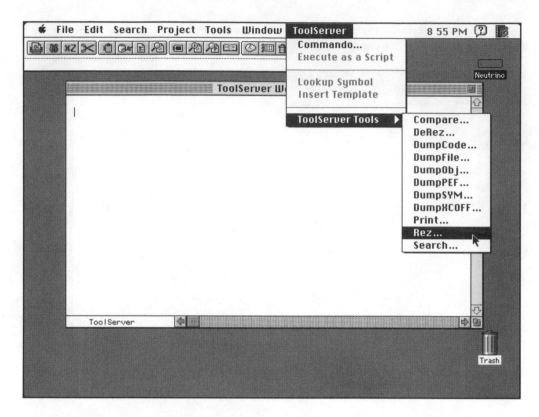

Figure 6.3 *Some MPW tools available from the ToolServer*

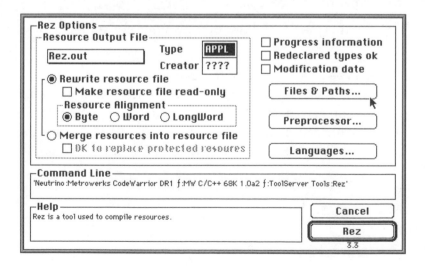

Figure 6.4 *The Rez Options window, where the output file's name, type, and creator is set*

Now go to the pop-up menu labeled with the default file name of Rez.out, and select Write Output to a New File from this menu. A Standard File dialog box appears. First ensure that you're in the SwitchBank ƒ folder. Type in the name **SwitchBank.π.rsrc** and press Return. Now that you've selected the output file's name, type, and creator, let's specify the input. Start by clicking on the Files & Paths button. Rez places another window titled Files & Paths... on the screen (see figure 6.5). We next guide Rez to the directory that contains the header files "SysTypes.r" and "Types.r." To do this, we click on the #Include Paths... button.

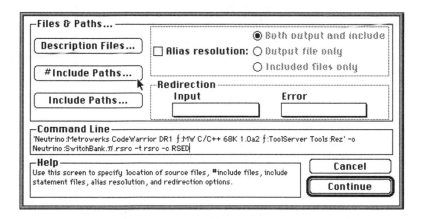

Figure 6.5 *The Files & Paths window, where the input file and search paths are selected*

Locate the folder RIncludes in the CodeWarrior:Apple Tools:MPW: Interfaces path. (The Apple Tools folder and its contents are on the CD-ROM, and are on your Mac's hard drive, depending upon the type of software installation you did). When you get there, click on the Add Current Directory button, and this name gets appended into a list at the bottom of the window (see figure 6.6).

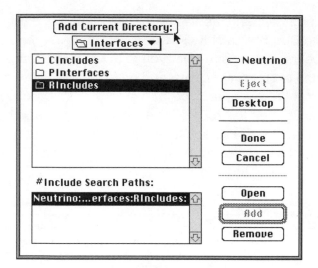

Figure 6.6   *Adding an include file directory to the file search path*

Click on the Done and Continue buttons and you'll end up back on the first screen. Take a brief glance to see that everything is set properly, then click on the Rez button. You should hear some hard disk activity, and the status pane indicates that Rez is active. No news in the Worksheet window is good news: it means the resource compilation ran successfully. Once the cursor changes from the rotating "beach ball" busy indicator back to an arrow, click on the WorkSheet window. You wind up back in CodeWarrior, but the ToolServer window remains open in case you want to run other MPW tools. If you're finished with Rez, go to the Tools menu in Metrowerks CodeWarrior and pick Stop ToolServer. The Worksheet window disappears when the ToolServer application quits. You do this because ToolServer uses up to 1.5M of RAM, which you'll want to put to use elsewhere.

Background Info

If the ToolServer complains of missing files or scripts, or the MPW tools don't appear in the hierarchial menu, the ToolServer software installation may have been done improperly. ToolServer requires that certain files be inside of specific directories to operate properly. Check the CodeWarrior documentation file, "How to add Tools," to determine if this is the problem.

A file named "SwitchBank.π.rsrc" should be present in the SwitchBank *f*
folder. Double-click on it to launch ResEdit, and examine the resources. If
everything appears in order, then it's time to start writing code.

The SwitchBank Program

Let's start with our definitions first:

```
#include <Types.h>
#include <ConditionalMacros.h>
#include <QuickDraw.h>
#include <Windows.h>
#include <Fonts.h>
#include <Controls.h>
#include <Dialogs.h>
#include <Menus.h>
#include <Devices.h>
#include <Memory.h>
#include <Files.h>
#include <Events.h>
#include <Desk.h>
#include <OSEvents.h>
#include <ToolUtils.h>
#include <DiskInit.h>
#include <Folders.h>

#include <AppleTalk.h>
#include <AppleEvents.h>
#include <EPPC.h>
#include <PPCToolBox.h>
#include <Processes.h>

/* Definitions */
#define LAST_MENU          4   /* Number of menus */
#define LAST_HANDLER       3   /* Number of Apple Event handlers - 1 */

#define MENU_BAR_ID        128   /* ID for MBAR resource */
#define APPLE_MENU         128   /* Menu ID for Apple menu */
```

```
#define FILE_MENU            129   /* Menu ID for File menu */
#define EDIT_MENU            130   /* Menu ID for Edit menu */
#define SWITCH_MENU          131   /* Menu ID for File Share control */
#define RESOURCE_ID          127   /* Starting index into the menu array */


#define ABOUT_BOX            1   /* About box menu item # in Apple menu */


#define I_QUIT               1   /* Quit item # in File menu */

/* Various constants */
#define NIL                  0L
#define FALSE                false
#define TRUE                 true

/* Coords for disk init dialog box */
#define INIT_X               112
#define INIT_Y               80

#define APPEND_MENU          0
#define CHAR_CODE_MASK        255
#define DEFAULT_VOL          0
#define IN_FRONT             (-1)
#define MAX_TRIES            6
#define NO_CURSOR            0L
#define LONG_NAP             60L
#define SYSTEM_7             0x0700
#define FILE_SHARING_CREATOR  'hhgg'
#define FILE_SHARING_TYPE    'INIT'

/* Resource IDs for our windows & dialogs */
#define ABOUT_BOX_ID         128
#define ERROR_BOX_ID         130
#define ERROR_MESS_ID        131

/* Resource ID for the message strings */
#define LOG_ID_STR           128
#define PROBLEM_STOPPING_FS    1   /* ID numbers of the messages */
#define PROBLEM_STARTING_FS    2
```

```
#define PROBLEM_ON_EJECT          3
#define DONT_EJECT_STARTUP_VOL     4
#define CANT_FIND_STARTUP_VOL      5
#define TROUBLE_WITH_SYS_INFO      6
#define CANT_LOCATE_FILE           7
#define PROBLEM_WITH_AE_HANDLER    8
#define SYSTEM_7_REQUIRED          9


/* Bit 9 in vMAttrib field = volume is shared */
#define PERSONAL_ACCESS_MASK       0x00000200L
#define SEND_MESSAGE               13 /* Send a message to file server */
#define SHUT_DOWN                  2  /* csCode to shut down server */
```

These declarations are from "SonOMunger.c" because, as stated earlier, we're reusing a lot of that code. Most Mac programmers keep handy a working "code skeleton" that implements basic application components, such as Toolbox initialization, the event loop, simple menu functions, and high-level event handlers. Writing a new program thus becomes a matter a fleshing out the details with application-specific custom functions. This also simplifies debugging, since you're building on a proven code foundation. Now we declare the functions we plan to use:

```
/* Function prototypes */
Boolean Check_System(void);             /* Standard application functions */
Boolean Do_Command (long mResult);
Boolean Init_Mac(void);
void Main_Event_Loop(void);
void Report_Error(OSErr errorCode);
void Report_Err_Message(long messageID);


Boolean Init_AE_Events(void);           /* High level Apple Events */
void Do_High_Level(EventRecord *AERecord);
pascal OSErr Core_AE_Open_Handler(AppleEvent *messagein, AppleEvent *reply,
                                long refIn);
pascal OSErr Core_AE_OpenDoc_Handler(AppleEvent *messagein,
                                 AppleEvent *reply, long refIn);
pascal OSErr Core_AE_Print_Handler(AppleEvent *messagein, AppleEvent *reply,
                                long refIn);
pascal OSErr Core_AE_Quit_Handler(AppleEvent *messagein, AppleEvent *reply,
```

```
                                long refIn);

/* Functions to handle details of file sharing */
Boolean File_Share_On(short vRefNum);
Boolean Find_File_Sharing(void);
Boolean Get_FS_Info(void);
void Stop_File_Sharing(void);
void Start_File_Sharing(void);
void Toggle_File_Sharing(void);
```

As you can see, our functions are broken out into the "generic" ones
we always reuse, plus the application-specific ones. Now for some data
structures:

```
/* Assorted structures for server trap */


typedef long    *LongIntPtr;


#if defined(powerc) || defined (__powerc)
#pragma options align=mac68k
#endif


struct DisconnectParam
    {
    QElemPtr    qLink;
    short       qType;
    short       ioTrap;
    Ptr         ioCmdAddr;
    ProcPtr     ioCompletion;
    OSErr       ioResult;
    LongIntPtr  scDiscArrayPtr;
    short       scArrayCount;
    short       reserved;
    short       scCode;
    short       scNumMinutes;
    short       scFlags;
    StringPtr   scMessagePtr;
    };
```

```c
#if defined(powerc) || defined(__powerc)
#pragma options align=reset
#endif


typedef struct DisconnectParam DisconnectParam;
typedef union SCParamBlockRec SCParamBlockRec;
typedef SCParamBlockRec *SCParamBlockPtr;


/* Structure for installing handlers into AE event dispatch table */
struct AEinstalls
   {
    AEEventClass theClass;
    AEEventID theEvent;
    AEEventHandlerProcPtr theProc;
   };
typedef struct AEinstalls AEinstalls;



/* Globals - standard */
WindowPtr            geventWindow;  /* our private window */
EventRecord          gmyEvent;
CursHandle           gtheCursor;    /* Current pointer icon */
Boolean              guserDone;
WindowPtr            gwhichWindow;
short                gwindowCode;


/* Application-specific globals */
short                gdragNDropFlag;
ProcessInfoRec       gprocess;
ProcessSerialNumber  gprocessSN;
long                 gSysDirID;
short                gsysVRefNum;
FSSpec               gthisFileSpec;
FSSpecPtr            gthisFileSpecPtr;
```

We define our usual gaggle of globals here. The high-level event structure for the dispatch table is recycled from "SonOMunger." The other data structures are used to set up a function that controls the file server software that's at the core of File Sharing. This code illustrates an important point. Note the use of the `#pragma options align=mac68k` statement. The 68K processor readily accesses data of any size (byte, word, or long word) at even memory addresses, while it can only access bytes at any memory address. Put another way, the 68K requires that most data be aligned on word (16-bit) boundaries. A 68K compiler typically adds padding bytes at certain points in a program's data structures to ensure that they are word-aligned. The PowerPC processor, on the other hand, favors memory accesses that conform to the data's size. In other words, it can readily access bytes at any address, words (16 bits) at every even address, and longs (32 bits) at every address divisible by four. Note the use of the verb *favors* here: The PowerPC can actually access data of any size at any address. However, aligned memory accesses require fewer bus cycles than unaligned ones, so for better performance PowerPC compilers insert padding bytes into data structures to achieve the preferred data alignment.

However, a data structure that's optimally aligned for the PowerPC processor might not be word-aligned and thus not usable by a 68K processor. On a Power Macintosh, you might wonder why you'd care about data alignment anyway. Recall that much of Power Mac's Toolbox routines are still implemented as 68K code, and the 68LC040 emulator expects the data to be word aligned. Also, there are still plenty of 68K-based Macs out there that your software should support. For example, suppose your program creates files with internal data structures that you expect a 68K Mac to read. Likewise, a networked Power Mac might transfer data through the network to 68K Macs for use. In both cases, proper data alignment is crucial.

To avoid this problem, the `#pragma options align=mac68k` statement tells the compiler to word-align the program's data structures. Performance may suffer on a PowerPC, but this data arrangement ensures that the 68K processor accesses will operate, especially for emulated Toolbox code. The `align=reset` directive immediately after `DisconnectParam` structure tells the compiler to resume arranging data in the PowerPC's preferred data alignment scheme. This is done to minimize the impact of misaligned data accesses on the PowerPC processor. Like the UPPs, the header files handle most of these alignment issues for you. However, for the custom function here—or any data structure you expect to pass the Macintosh OS or 68K Mac—you have to take care of the alignment problem yourself.

Now it's time to write our custom function:

```
/* Glue to call the ServerDispatch trap */
#if USES68KINLINES
#pragma parameter __D0 mySyncServerDispatch(__A0)
#endif
pascal OSErr mySyncServerDispatch(SCParamBlockPtr PBPtr)
 FOURWORDINLINE(0x7000, 0xA094, 0x3028, 0x0010);


/* = {                                               */
/*   0x7000, /* MOVEQ  #$00, D0         ; Input must be 0        */
/*   0xA094, /* _ServerDispatch        ; Hop to the trap        */
/*   0x3028,                                          */
/*   0x0010  /* MOVE.W ioResult(A0),D0  ; Move result to D0 because */
/*   }                                     ; File Sharing doesn't.    */


#ifdef powerc
/* Call the 68K code from the PowerPC through the Mixed Mode Manager */
static pascal OSErr mySyncServerDispatch(SCParamBlockPtr PBPtr)
{
ProcInfoType myProcInfo;
OSErr result;
   /* Need an RTS at the end to return ... */
static short code[] = {0x7000, 0xA094, 0x3028, 0x0010, 0x4E75};

    /* Build the procinfo (note use of register based calls) */
    myProcInfo = kRegisterBased
                        | RESULT_SIZE(SIZE_CODE(sizeof(OSErr)))
                        | REGISTER_RESULT_LOCATION(kRegisterD0)
                        | REGISTER_ROUTINE_PARAMETER(1,kRegisterA0,
                                    SIZE_CODE(sizeof(SCParamBlockPtr)));
```

```
    result = CallUniversalProc((UniversalProcPtr) code, myProcInfo, (PBPtr));
    return result;
} /* end mySyncServerDispatch() */
#endif
```

SyncServerDispatch() is a Toolbox routine that controls the file server software that implements AppleShare and File Sharing. Unfortunately, this routine escaped being defined in Apple's PowerPC libraries. Since I happened to know the trap word and glue code for SyncServerDispatch(), it seemed that I could define the routine myself. I wrote a function called mySyncServerDispatch() that uses the 68K assembly language code to implement the missing routine call. The conditional flags USES68KINLINES and powerc have CodeWarrior use either the original in-line 68K machine code when making the 68K version of the application, or use the PowerPC function when making the PowerPC application. By placing the 68K function definition before the PowerPC's, the 68K function serves double-duty as the PowerPC's function prototype. All the PowerPC function does is create the appropriate routine descriptor for mySyncServerDispatch() before calling the same 68K machine code. Let's see how this is done.

In the PowerPC version, we declare mySyncServerDispatch() as static to give its name file scope instead of global scope. We use the same in-line machine code as in the 68K version of the function, but with an important twist. On a 68K processor, the routine's code executes in-line, with execution resuming at the next instruction when the processor returns from the A trap exception. However, for the PowerPC version, we *call* this in-line code as a function. In order to return properly to the calling function, we add a 68K RTS instruction (0x4E75) to the code. We have to call the routine this way so that the Mixed Mode Manager can step in and handle the instruction set context switch.

Next, we construct the data structure myProcInfo which contains a description of mySyncServerDispatch()'s arguments. This routine is register based: That is, the argument and result get passed in 68K processor registers. MySyncServerDispatch() expects a pointer to a parameter block that contains a server control command in register A0, and the result of the operation is returned in register D0. Once myProcInfo is set up to describe this arrangement, we call CallUniversalProc(), and pass it the address of the routine call (the first element of the array code), myProcInfo, and the parameter block with the server command. When calling a 68K routine, as in this example, you can see that the 68K code pointer is a UPP. Therefore, it's unnecessary to create a routine descriptor for a 68K routine. This is why `CallUniversalProc()` takes the routine descriptor information as a separate argument. Generating code on the fly in the `code` array this way isn't the best implementation of the routine call, but it works adequately for this particular program.

We've made a change to our error reporting function:

```
void Report_Err_Message(long messageID)
{
unsigned char errorString[256];

    GetIndString((unsigned char *) errorString, LOG_ID_STR, messageID);
    if (errorString[0] == 0)        /* Is there a string present? */
       {
       SysBeep(30);            /* No, give up */
       return;
       } /* end if */
    ParamText(errorString, NIL, NIL, NIL);
    CautionAlert(ERROR_MESS_ID, NIL);

} /* end Report_Err_Message() */
```

Instead of accepting a pointer to a Pascal string, `Report_Err_Message()` now processes a message ID number. This message ID number corresponds to the ID number of a STR# resource that contains the relevant error message. This function uses `GetIndString()` to retrieve a string and passes it to the routines `ParamText()` and `CautionAlert()` for display. We do one safety check here. The Pascal string format has a length byte at the start of the string, and it is followed by the string data. The length byte says how many characters are in the string. If this value is zero, something's gone awry, and we bail out.

Our basic error function, `Report_Error()`, hasn't changed.

Here's the first of our application-specific functions:

```
Boolean Get_FS_Info(void)
{
gthisFileSpecPtr = &gthisFileSpec;
```

```
gprocessSN.highLongOfPSN = kNoProcess;
gprocessSN.lowLongOfPSN = kNoProcess;


gprocess.processInfoLength = sizeof(ProcessInfoRec); /* Store record size */
gprocess.processName = (unsigned char *) NewPtr(32); /* Allocate room for
                                                       the name */
gprocess.processAppSpec = gthisFileSpecPtr;          /* Direct towards our
                                                        storage */


/* Loop until all processes found */
while (GetNextProcess(&gprocessSN) == noErr)
    {
    if (GetProcessInformation(&gprocessSN, &gprocess) == noErr)
        {
        /* Is this process the File Sharing Extension? */
        if (gprocess.processType == FILE_SHARING_TYPE &&
            gprocess.processSignature == FILE_SHARING_CREATOR)
          return TRUE;
        } /* end if */
    } /* end while */

return FALSE;
}/* end Get_FS_Info() */
```

Get_FS_Info() searches the Mac OS process list, looking for a process whose file signature is the File Sharing Extension. You'll notice that we swiped most of this code from "process.c." This function assumes File Sharing is active, which means its process is present. If we discover such a process, **Get_FS_Info()** returns TRUE. The file name connected to this process is saved in the global **gprocess.processAppSpec**. If the process list is walked without finding a match, it returns FALSE.

```
Boolean File_Share_On(short volRefNum)
{
HParamBlockRec      ioHPB, volHPB;
GetVolParmsInfoBuffer    volInfoBuffer;
```

```
/* Get volume reference number */
   volHPB.volumeParam.ioCompletion = NIL; /* No completion routine */
   volHPB.volumeParam.ioNamePtr = NIL;    /* No volume name */
   volHPB.volumeParam.ioVRefNum = volRefNum;
   volHPB.volumeParam.ioVolIndex = 0;      /* 0 = Use only volRefNum to
                                              obtain the info */
   if (!PBHGetVInfo(&volHPB, FALSE))
      {
/* Get volume's characteristics */
      ioHPB.ioParam.ioCompletion = NIL;
      ioHPB.ioParam.ioNamePtr = NIL;
      ioHPB.ioParam.ioVRefNum = volHPB.volumeParam.ioVRefNum;
      ioHPB.ioParam.ioBuffer = (char *) &volInfoBuffer;
      ioHPB.ioParam.ioReqCount = sizeof(volInfoBuffer);
      if (!PBHGetVolParms(&ioHPB, FALSE))
         {
         if (volInfoBuffer.vMAttrib & PERSONAL_ACCESS_MASK)
            { /* The disk is shared */
            if (Get_FS_Info())      /* Look for File Sharing Ext */
               return TRUE;         /* Got the file info we need */
            } /* end if */
         } /* end if !PBHGetVolParms */
      } /* end if !PBHGetVInfo */
   return FALSE;
} /* end File_Share_On() */
```

This is part of the program's design to encourage users to drop all of their volume icons onto the SwitchBank application. `File_Share_On()` is used to determine if the volume dropped onto SwitchBank is shared or not. If `File_Share_On()` reports that the volume isn't shared, SwitchBank will eject it without interrupting File Sharing. The idea is to avoid excessive stopping and starting of the File Sharing process, which can fragment memory.

The routine `PBHGetVInfo()` takes the volume specification supplied to it via `volRefNum` and converts it to a volume reference number. This value, which is returned in `volHPB.volumeParam.ioVRefNum`, is used in the routine `PBHGetVolParms()` to obtain information about the target volume. If bit 9 in the `vMAttrib` field is set, the volume is being shared. We confirm this by calling `Get_FS_Info()`, which checks for the File Sharing Extension process. This also primes our global `gprocess.processAppSpec` with the file information associated with the process.

With these functions, we've obtained enough information about the File Sharing process to switch it off or on. Starting with shutting it off, we have:

```
/* Send a shut down immediately message to the File Sharing Server */
void Stop_File_Sharing(void)
{
DisconnectParam    serverBlock;
SCParamBlockPtr    serverBlockPtr;

/* Point to our message block */
     serverBlockPtr = (SCParamBlockPtr) &serverBlock;
     serverBlock.scCode = SHUT_DOWN;       /* Server command to shut down */
     serverBlock.scNumMinutes = 0;         /* Do it immediately */
     serverBlock.scFlags = SEND_MESSAGE;
     serverBlock.scMessagePtr = NIL;

     if (mySyncServerDispatch(serverBlockPtr) == noErr)
         {
         /* Let the OS get at the event */
         WaitNextEvent(everyEvent, &gmyEvent, LONG_NAP, NO_CURSOR);
         WaitNextEvent(everyEvent, &gmyEvent, LONG_NAP, NO_CURSOR);
         } /* end if */
     else
         Report_Err_Message(PROBLEM_STOPPING_FS);

} /* end Stop_File_Sharing() */
```

The function **Stop_File_Sharing()** does exactly what it describes. It accomplishes this by first loading the appropriate values into a parameter block that forms a server shutdown command with no time delay interval. Then it calls our custom function **mySyncServerDispatch()** with this parameter block. This issues the server shutdown command to the Mac OS.

What **Stop_File_Sharing()** executes next might not seem obvious, but it's part of the reality of cooperative multitasking. If SwitchBank plowed inexorably onwards, the shutdown command wouldn't take effect. That's because SwitchBank must surrender processor time so that the shutdown command percolates through the operating system, and for the File Sharing Extension process to respond to this command. Therefore, we call **WaitNextEvent()** to give processor time to the operating system and other

processes. If for some reason `mySyncServerDispatch()` reports an error, we
display an error message that explains the problem.

```
/* Launch the file that has the File Sharing application in it. */
/* The file name used for the launch was obtained from the process */
/*    when it's memory, or by searching the startup disk */
void Start_File_Sharing(void)
{
OSErr           launchErr;
LaunchPBPtr         thisAppPBPtr;
LaunchParamBlockRec  thisAppParams;

    gthisFileSpecPtr = &gthisFileSpec;
    thisAppPBPtr = &thisAppParams;
    thisAppParams.launchBlockID = extendedBlock;  /* Use new format */
    thisAppParams.launchEPBLength = extendedBlockLen;
    thisAppParams.launchFileFlags = 0;          /* Don't care about flags */
    thisAppParams.launchControlFlags = (launchNoFileFlags +
                                        launchContinue + launchDontSwitch);
/* Give it file name grabbed by Get_FS_Info() before File Sharing */
/*    Sharing was stopped */
    thisAppParams.launchAppSpec = gthisFileSpecPtr;
    thisAppParams.launchAppParameters = NIL;   /* Send just Open event */
    if ((launchErr = LaunchApplication(thisAppPBPtr)) == noErr)
        WaitNextEvent(everyEvent, &gmyEvent, SHORT_NAP, NO_CURSOR);
    else
        Report_Err_Message(PROBLEM_STARTING_FS);

} /* end Start_File_Sharing() */
```

`Start_File_Sharing()` undoes the work of `Stop_File_Sharing()`. First, it
takes the filename that it obtained from `Get_FS_Info()` or
`Find_File_Sharing()`, (described later) and puts it in a parameter block. We
also set control flags in this parameter block that specify our application
should continue running after the target application launches, and for the
target application (File Sharing Extension) not to switch to the foreground.
`Start_File_Sharing()` then calls the `LaunchApplication()` routine to start
the application embedded in the File Sharing Extension file. Again, we
have to call `WaitNextEvent()` so the operating system gets an opportunity
to handle the command.

Important

The initial version of SwitchBank sent a high-level Quit Application Apple Event to the File Sharing Extension process. However, I was informed by a seasoned Mac programmer that the politically correct way to stop this process was through file server commands, since File Sharing operates as a file server. Although I've had no problems stopping File Sharing through the Quit Application Apple Event, I don't ignore expert advice. For those who are interested in how this is done, here's the original `Stop_File_Sharing()` function. The code illustrates how to package a Quit Application Apple Event and send it to another application.

```
OSErr Stop_File_Sharing(void)
{
OSErr       err;
AppleEvent  thisEvent;
AEDesc      thisAddress;

if (File_Share_On()) /* Turn it off */
   {
   err = AECreateDesc(typeProcessSerialNumber, &gprocessSN,
             sizeof(processSN), &thisAddress);
   if (!err)
      err = AECreateAppleEvent(kCoreEventClass, kAEQuitApplication,
                &thisAddress, kAutoGenerateReturnID,
                kAnyTransactionID, &thisEvent);
   if (!err)
      err = AESend(&thisEvent, nil, kAENoReply + kAEAlwaysInteract +
            kAECanSwitchLayer, kAENormalPriority,
            kAEDefaultTimeout, nil, nil);
   if (!err)
      {
      AEDisposeDesc(&thisAddress);
      AEDisposeDesc(&thisEvent);
      } /* end if */
   /* Let the OS handle the event */
   WaitNextEvent(everyEvent, &myEvent, LONG_NAP, NO_CURSOR);
   } /* end if fileShareOn */

return err;
} /* end Stop_File_Sharing() */
```

The SwitchBank Controls menu lets you switch File Sharing off or on with just a keystroke. However, there's a problem here: What if the user started his Macintosh with File Sharing off, and wants to turn it on? In this situation, there's no File Sharing process running in memory that Get_FS_Info() can retrieve a filename from for LaunchApplication() to use. To close the door on this potential pitfall, I wrote the Find_File_Sharing() function:

```
Boolean Find_File_Sharing(void)
{
HParamBlockRec      searchPB;
FInfo               fileSharingExtInfo, fileSharingMaskInfo;
CInfoPBRec          searchSpec1, searchSpec2;
Point               nilPoint = {0, 0};

/* Set up creator and type for File Sharing Extension */
     fileSharingExtInfo.fdType = FILE_SHARING_TYPE;
     fileSharingExtInfo.fdCreator = FILE_SHARING_CREATOR;
     fileSharingExtInfo.fdFlags = 0;
     fileSharingExtInfo.fdLocation = nilPoint;
     fileSharingExtInfo.fdFldr = 0;

/* Set up masks */
     fileSharingMaskInfo.fdType = (OSType) 0xffffffff;
     fileSharingMaskInfo.fdCreator = (OSType) 0xffffffff;
     fileSharingMaskInfo.fdFlags = 0;
     fileSharingMaskInfo.fdLocation = nilPoint;
     fileSharingMaskInfo.fdFldr = 0;

/* 1st spec block */
/* Search by file type, not name */
   searchSpec1.hFileInfo.ioNamePtr = NIL;
/* Type & creator to look for */
   searchSpec1.hFileInfo.ioFlFndrInfo = fileSharingExtInfo;

/* 2nd spec block */
   searchSpec2.hFileInfo.ioNamePtr = NIL;
   searchSpec2.hFileInfo.ioFlFndrInfo = fileSharingMaskInfo; /* Mask */

/* Set up search call */
   searchPB.csParam.ioCompletion = NIL;
   searchPB.csParam.ioNamePtr = NIL;                    /* No volume name */
/* Search on startup volume */
   searchPB.csParam.ioVRefNum = gsysVRefNum;
```

```
        searchPB.csParam.ioMatchPtr = &gthisFileSpec;    /* Result goes here */
        searchPB.csParam.ioReqMatchCount = 1;            /* Look for 1 file */
   /* Search based on file characteristics */
        searchPB.csParam.ioSearchBits = fsSBFlFndrInfo;
        searchPB.csParam.ioSearchInfo1 = &searchSpec1;
        searchPB.csParam.ioSearchInfo2 = &searchSpec2;
        searchPB.csParam.ioSearchTime = 0;               /* Don't time out */
   /* Start at the beginning */
        searchPB.csParam.ioCatPosition.initialize = 0;
        searchPB.csParam.ioOptBuffer = NIL;   /* No search cache required */
        searchPB.csParam.ioOptBufSize = 0;

        if (PBCatSearchSync((CSParamPtr) &searchPB) == noErr)
           return TRUE;
        else
           {
           Report_Err_Message(CANT_LOCATE_FILE);
           return FALSE;
           } /* end else */


   } /* end Find_File_Sharing() */
```

In this function, we search for the File Sharing Extension on the startup volume, or boot disk. We begin by setting up the file's signature information (its creator and type) in a `fileSharingExtInfo` structure. This signature information is what we'll give the routine `PBCatSearchSync()` so it can locate the file. The `PBCatSearchSync()` routine performs high-speed searches on a volume's catalog file for specific file or directory information, and is ideal for the job. For more information, consult *Inside Macintosh: Files*. `PBCatSearchSync()` requires two specification blocks. The first contains search information and a start range, the second contains any masks to filter out information and a stop range. Our mask information, in the `fileSharingMaskInfo` structure, passes only the file's creator and type. Next, we assemble the parameter block that furnishes `PBCatSearchSync()` with the information needed to conduct the search. We supply it a pointer to our file specification global, `gthisFileSpec`, for the result to land in. We also provide the volume reference number of the startup volume, so that the search is conducted on the volume that has the System Folder. This is done because the File Sharing Extension resides in the Extensions folder, which in turn lies in the System Folder. If `PBCatSearchSync()` returns with a match, the global `gthisFileSpec` contains the filename, which is ready for use in `Start_File_Sharing()`.

Background Info

You might be wondering why `Get_FS_Info()` and `Find_File_Sharing()` both use the File Sharing Extension's signature information when they search, rather than just simply plugging in the name "File Sharing Extension." If you used a filename instead, it hampers the program's ability to operate in Macs overseas. That's because the File Sharing Extension's name varies in different languages, while its signature data never changes.

The next function implements the File Sharing toggle function used in SwitchBank's Controls menu. It's pretty simple, and it just calls the other functions discussed previously.

```c
void Toggle_File_Sharing(void)
{
   if (Get_FS_Info())              /* File Sharing already on (& in memory)? */
      Stop_File_Sharing();         /* Yes, turn it off */
   else                            /* No, look for the file */
      {
      if (Find_File_Sharing())     /* Find the File Sharing
                                          Extension file */
         Start_File_Sharing();     /* Launch it */
      } /* end else */

} /* end Toggle_File_Sharing() */
```

Some of the functions in SwitchBank, such as the one that installs the core Apple Event handlers, haven't changed and won't be covered here. For a complete source code listing, check the file "SwitchBank.c" on the CD-ROM, or appendix C. However, what has changed is the new Open Document handler, as shown below:

```c
/* High-level open document event */
pascal OSErr Core_AE_OpenDoc_Handler(AppleEvent *messagein,
                                 AppleEvent *reply, long refIn)
{
long            dummyResult;        /* Dummy variable for delay() */
register short  i, j;
Boolean         fileShareWasOn;
AEDesc          volDesc;            /* Container for sent volume names */
OSErr           volErr, highLevelErr;
long            numberOVolumes;     /* Number of volumes dropped onto us */
```

```
AEKeyword        ignoredKeyWord;       /* Bit buckets for high-level event info */
DescType         ignoredType;
Size             ignoredSize;
FSSpec           volFSS;               /* Container for volume names as FSSPecs */

   gtheCursor = GetCursor(watchCursor);       /* Change cursor */
   SetCursor(&**gtheCursor);
   fileShareWasOn = FALSE;

   if (!(highLevelErr = AEGetParamDesc(messagein, keyDirectObject,
                                  typeAEList, &volDesc)))
     {
     if ((highLevelErr = AECountItems(&volDesc, &numberOVolumes)) ==
                                    noErr)      /* How many? */
       {
       for (i = 1; ((i <= numberOVolumes) &&
                       (!highLevelErr)); ++i) /* Process each vol */
         {
         if (!(highLevelErr = AEGetNthPtr(&volDesc, i,
                                            typeFSS,
                                            &ignoredKeyWord,
                                            &ignoredType,
                                            (char *)&volFSS,
                                            sizeof(volFSS),
                                            &ignoredSize)))
            {
            if (volFSS.vRefNum != gsysVRefNum)
                     /* Chosen volume the boot drive? */
              {
              if (File_Share_On(volFSS.vRefNum))
                       /* This volume being shared? */

                {
                Stop_File_Sharing();
                fileShareWasOn = TRUE;
                } /* end if */
              j = 0;  /* Set retry count */
              while (((volErr = Eject(volFSS.name,
                                   volFSS.vRefNum)) != noErr) &&
                              (j < MAX_TRIES))
                {
```

```
                WaitNextFvent(everyEvent,
                                    &gmyEvent, SHORT_NAP, NO_CURSOR);
                Delay(10L, &dummyResult);
                j++;
                } /* end while */
            if (volErr == noErr)
                UnmountVol(volFSS.name,
                                        volFSS.vRefNum);
            else
                Report_Err_Message(PROBLEM_ON_EJECT);
            } /* end if != gsysVRefNum */
          else
              Report_Err_Message(DONT_EJECT_STARTUP_VOL);
          } /* end if !highLevelErr */
      } /* end for */
    } /* end if */
        /* Release memory copy of the AE parameter */
    highLevelErr = AEDisposeDesc(&volDesc);
    } /* end if !highLevelErr */

  if (fileShareWasOn)
    Start_File_Sharing();

  if (gdragNDropFlag >= 0)            /* Did user drag & drop onto us? */
    guserDone = TRUE;                 /* Yes, stop the application */

  SetCursor(&qd.arrow);              /* Restore the cursor */
  return highLevelErr;               /* Kick back any high-level
                                        problems to calling app */
} /* end Core_AE_OpenDoc_Handler() */
```

This function, like in "SonOMunger," gets called when objects get dropped on the application's icon. The handler uses the routine `AEGetParamDesc()` to fetch the message parameter out of the Open Document event sent to it and coerces the data into a descriptor list. The `AECountItems()` routine extracts the number of items in the list, and this value sets the duration of a `for` loop. The `for` loop uses the routine `AEGetNthPtr()` to obtain each volume name from the descriptor list, converting it into a file system specification as it does so. As in "SonOMunger," if `AEGetNthPtr()` reports an error, the loop stops. The target volume is now subjected to a battery of tests. First, its reference number is checked against the startup volume's reference number. If the two match, the user is attempting to eject the drive with the system software on it, which is a very bad idea. SwitchBank thus intervenes and warns the user of this. We could ignore this problem and allow the operation to fail when, because of the system software, the Toolbox `Eject()` routine detects the volume is busy. However, we can supply the user with a more informative error message and save some wasted processor cycles if we do this check now.

Next we look to see if the volume is being shared. If so, we call `Stop_File_Sharing()` to turn off File Sharing and set the flag `fileShareWasOn` to remind us that we did so. At last we call `Eject()` to eject the volume. The nice thing about this Toolbox routine is that it handles any type of volume: CD-ROM, floppy, and networked hard drives. If the Mac is extremely busy, `Eject()` might report an error because File Sharing hasn't had a chance to stop yet. So we wait a tenth of a second, call `WaitNextEvent()`, and retry the operation. The value of `MAX_TRIES` for this loop was determined empirically—a way of saying that I used SwitchBank on a Power Mac running under a heavy load and experimented until I found a value that worked best. If the eject fails, we warn the user.

When all of the work is done, we clean up by first disposing of the copy of the descriptor list made by `AEGetParamDesc()`. Then we check `fileShareWasOn` to see if File Sharing needs to be restarted, and call `Start_File_Sharing()` as required. Finally, we check a flag called `gdragNDropFlag` to determine if the application is already running, or was launched because of a drag and drop action. If the latter, then we flip the state of `guserDone` to make SwitchBank quit. If any of the high-level Apple Event routines have reported an error, we pass this value back to the calling application.

A new function in our stable of skeleton routines is `Check_System()`. As its name implies, it's used to check for specific features the application might need to operate properly:

```
Boolean Check_System(void)
{
SysEnvRec    machineInfo;          /* Record with machine-specific data */
short        sysVersion;           /* System version # */
short        versionRequested;     /* Version of SysEnvirons() to use */

    sysVersion = SYSTEM_7;
    versionRequested = 1;          /* MUST set this to get valid results */
```

```
        if (SysEnvirons(versionRequested, &machineInfo) == noErr)
            sysVersion = machineInfo.systemVersion;
        else
            {
            Report_Err_Message(TROUBLE_WITH_SYS_INFO);
            return FALSE;
            } /* end else */

        if (sysVersion < SYSTEM_7)                 /* Running System 7.0? */
            {
            Report_Err_Message (SYSTEM_7_REQUIRED);
            return FALSE;                          /* No. Sorry, can't run
                                                      without it  */

            } /* end if */


        return TRUE;
} /* end Check_System() */
```

The preferred method for investigating certain system features is to use the Gestalt Manager. However, the Gestalt Manager is available only under System 6.0.5 or later, which can be a problem if someone happens to launch SwitchBank on a Mac running an earlier version of the Macintosh OS. Because SwitchBank relies so heavily on certain System 7 features such as Apple Events, File Sharing, and the catalog search performed by `Find_File_Sharing()`, we must check the operating system version number. The solution is to call an older routine, `SysEnvirons()`. We use it to return the operating system version number, which we compare to see if it's System 7 or later. If not, `Check_System()` returns FALSE so that SwitchBank aborts the initialization phase. Once we've determined that System 7 is running, then we can use Gestalt Manager calls to look for specific features. Examples of how to use the Gestalt Manager to determine system-specific features abound in every volume of the new editions of *Inside Macintosh*, and volume VI of the old editions of *Inside Macintosh*. In our case, the check for the presence of System 7 is sufficient.

In `Do_Command()` we add an entry for SwitchBank's Controls menu, like so:

```
        case EDIT_MENU:
            SystemEdit(theItem - 1);
        break;
```

```
            case SWITCH_MENU:
                    Toggle_File_Sharing();
            break;

            default:
            break;
```

There are also some minor changes to `Main_Event_Loop()`. At the start of the function, we set `gdragNDropFlag = 1`. At the end of the **do** loop, we add:

```
            } /* end switch gmyEvent.what */
        } /* end if on next event */
    else                             /* Null event */
        ;                            /* Do idle or background stuff here */


/* Flag to determine whether app was launched by user or Open Apple Event */
        if (gdragNDropFlag >= 0)
            gdragNDropFlag--;
        } /* end do */

    while (guserDone == FALSE)
        ;                /* Loop until told to stop */
} /* end Main_Event_Loop() */
```

Here's where the flag `gdragNDropFlag` gets set. For a drag and drop operation, execution passes through the event loop twice (once for the Open Application Apple Event, and once for the Open Document Apple Event). The event loop decrements `gdragNDropFlag` until it goes negative, which occurs if the loop is traversed three times or more. At this point we can safely assume the application was launched by the user, and so `gdragNDropFlag` prevents `Core_AE_OpenDoc_Handler()` from stopping the application if a volume is dragged onto SwitchBank.

The initialization routine has changed:

```
Boolean Init_Mac(void)
{
Handle      theMenuBar;

/* Lunge after all the memory we can get */
    MaxApplZone();
```

```
/* Make sure we've got some master pointers */
   MoreMasters();
   MoreMasters();
   MoreMasters();
   MoreMasters();
   MoreMasters();
   MoreMasters();
   MoreMasters();
   MoreMasters();

/* Initialize managers */
   InitGraf(&qd.thePort);
   InitFonts();
   FlushEvents(everyEvent, 0);
   InitWindows();
   InitMenus();
   TEInit();
   InitDialogs(NIL);

/* Got our menu resources OK? */
   if ((theMenuBar = GetNewMBar(MENU_BAR_ID)) == NIL)
      return FALSE;

   SetMenuBar(theMenuBar);    /* Add our menus to menu list */
   DisposHandle(theMenuBar);
   AppendResMenu(GetMenuHandle(APPLE_MENU), 'DRVR'); /* Make Apple menu */
   DrawMenuBar();

/* Look for specific features or set up handlers this app needs */
   if (!Check_System())       /* Need System 7 */
      return FALSE;

   if (!Init_AE_Events())     /* Set up high-level event handlers */
      return FALSE;

   if (FindFolder(kOnSystemDisk, kSystemFolderType,
                  kDontCreateFolder, &gsysVRefNum, &gSysDirID) != noErr)
      {
      Report_Err_Message (CANT_FIND_STARTUP_VOL);
      return FALSE;
      } /* end if */
```

```
    InitCursor();                    /* Tell user app is ready */
    return TRUE;
} /* end Init_Mac() */
```

This time we build our menus by using `GetNewMBar()` and the MBAR re-source we made in "SwitchBank.r." This eliminates the array of MenuHandles and a `for` loop we used in "SonOMunger." However, if you want to add hierarchial menus in your application, you'll still have to use the `InsertMenu()` routine to set them up. We call `Check_System()` to see if the Mac is running System 7, followed by `Init_AE_Events()` to install our high-level event handlers. Finally, we call `FindFolder()`, a routine that obtains information on system directories such as the Preferences folder. If we pass this routine the constants `kOnSystemDisk` and `kSystemFolderType`, we get the startup volume reference number. From the earlier function descriptions, you'll recall that we needed this information for some error checking and the catalog search. The `main()` function hasn't changed at all. To examine the complete source code of the program, open the "SwitchBank.c" file in the SwitchBank ƒ folder, or check appendix C.

Creating the SwitchBank application uses the standard make operation we performed on "SonOMunger." Compile the "SwitchBank.c" file, and correct any errors. Add the libraries "MCWRuntime.Lib" and "InterfaceLib" to the project. Then, go to Edit menu and select Preferences. Pick the Project panel and change the application's name to SwitchBank, the creator to SWCH, and the memory size to 384K (see figure 6.7). Click on the SIZE flags pop-up menu here and uncheck the items acceptSuspendResumeEvents, and doesActivateOnFGSwitch. Confirm that the flag isHighLevelEventAware is checked on this menu. Now, make the application, and remember to rebuild the desktop database. The result should be an application with a knife-switch icon. You can launch the application, and from the Controls menu toggle File Sharing on or off. If you leave the application on the Desktop, you can drag and drop any volume icon onto SwitchBank. SwitchBank automatically launches, stops File Sharing if required, ejects the volume, restarts File Sharing, and quits.

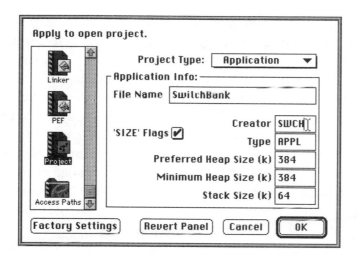

Figure 6.7 *Adjusting the project settings for the SwitchBank application*

The end result is a small utility application that makes my life easier. It also taught me a lot about the Power Mac.

Making a Fat Binary

You know I think that you should support 68K-based Macs, if only for the simple reason there are millions of them out there. For the next several years or so, count on them to outnumber the Power Macs. It makes sense to support this large existing hardware base with your software. However, you might be wondering how you're going to maintain and manage two copies of your application, one for each type of Mac. The first issue, maintenance, is simple. If you write the C code carefully, one set of source files can be used to generate both 68K and PowerPC machine code (or binaries). In fact, all of the programs presented in this book can be compiled on either version of CodeWarrior (both 68K and PowerPC) without modification.

The second issue appears to be more serious. How do you ensure that a 68K Mac owner gets a 68K version of your application and not the PowerPC version? The answer is that Apple's PowerPC application design enables you to create one copy of an application that runs on both a 68K Mac and a Power Mac. As you'll recall in chapter 5, a PowerPC application's code resides in a file's data fork, while a 68K application's code is composed of CODE resources in the file's resource fork. Both applications use a common set of resources such as MENU, WIND, DLOG, and others to implement the user interface. Because each program's code is in a different file fork, yet they draw on the same graphical resources, it's possible to combine the contents of the two forks to make what's known as a "fat binary," as shown in figure 6.8. Now each version of the Macintosh OS sees what it expects: the 68K Mac OS finds CODE resources in the application's resource fork, and the PowerPC Mac OS finds PowerPC code in the application's data fork. (Note: the Process Manager won't look for code fragments in an application unless a cfrg resource is present.) Due to smart planning on Apple's part, the issue of managing two different versions of the same application goes away, because one version will suffice. There are exceptions where it makes better sense to support two copies of the application. One case might be where the application is a large file, say, several megabytes. Making this application into a fat binary can double the file's size, resulting in a box of floppies and a lengthy installation for the user. In this situation, separate application binaries would keep the installation job to a manageable size and reduce the application's footprint on the system.

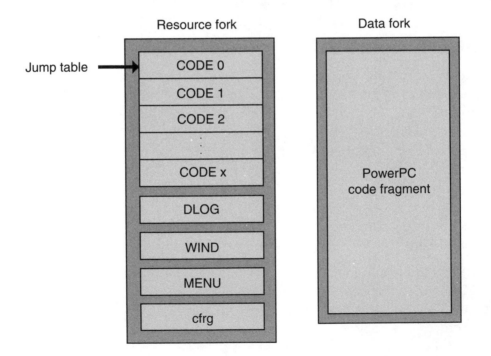

Figure 6.8   *The file structure for a fat binary application*

Making a fat binary with the Metrowerks CodeWarrior isn't difficult, and has two stages. By way of example, let's make "SwitchBank" into a fat binary. The first stage involves making the 68K version of the program. To begin, use Rez to compile "SwitchBank.r." Name this resource "SwitchBank.π.68K.rsrc." Next, make a project file with the 68K version of CodeWarrior and name it "SwitchBank.π.68K." Choose Add File... from the Project menu and pick "MacOS.lib" and "SwitchBank.c" to incorporate them into the project. Next, select Preferences from the Edit menu and go to the Project panel. Set the output file's type to 'rsrc' instead of 'APPL', and its creator to RSED. Name this output file "SwitchBank.π.PPC.rsrc." Now make the project "SwitchBank.π.68K," which generates the file "SwitchBank.π.PPC.rsrc." This results in a resource file composed of graphical resources (obtained from "SwitchBank.π.68K.rsrc"), and 68K CODE resources, as made by CodeWarrior. We've actually made a 68K application here, but it masquerades as resource file because of the file type we chose. This completes the first stage.

The second stage uses the results of the first stage, plus the output from compiling the same source code with the CodeWarrior PowerPC compiler. Start by creating a project in the PowerPC version of Metrowerks CodeWarrior, named "SwitchBank.π.PPC." Add the "SwitchBank.c" file, "MWCRuntime.Lib," and "InterfaceLib" to the project file. Go to Preferences item in the Edit menu and select the Project panel. Set the project type to application and name the output file "SwitchBank." Set the output file's type to 'APPL' and its creator to 'SWCH'. Go to the SIZE flags pop-up menu and check the following flag bits: canBackground, is32BitCompatible, and isHighLevelEventAware. Now make the PowerPC project, producing a native code application. This completes the second stage, and the end result is a fat binary application file called "SwitchBank." The one file runs on both 68K Macs and Power Macs.

As you probably suspect, by naming the 68K output file "SwitchBank.π.PPC.rsrc" in the first stage, we fool the PowerPC version of CodeWarrior into automatically copying all of the resources—including the 68K CODE resources—from this resource file into the PowerPC application at the completion of the second stage. You can confirm this by examining the file in ResEdit and seeing both cfrg and CODE resources. Although you could copy these resources using either ResEdit or Rez, the technique just described does the job using the two compilation stages you have to do anyway to make the 68K and PowerPC binaries.

There's one other thing we can do to "SwitchBank" so that it conserves memory on a Power Mac. CODE resources have an attribute bit set called Preload that makes the Resource Manager load them into memory automatically, whether they're used or not. We can fix this waste of memory with ResEdit. Launch ResEdit, and open the SwitchBank application. Open the CODE resource, and select all CODE segments but CODE 0. (For "SwitchBank," there's only CODE segment 1.) Choose Get Resource Info from the Resource menu, or type Command-I. A Get Info box appears. Under the Attributes section, uncheck the Preload checkbox (see figure 6.9). Save the file and quit ResEdit.

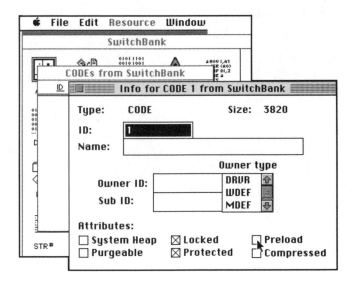

Figure 6.9   *Changing the Preload attribute on a CODE resource*

Important

The CodeWarrior application supports a number of high-level Apple Events, including the four core Apple Events. The *Metrowerks CodeWarrior User's Guide* describes the suite of Apple Events events that CodeWarrior provides. These events let you create projects, adjust some of the preference settings of both project and output files, add or remove files from a project, compile files, and specify an output file. This capability enables you to automate portions of the development cycle, which is valuable for large or complex projects. Here's a sample AppleScript that generates a fat binary:

```
(* 1st stage - Make 68K version of application *)
tell application "MW C/C++ 68K"
  activate
  open file "YourHardDisk:CodeWarrior:Code Examples ƒ:SwitchBank ƒ:SwitchBank.π.68K"
  (* Project file should already have  settings such as output file name and  its creator and type set*)
  Remove Binaries
  make project "SwitchBank.π.68K"
  close project "SwitchBank.π.68K"
  quit
end tell

(* 2nd stage - Make PPC version, using resources from 68K output file *)
tell application "MW C/C++ PPC"
  activate
  open file "YourHardDisk:CodeWarrior:Code Examples ƒ:SwitchBank ƒ:SwitchBank.π.PPC"
  (* Project file should already have  settings such as output file name and  its creator and type set*)
  Remove Binaries
  make project "SwitchBank.π.PPC"
  close project "SwitchBank.π.PPC"
  quit
end tell
```

This is just a basic script, with the pathnames to the compilers and projects hard-wired in. You'll have to edit these pathnames for this script to work on your system.

Handling a Code Fragment

Thus far we've seen how to supply the Mixed Mode Manager the information it needs to handle an instruction set switch when your custom function is called. Now it's time to go for an excursion into the Power Mac's basement, to get a glimpse of a code fragment close up. This brings us to the next utility, FlipDepth. Like SwitchBank, FlipDepth was a utility Extension that I wrote to make my life easier. My work and interests are often at odds on a Mac's screen. The reason is that I make my living writing, with an occasional bit of code writing thrown in. In these situations, I need the utmost in scrolling speed when I examine a lengthy chunk of text or code listing. The easiest fix, which costs you nothing, is to set the Mac's screen to black-and-white mode. This makes text scrolling very fast, because at this 1-bit pixel depth the Macintosh doesn't have as much data to pump to the screen at it does with color data. A color screen requires more bits per pixel, which means more data must be moved, and thus results in a slower scrolling process.

This wouldn't be an issue except that what I usually write about is heavy-duty graphics applications—the stuff that uses buckets of 24-bit pixels. So I was constantly clicking at the Monitors Control Panel, switching the Mac's screen depth from black-and-white to 24-bit color mode and back, depending upon what I was doing. If I could reduce the means of changing the screen depth to just a keystroke or two, it would make the job just a little easier. The real challenge is how to do this, of course.

Interlude: The Anatomy of a Trap

In chapter 5 we learned that the 68K Mac's Toolbox routines are accessed via a dispatch table. Because much of the Power Mac's Toolbox is still 68K code, this remains true, although portions of the underlying mechanism that accomplishes this has changed.

Background Info

The Power Mac's 68LC040 emulator is made up of two components: a dispatch table (not to be confused with the 68K Mac's dispatch table), and a PowerPC code block. This dispatch table has an array of 64K pairs of PowerPC instructions. The entries in the dispatch table correspond to 68K instructions. The main loop of the emulator fetches a 68K instruction word and uses it as a 16-bit unsigned index into the dispatch table. For simple 68K instructions, the first PowerPC instruction handles the operation and the second instruction jumps back to the emulator loop. For complex 68K instructions, the first PowerPC instruction starts the emulation process and the second instruction is a PC-relative branch into the code block. At this entry point are the PowerPC instructions that implement the 68K instruction. The emulator dispatch table also has entries for some of the A trap words, which point to native Toolbox routines. All 68K A traps get routed through the standard 68K Mac dispatch table, which exists on the Power Mac for compatibility. Execution either proceeds into the 68K emulator, or jumps to the emulator's dispatch table, and then to PowerPC code. By using the 68K dispatch table, existing Extensions and Control Panels that modify the trap tables still function.

The Mac Toolbox itself provides the means for us to reroute a Toolbox routine call to custom functions. Two routines, `NGetTrapAddress()` and `NSetTrapAddress()`, provide a high-level interface that lets us change a 68K dispatch table entry, no matter how the run-time architecture establishes the connection between the trap word and Toolbox routine's code. `NGetTrapAddress()` accepts a Toolbox trap word and Toolbox type (more on this later), and obtains from the trap dispatch table an address that's an entry point of the requested routine. `NSetTrapAddress()` accepts an address to your custom function, the Toolbox trap word and its type. It changes the dispatch table entry for this trap to point to your function. A bit of nomenclature here: these custom functions you write to modify a trap's behavior are called patch code because the term "patch" refers to fixing a hole in a wall by adding a little material, or fixing a software bug by adding a little code. Apple's system patches that fix bugs or add enhancements modify the dispatch table the same way to install additional code. If each patch does its job correctly, a Toolbox call can be reliably daisy-chained through several or more Extensions as well as the Toolbox routine itself.

Now when an application calls the modified Toolbox routine, your function gets called instead. Your function will handle the call one of two ways. The pseudo code for the first method looks like this:

```
My_Trap_Enhancement()
{
   Do_My_Stuff();
   Original_Trap_Routine();
} /* end */
```

This is called a *head patch*, because the function does its job first, then calls the Toolbox routine itself. Bear in mind that the pseudo code implies that the trap routine returns control to this function, when in reality it doesn't. Typically, **Do_My_Stuff()** performs its task, then jumps to **Original_Trap_Routine()**, never to return. You'll see an example of this shortly.

The second method uses this pseudo code:

```
My_Trap_Enhancement()
{
   result = Original_Trap_Routine();
   if (result == WHAT_WE_WANT)
        Do_My_Stuff();
} /* end */
```

This is called a *tail patch*, because we call the Toolbox routine first, then perhaps act on a result returned by the routine. For example, we might call **MenuSelect()**, and examine what it returns to act on a specific menu selection. Or, you might ignore what **Original_Trap_Routine()** does and instead perform a task based on the frequency that **Original_Trap_Routine()** gets called. We'll see an example of this shortly. Unlike the head patch, control does return to our function when the routine completes. On the 68K Mac, tail patches are considered evil because the return to your patch code can interfere with some of Apple's code patches that work by examining the return address on the stack. For the Power Mac, the issue of how the patch is applied to a trap is moot, because its architecture is fundamentally different.

There are just a few more details we need to be aware of before we write a line of code. The Macintosh OS divides its memory into two sections: a system partition (or system zone), and an application partition (or application zone). Naturally, the Mac OS uses the system partition for its own use. The system partition contains the operating system's global variables (known as *low-memory globals* because they occupy some of the lowest physical addresses in RAM), and the system heap. The system heap is where drivers, patch code, and other resources hang out. Resources loaded here are typically shared by all applications. The application partition is where the Process Manager loads and launches applications. This section of memory is in constant flux as applications load and unload.

Our patch code has an important requirement: it can't move in memory. If it moves, even by accident, the pointer in the dispatch table (or another Extension) winds up pointing at random data in memory. Thus a call to the patched Toolbox routine becomes a jump to nowhere, and the Mac crashes. We can lock our code in memory to prevent this, but we need to avoid creating an immoveable memory block that fragments the application partition. Thus, the system heap is an ideal place for our code.

Finally, there's the issue of accessing the global variables our patch code uses. At the very least, we need one global variable that stores the address we got from `NGetTrapAddress()`, so that we can call the original routine. For the 68K Mac run-time architecture, this is a tricky matter. As you recall from last chapter, register A5 points to an application's globals and jump table. When an application calls the patched Toolbox routine and our patch code executes, we have an immediate conflict of interest. Since our code is located somewhere else in memory, register A5 doesn't point to our globals. If we mess with A5 to correct this, there's the very real danger that we can mangle the application's A5 world. The application then loses track of its global variables and function references, which means certain death.

Important

Some more nomenclature: patch code belongs to a group of objects known as *stand-alone code*. Stand-alone code resources encapsulate pure machine code. These resources are loaded into memory and executed directly. This differs from an application, where the Process Manager first builds an A5 world for the application from its CODE 0 resource, then jumps to its `main()` in another

CODE resource. Because stand-alone code is executed without the benefit of any set up by the Process Manager, the value in A5 is meaningless. Also, stand-alone code has to be practically self-contained, because it can't rely on other resources being available, other than those in the operating system.

Typical resources that include stand-alone code are drivers (DRVRs), custom window handlers (WDEFs), custom menu handlers (MDEFs), Control Panel code (cdev), and Extension code (INIT). Remember that last type, because we'll be returning to it shortly.

Fortunately, there's an easy fix, that was first pioneered by Symantec's THINK C, and is used by Metrowerks CodeWarrior. When you create a stand-alone code resource with CodeWarrior, it assumes that such code might be running concurrently inside of an application. The code it generates has all the references to global variables and to functions made with respect to register A4, rather than A5. When our code is called, all we need to do is call some glue code provided in a header file that sets up A4 to point to our code (and thereby our globals) for us.

The Power Mac's new run-time architecture simplifies how you handle globals. Since each code fragment has a separate data space, and a TOC that points to objects within it, ready access to global data is built in. To locate a certain global, we first find the code fragment we want by asking for it by name, and then asking for the global itself by name. You'll appreciate this more when we look at the actual code in a moment.

There is one problem to avoid when you patch a trap on a Power Mac. You want to avoid creating a performance hit when you patch a trap. Let's see why. Certain Toolbox routines in the Macintosh OS get called often by other Toolbox routines. (For example, `NewWindow()` calls QuickDraw routines to create a window on the screen.) Because the Power Mac's Toolbox is an amalgam of 68K and PowerPC code, these routines might get called by a 68K Toolbox routine one time, and then by a PowerPC Toolbox routine the next. A problem arises if this heavily-called routine was only written in PowerPC code. The overhead of the Mixed Mode Manager performing the instruction set context switch for 68K routines calling this particular routine becomes considerable for small Toolbox routines, enough to seriously degrade performance. Apple's solution was to implement these critical routines as "fat traps." That is, the routine is written in both 68K and PowerPC code. Regardless of what routine calls the fat trap, no context switch is required, and so the performance hit is minimized. The point here is that on the Power Mac, for certain routines we have to write a fat trap. This is very convenient, because it allows us to compare how to do a patch for both system architectures. However, be aware that not all traps have to be fat. For example, a heavily called routine that does a lot of processing would probably be better off patched only with PowerPC code, where the performance boost of native execution readily compensates for the over-head of the Mixed Mode Manager switch. A rough rule of thumb is that the overhead of the Mixed Mode Manager context switch takes approximately fifty 68K instruction equivalents or five hundred PowerPC instruction equivalents. If your patch function is roughly larger than fifty 68K instruc-tions, then it's a candidate for being written as native code.

Writing a Fat Trap

With all of this information in hand, let's go write FlipDepth. Start a new project in the PowerPC version of CodeWarrior. Use the editor to start a new file. Type in the following:

```
#ifndef __TYPES__
    #include <Types.h>
#endif

#ifndef __MEMORY__
    #include <Memory.h>
#endif

#ifndef __GESTALTEQU__
    #include <gestaltequ.h>
#endif

#ifndef __FILES__
    #include <Files.h>
#endif
```

```
#ifndef __QUICKDRAW__
   #include <QuickDraw.h>
#endif

#ifndef __RESOURCES__
   #include <Resources.h>
#endif

#ifndef __ERRORS__
   #include <Errors.h>
#endif

#ifndef __FRAGLOAD__
   #include <FragLoad.h>
#endif

#ifndef __TEXTUTILS__
   #include <TextUtils.h>
#endif

#ifndef __RESOURCES__
   #include <Resources.h>
#endif

#ifndef __MEMORY__
   #include <Memory.h>
#endif

#ifdef __MWERKS__
   #ifndef powerc
      #include <A4Stuff.h>
   #endif
#endif
```

Save this in the file "INIT.h." These are the basic header files we need to make an Extension (INIT) stand-alone code resource. "INIT.h" serves as a template for all Extension code that we write. Now type:

```
/*
   Portions © 1994 Rock Ridge Enterprises. All Rights Reserved.
*/

/*
```

```
      This tells MixedMode.h that we want _real_ versions of
      the various RoutineDescriptor functions and not dummy
      stubs.
*/
#define USESROUTINEDESCRIPTORS 1

/*
   This #define is for testing only. Without it, only the
   68K version of our patch is called.
*/
#undef DO_PPC_CODE_ONLY

#include "Init.h"

#ifndef powerc
   #include <SetUpA4.h>
#endif

/* Headers required by our custom functions */
#include <SysEqu.h>
#include <Events.h>
#include <Windows.h>
#include <Palettes.h>

/*
   Some low memory globals. We'd rather not use these, but they're
   necessary because we'll be operating in a trap that doesn't move memory.
*/
#define lowMemKeyStroke    (*(KeyMap *) KeyMapLM)[0]
#define lowMemKeyModifiers (*(KeyMap *) KeyMapLM)[1]

/* Some constants that define the bits we'll see in KeyMap */
#define SHIFT_KEY          1L
#define CAPS_LOCK          2L
#define OPTION_KEY         4L
#define CONTROL_KEY        8L
#define COMMAND_KEY        0x8000L

#define KEY_COMBO          SHIFT_KEY + COMMAND_KEY
#define T_KEYCODE          0x0200L
#define BLACK_WHITE        128   /* First video mode ID in sResource list */
```

```
#define FALSE            false
#define TRUE             true
#define NIL              0L

#define kOldSystemErr        10000
#define kMinSystemVersion    (0x0605)
```

Here's our usual complement of header files, plus definitions for the address of a low memory global and some constants. The header files you see here define information required by our job-specific code that controls the screen depth. One important thing to note is that we set USESROUTINEDESCRIPTORS to 1 (true) immediately before we include any header files. (Actually, we need this to happen before the "MixedMode.h" header file is used.) If we don't, the routine NewFatRoutineDescriptor() is undefined for 68K generated code. We need this routine to build fat traps, so we have to set USESROUTINEDESCRIPTORS to signal any 68K compiler that we're serious about supporting two instruction sets. Also notice that for a 68K compilation (#ifndef powerc), the "SetUpA4.h" header file is used. Because we're using out of the ordinary settings here, you may want to avoid use of the precompiled header files (MacHeaders68K or MacHeadersPPC) until you precompile MacHeaders68K.c or MacHeadersPPC.c with the appropriate options set. Onward, we type:

```
/*============================*/
#define kPPCRezType      'PPC '
#define kPPCRezID        300


/*==========================
   The 68k code goes in a normal INIT resource.
   Be sure this is set to "system heap/locked".
==========================*/
#define kInitRezType     'INIT'
#define kInitRezID       300


/*==========================
   This is the name of the ppc fragment - for debugging only.
==========================*/
#define kInitName        "\pEricsInit"


/*==========================
   to save some screen space, we'll use "UPP" instead of "UniversalProcPtr"
==========================*/
typedef UniversalProcPtr    UPP;
```

Here are some more definitions, but now we're describing the characteristics of our generated code. Notice that we're declaring a resource type and ID number for a PowerPC code fragment here. What gives, when code fragments don't live in a file's resource fork? There are ways to access a code fragment in from a file's data fork, but occasionally it's easier to load it from a resource. Therefore, we must make the PowerPC code resemble a stand-alone code resource, so that the Mac OS treats it like one. This means that we must copy the PowerPC code fragment from a file's data fork into the resource fork, and then assign it a resource type and ID number. The resource type doesn't have to be 'INIT', because we'll use a 68K INIT resource to actually install the PowerPC resource. Instead, we'll make the resource type 'PPC' so we can recognize it as PowerPC code. Now it's time to define our function prototypes:

```
/*===========================
   PostEvent Information
=========================== */
enum
{
   kPostEventInfo = kRegisterBased
      | RESULT_SIZE(SIZE_CODE(sizeof(OSErr)))
      | REGISTER_RESULT_LOCATION(kRegisterD0)
      | REGISTER_ROUTINE_PARAMETER(1, kRegisterA0, SIZE_CODE(sizeof(short)))
      | REGISTER_ROUTINE_PARAMETER(2, kRegisterD0, SIZE_CODE(sizeof(long)))
};


typedef pascal OSErr ( *PostEventFuncPtr ) ( short eventNum, long eventMsg );
#define kPostEventFuncName "\pMyPostEventPPC"

/* Note separate functions */
short MyPostEvent68k( short eventNum, long eventMsg );
OSErr MyPostEventPPC( short eventNum, long eventMsg );


/*===========================
   GetMouse Information
=========================== */
enum
{
   kGetMouseInfo = kPascalStackBased
            | STACK_ROUTINE_PARAMETER(1, SIZE_CODE(sizeof(Point)))
};
```

```
typedef pascal void ( *GetMouseFuncPtr ) ( Point *mouseLoc );
#define kGetMouseFuncName "\pMyGetMouse"
void MyGetMouse ( Point *mouseLoc );   /* Only one function required */

/* Functions that change screen depth. Works one both platforms. */
void Change_Depth(long newDepth);
long Fetch_Depth(void);
```

Let's backtrack here a moment to explain why we're patching these two routines, `PostEvent()` and `GetMouse()`. I wanted to patch a trap that handled events, so that I could monitor the event stream for keystrokes. This way I could watch for the magic key combination that tells me the user wants to change the screen depth. `PostEvent()` is a Toolbox routine used by the Event Manager to place events in the event queue. It has two advantages: First, since it's actually responsible for creating the event stream, it's the perfect routine to monitor for keyboard events. Second, `PostEvent()` gets called frequently, so we can respond quickly to the user.

However, `PostEvent()` does have a down side. It's what's known as an Operating System routine (or trap). Operating System routines typically perform low-level functions such as file I/O, network I/O, and memory management. In the Mac's early days, such routines were *register-based*. That is, the calling function passes information to the Operating System routine by placing the values in certain processor registers. This "calling" arrangement means that we're going to have to write assembly language to examine any values passed into or returned from this type of routine. The other problem is that `PostEvent()` doesn't move memory. Put another way, the routine's memory demands are fixed, so it's not going to force the Memory Manager to purge memory, or relocate data items whenever it's called. Lots of Toolbox routines and applications count on `PostEvent()` and certain other low-level OS routines being well-behaved about memory this way. Whatever our patch does, it has to be very simple lest we unexpectedly jar the location of objects in memory and cause a system crash. The safest thing to do is have the patched `PostEvent()` routine detect the right combination of key presses, and set a global flag. We'll use this flag to signal another patched routine to actually change the screen depth.

The function that handles the depth change should be a Toolbox routine that doesn't have such strict memory requirements. That's because every application will be redrawing its chunk of the screen after the depth change, and this sort of thing definitely effects memory usage. Also, like `PostEvent()`, this routine should be called frequently for a fast response time. The routine `GetMouse()` fits these requirements.

`GetMouse()` is a *stack-based* Toolbox trap. That is, arguments are passed to this type of routine by pushing them on the stack. The result is typically returned on the stack, but there are exceptions. Ironically, `GetMouse()` is one of these exceptions, because it returns a result via a pointer you passed to the routine.

Important

Until now, I've used the term Toolbox loosely to mean any and all routines that implement services defined by the Mac API. For the moment, we'll have to make the distinction between Toolbox and OS traps. This is important because the 68K Trap Dispatcher maintains two different dispatch tables: one for Toolbox traps and one for OS traps.

Keep in mind the discussion of these routine's memory behavior is based on the Mac's 68K architecture. However, since much of the Toolbox is emulated 68K code, we can assume similar behavior on a Power Mac for the moment. This will change over time as more of the Toolbox is rewritten as native code. Also, if we want the Extension to operate on the installed base of 68K-based Macs, we need to follow the guidelines described above.

Background Info

Historically, the OS traps were designed to be register-based because it was expected that these low-level routines would only be accessed by system programmers writing in assembly language. Toolbox traps, on the other hand, were made stack-based to make them easy to access. This was because application programmers would use these high-level routines in their applications.

Nowadays, the distinction between the two trap types has blurred, since most compilers provide high-level access to OS traps using glue code. The definitions blur even further with the Power Macs, because all the routines pass their arguments through the PowerPC processor's registers.

Back to our code. Here's where the routine descriptors are built that describe the makeup of the traps we patch to the Mixed Mode Manager. Remember that our patch code will ultimately call the original trap, so we have to hand a routine descriptor to the Mixed Mode Manager so it can field an instruction set switch when one is required. We declare (no surprise) `PostEvent()` as a register-based routine and `GetMouse()` as a stack-based routine. We also define function prototypes for the routines and our patch code here. Observe that our `PostEvent()` patch code has both a PowerPC function and a 68K function. That's because for the 68K version, we have to do some processing in assembly language to retrieve `PostEvent()`'s arguments from the 68K processor registers. As you'll see, such gymnastics are unnecessary for the PowerPC version of the patch, thus, the two different versions of the same patch. We also declare our screen control functions, `Get_Depth()` and `Change_Depth()`, here. We don't need to set up routine descriptors for these functions because they are called locally inside the patch code. Finally, we declare two function name strings, `kPostEventFuncName` and `kGetMouseFuncName`. The Code Fragment Manager uses these strings to locate our patch functions.

```
/*============================
    This structure is shared between the PowerPC
    version of the code and the 68K version.

    Both the PowerPC code and the 68k code have a single
    global variable, "gGlobalsPtr". They point to the
    same area of memory.
============================*/

#ifdef powerc
    #pragma options align=mac68k
#endif

/*
    Note: do not move these fields around!
    The assembly code in PostEvent68kStub()
    depends on their locations. It must be
    compiled with the 68K packing conventions
*/
```

```
typedef struct
{
UPP            gOrigPostEvent;    /* Address of original PostEvent trap */
UPP            gOrigGetMouse;     /* Address of original GetMouse trap */
SysEnvRec      gSystemInfo;       /* Holds info on system config */
Boolean        gRequestFlag;      /* Flag that signals screen depth change */
GDHandle       gOurGDevice;       /* The GDevice of the screen */
short          gDevRefNum;        /* Driver number for video board's slot */
long           gOldScreenDepth;   /* Mode number for color screen setting */
} MyInitGlobals;

#ifdef powerc
   #pragma options align=reset
#endif


/*===========================
   Global Variables

   -- Each side of the code maintains its own pointer to the
      same block of memory.

   -- We reference the globals ptr by name, so these two must be
      changed together.
===========================*/
MyInitGlobals             *gGlobalsPtr;
#define kGlobalsSymName       "\pgGlobalsPtr"
```

Here's our globals block, called **MyInitGlobals**. Note that we use the **#pragma options align=mac68k** to force word-alignment on the data structures so **MyInitGlobals** can be used on a 68K processor (or the 68LC040 emulator). The globals hold the original trap routine addresses (as UPPs, of course) and other sundry variables such as the reference number to the device driver that controls the Mac's screen (**gDevRefNum**), and the logical device that manages it (**gOurGDevice**). Like our patch code, we also define a name string for the pointer to our globals. We'll pass this name to the Code Fragment Manager when we want to locate the globals block.

```
/*===========================
   An original trap is called differently from PowerPC
   code than from 68K code because CallOSTrapUniversalProc() isn't
   implemented for 68K code.
===========================*/
```

```
#ifdef powerc
   #define CallPostEvent(eventNum, eventMsg)\
   CallOSTrapUniversalProc( gGlobalsPtr->gOrigPostEvent, kPostEventInfo,\
    eventNum, eventMsg )
   #define CallGetMouse(mouseLoc)\
   CallUniversalProc( gGlobalsPtr->gOrigGetMouse, kGetMouseInfo, mouseLoc )
#else
   #define CallGetMouse(mouseLoc)\
   (*(GetMouseFuncPtr)gGlobalsPtr->gOrigGetMouse)( mouseLoc );
#endif

/* Custom function to place our patch code in the system heap */
Handle Get1ResourceSys( OSType rezType, short rezID );
```

These macros in the code above define a common way to call the original routines, whether from 68K code or PowerPC code. On the PowerPC side of the fence, we make the routine calls using either `CallOSTrapUniversalProc()` for an OS trap, or `CallUniversalProc()` for a Toolbox trap. The only difference between the two routines is that `CallOSTrapUniversalProc()` preserves some additional 68K registers for register-based traps. For the 68K side, we just pass a pointer to a function. Both techniques rely on addresses stored in the globals block. For the 68K code, we don't declare a macro for `PostEvent()`. That's because we'll use a separate function to extract the values out of this register-based routine.

Since we'll place our patch code in the system heap, we declare a custom function `Get1ResourceSys()` for this purpose.

```
   @@@@@@@@@@@@@@   68000 Exclusive Code   @@@@@@@@@@@@@@
*/
#ifndef powerc

/*============================
   Prototypes for 68k code
============================*/
OSErr       DoInitForOldMacs( void );
OSErr       DoInitForPPCMacs( void );
OSErr       CreateFatDescriptorSys( void *mac68Code, void *ppcCode,
                                    ProcInfoType procInfo, UPP *result );
OSErr       PatchTrapsForPPCMac( ConnectionID connID );

void        PostEvent68kStub( void );
pascal void GetMouse68kStub ( Point *mouseLoc );
```

We now define some processor-specific functions here. We'll use a 68K INIT resource to set up and install our patch code, no matter what processor is in the Mac.

```
/*===========================
   This is *always* the INIT's entry point. This is
   the only routine called by system software at startup.

   This requires that the INIT resource be set to
   System Heap/Locked.
===========================*/
void main( void )
{
long     oldA4;
Handle   initH = nil;        /* Handle to our own INIT resource */
OSErr    err = noErr;
long     ginfo;

   /*******************************
      Global variable support
      Place proper value for A4 into hole in INIT resource.
   *******************************/
   oldA4 = SetCurrentA4();       /* Get the proper value of A4 into A4 */
   RememberA4();                 /* save into self-modifying code */


   /*******************************
      Allocate our global variables
   *******************************/
   gGlobalsPtr = (MyInitGlobals*) NewPtrSysClear( sizeof(MyInitGlobals) );
   if ( !gGlobalsPtr )
      {
      err = memFullErr;
      goto DONE;
      }


   /*******************************
      Get some basic system information
   *******************************/
              ||
   err = SysEnvirons( 1, &gGlobalsPtr->gSystemInfo );
   if ( err )
      goto DONE;
```

```
/********************************
   Check the system version
********************************/
if ( gGlobalsPtr->gSystemInfo.systemVersion < kMinSystemVersion )
   {
   err = kOldSystemErr;
   goto DONE;
   }
```

Here's the start of the code that gets loaded and executed at boot time by the Macintosh OS. We first call the Metrowerks functions SetCurrentA4() and RememberA4(), which preserves register A4, then adjusts it to point at our code and thus our globals. Next, we allocate a block of zeroed memory in the system heap, using NewPtrSysClear(). If we succeed at obtaining the memory, we then call SysEnvirons() to determine what operating system we're running under. If it's less than System 6.0.5, we bail out, as we need the Gestalt Manager to tell us whether we're running on a Power Macintosh or not.

```
/********************************
   Get a handle to our own INIT resource
********************************/
initH = Get1Resource( kInitRezType, kInitRezID );
if ( !initH )
   {
   err = resNotFound;
   goto DONE;
   }


/********************************
   See if we're running on a PowerPC
********************************/
err = Gestalt( gestaltSysArchitecture, &ginfo );


/********************************
   Patch all the traps and get everything ready.
********************************/
if ( err || (ginfo == gestalt68k) )
   err = DoInitForOldMacs();
else
   err = DoInitForPPCMacs();
```

```
DONE:
if ( err )
   {
   /* Display "bad load" icon here */

   if ( gGlobalsPtr )
      DisposPtr( (Ptr)gGlobalsPtr );
   }
else
   {
   /* Display "good load" icon here */

   gGlobalsPtr->gOldScreenDepth = Fetch_Depth();

/* Make sure the init stays in memory when the INIT file closes */
   DetachResource( initH );
   } /* end else */

RestoreA4( oldA4 );              /* Restore previous value of A4 */
} /* end main() */
```

Now we fetch our INIT resource. It contains the code you see here, functions that patch the dispatch table, and our patch code. We load the resource into memory using `Get1Resource()`. Next, we use the Gestalt Manager to determine if we're running on a Power Mac. If not, we call the function `DoInitForOldMacs()` to perform the 68K patches. Otherwise, we call `DoInitForPPCMacs()` to do the PowerPC patches. If the patching operation fails, we clean up by releasing the memory allocated for our globals. If the patching process succeeds, we obtain the system's current screen depth for use by our screen control functions later. To ensure that the Resource Manager doesn't purge our INIT code from memory, we call `DetachResource()`. This routine severs the logical link between this resource and the Resource Manager, so that the resource remains in memory when the Resource Manager closes the file. Finally, we restore register A4 and exit.

Background Info

Extensions typically display an icon at the bottom of the Mac's screen as they load. The type of icon displayed indicates whether the Extension was able to install its patches or not. You can see stubs in the previous setup code where you would plug in such display functions.

```
/*==========================
    DoInitForOldMacs

    Initialization code for non-PowerPC Macs.
============================*/
OSErr DoInitForOldMacs( void )
{
    /* patch the trap */
    gGlobalsPtr->gOrigPostEvent = NGetTrapAddress( _PostEvent, OSTrap );
    NSetTrapAddress( (UPP)PostEvent68kStub, _PostEvent, OSTrap );
    gGlobalsPtr->gOrigGetMouse = NGetTrapAddress( _GetMouse, ToolTrap );
    NSetTrapAddress( (UPP)GetMouse68kStub, _GetMouse, ToolTrap );

    return noErr;
} /* end DoInitForOldMacs() */
```

Here's the mechanism where we modify the 68K Mac's dispatch table to point to our patch code. We first obtain the original address from the dispatch table using **NGetTrapAddress()**, and save it in our globals block. Next, we use **NSetTrapAddress()** to replace the address with a UPP (actually, a 68K procedure pointer) to our patch code. Notice that we specify the type of trap we're patching here (**OSTrap** or **ToolTrap**), so that the correct dispatch table gets modified. Now let's see how it's done for a Power Mac:

```
/*==========================
    DoInitForPPCMacs

    Initialization code for powerpc Macs.
============================*/
OSErr DoInitForPPCMacs( void )
{
OSErr        err = noErr;
Handle       ppcCodeH = nil;
SymClass     theSymClass;
```

```
Ptr            theSymAddr;
ConnectionID   connID = kNoConnectionID;
Str255         errName;
Ptr            mainAddr;

    /********************************
       Load the powerpc version of the code into
       memory. Since some of our trap patches may be
       called at interrupt time, don't use disk-based
       versions of the code.
    ********************************/
    ppcCodeH = Get1ResourceSys( kPPCRezType, kPPCRezID );
    if ( !ppcCodeH )
       return resNotFound;
    HLock( ppcCodeH );


    /********************************
       Open a connection with the code fragment we just loaded
    ********************************/
    err = GetMemFragment( *ppcCodeH, GetHandleSize(ppcCodeH), kInitName,
                          kLoadNewCopy, &connID, &mainAddr, errName );
    if ( err )
       {
       connID = kNoConnectionID;
       goto DONE;
       }
```

Since the container for our Code Fragment is a resource, we must first load it into memory with the Resource Manager. We do this using our custom function `Get1ResourceSys()`, which loads the fragment into the system heap and returns a handle, **ppcCodeH**, to it. `Get1ResourceSys()`, described later, adjusts memory accesses to the system partition and then calls the Resource Manager to load the resource into that partition. We lock this code in place using `HLock()`. Since our `PostEvent()` patch code might get called during an interrupt, it requires that the patch remain in memory at all times, which is why we load the fragment into the system heap and lock it in place. Now we pass the code fragment's handle to `GetMemFragment()`, which prepares the fragment for execution. We use `GetMemFragment()` over other Code Fragment Manager routines because it operates on fragments in memory. The constant **kLoadNewCopy** has `GetMemFragment()` make a new copy of any of the fragment's writable data (like our globals), and **connID** returns an ID value that specifies a connection to this fragment. We could also use the constant **kLoadLib**. The connection ID is analogous to the file reference number that the File Manager routines use for file I/O. You supply this connection ID to other Code Fragment routines to obtain information on fragments, or the addresses of functions or global data within fragments. Now it's time to find those globals:

```
/********************************
    find the global variable ptr that the powerpc
    code uses.
********************************/
err = FindSymbol( connID, kGlobalsSymName, &theSymAddr, &theSymClass );
if ( err )
    goto DONE;

/********************************
    Modify the powerpc global variable pointer to point
    to the area of memory we've already allocated.
********************************/
*(MyInitGlobals **)theSymAddr = gGlobalsPtr;
err = PatchTrapsForPPCMac( connID );

/********************************
    Cleanup
********************************/
DONE:
if ( err )
    {
        /* Close the code frag mgr connection if we got an error... */
    if ( connID != kNoConnectionID )
        CloseConnection( &connID );

        /* ...and release the memory we allocated */
    if ( ppcCodeH )
        ReleaseResource( ppcCodeH );
    } /* end if */
else
    {
        /* No error -> keep the ppc code around when file closes */
    DetachResource( ppcCodeH );
    } /* end else */

return err;
} /* end DoInitForPPCMacs() */
```

We use the Code Fragment Manager routine `FindSymbol()` to locate the PowerPC version our globals pointer, `gGlobalsPtr`. We pass it the connection ID obtained with `GetMemFragment()`, and the export name of our globals pointer in the string `kGlobalsSymName`. `FindSymbol()` returns the address of the pointer in **theSymAddr**. We then direct this pointer toward our globals block. Now that we can locate our globals, we call `PatchTrapsForPPCMac()` to patch the dispatch table. If all goes well, we call `DetachResource()` on the PowerPC resource to make the Resource Manager "forget" about the fragment and leave it in memory. If there is an error, we close the connection to the code fragment using `CloseConnection()`, and follow that with a call to `ReleaseResource()` to dispose of the code fragment.

Let's see how we patch traps on the PowerPC run-time architecture:

```
/*============================
   PatchTrapsForPPCMac
============================*/
OSErr PatchTrapsForPPCMac( ConnectionID connID )
{
   Ptr                symAddr;
   SymClass           symType;
   OSErr              err = noErr;
   UniversalProcPtr   upp = nil;

   /*
      Fat Patch _PostEvent
   */
   err = FindSymbol( connID, kPostEventFuncName, &symAddr, &symType );
   if ( err )
      return err;

   err = CreateFatDescriptorSys( PostEvent68kStub, symAddr,
                                 kPostEventInfo, &upp );
   if ( err )
      return memFullErr;

   gGlobalsPtr->gOrigPostEvent = NGetTrapAddress( _PostEvent, OSTrap );
   NSetTrapAddress( upp, _PostEvent, OSTrap );
```

```
/*
   Fat Patch _GetMouse
*/
err = FindSymbol( connID, kGetMouseFuncName, &symAddr, &symType );
if ( err )
   return err;

err = CreateFatDescriptorSys( GetMouse68kStub, symAddr,
                              kGetMouseInfo, &upp );
if ( err )
   return memFullErr;

gGlobalsPtr->gOrigGetMouse = NGetTrapAddress( _GetMouse, ToolTrap );
NSetTrapAddress( upp, _GetMouse, ToolTrap );

return noErr;
} /* end PatchTrapsForPPCMac() */
```

FindSymbol() greatly simplifies matters here. We provide this routine with the name of our patch code functions, and it returns the entry points to them in the code fragment. Since the course of execution could be hopping from one instruction set to another, we next build a routine descriptor for these functions. CreateFatDescriptorSys() is a custom function that places the descriptor information in the system heap. We'll examine its code shortly. We call this function with the address of our 68K patch code, the address of our PowerPC patch code, and the routine descriptor information provided at the start of the file. CreateFatDescriptorSys() returns a UPP that points to both the 68K patches and PowerPC patches. At this point, patching the Power Mac's dispatch table is nearly identical to how it's managed with the 68K dispatch table. The original trap address is copied from the dispatch table using NGetTrapAddress(), and it's replaced with the UPP to our patch code by calling NSetTrapAddress(). We could make this section of code more robust by performing the memory allocations (via CreateFatDescriptorSys()) and symbol locations in main(). This way, if there's a problem applying either of the patches, we have a chance to back out gracefully.

```
/*===========================
    CreateFatDescriptorSys

    Creates a fat routine descriptor in the system heap.
===========================*/
OSErr CreateFatDescriptorSys( void *mac68Code, void *ppcCode, ProcInfoType procInfo, UPP
*result )
{
THz    oldZone;
OSErr err = noErr;

    oldZone = GetZone();        /* Save current zone */
    SetZone( SystemZone() );    /* Get us in the system heap */

    #ifndef DO_PPC_CODE_ONLY
    *result = NewFatRoutineDescriptor( mac68Code, ppcCode, procInfo );
    #else
    *result = NewRoutineDescriptor( ppcCode, procInfo, kPowerPCISA ); /* debugging only
*/
    #endif

    SetZone( oldZone );

    return ( *result ? noErr : memFullErr );
} /* end CreateFatDescriptorSys() */
```

Here's that custom function that generates routine descriptors in the
system heap. We begin by saving the current zone (or memory partition).
This is done by first calling GetZone() to obtain a pointer to this zone, and
saving it in oldZone. Then we change the zone that we'll operate in to the
system zone. To do this, we call SystemZone() to get a pointer to this zone,
and make it the active zone by passing the pointer to SetZone(). Now when
we generate a new data structure, such as our fat descriptor, the memory
gets drawn from the system heap. Then we call
NewFatRoutineDescriptor(), which makes the UPP containing a fat descriptor. Once that's done, we restore the current zone by passing oldZone to
SetZone(), and exit.

```
/*===========================
    PostEvent68kStub
===========================*/
```

```
asm void PostEvent68kStub( void )
{
     // Reserve space on stack for "real" PostEvent address
  sub.l       #4, SP

     // Save registers (not A0 & D0, though)
  movem.l     A1-A5/D1-D7, -(SP)

     // Push A0 & D0 on stack for call to MyPostEvent68k below
     // We must do this before SetUpA4 since it modifies registers
  move.l      D0, -(SP)        // push event message
  move.w      A0, -(SP)        // push event code

  jsr         SetUpA4          // give us global access

     // Put address of "real" postevent in place reserved on stack
     // Note that it is the first field in the gGlobals structure
  move.l      gGlobalsPtr, A0
  move.l      (A0), 54(SP)

     // Call MyPostEvent68k
     // Parameters are on the stack already
     // D0.w returns with the new event code
  jsr         MyPostEvent68k

  move.w      D0, A0           // A0.w = event code
  add.l       #2, SP           // Clear old event code from stack
  move.l      (SP)+, D0        // Restore event message from stack

     // restore registers
  movem.l     (SP)+, A1-A5/D1-D7

     // Jump directly to original PostEvent code
     // The address was placed on the stack in the above code
  rts
} /* end PostEvent68kStub() */

pascal void GetMouse68kStub( Point *mouseLoc )
{
long     oldA4;
```

```
    oldA4 = SetUpA4();
    MyGetMouse ( mouseLoc );
    RestoreA4( oldA4 );
} /* end GetMouse68kStub() */

#endif      /* 68K code */
```

These are the 68K code stubs for our patch code. These stubs minimally fix up register A4 to point to our globals before calling our patch code, and restore A4 when they exit. As you'll see in a moment, for OS traps the stub has a lot more work to do. `PostEvent68kStub()` is the entry point for the 68K `PostEvent()` patch code and is a head patch. We use CodeWarrior's built-in assembler to write 68K machine code that fetches the contents of register A0, which contains the event code (or type), and the contents of register D0, which holds the event's message. It's a nasty business, since we have to keep careful track of where things are on the stack. There are two things to be aware of with the CodeWarrior's built-in assembler. First, you can't place assembly language instructions directly in-line with C code, as you can with Symantec's THINK compiler. The assembly language code must be wrapped inside a function. This function is declared `asm`, as you can see in the code. Second, to comment assembly-language statements you use C++ style comments, where each comment is lead with a double-slash (//).

When `PostEvent68kStub()` gets called, we first save room on the stack where we'll stow the address of the original `PostEvent()` trap. Then we save most of the processor registers. Next, we retrieve `PostEvent()`'s arguments out of register A0 and D0 and push them onto the stack, for use in our patch function `MyPostEvent68K()`. Now we call `SetUpA4()` to fix up register A4 so we can get at our globals. This lets us obtain the pointer to our globals block, `gGlobalsPtr`. Once that's done, we fetch the address of the original `PostEvent()` from `gOrigPostEvent` and drop it on the stack. Since `gOrigPostEvent` starts the globals block, we don't need an offset from the pointer to access it. We stuff this address into the location on the stack where we allocated room for it. Because of all of the items we've pushed onto the stack so far, this location is 54 bytes from the current stack top.

With all the preliminary setup done, we at last call `MyPostEvent68k()`, the patch code which processes the event. When it returns, we place the event code it returns back into A0. We then toss the original event code into the bit bucket (since **MyPostEvent68k()** might have changed it), move the original event message back into D0, and restore the registers. At the end of all this work, the address of the original **PostEvent()** has moved to the top of the stack, and so that routine gets called when our function exits.

Since **GetMouse()** is a stack-based routine, we only have to set up access to our globals using **SetUpA4**() before calling the real patch code in **MyGetMouse()**. We restore A4 as the function exits.

```
/*

   @@@@@@@@@@@@@@@ Shared Code   @@@@@@@@@@@@@@@@

   This code gets compiled into both 68k and powerpc object code.
   The 68k code gets called from 68k patches & code.
   The powerpc code gets called from powerpc patches & code.

   If these routines were very large, or called infrequently, we could
   just have a single version that is called by the "other" object code,
   but it's not worth the hassle & context switch.
*/
Handle Get1ResourceSys( OSType rezType, short rezID )
{
   THz         oldZone;
   Handle      h;

   oldZone = GetZone();
   SetZone( SystemZone() );
   h = Get1Resource( rezType, rezID );
   SetZone( oldZone );
   return h;
}


/* Our custom GetMouse function. We do our screen stuff here because
   _GetMouse is allowed to move memory, and is called frequently.
*/

void MyGetMouse( Point *pt )
{
long   currentDepth;
```

```
  if ( gGlobalsPtr->gRequestFlag )            /* Event is for us ? */
    {
    gGlobalsPtr->gRequestFlag = FALSE;      /* Clear flag */
    currentDepth = Fetch_Depth();
    if ((currentDepth == BLACK_WHITE) &&
        (currentDepth != gGlobalsPtr->gOldScreenDepth))
        Change_Depth(gGlobalsPtr->gOldScreenDepth);
    else
        Change_Depth(BLACK_WHITE);
    } /* end if */

  CallGetMouse( pt );                        /* Hop to original GetMouse() */

} /* end ourGetMouse() */
```

Most of the functions here, with the exception of the PostEvent() patch code, get compiled for both processors. The resulting machine code goes into separate resources ('INIT' for 68K code and 'PPC' for PowerPC code) to build the fat trap, with a fat descriptor pointing to the function entry points in each resource.

The function Get1ResourceSys() loads the specified resource into the system heap.

MyGetMouse() is the patch code for the GetMouse() routine. When it's called, it checks to see if gRequestFlag has been set. If so, it knows that the user requests a screen depth change. The function first clears this flag so that it won't respond again the next time the routine gets called. MyGetMouse() next has Fetch_Depth() determine the current screen depth. This is checked against the constant BLACK_WHITE and the screen depth saved when the Extension loaded. If the screen depth isn't black-and-white, then it calls Change_Depth() to set the screen that way. If the screen is black-and-white, Change_Depth() gets called to switch the screen depth back to the original mode. The reason for the complicated if statement is to head off potential trouble if you start the Mac with the screen in black-and-white mode. In this case, FlipDepth has no idea what other screen depths the display supports, so the code locks the screen into this mode. If we didn't, Change_Depth() would be called with a garbage value, which might result in an interesting, if unusable, display. Once we've changed the screen depth, we call the original GetMouse() to finish the call.

```
short MyPostEvent68k( short eventNum, long eventMsg )
{
short newEventCode = eventNum;

    if ( (eventNum == keyDown) || (eventNum == autoKey) )
        {
        if ( (lowMemKeyModifiers == KEY_COMBO) &&
           (lowMemKeyStroke == T_KEYCODE) )
            {
            newEventCode = nullEvent;          /* Suppress the event */
            gGlobalsPtr->gRequestFlag = TRUE;
            } /* end if KEY_COMBO && T_KEYCODE */
        } /* end if */

    return newEventCode;
} /* end MyPostEvent68k() */


#ifdef powerc
OSErr MyPostEventPPC( short eventNum, long eventMsg )
{
OSErr result;

    if ( (eventNum == keyDown) || (eventNum == autoKey) )
        {
        if ( (lowMemKeyModifiers == KEY_COMBO) &&
           (lowMemKeyStroke == T_KEYCODE) )
            {
            eventNum = nullEvent;              /* Suppress the event */
            gGlobalsPtr->gRequestFlag = TRUE;
            } /* end if KEY_COMBO && T_KEYCODE */
        } /* end if */

    result = CallPostEvent(eventNum, eventMsg);
    return result;
} /* end MyPostEventPPC() */


#endif
```

These functions are the 68K and PowerPC versions of the PostEvent()
patch. Basically, they watch the event code (or its type) passed to the
routine. Since we're looking for a special key-combination, the code ignores
all events but key down and auto key events. If a keyboard event occurs,

we examine a low memory global, **KeyMapLM,** to determine what keys were pressed. We'd rather not use a low memory global because it introduces an absolute address in our code, but other routines that could do the job also happen to move memory.

Hazard

Apple will eventually phase out certain low memory globals, because they hamper moving the Mac OS to a preemptive multitasking operating system. Therefore, the use of low memory globals is strongly discouraged. However, for the FlipDepth example we had two choices. First, perform a safe head-patch on **PostEvent()** and use a low-memory global (that will probably be supported for awhile longer on the Power Mac) to obtain the modifier keys. In short, FlipDepth as implemented here works reliably on both architectures now and for the immediate future. Or, we avoid using the low-memory global by performing a tail-patch on a Toolbox call such as **GetOSEvent()**, to capture both the event and the modifier keys. This might buy us trouble immediately if our tail patch interferes with Apple's patch software. When you're dealing with the Mac OS at this level, sometimes there are no easy choices.

If Command-Shift-T was pressed, it's a request to change the screen depth. We respond by first discarding the event by zeroing the event code. If we didn't do this, the keyboard event gets forwarded to the application, which might respond in undesirable ways. Then, we set the global **gRequestFlag** and exit.

Before we could call the 68K version of this function, we had to do some scary assembly code to position the arguments onto the stack where we could use them. This isn't the case for the PowerPC version. Even though **PostEvent()** is register-based, when **MyPostEventPPC()** gets called, these values appear in the function's arguments, as if the routine were stack-based. This simplifies use of the OS trap routines immensely, thanks to the Mixed Mode Manager. As a final note, when **MyPostEvent68k()** exits, it has to traverse more assembly code to clean up the stack, restore register A4, and jump to the original **PostEvent()**. The PowerPC version calls the **CallPostEvent()** macro and exits.

But I digress. Onward to the screen depth control software:

```c
/*  Get the current screen depth. Also get the GDevice of main screen and its
    device number (to use the driver) */
long Fetch_Depth(void)
{
long      screenDepth;                   /* Current bit depth of our screen */
GDHandle thisGDevice;

    /* Get start of GDevice list */
    thisGDevice = GetMainDevice();              /* Get GDevice of main screen */
    gGlobalsPtr->gOurGDevice = thisGDevice;
    screenDepth = (**thisGDevice).gdMode;         /* Get pixel's size */
    gGlobalsPtr->gDevRefNum = (**thisGDevice).gdRefNum; /* Driver # */
    return screenDepth;

} /* end Fetch_Depth() */
```

Fetch_Depth()'s job is to find the Mac's main active screen. It uses a call to
the routine **GetMainDevice()**, which fetches the GDevice for the main
screen. A GDevice is a data structure used to maintain a screen. It stores
such information as the screen's size, the device driver controlling the
display hardware, its current color palette, and what pixel depth the screen
is at. Next, we obtain the driver reference number and current screen mode
from this GDevice, and place this data in the globals **gdRefNum** and **gdMode** .
The mode value is the ID number of a special resource used to handle the
screen.

```c
void Change_Depth(long newDepth)
{
GrafPtr     oldPort;
Rect        ourGDRect;
RgnHandle   thisScreenBoundary;
GrafPtr     theBigPicture;
WindowPtr   theFrontWindow;

    HideCursor();                     /* Hide pointer since its depth will change */
    InitGDevice(gGlobalsPtr->gDevRefNum, newDepth, gGlobalsPtr->gOurGDevice);
/* At last we change the screen depth! */
    theFrontWindow = FrontWindow();
    ActivatePalette(theFrontWindow);   /* Use active window's color palette */
    AllocCursor();                     /* Draw cursor at new screen depth */
    ShowCursor();                      /* Put it back on-screen */
```

```
/* The desktop's still a mess: redraw it */
   thisScreenBoundary = NewRgn();        /* Get a region to hold this screen */
   if (!MemError())                      /* Trouble? */
      {                                  /*No */
      ourGDRect = (**gGlobalsPtr->gOurGDevice).gdRect;
      RectRgn(thisScreenBoundary, &ourGDRect);   /* Get gDevice boundary */
      GetPort(&oldPort);                 /* Save current port */
      GetWMgrPort(&theBigPicture);       /* Get Desktop's port */
      SetPort(theBigPicture);            /* Make it the current port */
      DrawMenuBar();
      PaintOne(NIL, thisScreenBoundary);     /* Paint the background */
  /* Now the other windows */
      PaintBehind( *(WindowPeek *) WindowList, thisScreenBoundary);
      SetPort(oldPort);
      DisposeRgn(thisScreenBoundary);
      } /* end if !MemError() */
   else
      SysBeep(30);                       /* Couldn't make the region, complain */

} /* end Change_Depth() */
```

Last but not least, here's the function that does the actual screen change. The second line of code, where `InitGDevice()` is called, does the actual depth change. We pass this routine the device reference number so that it can communicate with the driver controlling the screen's display hardware, the new screen mode value, and the GDevice that manages the screen. `Fetch_Depth()` conveniently obtained the display's driver reference number and its associated GDevice that we now use in the `InitGDevice()` call. The rest of the code in this function basically cleans up the screen after the depth change.

Let's talk about those screen modes a bit more. The screen mode number derives from the ID numbers of special resources (called sResources, because they're Slot Manager resources) in a display board's firmware, or in firmware that manages the Mac's built-in video circuits. Each different pixel depth that the display supports has its own sResource ID number. These sResources contain information that describes the screen's characteristics to both the operating system and the device driver for a particular screen depth (say, 8 bits per pixel).

What's key here is that these sResources are handled a lot like actual resources, where the first available ID number begins at 128. The Macintosh API dictates that the first screen mode is always black-and-white, and thus its mode sResource value must always be 128. If we call `InitGDevice()` with a mode value of 128, the screen turns black-and-white. How do we handle other screen depths? We punt on that issue, because there's no guarantee as to what pixel depth the next sResource (ID = 129) supports. A display board might support 1-, 2-, 4-, and 8-bit color, and so its sResource IDs would be 128, 129, 130, and 131, respectively. Another board might support 1-, 8-, 16-, and 32-bit screen modes, and its sResources would also be 128, 129, 130, 131. What FlipDepth does is grab the current screen mode (and thus its sResource ID number) when the Extension loads and saves it in the globals block. We simply pass this value—whatever screen depth it represents—to `InitGDevice()` whenever the user wants to leave black-and-white mode. While this all sounds complicated, the code shows that it's fairly simple. The big payoff is that this mechanism is hardware independent: this identical code works on Mac IIs, PowerBooks, Quadras, and Power Macs.

Important

Why don't I use the high-level routines HasDepth() and SetDepth(), which obtains a screen mode and sets a screen's mode, respectively? I wrote this code long before these routines appeared on the scene. Also, the initial release of these routines was slightly buggy. However, to make the code more bulletproof, I would probably call HasDepth() to double-check that a black-and-white screen exists on the system in the initialization section of FlipDepth. However, as a fast hack for a screen utility, this code has served me well for many years.

The rest of this function handles repainting the screen after the depth changes. We start by hiding the cursor, and do the depth change. Next, we fix up the color palette so that it uses the color palette of the foreground application (which owns the front window) with a call to `ActivatePalette()`. Then we fix the cursor's pixel depth.

Redrawing the screen itself requires that we obtain a region that we'll use to map the desktop onto so that we can redraw the background pattern. We use `NewRegion()` to make this region structure. We plug into this region the boundaries defined by the screen's GDevice, using `RectRgn()`. The current drawing port is saved, and we use `GetWMgrPort()` to fetch the port that handles the entire desktop. We make this the current drawing port and call `DrawMenuBar()` to reconstruct the menus. `PaintOne()` is a Window Manager routine that, when called with a value of NIL for the window argument, knows that the "window" is the desktop and paints it with the background pattern. `PaintBehind()` then redraws all the windows in the region. At this point, the Mac's screen is rebuilt, so we clean up by restoring the port and releasing the memory used to make the region.

Building a Fat Trap

At last, we're ready to use this code to build our fat trap. Let's start by saving the code into a file called "FlipDepth.c." Create a new project called "FlipDepth.π.PPC," and add "FlipDepth.c" to it, followed by "InterfaceLib" from the MacOS folder. Before we compile the code, we have to change the project's preferences so that we can generate a shared library. We make a shared library because the result must be stand-alone code. If we don't, the linker will add some run-time code that prepares the code fragment for execution as an application when it loads.

Select Preferences from Metrowerks CodeWarrior's Edit menu, and go to the Linker panel. In the Entry Points section of the panel, clear all three text boxes of the Initialization, Main, and Termination default entry point names. Next, in the PEF panel, go to the Export Symbols pop-up menu item and select All Globals. Next, choose Context for both the Shared Code and Shared Data pop-up menu items. Now, go the Project panel. Click on the Project Type pop-up menu and choose Shared Library. The window's contents will change, displaying items that modify the shared library's characteristics. Type in the name **INIT #1.lib** for the library's name and leave the file's type and creator alone, other than to confirm that the file type is shlb. Save all of these settings by clicking on the OK button. Click on the Make button in the Toolbar, or select Make from the Project menu to compile the code and create the library. Don't select Build Library from the

Project menu: It's for generating libraries that are to be linked to other Metrowerks projects. If all has gone well, you should have a file "INIT #1.lib" in your CodeWarrior folder. If a file doesn't appear, recheck the settings in the PEF panel.

Unfortunately, there's a problem here. To progress further, we need to move the PowerPC code out of the file's data fork and into the resource fork, so it looks like a resource. Mathemæsthetic's Inc.'s Resourcer is a resource editor similar to ResEdit that lets you cut and paste between file forks. However, with CodeWarrior in hand, we can manage this ourselves. Start a new project and type:

```c
#include <Types.h>
#include <QuickDraw.h>
#include <Windows.h>
#include <Fonts.h>
#include <Memory.h>
#include <ToolUtils.h>
#include <StandardFile.h>
#include <Errors.h>
#include <Resources.h>

/* Various constants */
#define NIL             0L
#define FALSE           false
#define TRUE            true
#define DEFAULT_VOL     0
#define ONE_FILE_TYPE   1
#define POWER_PC_FRAG   'PPC '                   /* Resource type */
#define FRAG_ID         300                      /* Resource ID */

void Move_Fork(short input);
void main(void);

void Move_Fork(short input)
{
OSErr       fInputErr;
long        codeFragSize;
Handle      fragBuff;

    fInputErr = GetEOF(input, &codeFragSize);        /* Get file length */
    if ((fragBuff = NewHandle(codeFragSize)) != NIL)  /* Enough memory? */
```

```
        {                                              /* Read in fragment */
    if (!(fInputErr = FSRead(input, &codeFragSize, *fragBuff)))
        {                                              /* Treat as a resource */
        AddResource(fragBuff, POWER_PC_FRAG, FRAG_ID, NIL);
        if (!ResError())                               /* No trouble? */
          {
          WriteResource(fragBuff);        /* Write frag to resource fork */
          if (ResError())
             SysBeep(30);
          } /* end if !ResError */
        } /* !fInputErr */
     } /* end if != NIL */
  ReleaseResource(fragBuff);              /* Free the memory */
} /* end Move_Fork() */
```

The function **Move_Fork()** performs the operations necessary to copy the
PowerPC code from the data fork to the resource fork. Let's see how this is
done. We first use the **GetEOF()** routine to obtain the size of the file's data
fork. This size value gets passed to **NewHandle()** to create a buffer large
enough to hold the code fragment. The code then gets read into this buffer
with **FSRead()**. With the code fragment in memory, we use **AddResource()** to
create a resource entry for the data in the resource fork of a file we've
opened. We use **WriteResource()** to write the PowerPC code into the file's
resource fork. Finally, we call **ReleaseResource()** to discard the memory
used by **fragBuff**, since this buffer is now considered a resource by the
Mac OS. To change the resource's type and ID number, you can edit the
definitions for **POWER_PC_FRAG**, and **FRAG_ID**.

Now let's add **main()** where we open and close the files:

```
void main(void)
{
unsigned char       fileName[14] = {"\pKlepto.π.rsrc"};
OSType              fileCreator = {'RSED'}; /* Output file's creator */
OSType              fileType = {'rsrc'};    /* Output file's type */
OSErr              fileError;
short              inFileRefNum, outFileRefNum;
StandardFileReply  inputReply, outputReply;
short              oldVol;
SFTypeList         shlbType = {'shlb'};    /* File type for shared library */
CursHandle         theCursor;              /* Current pointer icon */
```

```
/* Lunge after all the memory we can get */
   MaxApplZone();

/* Make sure we've got some master pointers */
   MoreMasters();
   MoreMasters();
   MoreMasters();
   MoreMasters();

/* Initialize managers */
   InitGraf(&qd.thePort);
   InitFonts();
   FlushEvents(everyEvent, 0);
   InitWindows();
   InitMenus();
   TEInit();
   InitDialogs(NIL);

/* Open the input file */
   StandardGetFile(NIL, ONE_FILE_TYPE, shlbType, &inputReply);
   if (inputReply.sfGood)
      {
      GetVol (NIL, &oldVol);            /* Save current volume */
      if ((fileError = FSpOpenDF (&inputReply.sfFile, fsCurPerm,
                                  &inFileRefNum)) != noErr)
        {
        SysBeep(30);
        return;
        } /* end if error */

/* Open the output file */
      StandardPutFile("\pSave code fragment in:", fileName, &outputReply);
      if (outputReply.sfGood)
        {
        SetVol(NIL, outputReply.sfFile.vRefNum);
        fileError = FSpCreate(&outputReply.sfFile, fileCreator,
                              fileType, smSystemScript);
        switch(fileError)
          {
          case noErr:
          break;
          case dupFNErr:                /* File already exists */
```

```
        if ((fileError = FSpDelete(&outputReply.sfFile)) == noErr)
                {
                if ((fileError = FSpCreate(&outputReply.sfFile,
                                           fileCreator,
                                           fileType,
                                           smSystemScript)) != noErr)
                    {
                    SysBeep(30);
                    FSClose(inFileRefNum);
                    SetVol(NIL, oldVol);
                    return;
                    } /* end if != noErr */
                } /* end == noErr */
            else
                {
                SysBeep(30);
                FSClose (inFileRefNum);
                SetVol(NIL, oldVol);
                return;
                } /* end else */
        break;    /* end case dupFNErr */
        default:
            SysBeep(30);
            FSClose(inFileRefNum);           /* Close the input file */
            SetVol(NIL, oldVol);             /* Restore original volume */
            return;
        } /* end switch */

/* Open file's data fork. We do this only to get a file ref number */
        if (!(FSpOpenDF (&outputReply.sfFile, fsCurPerm, &outFileRefNum)))
            {
/* MUST create resource map in resource fork or no resource writing occurs */
            FSpCreateResFile (&outputReply.sfFile, fileCreator,
                            fileType, smSystemScript);
            if (!ResError())
                {  /* Open resource fork */
                FSpOpenResFile (&outputReply.sfFile, fsCurPerm);
                if (!ResError())
                    {
                    theCursor = GetCursor(watchCursor);     /* Change cursor */
                    SetCursor(&**theCursor);
                    Move_Fork(inFileRefNum);
```

```
                        FSClose(outFileRefNum);
                        SetCursor(&qd.arrow);                    /* Restore cursor */
                    } /* end if !ResError */
                } /* end if !ResError */
            FlushVol (NIL, outputReply.sfFile.vRefNum);
                } /* end if !FSpOpenDF */
            } /* end if outputReply.sfGood */
        FSClose (inFileRefNum);
        SetVol(NIL, oldVol);                        /* Restore current volume */
    } /* end if inputReply.sfGood */

} /* end main() */
```

You'll notice there's no event loop in this program. That's OK, because the Standard File Dialog boxes have enough built-in smarts to manage most of the events required to make a file selection, and `Move_Fork()` manages all of the file I/O. That's all we need for this quick and dirty little program. Once you get past the initialization code, you can see most of the code came from the `Ask_File()` function in SonOMunger. I did remove all the error reporting calls, replacing them with SysBeep(30) to simplify things.

The code for picking and opening the input file remains the same as SonOMunger's, except that `StandardGetFile()` filters out all files but types of 'shlb'. The code for opening the output file is the same, up to a point. We first open the output file using `FSpOpenDF()`, only so that we can get a file reference number in order to close the file when we're done. Next, we call `FSpCreateResFile()` to create a resource reference map in the file's resource fork. If we fail to perform this step, no resource writing can be done to the file. The final step before calling `Move_Fork()` is to open the resource fork using `FSpOpenResFile()`. Note that the resource file routines report errors back through the `ResError()` function. These routines also don't use a file reference number. That's because once a link is established between the file and the Resource Manager, it persists through all subsequent resource routines until the file is closed.

Since this code steals PowerPC code from a file's data fork, name this program's file "Klepto.c." Create a new project called "Klepto.π," and set its preferences as an application, using the factory defaults, other than to name the output file "Klepto." Compile and make the application. That's right: you didn't build any resources with Rez in order to make "Klepto." Since "Klepto" doesn't use any special resources, and the resources for Standard File Dialog boxes come from the System file, the program code runs as it is.

Double-click on Klepto to launch it, and a Standard File Dialog box appears. The only file that should appear in the dialog is our shared library file, "Init #.lib." Click on the Open button or press Return to choose the file. Immediately, a second Standard File Dialog box appears. Type in the name **FlipDepth.π.rsrc**, and press Return. Klepto should quit shortly, leaving you a resource file with the given name. If you double-click on this file, ResEdit launches, and you can examine the PPC resource to see the PowerPC code within it.

We named the output file "FlipDepth.π.rsrc" to pull the same trick that we did with SwitchBank project files to create a fat binary application. When we make the 68K version of our Extension, CodeWarrior will copy this file's resources—and thus the PowerPC code in it—to the Extension file.

Let's finish the job. Launch the 68K version of Metrowerks CodeWarrior, and create a project called "FlipDepth.π." Add the files "FlipDepth.c" and "MacOS.lib" to the project. Select Preferences from the Edit menu, and choose the Processor panel. Click on the Code Model pop-up menu and select Small. In the Linker panel, go to the Linker Info section and check the item Link Single Segment. Finally, pick the Project panel. For the Project Type, click on the pop-up menu and choose Code Resource. The panel's contents will change. In the Code Resource section, type **FlipDepth** for the file's name. For the ResType item, type in **INIT**, and for the ResID item type in **300**. This sets up the resource's type and ID number. The last thing to do is set the output file's type and creator. Go to the Creator item and type **????**, and for the Type item enter **INIT**. Finally, go to the Resource flags and click on the pop-up menu. Check the System Heap and Locked items. These settings ensure that the Resource Manager loads the 68K code resource into the system heap, and locks it in place. Click on the OK button to save the new settings.

Now make the project. "FlipDepth.c" should compile, and a "FlipDepth" file should appear, sporting the generic puzzle piece Extension icon. If the linker should report problems, double-check the Linker panel and Project panel settings. Drag "FlipDepth" to the System Folder, and the Finder should request to place the file in the Extensions folder. Make sure that the Mac is currently set in a mode other than black-and-white, and reboot. When the desktop appears, try typing Command-Shift-T. The Mac's screen should toggle to the black-and-white mode and back to the color mode.

Summary

In this chapter, we've seen how to apply the knowledge we've gained about the PowerPC run-time architecture to solve specific programming problems, especially to guarantee an orderly switch from one instruction set to another when calling your custom function. As we've walked through the code of these two programs, you can see that doing this isn't difficult. Furthermore, it should be obvious that access to the global data of any program and OS Toolbox routines is far simpler than it is with the 68K architecture. This goes a long way toward helping developers write more Power Macintosh software.

Now that we have develped our programs, let's get to the "other" stuff: debugging.

The Art of Debugging

The material in this chapter will be of no interest to those programmers who write perfect programs, every time.

Seriously though, it is inevitable that program code has bugs. Programming is where you give the computer precise directions in what amounts to a second language for you. Despite C's elegant terseness of syntax (or because of it), there's the inevitable conversational misstep that causes the Mac to freeze up like a social misfit at a debutante's ball. In this chapter we'll look at the high-level debugging tools CodeWarrior provides in the form of MW Debug, a low-level debugger called The Debugger, and finish with some common sense debugging techniques. Bear in mind that the PowerPC versions of these tools are changing rapidly, and some features and capabilities may differ from what you see here.

> **Important**
>
> This text was written using the full version of Metrowerks CodeWarrior. You'll have to use slightly different steps when using the limited version on the CD; the limited version can only work with the sample files provided on the CD so the commands Add File... and New Project are not available.
>
> So, if you are following along using the limited version of CodeWarrior that's on the CD, when the text tells you to use the New Project or the Add File... command, you should instead open the related project file and keep it open throughout the exercise. All the associated files will already be in the project and so you won't need the Add File... command. Then, you can follow the same procedures as if you were using the full version of CodeWarrior.

About Debuggers

You've just completed writing that next killer application that users will flock to, with their wallets open. The code passes muster with Metrowerks CodeWarrior's C compiler, and after a few minor revisions the linker approves too. But when you launch the application, either from within CodeWarrior or by double-clicking on the resulting file, you get the infamous "bomb box," complete with a sizzling bomb icon. This dialog box is produced by the System Error Handler, which the operating system calls when it detects a fatal error or exception. This assumes that the cause of the error hasn't seriously trashed the operating system in the process. You might be spared the pyrotechnics, and the Mac instead simply seizes up with no warning at all. Despite this, consider yourself lucky that such a bug manifests itself so rapidly. It's those slowly ticking logic bombs lurking within the program code that go off minutes or hours later which can drive seasoned programmers to drink—and I don't mean Jolt cola, either.

No matter what type of program bug it is, or how long it takes the bug to bite, programmers rely on their wits, intuition, and debuggers to rid their code of these pests. A debugger is a highly-specialized program designed to help you track down program bugs, hence the name. The debugger program installs its own exception handlers or uses advanced system routines so that when an exception occurs, it can seize control and halt the program. You then use the debugger to investigate the exception's cause by examining the program's variables and data structures. If necessary, you can have the debugger take charge at designated points in the program, and single-step through the program's instructions, tracing the path of execution up to the crash. These debugger features enable you to reconstruct the crash scene. This usually gives you a good idea of where the bug is and how to fix it.

Background Info

It's nomenclature time again. Debuggers generally fall into two categories: hardware and software. A hardware debugger uses dedicated hardware to perform the debugging process, and a software debugger is a special computer program.

A typical hardware debugger is an In Circuit Emulator, or ICE for short. As its name implies, an ICE is a dedicated set of hardware that connects in-line with the test computer's processor, or replaces the processor entirely with custom circuitry. Special software lets you halt a program's execution based on hardware accesses, such as read/write operations to a memory location or an I/O port. Such fine control is possible because the ICE hardware eavesdrops on the bus signals and detects when a bus access touches the memory locations you request. An ICE is not usually necessary for development at the application level. It's used by the hardware and firmware designers as they build the prototype computer system and its ROM code. Since we're debugging programs here, not building a computer, this is the last mention of hardware debuggers.

Software debuggers are used to debug applications or software components such as plug-in modules or stand-alone code resources. These software debuggers may be further subdivided into two categories: low-level and high-level. A low-level debugger operates by using as few of the operating system resources as it can. Because of this, these debuggers are very robust. They continue to function even though a buggy application may have done heavy damage to the operating system. On the other hand, such debuggers typically have a minimalist interface and display. You can examine the program, but usually only as machine code instructions, and you need to know memory addresses of a program variable to view its contents.

High-level debuggers rely heavily on the operating system to provide services such as windows and menus. In turn, they provide an easier to use interface and a sophisticated display. They can show a test program's code as either source or assembly language statements. Variables can be monitored simply by knowing the variable's name, not its memory location. Their values can be displayed in a variety of formats. On the other hand, since these capabilities depend on the operating system's health, substantial damage to it by a program error causes high-level debuggers to go down in flames along with the buggy program. Another limitation is that you can't debug certain types of code: Extensions, MDEF (menu definition handlers), completion functions, or interrupt tasks. That's because some of these code types function on the fringes of the operating system (such as an Extension or interrupt task), and others pose reentrancy problems (you can't debug a new menu handler when the debugger itself uses menus).

Despite these limitations, a high-level debugger is a good way to confirm a program works as it should. Also, it's very good at quickly locating the vicinity of the problem code, which helps reduce the time it takes to zero in and fix the problem. Also, a low-level debugger requires that you learn a lot of details about the processor, the operating system, and the compiler's output before you can make sense of what's going on. In short, a low-level debugger has a steep learning curve, while high-level debuggers only require that you know the programming language.

Both types of debuggers let you step through the statements one line at a time, or set control points called *breakpoints*. A breakpoint marks the program statement where the program halts execution (or breaks), and the debugger program resumes control. Breakpoints thus allow you to run a program up to a suspect location. You can examine critical program variables and begin single-stepping from the breakpoint location to gather additional information.

So far, we've been talking about debuggers that run on the one target machine. There is another category of debugger here: a two-machine debugger. A two-machine debugger uses a small code "nub" on the target machine, while the debugger itself runs on a different machine (called the host). The host machine communicates to the nub on the target via a wire, typically a serial cable. The big advantage to a two-machine debugger is that the host can support a high-level front end, while the low-level nub can usually survive the target machine's operating system being destroyed. A two-machine debugger can also provide source-level debugging for virtually any code in the target system. The big disadvantage is that this type of debugger is that it requires two machines. Apple's initial PowerPC debugger, Macintosh Debugger for PowerPC, is a two-machine debugger.

Metrowerks CodeWarrior's debugging application, called MW Debug, is a high-level debugger. You can single-step through the source code, and set breakpoints. MW Debug also displays the contents of variables, and lets you change their value. This way, as you step through the program, you observe what the code is actually doing and what values it's working with. By changing the values of function results, you can force the program through an error handler to check the application's robustness. MW Debug also allows you to examine a program as assembly language instructions.

Currently MW Debug can debug applications or shared libraries. If, however, you're writing stand-alone code resources or accelerated code resources, then you'll have to use a low-level debugger.

Using the CodeWarrior Debugger

In order for MW Debug to display variables and trace through the source code, it requires specific information about your program. You supply this vital data by preparing the program for debugging in Metrowerks CodeWarrior. This preparation involves only a few changes to the project's preferences settings, and simply recompiling the program to make a new version. Along with the new executable application file, CodeWarrior also generates a symbols file. This symbols file contains the names of the variables and functions used in your program, plus their location in both the source code file and in the application file. MW Debug uses this symbol file information to manage the debugging session.

The symbols file CodeWarrior makes has the same name as the application's name, plus an extension of .SYM for the 68K code, and .xSYM for the PowerPC code. For example, let's assume we compile the source file in project "Klepto.π" for debugging, and name the application Klepto. The resulting symbols file is "Klepto.SYM" for the 68K version of CodeWarrior, and "Klepto.xSYM" for the PowerPC version of Metrowerks CodeWarrior.

Let's take the "SwitchBank" program and run through parts of it with MW Debug. First, launch CodeWarrior by double-clicking on the "SwitchBank.π.PPC" project file. Go to the Project window, and in "SwitchBank.c" file slot, click on the area beneath the bug icon. A small dot appears (see figure 7.1). This dot is the Generate SYM Info marker. Whenever the linker generates an output file, it creates the required symbolic debug information for the marked file. You can choose one or more files for debugging.

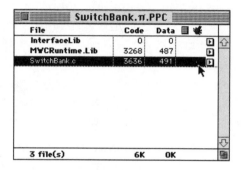

Figure 7.1 *Marking a file for debug output*

Now that we've marked the source file, we need the CodeWarrior linker to actually generate the debug information. Select Preferences from the Edit menu, and select the Linker Panel. Under the Link Options section, click on the Generate SYM File item to check it. Also check the Use Full Path Names item (see figure 7.2). The Full Path Names has the linker generate a complete path specification for a file, such as Tachyon:CodeWarrior:CodeExamples *f*: SwitchBank *f*:SwitchBank.c. While checking this item isn't necessary, it helps MW Debug locate the files it needs, especially if they're located somewhere other than the CodeWarrior folder or project folder. Users working with the 68K version of Metrowerks CodeWarrior also have to check the Generate A6 Stack Frames item.

Remaking the application is the last step in the preparation sequence. Choose Make from the Project menu or type Command-M. CodeWarrior first recompiles the source, and then the linker produces the application file and the symbols file. Quit CodeWarrior.

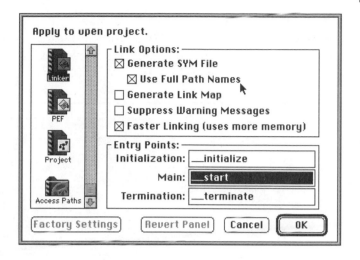

Figure 7.2 *Setting the linker to produce symbols for the debugger*

Important

Before you start the CodeWarrior source debugger, check that you have installed the auxiliary files it requires to operate. For a Power Mac, the file "PPCTraceEnabler" should be in the Extensions folder, and the application file "DebugServices for PowerPC" should be in the Startup Items folder. For 68K Macs, the file "DebuggerINIT" should be in the Extensions folder. If these files aren't present, look for them in the Debugger *f* folder on the CodeWarrior CD, inside the folder appropriate for your compiler. For example, if you own the PowerPC version of Metrowerks CodeWarrior, you would go to the CodeWarrior: MWC/C++ PPC:Debugger *f*: Put these in PPC System Folder! Copy the files to the pertinent System Folders and reboot the Mac.

To launch CodeWarrior's high-level debugger, double-click on the MWDebug application, or drag the project's .xSYM file icon onto the MW Debug icon. MW Debug launches, and after a brief interval, two windows appear (see figure 7.3) The frontmost window, titled SwitchBank, is the Program Window. It displays the source code file that has the active function (in this case, `main()`). The other window, titled SwitchBank.xSYM, is the File window. It's used to select other source files in the project, so that you can examine them and set up breakpoints. The floating Toolbar provides ready access to often-used items in the Control menu. If you're more comfortable using the keyboard to step through a debugger, you can get rid of the Toolbar by clicking on its Close box.

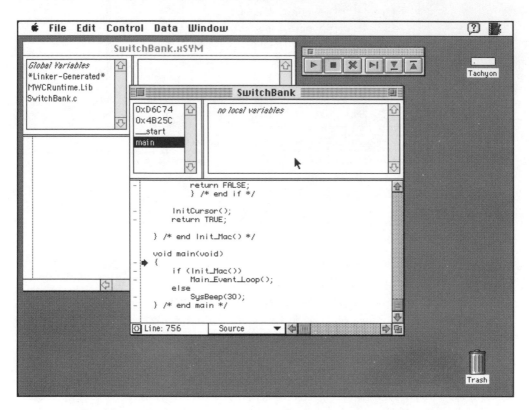

Figure 7.3 *MW Debug displaying the Program and File windows*

Let's take a closer look at the Program Window (see figure 7.4). It's composed of three panes, or sections. The bottom section is the Source Pane. It shows the source code of the active function. It's where you step through your program, one line at a time. Tick marks on the pane's left indicate executable statements. The small arrow adjacent these marks points to the currently executing statement.

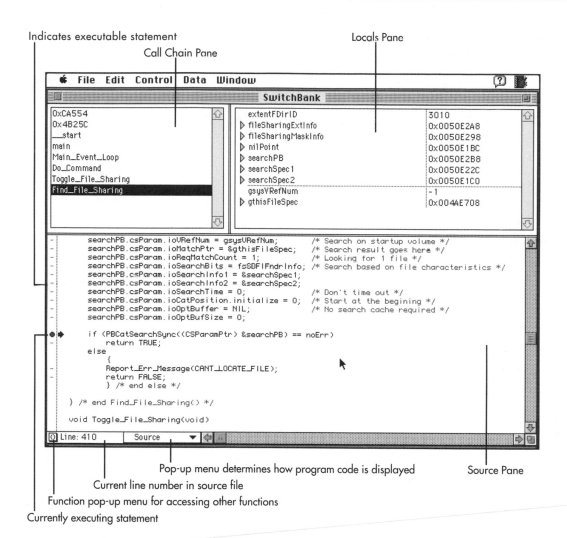

Indicates executable statement

Call Chain Pane

Locals Pane

```
 ▲ File  Edit  Control  Data  Window                                    ⑦  ▨
▱                                   SwitchBank                                   ▱
OxCA554                        ⇧  │  extentFDirID                    3010      ⇧
0x4B25C                           │ ▷ fileSharingExtInfo             0x0050E2A8
_start                            │ ▷ fileSharingMaskInfo            0x0050E298
main                              │ ▷ nilPoint                       0x0050E1BC
Main_Event_Loop                   │ ▷ searchPB                       0x0050E2B8
Do_Command                        │ ▷ searchSpec1                    0x0050E22C
Toggle_File_Sharing               │ ▷ searchSpec2                    0x0050E1C0
Find_File_Sharing                 │   gsysVRefNum                    -1
                                  │ ▷ gthisFileSpec                  0x004AE708
                               ⇩  │                                             ⇩
──────────────────────────────────────────────────────────────────────────────
 -      searchPB.csParam.ioVRefNum = gsysVRefNum;       /* Search on startup volume */      ⇧
 -      searchPB.csParam.ioMatchPtr = &gthisFileSpec;   /* Search result goes here */
 -      searchPB.csParam.ioReqMatchCount = 1;           /* Looking for 1 file */
 -      searchPB.csParam.ioSearchBits = fsSBFlFndrInfo; /* Search based on file characteristics */
 -      searchPB.csParam.ioSearchInfo1 = &searchSpec1;
 -      searchPB.csParam.ioSearchInfo2 = &searchSpec2;
 -      searchPB.csParam.ioSearchTime = 0;              /* Don't time out */
 -      searchPB.csParam.ioCatPosition.initialize = 0;  /* Start at the begining */
 -      searchPB.csParam.ioOptBuffer = NIL;             /* No search cache required */
 -      searchPB.csParam.ioOptBufSize = 0;

●▶     if (PBCatSearchSync((CSParamPtr) &searchPB) == noErr)
           return TRUE;
 -      else
            {
            Report_Err_Message(CANT_LOCATE_FILE);
            return FALSE;
            } /* end else */

      } /* end Find_File_Sharing() */

      void Toggle_File_Sharing(void)
                                                                                ⇩
▱ Line: 410        Source      ▼  ⬅▮▮▮                                        ➡▱
```

Pop-up menu determines how program code is displayed

Source Pane

Current line number in source file

Function pop-up menu for accessing other functions

Currently executing statement

Figure 7.4 *Details of the Program Window*

At the Source Pane's bottom left is an indicator and controls. The small braces or Function icon operates like its counterpart in the CodeWarrior editor window. When you click on it, a pop-up menu appears that displays all of the functions in this file. The checkmark in this menu flags the active function. If you select another function, the Source Pane displays the source code of that function, starting at its entry point. Next to the Function icon is an indicator that shows, for this file, the source line number of the currently executing statement. Finally, there's a pop-up menu that lets you change the Source Pane's display from C source code to the corresponding assembly language statements generated by the compiler (see figure 7.5). You can single-step through 68K or PowerPC assembly language code and set breakpoints if you choose to do so.

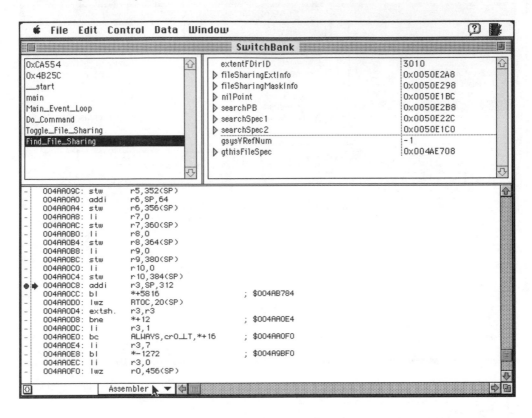

Figure 7.5 *Viewing the program's code as PowerPC assembly language*

The pane in the Program Window's upper left is termed the Call Chain Pane. It displays the list of functions called prior to the function shown in the Source Pane. In figure 7.5, the highlighted name, `Find_File_Sharing`, is the active function. From the list, we can see the `main()` called `Main_Event_Loop()`, `Do_Command()`, and `Toggle_File_Sharing()` before calling `Find_File_Sharing()`. The Source Pane's output is tied to the highlighted choice in the Call Chain Pane. Clicking on another function name in the Call Chain Pane highlights that name and immediately takes you to that function in the Source Pane. The Source Pane displays this function's source code at the point where it called the next function in the chain.

The pane in the upper right portion of the Program Window is the Locals Pane. It lists the function's local variables, plus any static or global variables referenced by the function. A dashed line separates the function's local variables (at the top of the pane) from the global variables (at the pane's bottom). When the flow of execution moves to a different function, the Locals Pane's contents are updated accordingly. Like the Source Pane, the Locals Pane always displays the variables of the function highlighted in the Call Chain Pane.

The small triangles to the variable name's left indicate that it is a structure. When you click on the triangle, the variable expands to show all of the structure's elements. Clicking on the triangle again hides the structure's elements. When you hold down the Option key when expanding a handle to a structure, the multiple dereferences are processed so that the display shows the structure's data elements. If the size of the Locals Pane is too confining, especially for large data structures, just double-click on the variable name. A new, independent window appears, displaying the entire structure. You can create as many independent windows as you want (see figure 7.6).

The current value of each variable appears to its right. If the displayed format of the variable's data is unsuitable, you can change it. First, click on the value to highlight it. Then, go to MW Debug's Data menu and choose another data type, say, character. The value is shown in the new format. If you intend to single-step through PowerPC assembly language instructions, the Locals Pane still displays the variable's contents as you continue through the program.

You can edit the contents of certain variables by double-clicking on the value. The data becomes framed, which indicates that you can enter a new value. The types of data you can enter are decimal, hexadecimal, floating-point, characters, and strings. Character data must be enclosed in quotes, and Pascal strings must include the "\p" escape sequence. The values of pointers to data structures can't be edited.

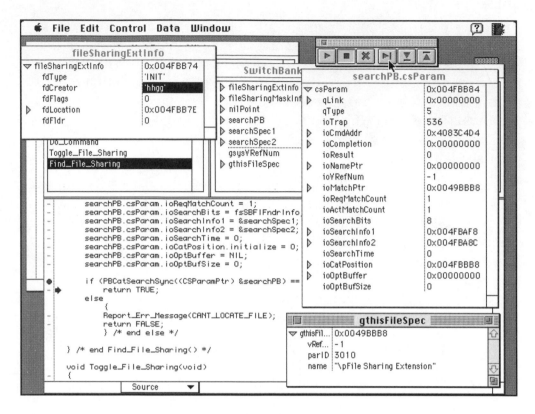

Figure 7.6 *Displaying data structures in their own windows*

The File Window operates basically like the Program Window. However, while the Program Window is focused on the active function in a file, the File Window is oriented toward dealing with the program's files as a whole. The bottom area is the Source Pane, and it displays the contents of the selected file. The upper left pane is the File Pane, which displays the names of the files used to produce the application. The upper right pane is the Globals Pane, and displays the global and static variables that are shared across all of the files (see figure 7.7). Notice that for array `AEInstalls[]`, you get a special window where you can alter the array's size and bind it to an address, a variable, or a register.

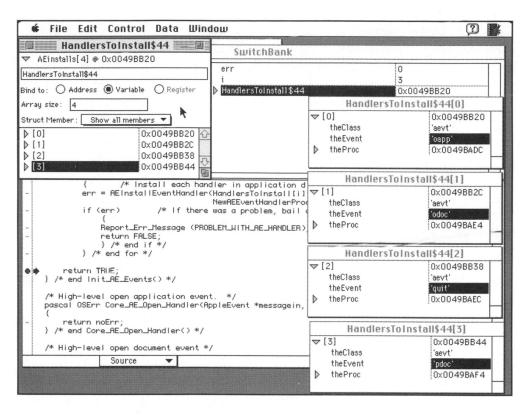

Figure 7.7 *The File Window, with a display of the application's high-level event dispatch table*

Now it's time to control the program. You do this using commands from the Control menu. The Run, Stop, and Kill commands provide gross program control. The Run command simply starts the program from `main()`, or the location where the program was halted. The Stop command suspends program execution. If you issue another Run command, the program resumes execution from this point. The Kill command terminates the program under test. If you issue a Run command after a Kill command, the program's execution starts over in `main()`.

The Step Over, Step Into, and Step Out commands apply fine control over the test program. The Step Over command executes program code, a line at a time. You'll use the Step Over command frequently to single-step through a program, observing the results of Toolbox calls and tracking the direction of C control statements. If the current line of code is a function or Toolbox trap, MW Debug calls the function or trap, returns, and advances to the next source line. In this sense, the debugger appears to "step over" function calls, even though their code actually executes. The Step Into command, when invoked, carries you inside the function called by the current source line. This allows you to examine what values get passed to the target function, and examine the operation of that function's code. Note: You can Step Into the code of libraries or other files that don't supply a symbols file, but you can only view the trace as assembly language in the Source Pane. The Step Out command executes the remaining code in the current function and halts the program once it returns to the calling function.

The VCR-style button icons on the Toolbar correspond to the gross and fine program control commands on the Control menu. The three icons that make up the Toolbar's left correspond to the Run, Stop, and Kill commands, while the trio of icons on the right represent Step Over, Step In, and Step Out.

To mark or place a breakpoint in a program, use the Function icon to jump to a suspect function. Next, scroll through the source code to the questionable statement. Place the pointer on the statement's tick mark (it's located on the left side of the Source Pane) and click on it. A circle appears, replacing the tick mark. The circle indicates that a breakpoint is set for this statement (see figure 7.8). You can set as many breakpoints as you like. To remove a breakpoint, click on the circle again. To remove all of the breakpoints at once, choose Clear All Breakpoints from the Control menu. There isn't a way to obtain the locations of all the breakpoints at once.

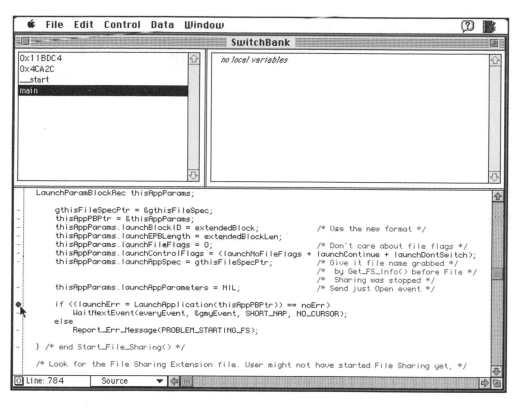

Figure 7.8 *Setting a breakpoint*

Important

MW Debug uses the files "DebugServices for PowerPC" application and "PPCTraceEnabler" Extension to access the Power Mac's debugging facilities. DebugServices for PowerPC is a background-only application written by Apple that provides a low-level debugging API to set/reset breakpoints, kill processes, and perform memory reads and writes. MW Debug uses low-level message blocks (via the PPCToolbox) to communicate with this application. DebugServices controls the test application, and returns information about its behavior back to MW Debug.

PPCTraceEnabler is a native Extension written by Apple. It gives DebugServices access to the single-step trace bit in the 601 processor's Machine State Register (MSR). The MSR is a supervisor-level register, and is not normally accessible by user-level application code. The PPCTraceEnabler Extension sets up this access. On 68K Macs, the DebuggerINIT, also written by Apple, patches the appropriate entries in the dispatch table to provide low-level debugging services to MW Debug.

For your application to be controlled properly by MW Debug, it must have the canBackGround bit set in the SIZE resource, and the program must make frequent calls to `WaitNextEvent()`. For more information on the SIZE resource, see chapters 4 and 6.

MW Debug remembers the size and location of the Program and File Windows, and the locations of all the breakpoints. This information is stored in a file with an extension of .xdbg. Continuing with our earlier example, if we debug the application Klepto and set some breakpoints, MW Debug produces a file named "Klepto.xdbg." If you want to quit MW Debug, and resume the job later with all the breakpoints in place, don't delete the .xdbg file.

Since we've got SwitchBank up and running under MW Debug, let's do a short tour. In the Program Window, click on the Function icon and select `Init_Mac()` from the pop-up menu. Scroll through `Init_Mac()`'s code and set a breakpoint on the statement containing the Apple Event initialization function, `Init_AE_Events()`, as shown in figure 7.9. Now pick Run from the Control menu, or type Command-R. After a short delay, SwitchBank should halt in `Init_Mac()`, at the call to `Init_AE_Events()`. Note: If you hold down the Option key when you set a breakpoint marker, the program automatically executes to that breakpoint, unless it encounters another breakpoint.

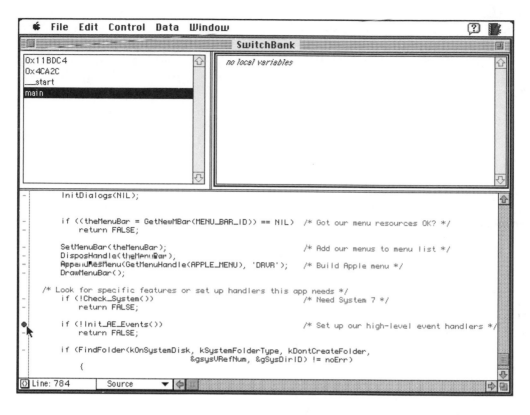

Figure 7.9 *Setting a breakpoint for the Apple Event initialization function*

If we wanted to step over this function, we'd simply pick Step Over in the Control menu or type Command-S. (After single-stepping through lots of code, you'll soon appreciate this command's keyboard equivalent.) However, let's examine what this function does. Type Command-T to step into `Init_AE_Events()`. The Source Pane now displays this function's entry point (figure 7.10).

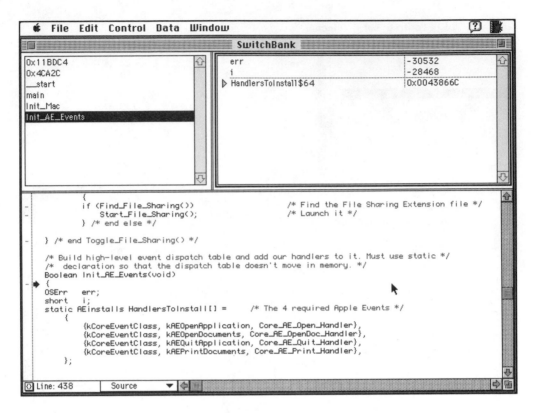

Figure 7.10   *Inside the Apple Event initialization function*

Type Command-S several times and watch the variable i get initialized by the for loop. Single-step and observe the result passed back by AEInstallEventHandler(), and how the if statement within the loop checks for an error result. Step through the loop once or twice, and when the execution pointer arrives back at the if statement again, go to the Locals Pane and type a negative number in err's value area to simulate an error (see figure 7.11).

When you single step this time, the flow of execution calls Report_Err_Message() instead, and Init_AE_Events() returns immediately with a value of FALSE. If you continue to single-step, you'll see Init_Mac() also return immediately with a FALSE value, and then main() calls SysBeep(), and exits. This is admittedly a simple example, but it shows what you can do with MW Debug.

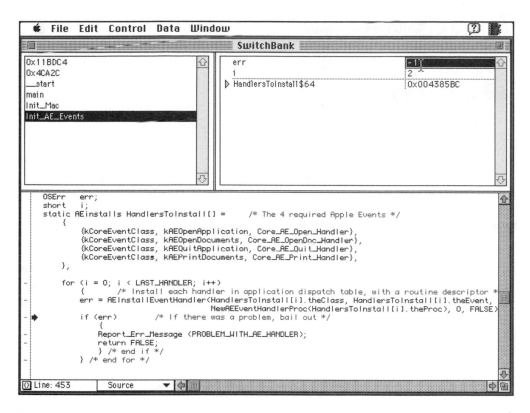

Figure 7.11 *Changing the value of err*

Let's look at another section of SwitchBank. If you had let SwitchBank terminate from the last example, the Source Pane in MW Debug's Program Window states that SwitchBank is not running. Go to the Control menu and choose Clear All Breakpoints. Type Command-R to run SwitchBank again. After a brief delay, the Program Window's panes should fill with source code. The Source Pane should be positioned in main(), ready to go. Click on the Function icon and pick **Core_AE_OpenDoc_Handler()**. You'll wind up at the entry point to this function, as shown in figure 7.12. Now set a breakpoint at the first executable statement in the function.

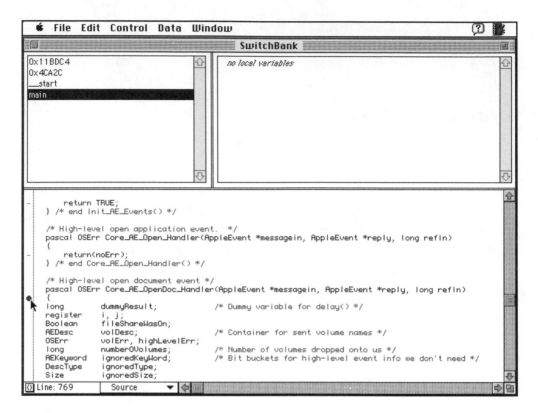

Figure 7.12 *Adding a breakpoint to the high-level Open Document function*

Once that's done, type Command-R to run SwitchBank. The panes in the Program Window should clear, and the Source Pane contains a message stating that SwitchBank is executing. So far, so good. Now we need to create a high-level Open Document Apple Event. Go to the edge of Program Window, hold down the Option key, and click on the desktop pattern. MW Debug's two windows should disappear, leaving a clear view of the Macintosh desktop. If you pull down the Application menu, you can see that MW Debug and SwitchBank are running, but not visible. The SwitchBank icon doesn't appear to be active (it doesn't display the "hollow" icon that active applications use), but that's because MW Debug had the Process Manager launch SwitchBank behind the Finder's back. Not knowing this, the Finder hasn't updated SwitchBank's Desktop icon to reflect this fact. Click on the startup volume's icon, drag it to the SwitchBank folder, and drop it onto SwitchBank. MW Debug should reappear, with SwitchBank's execution suspended inside the `Core_AE_OpenDoc_Handler()` function. You can single-step through this function, and observe how information is obtained from the Apple Event message. You'll also see SwitchBank's safety logic balk at ejecting a drive with the active system software on it. When you're done experimenting with SwitchBank, quit MW Debug, which also terminates SwitchBank.

Debugging a shared library file requires that you open it in MW Debug first, followed by the application that's linked to the library. An example should help illustrate the procedure. Suppose that you're working on a set of handy utility functions in a shared library named "CoolLib." First, mark the source file for debugging in the Project window, and set the linker preferences so that an .xSYM file is produced. Make the shared library, which results in the files "CoolLib" and "CoolLib.xSYM." You also have to prepare the test application that gets linked to your library. Mark the file for debugging in the Project Window and use the same linker settings as you did for "CoolLib." Make the test application. Let's call the output of this project "TestApp" and "TestApp.xSYM." Now you have all the components you need to debug the shared library.

To start the debugging session, first drag "CoolLib.xSYM" to MW Debug. MW Debug launches, and a File Window for the library file appears. Option-click on the desktop to hide the MW Debug window, and drag "TestApp.xSYM" onto the hollow MW Debug icon. TestApp should launch, and you have three windows on-screen: the File Window for "CoolLib.xSYM," the File Window for "TestApp.xSYM," and the Program Window for TestApp (see figure 7.13). Next, you set breakpoints in the shared library code using the CoolLib.xSYM window. To reach the breakpoint so that you can begin code tracing, start TestApp in the Program Window by selecting Run from the Control menu.

MW Debug also offers some surprisingly low-level debugger features. If you select the Show Registers item under the Windows menu, a window displaying the processor registers for either the 68K or PowerPC processor appears. Better still, by double-clicking on a register value, the value is framed so that you can modify the register's contents (see figure 7.14). Since you're messing with the state of the processor itself, use this capability with extreme caution. Another menu item, Show FPU Registers, lets you examine the floating-point registers of the 68040 or PowerPC. Finally, a Show Collection item creates a Collection window that acts as a container for any program variables you examine constantly. To use it, open a collection window with this menu command. Click on the desired variables and choose Copy to Collection from the data menu. Then position the Collection window where you can keep an eye on it and the variables you're monitoring.

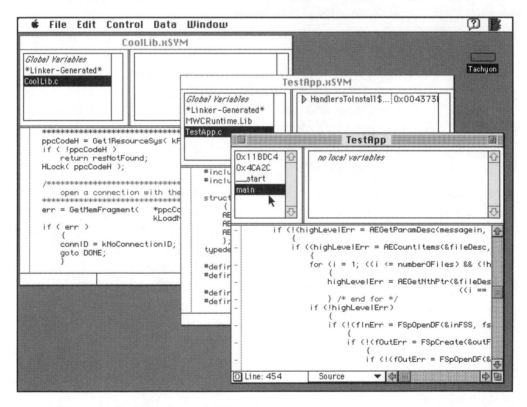

Figure 7.13 *Debugging a shared library*

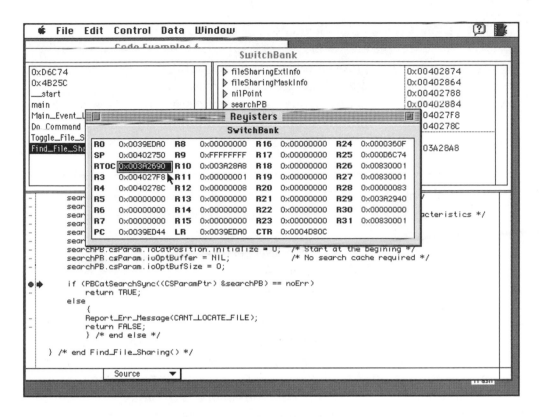

Figure 7.14   *Changing the TOC register on the PowerPC processor in MW Debug*

A Low-Level Debugger

For Power Mac program debugging, there are two low-level debuggers available. The first is Apple's own Macsbug, version 6.5. It's actually a 68K program that runs in the Power Mac emulator. It's still oriented around 68K processor debugging, since the debugger shows the 68K processor registers and stack. The capabilities of Macsbug can be expanded through the use of special resources called dcmds. Certain of these dcmds are used to disassemble PowerPC code, and display the PowerPC processor registers. Since Apple hasn't published any of these dcmds yet, we'll have to pass on Macsbug for now.

However, there's another low-level debugger available that gives you access to the 601 registers, displays native instructions, and lets you debug a native program. It's appropriately named The Debugger and is written by Steve Jasik of Jasik Designs. Because it's a low-level debugger, The Debugger can be used to debug stand-alone code such as Extensions. For a low-level debugger, it sports some sophisticated high-level debugger features, including windows and menus.

Background Info

How does The Debugger provide a high-level system interface? The Debugger copies the required system resources into a private area owned by it. This enables The Debugger to provide high-level debugger services, yet still continue to function when the operating system gets mangled by a program bug.

For a 68K program, The Debugger automatically reads the .SYM files that CodeWarrior made for the application and provides a source code display (see figure 7.15). The Sigma symbols ($\sum$) to the left of the source code indicate executable statements. If you highlight a statement and type Command-B, a small bullet symbol appears that indicates a breakpoint has been set. You can mark either C source statements or 68K instructions with breakpoints. By holding down the Command key and clicking on the source window, you can toggle the view between C source code, and C source interspersed with 68K machine code instructions. You can single-step through the program as either 68K assembly or C source code, viewing the processor registers, and the stack. The one feature lacking is a ready view of variable names and their values.

On the Power Mac, you can view source code and PowerPC machine code instructions. You can view the 601 processor registers and set breakpoints. A "training wheels" feature attaches comments beside each instruction to assist you in learning the PowerPC machine code (see figure 7.16).

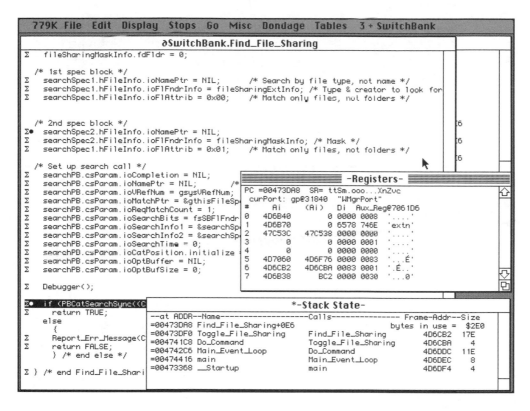

Figure 7.15 *The Debugger displaying a 68K program as source code; the bullet symbols mark breakpoints*

On either a 68K Macintosh or a Power Mac, you can activate a continuous step mode in The Debugger, and watch it run through the program. The stack and register displays are automatically updated. Pressing Command-period stops the continuous trace.

Because The Debugger can use Metrowerks CodeWarrior symbol files, this makes it a valuable companion to MW Debug. However, because both MW Debug and The Debugger use PPCTraceEnabler, you can't use MW Debug while The Debugger is present. However, you can use the two programs in concert to track down a bug. The Debugger typically displays a dialog box at boot time that asks whether or not to install the program. For a first-time debug run on your program, say no to the installation and use MW Debug to find the problem area. Reboot the Mac, and this time let The Debugger install. Don't use MW Debug this time: instead, launch the program and type Option-\ to bring up The Debugger. Now set your breakpoints or single-step through the program.

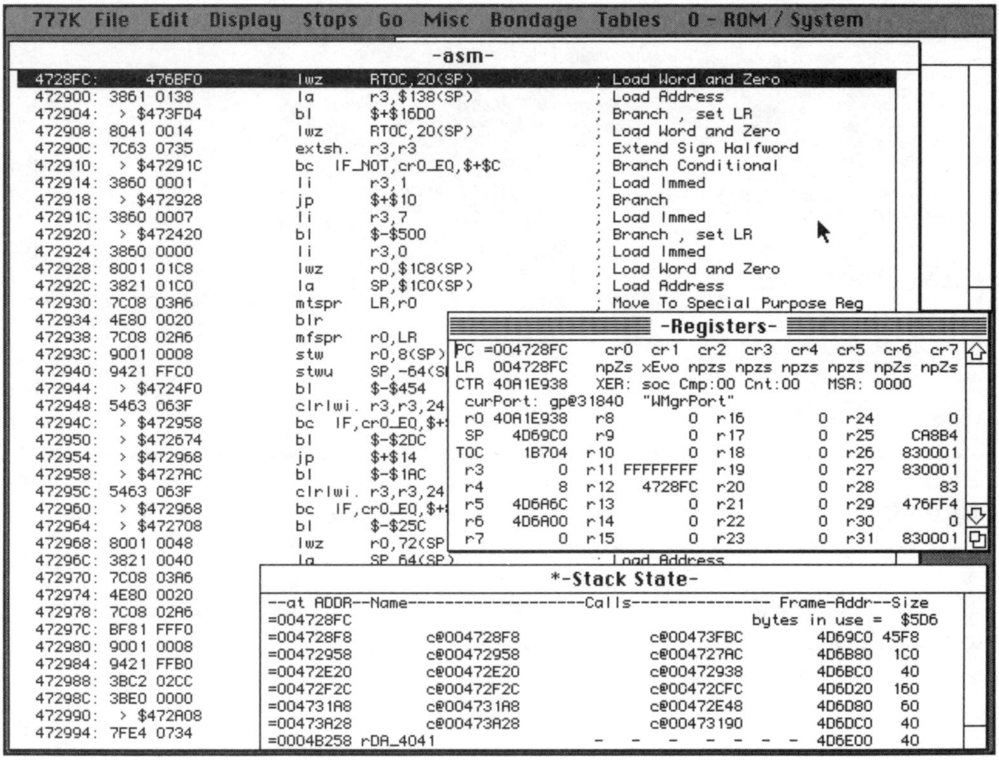

Figure 7.16   *The Debugger displaying a 601 program as machine code*

Debugging Techniques

To the uninitiated, the debugging process might seem arcane, but essentially what it amounts to is gathering information or clues. You observe the program's behavior carefully up to the moment it crashes, taking note of what events trigger the crash. The debugging tools mentioned here serve an important purpose—they help you prod the remains for additional information, or let you take the program for a tightly controlled stroll over the brink.

This information allows you to determine two things, where the program crashed, and why that particular statement caused the crash. It might seem that all you really need to know is where the program crashed, but sometimes that's not the complete picture. After all, a `for` loop that reads control values out of an array is going to work flawlessy—up until a logic error has the loop read past the end of the array.

There's no exact formula or procedure that you can follow to track down and fix program bugs. Debugging techniques vary on case-by-case situation since each program is unique. The best technique to minimize program bugs is to code defensively, especially in the user interface code. Remember that the user might perform actions in any sequence. Also, initialize the program with a set of reasonable defaults, since the user might not explore that portion of program where the values of key variables get set. From my own experience writing shareware, it's definitely worth having outside testers try out the program in the early phases. Their efforts invariably point out holes in the interface code. Keep an open mind to the testers' critiques of the program. They often make worthwhile suggestions that can streamline the interface, which in turn results in simpler and more solid interface code.

I mentioned this rule earlier in the book when we wrote our first program, but it's worth repeating: *Always check for errors.* Many Toolbox routines return a value that indicates whether or not the request completed successfully. In case of a failure, the value returned often indicates what condition caused the error, such as the program ran out of memory, or the disk is full. Note that the status of calls to the Resource Manager are returned by the function `ResError()`, and that you can obtain the status of some QuickDraw calls using `QDError()`. One of the first functions I add to a new program is `Report_Error()`, so that it can trap any major errors I make when calling unfamiliar Toolbox routines.

I realize it's difficult trying to code for all the possibilities. For example, the apparently simple act of saving a file to disk involves an army of safety checks. You have to see if a file of the same name exists, ask to overwrite the existing file or not, see if there's enough room on the volume to save the data, and then constantly monitor the file I/O routines during the save operation. Use MW Debug to modify the results of Toolbox calls so that your error handling code gets thoroughly tested. The benefits from such an effort are a reliable program and robust code that can be reused in future projects.

Of course, if you're doing a quick and dirty in-house program hack, such as the Klepto application, then you needn't be as exhaustive monitoring the results of the Toolbox routines. Nevertheless, you'll notice that even Klepto performs some safety checks. A lot of Klepto's file setup code came out of the SonOMunger program, and I just replaced the `Munge_File()` function with `Move_Fork()`. This let me knock out a solid and reliable utility program in a short time. However, if you're writing code that you expect other folks to use, do them a favor and do all the safety checking. They might not like getting warning or error messages, but users have no patience at all with a program that bombs.

A Bug Taxonomy

There are countless categories and types of bugs. Here I would like to discuss three particular bugs that can be divided into several broad categories. First there are the logic bugs, which are flaws in the algorithms and plague programmers no matter what platform they're working on. Second is where the Toolbox is called improperly, which either crashes the Mac quickly, or creates hidden damage to the operating system so that trouble rears its ugly head hundreds of instructions later. Finally, there are those bugs that manifest themselves because of side effects that occur in the Mac run-time environment. I will provide some general guidelines for each.

Logic bugs can sometimes be found without resorting to debuggers. A "code walkthrough," where you explain the operation of the program to a coworker or friend often uncovers gaps or flaws in a program's logic. Also, sit down with a program listing and some paper, and step through the listing line by line, jotting down the values of variables as you manually evaluate each statement. This process, though tedious, can spot some problems. It's also valuable in making you really look at the code, rather than skimming through it with a program editor.

During the program's development phase, add code that does limit checks on arrays and other program resources. The overhead of this type of code slows the program, but it will pay for itself when it snares a bug or two while the program is taking form. Limit checks also help in those situations where you're trying to integrate portions of the application that were written by different programmers. Bracket the limit check code with conditional compilation statements so that it can be quickly eliminated during the final build of the shipping application.

Finally, use CodeWarrior's compiler to help eliminate logic bugs caused by typos, such as the `if` statement that uses a single equals sign for the comparision. Check the Extended Error Checking item in the Language preferences panel so that the compiler looks for this type of error and other syntax problems. Don't hesistate to use MW Debug to step through the code and see what's going on. If you've already done a code walkthrough and have some values you can reference, then MW Debug's Locals Pane can uncover a problem quickly.

The next category of bug occurs when you call the Macintosh Toolbox routines improperly. If you're lucky (and usually are), such mistakes take out the Mac fast. You might think that making this sort of goof would be difficult, given the copious documentation on the Toolbox routines. However, such errors do have a way of sneaking up on you.

One type of improper Toolbox usage is calling a routine with arguments that are the wrong size (say, passing a `long` where a `short` was expected). For performance reasons, the Toolbox routines don't perform any argument checks. On the 68K Mac, where the arguments are usually passed on the stack, pushing the wrong-sized argument mangles the stack. The Mac dies when the routine attempts to return and first pops a proper-sized argument value off the stack, which skews the return address. 68K Macs seize up solid on this type of mistake.

Part of this problem stems from the ambiguity in the size of an integer variable. Depending upon the development tools you use and their settings, an `int` could be 16 or 32 bits in size. My recommendation: Remove `int` from your C vocabulary. Declare variables as `short` or `long` instead. Most debuggers, such as The Debugger provide a built-in function called Discipline, which performs on-the-fly size checking on any routine your application calls.

This type of problem shouldn't occur as often on the Power Macintosh for a number of reasons. As you saw in chapter 5, Toolbox arguments get stuffed into PowerPC registers rather than pushed on the stack, so a wrong-sized argument isn't as lethal as it would be on the 68K architecture, although it's possible to hose the 68LC040 emulator this way. Finally, the ANSI C requirement for Power Mac software reduces this problem because of function prototypes. The header files for all of the Toolbox routines contain function prototypes, and so an argument mismatch in your code is quickly recognized and flagged by the compiler. If you haven't yet checked the Require Function Prototypes item in the Language preferences panel, do yourself a favor and set it now.

Another type of Toolbox usage error is where you simply don't supply all the information the routine requires. Guess what happens when that routine uses random data as a source of information? This sort of mistake crops up on those Toolbox routines that use selectors or parameter blocks to pass information.

Background Info

Routines that have selectors operate as follows: they use a single trap word that acts as the entry point into a package of related system services. The selector is a value passed to the routine that specifies the desired service in the package to use. Toolbox routines that fall into this group belong to the Standard File, Alias, Sound, List, Process, Apple Events, Slot, and File Manager. Sometimes it appears that a routine doesn't use a parameter block or selector, such as in the case of the Apple Event and File I/O routines we used in the chapters 4 and 6. However, if you dissect the header files, and pay close attention to what the in-line 68K assembly macros do, you'll see that these routines actually use selectors.

When you use such calls, pay close attention to what arguments the routine requires. I once spent an afternoon trying to figure out why the Slot Manager call `SNextTypeSRsrc()` in my program was reading video `sResources` from a second display board in a Mac II, rather than the one I wanted. (sResources are special code objects used in expansion board firmware, and are accessed like regular resources, using a name and ID number.) I eventually discovered that I wasn't supplying a value for an argument handling the sResource's ID, called spID. So SNextTypeSRsrc() looked for the next video resource, indexing off the large nonsense value left in spID. With relentless logic, SNextTypeSRsrc() dutifully went to the next slot with a video board in the Mac and found the next sResource for me. Adding a statement to zero spID fixed the bug.

Another gotcha lurks in the optional completion functions some Toolbox routines expect. Even if you don't use use an I/O completion function with the call to PBCatSearchSync() or similar Toolbox routines, place a value of NIL in the parameter block to make the fact perfectly clear to the Macintosh OS. Finally, some routines pass results back to you via a pointer to a buffer you provide. Not to single out PBCatSearchSync() here, but you'll recall this routine places the search results in a buffer we allocated for it. Be sure to set up this buffer, or else the routine will hammer at some random memory location with the data you requested.

The last type of bug is what I loosely term "side-effect" bugs. These occur because of side effects induced by certain Toolbox calls or the Mac OS. These bugs are hard to find, because there's nothing obviously wrong with the code. Also, the bug may only bite based upon the application's memory usage and the state of the operating system at certain times. One bug of this type is the memory leak. Certain Toolbox routines create copies of buffers that you're then expected to dispose of. If you don't, eventually the application's memory dries up. As an example of this, look again at the use of the AEGetParamDesc() or GetNewDialog(). Both allocate buffers that you must delete when you're finished using them. You might lump this sort of problem under the improper use of the Toolbox, but I make the distinction because you're not actually calling the routines improperly. The program won't crash, but it will eventually run out of memory. This can mislead you as to the real root of the problem. Again, this sort of bug can be avoided by a thorough understanding of what each Toolbox call does.

The other side effect issue is where a Toolbox call or the allocation of a buffer cause the Memory Manager to shuffle things around in memory. For example, if you're accessing a PICT resource (usually to display an image), trouble can occur if the image data gets moved. Here's code that shows how to update a PICT image in a window:

```
/* Globals */
WindowPtr        gBannerWindow;
PicHandle        gThePict;

/Locals */
Rect             thisFrame;
GrafPtr          oldPort;
WindowPtr        whichWindow;

main event loop code...

   case updateEvt:                          /* Update the window */
   whichWindow = (WindowPtr) myEvent.message;
   if (whichWindow == gBannerWindow)        /* It's the banner window */
      {
      BeginUpdate(whichWindow);             /* Start the update */
      GetPort(&oldPort);
      SetPort(whichWindow);
      if (gThePict != NIL)                  /* Do we have the image? */
         {
         thisFrame = (*gThePict)->picFrame; /* Get PICT's frame rect */
         DrawPicture(gThePict, &thisFrame); /* Display image */
         } /* end if */
      else
         {
         SysBeep(30);
         } /* end else */
      SetPort(oldPort);                     /* Restore port */
      EndUpdate(whichWindow);               /* Update completed */
      } /* end if == gBannerWindow */
   break;
```

This code works fine as long as the PICT resource **gThePict** stays put. However, if the image data gets relocated—perhaps because of a Toolbox call—the statement that uses a pointer to obtain the display rectangle out of gThePict is liable to pass junk masquerading as a `Rect` to `DrawPicture()`. We either have to use a handle to extract the rectangle information out of gThePict, or lock it in memory, like so:

```
/* Banner intialization code */
Rect            theFrame;
Handle          theLogo;

    (hasColor) ? (theLogo = GetNamedResource('PICT', "\pColor Banner"))
               : (theLogo = GetNamedResource('PICT', "\pB&W Banner"));
    if (ResError() == noErr)
        {
        gThePict = (PicHandle) theLogo;
        HLock((Handle) gThePict);
        theFrame = (*gThePict)->picFrame;
        SizeWindow(gBannerWindow, theFrame.right, theFrame.bottom, TRUE);
        } /* end if == noErr */
```

For 68K Macs, there are lists in *Inside Macintosh* of those Toolbox routines that move memory, and thus trigger these memory relocation problems described here. There are other less obvious interactions that Toolbox calls or the Mac OS can do to objects in memory. A good reference work on this subject for the 68K Macs is Scott Knaster's *How to Write Macintosh Software*.

It's still too early to see what new interactions and side effects the new Macintosh run-time architecture will bring to the party. However, I can offer one bit of advice here: If the Power Mac seizes up solid, you've got a function that you failed to provide a UPP for, or, you've mangled the routine descriptor that the UPP uses.

Debugging Miscellany

To close this chapter, I'll mention some facts that don't seem to fit anywhere else.

When testing fat trap code, you have to ensure that both sections of the trap get called. This is because the Mixed Mode Manager attempts to avoid an instruction set context switch whenever possible. In the case of

FlipDepth, the Power Mac's Event Manager is still emulated 68K code. Therefore, the Mixed Mode Manager always calls the 68K side of the fat trap. To test the PowerPC patches in FlipDepth, I had to compile a PowerPC-only version of the patches to guarantee that the native version of the patch gets called. For "FlipDepth.c," in the declarations area at the start of the file, locate the flag `DO_PPC_CODE_ONLY`. (There's a statement that undefines it located here.) Edit the statement to define `DO_PPC_CODE_ONLY`, and recompile the project with the PowerPC version of CodeWarrior. This ensures that only a PowerPC version of the routine descriptor is generated, and not a fat routine descriptor. As a example of this technique, here's the specific code from FlipDepth:

```
/*============================
   CreateFatDescriptorSys

   Creates a fat routine descriptor in the system heap.
============================*/
OSErr CreateFatDescriptorSys( void *mac68Code, void *ppcCode, ProcInfoType procInfo, UPP *result )
{
THz    oldZone;
OSErr err = noErr;

   oldZone = GetZone();         /* Save current zone */
   SetZone( SystemZone() );     /* Get us in the system heap */

   #ifndef DO_PPC_CODE_ONLY
   *result = NewFatRoutineDescriptor( mac68Code, ppcCode, procInfo );
   #else
   *result = NewRoutineDescriptor( ppcCode, procInfo, kPowerPCISA ); /* debugging only */
   #endif

   SetZone( oldZone );

   return ( *result ? noErr : memFullErr );
} /* end CreateFatDescriptorSys() */
```

It's possible to test the 68K portion of a fat binary application on a Power Mac. To do this, open the application with ResEdit and then open the cfrg resource. There will only be one, of ID 0. Select Get Resource Info from the

Resource menu, or type Command-I. When the Info box appears, change the ID number to something other than zero. Without a cfrg resource of ID 0, the operating system is fooled into thinking the application is a 68K application, and so it loads and executes the 68K CODE resources. To test the PowerPC side of the program, change the cfrg resource ID back to 0. Of course, you'll want to test the application on some real 68K Macs to eliminate timing and emulator side effects. Testing on a 68K Mac can help flush out some improper Toolbox usage bugs as well.

Occasionally you'll want a debugger to break into the execution of an application at certain points. To do this, there are specialized statements that you can add to the program code to cause an exception and invoke a high-level or low-level debugger. These statements are:

```
Debugger();                 /* Trigger the debugger */
DebugStr("\perror msg");    /* Trigger debugger, display error message */

Debugger68K();              /* Trigger 68K debugger */
DebugStr68K("\perror msg"); /* Trigger 68K debugger, show error message */

SysBreak();                 /* Break into high-level debugger */
SysBreakStr("\perror msg"); /* Break into debugger with message */
```

The **Debugger()** statement typically invokes a low-level debugger on both Power Macs and 68K Macs. **DebugStr()** accomplishes the same end, but also presents a message string when the debugger kicks in. The message can inform you which **DebugStr()** statement out of several was executed. **Debugger68k()** and **DebugStr68K()** operate similarly, but invoke a 68K debugger such as Macsbug, even if a native PowerPC debugger is present. **SysBreak()** and **SysBreakStr()** act as breakpoints that transfer execution from the test program to a high-level debugger. However, be aware that the implementation of these statements varies. On a 68K Mac, **SysBreak()** and **SysBreakStr()** switch control back to MW Debug if it is running. On a Power Mac, the **Debugger()** statements swap execution from the program to MW Debug. This behavior is consistent with Apple's own source debugger tool, SourceBug. If MW Debug isn't running, then a native debugger such as The Debugger takes control.

Get to know AppleScript. It can help you set up test events for debugging high-level event handlers. It's also useful for writing scripts to automate parts of the development cycle.

Finally, there are a couple of shareware/freeware utilities that can expedite the debugging process. MacErrors, by Marty Wachter and Phil Kearney, is a small application that translates those cryptic error codes into an readable explanation. If a File Manager routine reports a -43, you type this value into MacErrors and press Return. MacErrors explains that the error number means "file not found; folder not found." This message should pinpoint the trouble to that part of your file I/O code that handles a FSSpec or related data structure.

Sometimes, you just want to break into the debugger immediately as the program runs. Paul Mercer's Programmer's Key is an Extension that, when you press the Command key and Power key simultaneously, it generates an exception that drops you into the debugger.

Enough Debugging

In this chapter, you've received an overview of the types of debuggers. We've looked at two PowerPC debuggers for testing your native applications and we've talked about the various types of bugs. So be careful as you are writing your code and you'll eliminate much of the debugging task. Proper use of the available debugging tools will minimize the job of finding and eliminating those pesky bugs that do sneak in.

Finally, our journey is at an end. I've provided a few tips that should help you get started in Power Macintosh programming. Currently, the Power Mac has only been on the market for several months and technical information on them is sparse. As the number of Power Macs grows, so will the body of information on programming and debugging techniques. Until then, I hope this book provides valuable programming information in these initial days of the Power Mac.

The PowerPC RISC Processor Family

Power Macintoshes are based on the PowerPC 601, the first member in a new line of RISC microprocessors jointly developed by Apple, IBM, and Motorola. The PowerPC processor family is designed to be a low-cost processor architecture that supports a wide range of applications from embedded applications (such as in automobiles) to hand-held Personal Digital Assistants (PDAs), to desktop computers. It accomplishes this by providing high performance processing, while portions of the processor's design are tailored for the target application. For example, a PowerPC fabricated for a desktop computer might have a large cache, while a PDA version might reduce the cache size and eliminate multiprocessing features to

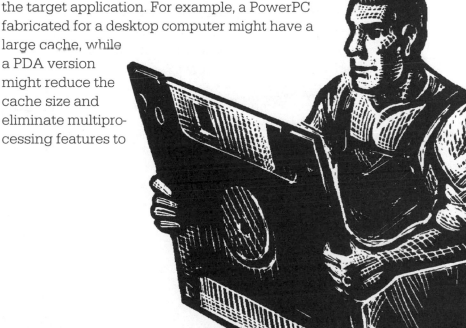

minimize power consumption. Currently, there are two members in the PowerPC family, with two more in the design stage. The previously mentioned PowerPC 601 targets mid-range desktop computers, such as Apple's Power Macs and IBM's forthcoming Power Personal desktop systems. The PowerPC 603 is a low-power implementation of the PowerPC processor that's optimized for use in notebook and sub-notebook computers and low-end desktop systems.

Several aspects of the PowerPC design allow it to achieve the diametrically opposed goals of high performance and low cost. First, the RISC design itself facilitates high instruction throughput. By using basic, fixed-length instructions, RISC processors have a simple hardware instruction decoder that can dispatch instructions in one clock cycle. This differs from the Complex Instruction Set Computing (CISC) processor, whose decoder is more complex and requires several clock cycles to read in variable-length instructions and dispatch them. By dispatch, we mean that the decoder passes the translated instruction on to the appropriate sections of the processor for execution. These sections, which are organized around the instruction's purpose (such as integer math, floating-point math, and program branches), are called execution units. Note that while it takes only one clock cycle to dispatch an instruction, it might take one or more clock cycles for the instruction to actually execute.

The RISC design also uses pipelining to improve instruction throughput. A pipeline is where the instruction's execution is broken into several stages inside the execution unit. To illustrate this, suppose the decoder dispatches the translated instruction to the pipeline in, say, a floating-point execution unit. Each stage in the floating-point unit's pipeline handles a portion of the instruction's execution. For example, the first stage of the floating-point pipeline might obtain the first number from a register, the second stage would obtain the second number from another register, the third stage would perform the calculation, and the fourth stage would write the result into a register. Pipelines improve throughput by processing several instructions at once, where each instruction is at a different stage of execution in a different section of the pipeline. As long as the various pipelines are kept filled, instruction processing occurs at a constant rate. Under ideal conditions when the processor's on-chip cache keeps the pipelines full, one instruction completes execution for every tick of the processor clock.

The PowerPC processor architecture levers off the pipeline concept by using multiple execution units. Furthermore, the instruction set was carefully designed so that most instructions don't overlap, or depend, on other instructions. This way a floating-point unit can work concurrently on its floating-point instructions as an integer unit works on its set of instructions.

To reduce design costs, the PowerPC architecture was based on IBM's POWER (Performance Optimization With Enhanced RISC) 64-bit architecture. This decision gave the PowerPC designers a ready-made instruction set and RISC processor core for the chip. Where the PowerPC architecture differs from POWER's is its support for multiple processors and single-precision (32-bit) floating-point instructions. (POWER's 64-bit floating-point instructions are also supported.) The PowerPC 601 implements most POWER instructions (certain complex or nonscalable POWER instructions were deleted), and thus a host of IBM software development tools were immediately available to write PowerPC software.

Another cost reduction was that the initial PowerPC processor bus is based on the bus of the Motorola's 88110 RISC processor. This bus has high throughput and also supports multiprocessing. This decision provided another ready-made portion of the PowerPC design.

Expect future versions of the PowerPC processor to be faster. They'll do this using new aggressive process methodologies, higher clock rates, larger pipelines, and more execution units. They will also use a different bus and possibly support fewer of the POWER instructions. For now, let's look at the current members of the PowerPC family.

PowerPC 601

The PowerPC 601 packs 2.8 million transistors onto a die that's 132 mm^2. It's fabricated using a 3.6 volt, 0.65-micron four-metal layer CMOS process in IBM's microprocessor foundry in Burlington, Vermont. Early versions of the 601 operate at clock speeds from 50 MHz to 80 MHz. At 66 MHz, the 601 dissipates 9 watts of power, peak. A new 100 MHz version of the 601 uses a 0.5-micron process that reduces the die to 74 mm^2 and lowers power consumption to 4 watts.

The 601 is a 32-bit implementation of the 64-bit PowerPC architecture. It has a 32-bit address bus that can access 4G of physical memory. A built-in Memory Management Unit (MMU) supports 52-bit virtual addresses. The 601 supports 64-bit data and has a 64-bit data bus. It has a massive 32K on-chip unified cache. The term unified means that both data and code occupy the cache. Additional buffers and arbitration logic are required to keep both data and code moving in and out of the cache. Three independent execution units (integer, floating-point, and branch unit) allow up to three different types of instructions to execute at once on the 601.

The 601 can be viewed as a bridge chip for moving from the POWER architecture to the PowerPC architecture. For IBM, POWER workstation applications can be migrated quickly to PowerPC systems, although future PowerPC desktop systems will support other operating systems such as OS/2. It is also a bridge for Apple's shift from CISC to RISC computing. It supplies formidable processing power, enough to operate the 68LC040 emulator that makes much of the Power Mac's system software possible.

PowerPC 603

The PowerPC 603 is the 601's low-power sibling. It uses a 3.3 volt, 0.5-micron four-metal-layer static CMOS technology to place 1.6 million transistors on a die 85.1 mm^2. At 3.3 volts and 80 MHz, the 603 dissipates 3 watts, peak. The 603 is manufactured at IBM's Burlington facililty and Motorola's MOS-11 plant.

Like the 601, the 603 is a 32-bit version of the PowerPC architecture, with a 32-bit address bus and 64-bit data bus. The 603 also uses the same pipelined architecture and thus is able to dispatch three instructions at a time.

The 603 differs from the 601 in several ways. First, it uses a Harvard architecture, where data and code are treated separately. It has two independent 8K caches—one for code and one for data—each with its own MMU. The smaller cache size is offset by the reduced complexity of the circuitry required to manage the caches. The arbitration logic needed to manage the 601's unified cache is gone, and the temporary buffers are smaller. The net result is that the 603 musters nearly the same performance as the 601 while using fewer transistors. Also, because the 603 is expected to be used in small, portable systems, the multiprocessor support has been stripped from the design.

Next, the 603 has five, rather than three execution units. It's important to note that these two extra units provide support functions to manage the energy saving features and data transfer rather than execute instructions. It still has the same integer, floating-point, and branch units. The first new execution unit is a load/store execution unit that manages data transfers between the data cache and various registers. It executes the load and store instructions, thus freeing the integer unit of the burden of computing effective addresses. The other execution unit is a system register unit that handles the power-saving functions in the 603.

The 603 uses static logic, so the contents of registers and the caches are preserved even when the clock to the processor is stopped to conserve power. The 603 provides three different power-saving modes that implement different levels of energy consumption. These modes are under software control. Dynamic power management logic switches off idle subsystems or execution units. The power management logic watches the instruction stream and powers up an idle unit—say, the branch unit—on an incoming branch instruction.

Finally, the 603 has a phased lock loop (PLL) clock multiplier circuit. This enables the 603 to operate reliably even though the system clock might be slowed to reduce a notebook computer's overall power consumption. Also, it acts as a multiplier so that the processor can operate at 66 MHz internally, while the rest of the system runs at 33 MHz.

The 603's low power consumption, combined with its near 601 performance, makes it suitable for notebook and PDA designs. Because it is code compatible with the 601, applications written for Power Macs or Power Personal systems should run on these low-power systems with little or no modifications.

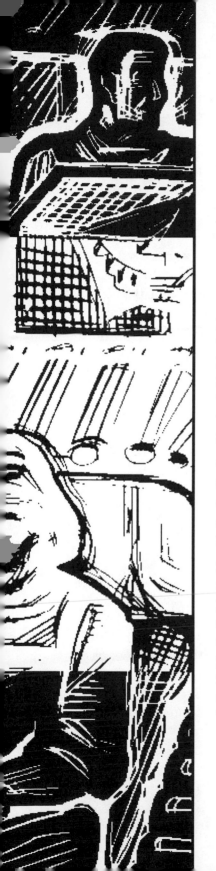

Porting to the Power Mac

In this book, we've looked at how to write a Macintosh application so that the C code compiles and runs on both 68K-based Macs and Power Macs. This is fine if you're starting a program from scratch. Of course, the luxury of writing programs this way doesn't exist for those vendors with software already on the market. For these folks, the real issue becomes: How hard is it to port existing Mac code to a Power Macintosh?

Overall, porting working Mac C code isn't difficult. There will be some problem areas for certain types of applications. This appendix covers those details.

The program's code should be ANSI C compliant. This is because the PowerPC compilers originated from ANSI C compilers. However, the ANSI C function prototyping is an asset here, because it can flag problems with improperly written calls to functions or Toolbox routines.

Some portions of the program might rely on certain compiler dependencies to operate. Obviously such program elements should be removed. One such dependency is the size of the `int` variable, which can be 16 or 32 bits, depending upon a compiler's settings. Eliminate `int` variables from your source code and explicitly declare them as `short` or `long`. If you've ported the code from another platform, most of these dependencies have probably been eliminated. The name `powerc` is defined for use in conditional compilation.

The application code must be well-behaved. That is, it only accesses the hardware through the Toolbox, not by hammering at certain addresses. Also, it must be 32-bit clean. The various hardware configurations that make up the Mac line should have discouraged the former, and retooling an application to work with System 7 should have taken care of the latter.

The use of low memory globals is strongly discouraged. To this end, the "SysEqu.h" header file has been eliminated. In its place you should use the header file "LowMem.h." While direct accesses to these areas of memory are still supported for the moment, you should start using the "accessor functions" in "LowMem.h" to obtain these values. For example, instead of obtaining the value of A5 from the global `CurrentA5` (address 0x904), use the function `LMGetCurrentA5()` and let the Power Mac OS return a value for you.

Forget about using segments. They're not necessary for the PowerPC runtime environment. The `#pragma segment` directive is ignored by most PowerPC compilers.

If you use callback or completion routines, such as those used in the high-level event handlers, custom window controls, or an event filter function in a dialog box, you'll need to build a UPP for the function. This enables the Mixed Mode Manager to deal appropriately with your code when it's called by the Macintosh OS. Basically, if the function is accessed using a ProcPtr, it better have UPP set up for it. Fortunately, the PowerPC header files provide macros that handle most of these details for you. Search for functions prefaced with "New" or "Call" in the header files that you use with the program. If you're writing a custom PowerPC plug-in module to enhance a 68K application (as Adobe did with Photoshop 2.5), you'll have to write the

UPPs yourself. See chapter 6 for details. If you're writing a PowerPC plug-in module for a PowerPC application, then you can use PowerPC procedure pointers and avoid the overhead of a mode switch or using UPPs.

If you're passing data structures to the Toolbox, remember that it's mostly emulated 68K code and so you have to word-align the data for it. Use the compiler declaration `#pragma options align=mac68k` to achieve this. Don't forget to use `#pragma options align=reset` after such structures to provide optimal PowerPC data alignment. If the program and its data is expected to run on 68K Macs as well as Power Macs, you'll need to enforce word-alignment throughout the program. This is also true if you expect to exchange files with 68K Macs.

If your program makes heavy use of floating-point math you'll have to make some modifications. The `extended` 80- or 96-bit values, and the 64-bit `comp` used by SANE are not supported in the PowerPC hardware. For compatibility, the PowerPC SANE implementation supports these data types in emulation. To obtain fastest processing, you'll want to rewrite the code to support the processor's native 32- or 64-bit values. These data types are declared `float` or `double`, respectively. A 128-bit `long double` type is supported, but only in software, not in the hardware. Discontinue use of the "sane.h" and "math.h" header files. Instead, use the functions provided in the header file "fp.h," which provides data conversions and transcendental math functions. These functions follow the Floating-Point C Extensions (FPCE) specification, which defines support for IEEE 754/854 floating-point math. As a developing standard, this should enable the program to be ported to other platforms. The "fpenv.h" header file provides functions used to set the floating-point environment. Note: Metrowerks predefines the name `__ieeedoubles__`. If it is defined (set to 1), the CodeWarrior compiler generates PowerPC 32- and 64-bit values for `float` and `double`. If this name is not defined, the compiler generates 80- and 96-bit values that SANE routines use. This allows the same code to be supported on 68K Macs and Power Macs, but you might have to rework the code anyway to compensate for the loss in precision.

Be aware that if you've fine tuned the application's processing around the 68K environment, you might need to do some readjustments for the

PowerPC. The Power Macs use a new Memory Manager that's been optimized for a RISC processor; it might have an impact on a program that's adapted for the old Memory Manager. Likewise, calling some Toolbox routines can create an ISA context switch. Be careful of making Toolbox calls in tight loops. If the loop isn't running as fast as expected, a mode switch is probably occurring.

The `pascal` keyword is ignored by PowerPC compilers. This keyword was used to reorder how a C function's arguments get passed to the target function. It's primarily used when calling Toolbox functions whose interface was based on the Pascal programming language. This isn't a big issue, since C calling conventions are the norm for the Power Mac software, and the Mixed Mode Manager sorts the rest out for you. However, be aware that Pascal automatically passes arguments larger than 4 bytes by reference, and you'll have to declare such arguments as pointers in C.

Avoid patching traps if you can help it. The Power Macintosh's new run-time architecture allows the ready enhancement of applications and other code fragments without resorting to trap patches. If you must patch, take into consideration what the code is doing, versus the overhead of the Mode switch. Write a fat patch if necessary.

Program Listings

Chapter 3

munger.c

```c
#include <stdio.h>

#define CR 0x0D
#define LF 0x0A

FILE *istream, *ostream;

void main(void)
{
short   crflag;
long    icount, ocount;
char    ifile[64], ofile[64];                    /* Path
➥names must be 64 chars or less */
int     nextbyte;
```

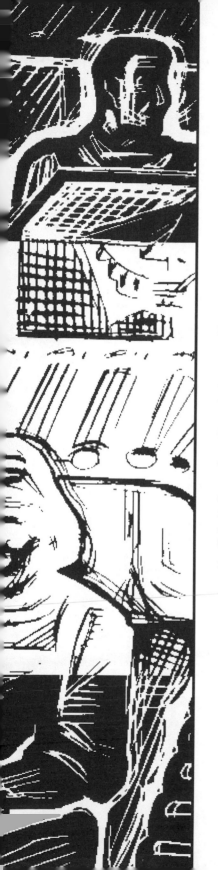

```
        printf ("Enter input file: ");
        gets (ifile);
        if ((istream = fopen(ifile, "rb")) == NULL)    /* Open the file OK? */
                {
                printf ("\nError opening input\n");     /* NO, say so */
                return;                                 /* Bail out */
                } /* end if */

        printf ("Enter output file: ");
        gets(ofile);
        if ((ostream = fopen(ofile, "wb")) == NULL)     /* Can we write an output file */
                {
                fclose (istream);                       /* NO. First close input file */
                printf ("\nError opening output\n");    /*   then warn, and bail out */
                return;
                } /* end if */

        icount = 0L;                                    /* Set counters */
        ocount = 0L;
        crflag = 0;

        while((nextbyte = fgetc(istream)) != EOF)       /* Read char.s until end of file */
                {
                icount++;                               /* Bump input char counter */
                switch (nextbyte)                       /* What char was read? */
                        {
                        case CR:
                        if (crflag >= 1)                /* Two in a row, end of paragraph */
                                {
                                fputc(nextbyte, ostream); /* Write two CRs to the output */
                                fputc(nextbyte, ostream);
                                crflag = 0;             /* Reset the flag */
                                ocount++;
                                } /* end if */
                        else
                                crflag++;               /* Bump the flag, and toss the CR */
                        break;
                        case LF:                        /* Toss LF, but don't touch crflag */
                        break;
                        default:
                                fputc(nextbyte, ostream); /* All other char.s get written */
                                ocount++;
                                crflag = 0;             /* Clear the flag */
                        } /* end switch */
                } /* end while */
```

```
fclose (istream);                                    /* Clean up */
fclose (ostream);
printf("Bytes read:    %ld\n", icount);
printf("Bytes written: %ld\n", ocount);
} /* end main() */
```

process.c

```
#include <processes.h>
#include <memory.h>
#include <strings.h>
#include <stdio.h>


void main (void)
{
register int          i;
ProcessInfoRec        thisProcess;
ProcessSerialNumber   process;
FSSpec                thisFileSpec;
unsigned char         typeBuffer[5] = {0};
unsigned char         signatureBuffer[5] = {0};

thisProcess.processAppSpec = &thisFileSpec;              /* Aim pointer at our storage */
thisProcess.processInfoLength = sizeof(ProcessInfoRec);  /* Store record size */
thisProcess.processName = (unsigned char *) NewPtr(32);  /* Allocate room for the name */
process.highLongOfPSN = kNoProcess;                      /* Clear process serial number */
process.lowLongOfPSN = kNoProcess;

while (GetNextProcess(&process) == noErr)                /* Loop until all processes found */
    {
    if (GetProcessInformation(&process, &thisProcess) == noErr) /* Obtain detailed info */
        {
        for (i = 0; i <= 3; i++)            /* Copy type & sig info into string buffers */
            {
            typeBuffer[i] = ((char *) &thisProcess.processType)[i];
            signatureBuffer[i] = ((char *) &thisProcess.processSignature)[i];
            } /* end for */
        printf ("Process SN: %ld, %ld, Type: %s, Signature: %s, Name: ",
            thisProcess.processNumber.highLongOfPSN,
            thisProcess.processNumber.lowLongOfPSN,
            typeBuffer,
            signatureBuffer);
        printf (" %s \n", P2CStr(thisProcess.processName));    /* Print the name */
        } /* end if */
```

```
      } /* end while */
} /* end main() */
```

Chapter 4

hello1.c

```c
#include <Types.h>
#include <QuickDraw.h>
#include <Fonts.h>
#include <Windows.h>
#include <Memory.h>
#include <Events.h>
#include <OSUtils.h>


#define TRUE         true
#define FALSE        false


#define NIL          0L
#define IN_FRONT     (-1)
#define IS_VISIBLE   TRUE
#define NO_CLOSE_BOX FALSE


void main(void)
{
WindowPtr   thisWindow;
Rect        windowRect;

/* Lunge after all the memory we can get */
   MaxApplZone();
   MoreMasters();
   MoreMasters();

/* Initialize the various Managers */
   InitGraf(&qd.thePort);
   InitFonts();
   FlushEvents(everyEvent, 0);
   InitWindows();

/* Set up the window */
   windowRect.top = windowRect.left = 40;
   windowRect.bottom = 200;
   windowRect.right = 300;
```

```
    if ((thisWindow = NewWindow(NIL, &windowRect,
        "\pHello world", IS_VISIBLE, documentProc,
        (WindowPtr) IN_FRONT, NO_CLOSE_BOX, NIL)) != NIL)
        {
        SetPort(thisWindow); /* Make window current drawing port */
        MoveTo (20, 20);
        DrawString("\pHello world");
        InitCursor();

        while (!Button())    /* Wait until mouse button clicked */
            ;

        DisposeWindow(thisWindow);
        } /* end if */
    else
        SysBeep(30);

} /* end main() */
```

macmunger.c

```
#include <Types.h>
#include <QuickDraw.h>
#include <Windows.h>
#include <Fonts.h>
#include <Controls.h>
#include <Dialogs.h>
#include <Menus.h>
#include <Devices.h>
#include <Memory.h>
#include <Events.h>
#include <Desk.h>
#include <OSEvents.h>
#include <OSUtils.h>
#include <ToolUtils.h>
#include <TextUtils.h>
#include <StandardFile.h>
#include <Errors.h>
#include <Resources.h>
#include <DiskInit.h>

/* Resource ID numbers */
#define LAST_MENU       3    /* Number of menus */
```

```
#define APPLE_MENU      128  /* Menu ID for Apple menu */
#define FILE_MENU       129  /* Menu ID for File menu */
#define EDIT_MENU       130  /* Menu ID for Edit menu */
#define RESOURCE_ID     127  /* Starting index into the menu array */


#define ABOUT_BOX       1    /* About box menu item # in Apple menu */


#define OPEN_FILE       1    /* Open item # in File menu */
/*----------------------*/   /* Separator line is item # 2 */
#define I_QUIT          3    /* Quit item # in File menu */


#define ABOUT_BOX_ID    128  /* Resource IDs for our windows & dialogs */
#define STATUS_BOX_ID   129
#define ERROR_BOX_ID    130


/* Various constants */
#define NIL             0L
#define FALSE           false
#define TRUE            true


#define INIT_X          112  /* Coords for disk init dialog box */
#define INIT_Y          80


#define APPEND_MENU     0
#define CHAR_CODE_MASK  255
#define IN_FRONT        -1
#define NO_CURSOR       0L
#define ONE_FILE_TYPE   1
#define LONG_NAP        60L


#define CR              0x0D
#define LF              0x0A
/* Function prototypes */
Boolean Do_Command (long mResult);
Boolean Init_Mac(void);
void Main_Event_Loop(void);
void Report_Error(OSErr errorCode);

/* Application-specific functions */
void Ask_File(void);
void Munge_File(short input, short output, unsigned char *fileName);
```

```c
/* Globals */
MenuHandle  gmyMenus[LAST_MENU+1];   /* Handle to our menus */
EventRecord gmyEvent;                /* Holds event returned by OS */
WindowPtr   geventWindow;            /* Our private window */
Boolean     guserDone;               /* Indicates user wants to quit */
CursHandle  gtheCursor;              /* Current pointer icon */
short       gwindowCode;
WindowPtr   gwhichWindow;            /* The window that got an event */

OSType      gfileCreator = {'MUNG'}; /* Output file's creator */
OSType      gfileType = {'TEXT'};    /* Output file's type */
void Report_Error(OSErr errorCode)
{
unsigned char errNumString[8];

   NumToString((long) errorCode, errNumString);
   ParamText(errNumString, NIL, NIL, NIL);
   StopAlert(ERROR_BOX_ID, NIL);
} /* end Report_Error() */

void Munge_File(short input, short output, unsigned char *fileName)
{
long          amount;
unsigned char buffer;
short         crflag;
long          icount, ocount;
unsigned char inNumString[12], outNumString[12];
DialogPtr     statusDialog;

   amount = 1L;
   crflag = 0;
   icount = 0;
   ocount = 0;
   while (FSRead(input, &amount, &buffer) == noErr)
      {
      icount++;                      /* Bump input char counter */
      switch (buffer)                /* What char was read? */
         {
         case CR:
            if (crflag >= 1)         /* Two in a row, end of paragraph */
               {
               FSWrite(output, &amount, &buffer);  /* Write two CRs */
               FSWrite(output, &amount, &buffer);
```

```
              crflag = 0;                          /* Reset the flag */
              ocount++;
              } /* end if */
          else
              crflag++;                            /* Bump the flag, and toss the CR */
        break;  /* end case CR */
        case LF:                                   /* Toss LF, but don't touch crflag */
        break;  /* end case LF */
        default:
            FSWrite(output, &amount, &buffer);
            ocount++;
            crflag = 0;                            /* Clear the flag */
        } /* end switch */
    } /* end while */

/* Display processing statistics */
   if ((statusDialog = GetNewDialog(STATUS_BOX_ID, NIL,
                             (WindowPtr) IN_FRONT)) != NIL)

    {
    NumToString(icount, inNumString);   /* Convert bytes read to string */
    NumToString(ocount, outNumString);
    ParamText (fileName, inNumString, outNumString, NIL);
    DrawDialog(statusDialog);
    Delay (120L, NIL);
    DisposDialog(statusDialog);
    } /* end if != NIL */
   else
    SysBeep(30);


} /* end Munge_file() */

void Ask_File(void)
{
unsigned char    fileName[14] = {"\pMunge.out"};
short            inFileRefNum, outFileRefNum;
OSErr            fileError;
short            oldVol;
SFTypeList       textType = {'TEXT'};


StandardFileReply inputReply, outputReply;

/* Open the input file */
   StandardGetFile(NIL, ONE_FILE_TYPE, textType, &inputReply);
```

```c
    if (inputReply.sfGood)
      {
      GetVol (NIL, &oldVol);              /* Save current volume */
      if ((fileError = FSpOpenDF (&inputReply.sfFile, fsCurPerm,
                               &inFileRefNum)) != noErr)
        {
        Report_Error(fileError);
        return;
        } /* end if error */

/* Open the output file */
      StandardPutFile ("\pSave text in:", fileName, &outputReply);
      if (outputReply.sfGood)
        {
        SetVol(NIL, outputReply.sfFile.vRefNum);
        fileError = FSpCreate(&outputReply.sfFile, gfileCreator, gfileType,
                            smSystemScript);
        switch(fileError)            /* Process result from File Manager */
          {
          case noErr:
          break;
          case dupFNErr:           /* File already exists, wipe it out */
             if ((fileError = FSpDelete(&outputReply.sfFile)) == noErr)
                {
                if ((fileError = FSpCreate(&outputReply.sfFile,
                                          gfileCreator, gfileType,
                                          smSystemScript)) != noErr)
                  {
                  Report_Error(fileError);
                  FSClose (inFileRefNum);
                  SetVol(NIL, oldVol);
                  return;
                  } /* end != noErr */
                } /* end if == noErr */
             else
                {
                Report_Error(fileError);
                FSClose (inFileRefNum);
                SetVol(NIL, oldVol);
                return;
                } /* end else */
           break;   /* end case dupFNErr */
```

```
                   default:                    /* Unknown error, try to abort cleanly */
                      Report_Error(fileError);
                      FSClose (inFileRefNum); /* Close the input file */
                      SetVol(NIL, oldVol);    /* Restore original volume */
                      return;
                   } /* end switch */

     /* Open data fork */
           if (!(FSpOpenDF (&outputReply.sfFile, fsCurPerm, &outFileRefNum)))
               {
               gtheCursor = GetCursor(watchCursor);   /* Change the cursor */
               SetCursor(&**gtheCursor);
               Munge_File (inFileRefNum, outFileRefNum, (unsigned char *)
                           inputReply.sfFile.name);
               FSClose (outFileRefNum);
               SetCursor(&qd.arrow);                   /* Restore the cursor */
               } /* end if !fileError */
           FlushVol (NIL, outputReply.sfFile.vRefNum);
           } /* end if outputReply.sfGood */
        FSClose (inFileRefNum);
        SetVol(NIL, oldVol);
        } /* end if inputReply.sfGood */


} /* end Ask_File() */
Boolean Do_Command (long mResult)
{
unsigned char   accName[255];
short           itemHit;
Boolean         quitApp;
short           refNum;
DialogPtr       theDialog;
short           theItem, theMenu;
GrafPtr         savePort;       /* place to stow current GrafPort when */
                                /*    Desk Accessory (DA) is activated */

    quitApp = FALSE;            /* Assume Quit not chosen */
    theMenu = HiWord(mResult); /* Extract the menu selected */
    theItem = LoWord(mResult); /* Get the item on the menu  */

    switch (theMenu)
       {
       case APPLE_MENU:
```

```
            if (theItem == ABOUT_BOX)              /* Describe ourself */
                {
                if ((theDialog = GetNewDialog(ABOUT_BOX_ID, NIL,
                                        (WindowPtr) IN_FRONT)) != NIL)
                    {
                    ModalDialog(NIL, &itemHit);
                    DisposDialog(theDialog);
                    } /* end if != NIL */
                else
                    SysBeep(30);
                } /* end if theItem == ABOUT_BOX */
            else                                    /* It's a DA */
                {
                GetPort(&savePort);                 /* Save port (if DA doesn't) */
                GetMenuItemText(gmyMenus[(APPLE_MENU - MENU_RESOURCE)],
                        theItem, accName);
                refNum = OpenDeskAcc(accName);   /* Start it */
                SetPort(savePort);                  /* Done, restore the port */
                }
            break; /* end APPLE_MENU case */

        case FILE_MENU:
            switch(theItem)
                {
                case OPEN_FILE:
                    Ask_File();                     /* Obtain file info & process */
                    break;
                case I_QUIT:                        /* User wants to stop */
                    quitApp = TRUE;
                    break;
                } /* end switch */
            break; /* end FILE_MENU case */

        case EDIT_MENU:                             /* Pass events to OS */
            SystemEdit(theItem - 1);
            break;
        default:
            break;
        } /* end switch */

    HiliteMenu(0);          /* Switch off highlighting on the menu just used */
    return quitApp;
} /* end Do_Command() */
```

```
void Main_Event_Loop(void)
{
Point    where;

    FlushEvents(everyEvent, 0);        /* Clear out left over events */
    guserDone = FALSE;

    do
        {
        if (WaitNextEvent(everyEvent, &gmyEvent, LONG_NAP, NO_CURSOR))
            {                          /* We have an event... */
            switch(gmyEvent.what)      /* Field each type of event */
                {
                case mouseDown:        /* In what window, and where?? */
                    gwindowCode = FindWindow(gmyEvent.where, &gwhichWindow);
                        switch(gwindowCode)
                        {
                        case inSysWindow: /* It's a Desk Accessory (DA) */
                            SystemClick(&gmyEvent, gwhichWindow);
                        break;
                        case inDrag:      /* Drag the window */
                        break;
                        case inGrow:      /* Change the window's size */
                        break;
                        case inContent:   /* Bring window to front if it's not */
                        break;
                        case inMenuBar:   /* In a menu, handle the command */
                            guserDone = Do_Command(MenuSelect(gmyEvent.where));
                        break;
                        } /* end switch gwindowCode */
                    break; /* end mouseDown */
                case keyDown:
                case autoKey:            /* Command key hit, pass to MenuKey */
                    if((gmyEvent.modifiers & cmdKey) != 0)
                        guserDone = Do_Command(MenuKey((char) (gmyEvent.message
                                    & CHAR_CODE_MASK)));
                    break; /* end key events */
                case updateEvt:          /* Update the window */
                    gwhichWindow = (WindowPtr) gmyEvent.message;
                    break;
                case diskEvt:            /* Handle disk insertion event */
                    if (HiWord(gmyEvent.message) != noErr)
                        {
```

```
                    DILoad();
                    where.h = INIT_X;
                    where.v = INIT_Y;
                    DIBadMount(where, gmyEvent.message);
                    DIUnload();
                    } /* end if != noErr */
              break; /* end disk event */
              case activateEvt:        /* Activate event */
                    gwhichWindow = (WindowPtr) gmyEvent.message;
              break;
              default:
              break;
              } /* end switch gmyEvent.what */
           } /* end if on next event */
        } /* end do */

   while (guserDone == FALSE);        /* Loop until told to stop */
} /* end Main_Event_Loop() */

Boolean Init_Mac(void)
{
short i;

/* Lunge after all the memory we can get */
   MaxApplZone();

/* Make sure we've got some master pointers */
   MoreMasters();
   MoreMasters();
   MoreMasters();
   MoreMasters();

/* Initialize managers */
   InitGraf(&qd.thePort);
   InitFonts();
   FlushEvents(everyEvent, 0);
   InitWindows();
   InitMenus();
   TEInit();
   InitDialogs(NIL);

/* Loop to setup menus */
   for (i = APPLE_MENU; i < (APPLE_MENU + LAST_MENU); i++)
```

```
      {
         gmyMenus[(i - RESOURCE_ID)] = GetMenu(i); /* Get menu resource */
         if (gmyMenus[(i - RESOURCE_ID)] == NIL)   /* Didn't get resource? */
            return FALSE;                          /* No, bail out */
      }; /* end for */

/* Build Apple menu */
   AppendResMenu(gmyMenus[(APPLE_MENU - RESOURCE_ID)], 'DRVR');


/* Add the menus */
   for (i = APPLE_MENU; i < (APPLE_MENU + LAST_MENU); i++)
      InsertMenu(gmyMenus[(i - RESOURCE_ID)], APPEND_MENU);

   DrawMenuBar();
   InitCursor();                                   /* Tell user app is ready */
   return TRUE;
} /* end Init_Mac() */

void main(void)
{
   if (Init_Mac())
      Main_Event_Loop();
   else
      SysBeep(30);
} /* end main */
```

SonOMunger.c

```
#include <Types.h>
#include <QuickDraw.h>
#include <Windows.h>
#include <Fonts.h>
#include <Controls.h>
#include <Dialogs.h>
#include <Menus.h>
#include <Devices.h>
#include <Memory.h>
#include <Events.h>
#include <Desk.h>
#include <OSEvents.h>
#include <OSUtils.h>
#include <ToolUtils.h>
#include <TextUtils.h>
#include <StandardFile.h>
```

```c
#include <Errors.h>
#include <Resources.h>
#include <DiskInit.h>

#include <AppleTalk.h>
#include <AppleEvents.h>
#include <EPPC.h>
#include <PPCToolBox.h>
#include <Processes.h>

struct AEinstalls
    {
     AEEventClass theClass;
     AEEventID theEvent;
     AEEventHandlerProcPtr theProc;
    };
typedef struct AEinstalls AEinstalls;

#define LAST_HANDLER      3         /* Number of Apple Event handlers - 1 */
#define LAST_MENU         3         /* Number of menus */

#define APPLE_MENU        128       /* Menu ID for Apple menu */
#define FILE_MENU         129       /* Menu ID for File menu */
#define EDIT_MENU         130       /* Menu ID for Edit menu */
#define RESOURCE_ID       127       /* Starting index into the menu array */

#define ABOUT_BOX         1         /* About box menu item # in Apple menu */

#define OPEN_FILE         1         /* Open item # in File menu */
/*------------------------*/          /* Separator line is item # 2 */
#define I_QUIT            3         /* Quit item # in File menu */

#define ABOUT_BOX_ID      128       /* Resource IDs for our windows & dialogs */
#define STATUS_BOX_ID     129
#define ERROR_BOX_ID      130
#define ERROR_MESS_ID     131

/* Various constants */
#define NIL               0L
#define FALSE             false
#define TRUE              true

#define INIT_X            112       /* Coords for disk init dialog box */
```

```c
#define INIT_Y          80

#define APPEND_MENU     0
#define CHAR_CODE_MASK  255
#define DEFAULT_VOL     0
#define IN_FRONT        -1
#define NO_CURSOR       0L
#define ONE_FILE_TYPE   1
#define SHORT_NAP       60L

#define CR              0x0D
#define LF              0x0A

/* Function prototypes */
Boolean Do_Command (long mResult);
Boolean Init_Mac(void);
void Main_Event_Loop(void);
void Report_Error(OSErr errorCode);
void Report_Err_Message(unsigned char *errMess);

/* High-level Apple Event functions */
Boolean Init_AE_Events(void);              /* Install the handlers */
void Do_High_Level(EventRecord *AERecord); /* Post high-level event to the dispatch table */
pascal OSErr Core_AE_Open_Handler(AppleEvent *messagein, AppleEvent *reply, long refIn);
/* Handlers */
pascal OSErr Core_AE_OpenDoc_Handler(AppleEvent *messagein, AppleEvent *reply, long refIn);
pascal OSErr Core_AE_Print_Handler(AppleEvent *messagein, AppleEvent *reply, long refIn);
pascal OSErr Core_AE_Quit_Handler(AppleEvent *messagein, AppleEvent *reply, long refIn);

/* Application-specific functions */
void Ask_File(void);
OSErr Munge_File(short input, short output, unsigned char *fileName);

/* Globals */
MenuHandle    gmyMenus[LAST_MENU+1];  /* Handle to our menus */
EventRecord   gmyEvent;               /* Holds the event returned by the OS */
WindowPtr     geventWindow;           /* Our private window */
Boolean       guserDone;              /* Indicates user wants to quit (== TRUE) */
CursHandle    gtheCursor;             /* Current pointer icon */
short         gwindowCode;
WindowPtr     gwhichWindow;           /* The window that got an event */
```

```c
OSType        gfileCreator = {'MUNG'}; /* File type and creator for our output file */
OSType        gfileType = {'TEXT'};


void Report_Err_Message(unsigned char *errMess)
{

   ParamText(errMess, NIL, NIL, NIL);
   CautionAlert(ERROR_MESS_ID, NIL);
} /* end Report_Err_Message() */

/* Function to report error conditions. Error ID only. */
void Report_Error(OSErr errorCode)
{
unsigned char errNumString[8];

   NumToString((long) errorCode, errNumString);
   ParamText(errNumString, NIL, NIL, NIL);
   StopAlert(ERROR_BOX_ID, NIL);
} /* end Report_Error() */

/* Function to read and write a file. Passed in are the input and output file's volume */
/*   reference numbers, and the name string of the input file */
OSErr Munge_File(short input, short output, unsigned char *fileName)
{
long          amount;
unsigned char buffer;
short         crflag;
long          dummyResult;
OSErr         fInOutErr;
long          icount, ocount;
unsigned char inNumString[12], outNumString[12];
DialogPtr     statusDialog;

   amount = 1L;
   crflag = 0;
   icount = 0;
   ocount = 0;
   while (FSRead(input, &amount, &buffer) == noErr)
     {
     icount++;                          /* Bump input char counter */
     switch (buffer)                    /* What char was read? */
       {
       case CR:
```

```
                    if (crflag >= 1)              /* Two in a row, end of paragraph */
                      {
                      if (!(fInOutErr = FSWrite(output, &amount, &buffer)))
                         {
                         if ((fInOutErr = FSWrite(output, &amount, &buffer)) != noErr)
                            {
                            Report_Error(fInOutErr);
                            return fInOutErr;
                            } /* end if != */
                         } /* end if ! */
                      else
                         {
                         Report_Error(fInOutErr);
                         return fInOutErr;
                         } /* end else */
                      crflag = 0;           /* Reset the flag */
                      ocount++;
                      } /* end if */
                    else
                      crflag++;              /* Bump the flag, and toss the CR */
                 break; /* end case CR */
                 case LF:                    /* Toss LF, but don't touch crflag */
                 break;    /* end case LF */
                 default:                    /* Write a character out */
                    if ((fInOutErr = FSWrite(output, &amount, &buffer)) != noErr)
                       {
                       Report_Error(fInOutErr);
                       return fInOutErr;
                       } /* end if */
                    ocount++;
                    crflag = 0;              /* Clear the flag */
                 break;
                 } /* end switch */
              } /* end while */

   /* Display processing statistics */
      if ((statusDialog = GetNewDialog(STATUS_BOX_ID, NIL, (WindowPtr) IN_FRONT)) != NIL)
         {
         NumToString(icount, inNumString);    /* Convert bytes read to string */
         NumToString(ocount, outNumString);
         ParamText (fileName, inNumString, outNumString, NIL);
         DrawDialog(statusDialog);
         Delay (120L, &dummyResult);
```

```
        DisposDialog(statusDialog);
        } /* end if != NIL */
    else
        SysBeep(30);

    return fInOutErr;
} /* end Munge_file() */

/* Obtain info on file to munge and output file */
void Ask_File(void)
{
unsigned char      fileName[14] = {"\pMunge.out"};
short              inFileRefNum, outFileRefNum;
OSErr              fileError;
short              oldVol;
SFTypeList         textType = {'TEXT'};
StandardFileReply inputReply, outputReply;

/* Open the input file */
    StandardGetFile(NIL, ONE_FILE_TYPE, textType, &inputReply);
    if (inputReply.sfGood)
        {
        GetVol (NIL, &oldVol);              /* Save current volume */
        if ((fileError = FSpOpenDF (&inputReply.sfFile, fsCurPerm, &inFileRefNum)) != noErr)
            {
            Report_Error(fileError);
            return;
            } /* end if error */

/* Open the output file */
        StandardPutFile ("\pSave text in:", fileName, &outputReply);
        if (outputReply.sfGood)
            {
            SetVol(NIL, outputReply.sfFile.vRefNum); /* Make the destination volume current */
            fileError = FSpCreate(&outputReply.sfFile, gfileCreator, gfileType,
smSystemScript);
            switch(fileError)                         /* Process result from File Manager */
                {
                case noErr:
                break;
                case dupFNErr:                        /* File already exists, wipe it out */
                    if ((fileError = FSpDelete(&outputReply.sfFile)) == noErr)
                        {
```

```
                if ((fileError = FSpCreate(&outputReply.sfFile, gfileCreator,
                                           gfileType, smSystemScript)) != noErr)
                    {
                    Report_Error(fileError);
                    FSClose (inFileRefNum);
                    SetVol(NIL, oldVol);
                    return;
                    } /* end if != noErr */
                } /* end == noErr */
            else
                {
                Report_Error(fileError);
                FSClose (inFileRefNum);
                SetVol(NIL, oldVol);
                return;
                } /* end else */
        break;   /* end case dupFNErr */
        default:                        /* Unknown error, try to abort cleanly */
            Report_Error(fileError);
            FSClose (inFileRefNum); /* Close the input file */
            SetVol(NIL, oldVol);    /* Restore original volume */
            return;
        } /* end switch */

/* Open data fork */
        if (!(FSpOpenDF (&outputReply.sfFile, fsCurPerm, &outFileRefNum)))
            {
            gtheCursor = GetCursor(watchCursor);   /* Change the cursor */
            SetCursor(&**gtheCursor);
            Munge_File (inFileRefNum, outFileRefNum, (unsigned char *) inputReply.sfFile.name);
            FSClose (outFileRefNum);
            SetCursor(&qd.arrow);                  /* Restore the cursor */
            } /* end if !fileError */
        FlushVol (NIL, outputReply.sfFile.vRefNum);
        } /* end if outputReply.sfGood */
    FSClose (inFileRefNum);
    SetVol(NIL, oldVol);                           /* Restore current volume */
    } /* end if inputReply.sfGood */

} /* end Ask_File() */


Boolean Init_AE_Events(void)
{
```

```
OSErr err;
short i;
static AEinstalls HandlersToInstall[] =  /* The 4 required Apple Events */
   {
      {kCoreEventClass, kAEOpenApplication, Core_AE_Open_Handler},
      {kCoreEventClass, kAEOpenDocuments, Core_AE_OpenDoc_Handler},
      {kCoreEventClass, kAEQuitApplication, Core_AE_Quit_Handler},
      {kCoreEventClass, kAEPrintDocuments, Core_AE_Print_Handler}
   };

   for (i = 0; i < LAST_HANDLER; i++)
     {
     err = AEInstallEventHandler(HandlersToInstall[i].theClass,
                                 HandlersToInstall[i].theEvent,
             NewAEEventHandlerProc(HandlersToInstall[i].theProc),
                                             0, FALSE);
      if (err)    /* If there was a problem, bail out */
        return FALSE;
      } /* end for */

   return TRUE;
} /* end Init_AE_Events() */

/* High-level open application event.  */
pascal OSErr Core_AE_Open_Handler(AppleEvent *messagein, AppleEvent *reply, long refIn)
{
    return noErr;
} /* end Core_AE_Open_Handler() */

/* High-level open document event */
pascal OSErr Core_AE_OpenDoc_Handler(AppleEvent *messagein, AppleEvent *reply, long refIn)
{
short          i, j;
AEDesc         fileDesc;
OSErr          highLevelErr;
AEKeyword      ignoredKeyWord;
DescType       ignoredType;
Size           ignoredSize;
long           numberOFiles;
unsigned char  outFileName[64];
FSSpec         inFSS, outFSS;
short          inFileRefNum, outFileRefNum;
OSErr          fInErr, fOutErr, mungeResult;
```

```
    gtheCursor = GetCursor(watchCursor);     /* Change the cursor to indicate we're busy */
    SetCursor(&**gtheCursor);
    mungeResult = 0;                          /* Clear result so for loop will operate */
/* Get parameter info (a list of file names) out of Apple Event*/
    if (!(highLevelErr = AEGetParamDesc(messagein, keyDirectObject, typeAEList, &fileDesc)))
        {
        if ((highLevelErr = AECountItems(&fileDesc, &numberOFiles)) == noErr) /* Count files */
            {
            for (i = 1; ((i <= numberOFiles) && (!highLevelErr) && (!mungeResult)); ++i)
                {
                if (!(highLevelErr = AEGetNthPtr(&fileDesc, i, typeFSS,
                                            &ignoredKeyWord, &ignoredType,
                                            (char *)&inFSS, sizeof(inFSS),
                                            &ignoredSize))) /* Get each name */
                {
/* Copy input file name to file output name */
                    for (j = 1; (j <= inFSS.name[0]); j++)
                        {
                        outFileName[j] = inFSS.name[j];
                        } /* end for */
                    outFileName[j] = '.';               /* Tack on a '.out' extension */
                    outFileName[j + 1] = 'o';
                    outFileName[j + 2] = 'u';
                    outFileName[j + 3] = 't';
                    outFileName[0] = (j + 3);           /* Update the string's length */
                    if (!(fInErr = FSpOpenDF(&inFSS, fsCurPerm, &inFileRefNum)))
                        {
                        if ((fOutErr = FSMakeFSSpec(DEFAULT_VOL, NIL, outFileName, &outFSS)) == fnfErr)
                            {
                            if (!(fOutErr = FSpCreate(&outFSS, gfileCreator,
                                                    gfileType, smSystemScript)))
                                {
                                if (!(fOutErr = FSpOpenDF(&outFSS, fsCurPerm, &outFileRefNum)))
                                    {
                                mungeResult = Munge_File(inFileRefNum, outFileRefNum,
                                                    inFSS.name);  /* Process the data */
                                FlushVol(NIL, outFileRefNum);
                                FSClose(outFileRefNum);
                                } /* end if !fOutErr */
                            else
                                Report_Err_Message("\pError opening output file");
                            } /* end if !fOutErr */
                        else
```

```
                        {
                          Report_Err_Message("\pError creating output file");
                        } /* end else */
                    } /* end if == fnfErr */
                else
                    { /* No error means a file already has that name */
                    if (fOutErr == noErr)
                      Report_Err_Message("\pCan't write, file already exists");
                    } /* end else */
                FSClose(inFileRefNum);
                } /* end if !fInErr */
            else
                Report_Err_Message("\pError opening input file");
            } /* end if !highlevelErr */
        } /* end for */
      } /* end if == noErr */
   highLevelErr = AEDisposeDesc(&fileDesc);  /* Dispose of the copy made by AEGetParamDesc() */
   } /* end if !highLevelErr */

SetCursor(&qd.arrow);          /* Restore the cursor */
guserDone = TRUE;              /* We're done, stop the application */
return highLevelErr;
} /* end Core_AE_OpenDoc_Handler() */


/* High-level print event */
pascal OSErr Core_AE_Print_Handler(AppleEvent *messagein, AppleEvent *reply, long refIn)
{
    return errAEEventNotHandled;  /* No printing done here, so no print handler */
} /* end Core_AE_Print_Handler() */


/* High-level quit event   */
pascal OSErr Core_AE_Quit_Handler(AppleEvent *messagein, AppleEvent *reply, long refIn)
{
    guserDone = TRUE;              /* Tell main event loop we want to stop */
    return noErr;
} /* Core_AE_Quit_Handler() */


void Do_High_Level(EventRecord *AERecord)
{
   AEProcessAppleEvent(AERecord);
} /* end Do_High_Level() */


/* Handle a command thru menu activation. Don't forget to unhighlight the
```

```
      selection to indicate the application is done. (Menu is highlighted
      automatically by MenuSelect.) */

Boolean Do_Command (long mResult)
{
unsigned char  accName[255];
short          itemHit;
Boolean        quitApp;
short          refNum;
DialogPtr      theDialog;
short          theItem, theMenu;
GrafPtr        savePort;        /* place to stow current GrafPort when we activate a
                                   Desk Accessory (DA) */

   quitApp = FALSE;             /* Assume Quit not activated */
   theMenu = HiWord(mResult);   /* Extract the menu selected */
   theItem = LoWord(mResult);   /* Get the item on the menu  */

   switch (theMenu)
      {
      case APPLE_MENU:
         if (theItem == ABOUT_BOX)             /* "About..." selected, describe ourself */
            {
            if ((theDialog = GetNewDialog(ABOUT_BOX_ID, NIL, (WindowPtr) IN_FRONT)) != NIL)
               {
               ModalDialog(NIL, &itemHit);
               DisposDialog(theDialog);
               } /* end if != NIL */
            else
               SysBeep(30);
            } /* end if theItem == ABOUT_BOX */
         else                                  /* It's a DA */
            {
            GetPort(&savePort);                /* Save port (in case the DA doesn't) */
            GetMenuItemText(gmyMenus[(APPLE_MENU - RESOURCE_ID)], theItem, accName);
            refNum = OpenDeskAcc(accName);   /* Start it */
            SetPort(savePort);                 /* Done, restore the port */
            }
      break; /* end APPLE_MENU case */

      case FILE_MENU:
         switch(theItem)
            {
```

```
          case OPEN_FILE:
             Ask_File();
             break;
          case I_QUIT:
             quitApp = TRUE;
          break;
          } /* end switch */
     break; /* end FILE_MENU case */

     case EDIT_MENU:
        SystemEdit(theItem - 1);
     break;
     default:
        break;
     } /* end switch */

  HiliteMenu(0);         /* Switch off highlighting on the menu just used */
  return quitApp;
} /* end Do_Command() */

/* The main chunk of code that processes events as they occur. Execution remains in */
/*   this loop until Do_Command returns TRUE, indicating the user wants to quit. In */
/*   most cases, an event should call a subroutine to handle the event, but in this */
/*   example the actions are so simple most code can be placed in-line. */
void Main_Event_Loop(void)
{
Point      where;

  FlushEvents(everyEvent, 0);      /* Clear out left over events */
  guserDone = FALSE;

  do
     {
     if (WaitNextEvent(everyEvent, &gmyEvent, SHORT_NAP, NO_CURSOR))
        {                           /* We have an event... */
        switch(gmyEvent.what)       /* Field each type of event */
           {
           case mouseDown:          /* In what window, and where?? */
              gwindowCode = FindWindow(gmyEvent.where, &gwhichWindow);
                 switch(gwindowCode)
                 {
                 case inSysWindow: /* It's a Desk Accessory (DA) */
                    SystemClick(&gmyEvent, gwhichWindow);
```

```
                        break;
                        case inDrag:        /* Drag the window */
                        break;
                        case inGrow:        /* Grow the window, if size has changed */
                        break;
                        case inContent:    /* Bring window to front, and that's all */
                        break;
                        case inMenuBar:    /* In a menu, handle the command */
                            guserDone = Do_Command(MenuSelect(gmyEvent.where));
                        break;
                        } /* end switch gwindowCode */
                    break; /* end mouseDown */
                case keyDown:
                case autoKey:              /* Command key pressed, pass to MenuKey */
                    if((gmyEvent.modifiers & cmdKey) != 0)
                        guserDone = Do_Command(MenuKey((char) (gmyEvent.message
                                    & CHAR_CODE_MASK)));
                     break; /* end key events */
                case updateEvt:            /* Update the window */
                        gwhichWindow = (WindowPtr) gmyEvent.message;
                     break;
                case diskEvt:              /* Handle disk insertion event */
                    if (HiWord(gmyEvent.message) != noErr)
                        {
                        DILoad();
                        where.h = INIT_X;
                        where.v = INIT_Y;
                        DIBadMount(where, gmyEvent.message);
                        DIUnload();
                        } /* end if != noErr */
                break; /* end disk event */
                case activateEvt:          /* Activate event */
                        gwhichWindow = (WindowPtr) gmyEvent.message;
                break;
                case kHighLevelEvent:   /* Handle Apple Event */
                        Do_High_Level(&gmyEvent);
                break;
                default:
                break;
                } /* end switch gmyEvent.what */
            } /* end if on next event */
        } /* end do */
```

```
   while (guserDone == FALSE);                              /* Loop until told to stop */
} /* end Main_Event_Loop() */


Boolean Init_Mac(void)
{
short i;

/* Lunge after all the memory we can get */
   MaxApplZone();

/* Make sure we've got some master pointers */
   MoreMasters();
   MoreMasters();
   MoreMasters();
   MoreMasters();
   MoreMasters();
   MoreMasters();
   MoreMasters();
   MoreMasters();

/* Initialize managers */
   InitGraf(&qd.thePort);
   InitFonts();
   FlushEvents(everyEvent, 0);
   InitWindows();
   InitMenus();
   TEInit();
   InitDialogs(NIL);

   for (i = APPLE_MENU; i < (APPLE_MENU + LAST_MENU); i++) /* Loop to setup menus */
     {
     gmyMenus[(i - RESOURCE_ID)] = GetMenu(i); /* Get menu resource */
     if (gmyMenus[(i - RESOURCE_ID)] == NIL)    /* Didn't get resource? */
       return FALSE;                            /* No, sure didn't, bail out */
     }; /* end for */

   AppendResMenu(gmyMenus[(APPLE_MENU - RESOURCE_ID)], 'DRVR'); /* Build Apple menu */

   for (i = APPLE_MENU; i < (APPLE_MENU + LAST_MENU); i++)        /* Add the menus */
     InsertMenu(gmyMenus[(i - RESOURCE_ID)], APPEND_MENU);

   DrawMenuBar();
```

```
    if (!Init_AE_Events())                    /* Set up our high-level event handlers */
        return FALSE;

    InitCursor();                             /* Tell user app is ready */
    return TRUE;
} /* end Init_Mac() */


void main(void)
{
    if (Init_Mac())
        Main_Event_Loop();
    else
        SysBeep(30);
} /* end main */
```

Chapter 6

SwitchBank.c

```
/* SwitchBank - Apple Event application that can eject "captive    */
/*     volumes". (The volume, usually a CD, can't be              */
/*     ejected because File Sharing (FS) is on.)                  */
/*                                                                */
/* Creation date:                              23-Jan-94   */
/* Added server call to halt FS, instead of using a               */
/*     Quit Apple Event (I'm told this is the safer               */
/*     way to do this.)                         26-Jan-94   */
/* Changed code to look at volume to see if it's shared,          */
/*     rather than just snoop for the File Sharing                */
/*     Extension. This way we can eject other volumes             */
/*     without restarting FS frequently, thereby                  */
/*     fragmenting the heap. This also lets us eject              */
/*     a volume as FS starts up, without interfering  30-Jan-94   */
/*     with that operation.                                       */
/* Changed code to use FindFolder() to locate startup  24-Feb-94   */
/*     volume. Also moved error messages into strings.            */
/*     Fixed a bug where the program wasn't releasing             */
/*     the memory used by AEGetParamDesc().                       */

#include <Types.h>
#include <QuickDraw.h>
#include <Windows.h>
#include <Fonts.h>
```

```
#include <Controls.h>
#include <Dialogs.h>
#include <Menus.h>
#include <Devices.h>
#include <Memory.h>
#include <Files.h>
#include <Events.h>
#include <Desk.h>
#include <OSEvents.h>
#include <ToolUtils.h>
#include <DiskInit.h>
#include <Folders.h>

#include <AppleTalk.h>
#include <AppleEvents.h>
#include <EPPC.h>
#include <PPCToolBox.h>
#include <Processes.h>

/* Definitions */
#define LAST_MENU               4               /* Number of menus */
#define LAST_HANDLER            3               /* Number of Apple Event handlers - 1 */

#define MENU_BAR_ID             128             /* ID for MBAR resource */
#define APPLE_MENU              128             /* Menu ID for Apple menu */
#define FILE_MENU               129             /* Menu ID for File menu */
#define EDIT_MENU               130             /* Menu ID for Edit menu */
#define SWITCH_MENU             131             /* Menu ID for File Share control */
#define RESOURCE_ID             127             /* Starting index into the menu array */

#define ABOUT_BOX               1               /* About box menu item # in Apple menu */

#define I_QUIT                  1               /* Quit item # in File menu */

/* Various constants */
#define NIL                     0L
#define FALSE                   false
#define TRUE                    true

#define INIT_X                  112             /* Coords for disk init dialog box */
#define INIT_Y                  80

#define APPEND_MENU             0
```

```c
#define CHAR_CODE_MASK          255
#define DEFAULT_VOL             0
#define IN_FRONT                (-1)
#define MAX_TRIES               6
#define NO_CURSOR               0L
#define LONG_NAP                60L
#define SYSTEM_7                0x0700
#define FILE_SHARING_CREATOR    'hhgg'
#define FILE_SHARING_TYPE       'INIT'


#define ABOUT_BOX_ID            128              /* Resource IDs for our windows & dialogs */
#define ERROR_BOX_ID            130
#define ERROR_MESS_ID           131


#define LOG_ID_STR              128              /* Resource ID for the message strings */
#define PROBLEM_STOPPING_FS     1                /* ID numbers of the messages */
#define PROBLEM_STARTING_FS     2
#define PROBLEM_ON_EJECT        3
#define DONT_EJECT_STARTUP_VOL  4
#define CANT_FIND_STARTUP_VOL   5
#define TROUBLE_WITH_SYS_INFO   6
#define CANT_LOCATE_FILE        7
#define PROBLEM_WITH_AE_HANDLER 8
#define SYSTEM_7_REQUIRED       9


#define PERSONAL_ACCESS_MASK    0x00000200L      /* Bit 9 in vMAttrib field = volume is shared */
#define SEND_MESSAGE            13               /* Send a message to the file server */
#define SHUT_DOWN               2                /* csCode to shut down the server */

/* Function prototypes */
Boolean Check_System(void);                      /* Standard application functions */
Boolean Do_Command (long mResult);
void Main_Event_Loop(void);
Boolean Init_Mac(void);
void Report_Error(OSErr errorCode);
void Report_Err_Message(long messageID);


Boolean Init_AE_Events(void);                    /* High level Apple Events */
void Do_High_Level(EventRecord *AERecord);
pascal OSErr Core_AE_Open_Handler(AppleEvent *messagein, AppleEvent *reply, long refIn);
/* Handlers */
pascal OSErr Core_AE_OpenDoc_Handler(AppleEvent *messagein, AppleEvent *reply, long refIn);
pascal OSErr Core_AE_Print_Handler(AppleEvent *messagein, AppleEvent *reply, long refIn);
```

```c
pascal OSErr Core_AE_Quit_Handler(AppleEvent *messagein, AppleEvent *reply, long refIn);

Boolean File_Share_On(short vRefNum);              /* Functions to handle details of file sharing */
void Stop_File_Sharing(void);
void Start_File_Sharing(void);
void Toggle_File_Sharing(void);
Boolean Get_FS_Info(void);
Boolean Find_File_Sharing(void);

/* Assorted structures for server trap */
typedef long    *LongIntPtr;

#if defined(powerc) || defined (__powerc)
#pragma options align=mac68k
#endif

struct DisconnectParam
    {
    QElemPtr    qLink;
    short       qType;
    short       ioTrap;
    Ptr         ioCmdAddr;
    ProcPtr     ioCompletion;
    OSErr       ioResult;
    LongIntPtr  scDiscArrayPtr;
    short       scArrayCount;
    short       reserved;
    short       scCode;
    short       scNumMinutes;
    short       scFlags;
    StringPtr   scMessagePtr;
    };

#if defined(powerc) || defined(__powerc)
#pragma options align=reset
#endif

typedef struct DisconnectParam DisconnectParam;
typedef union SCParamBlockRec SCParamBlockRec;
typedef SCParamBlockRec *SCParamBlockPtr;

/* Structure for installing handlers into AE event dispatch table */
struct AEinstalls
```

```
      {
       AEEventClass theClass;
       AEEventID theEvent;
       AEEventHandlerProcPtr theProc;
      };
     typedef struct AEinstalls AEinstalls;

     /* Globals - standard */
     WindowPtr          geventWindow;          /* our private window */
     EventRecord        gmyEvent;
     CursHandle         gtheCursor;            /* Current pointer icon */
     Boolean            guserDone;
     WindowPtr          gwhichWindow;
     short              gwindowCode;

     /* Application-specific globals */
     short              gdragNDropFlag;
     ProcessInfoRec     gprocess;
     ProcessSerialNumber gprocessSN;
     long               gSysDirID;
     short              gsysVRefNum;
     FSSpec             gthisFileSpec;
     FSSpecPtr          gthisFileSpecPtr;

     /* Glue to call the ServerDispatch trap */
     #if USES68KINLINES
     #pragma parameter __D0 mySyncServerDispatch(__A0)
     #endif
     pascal OSErr mySyncServerDispatch(SCParamBlockPtr PBPtr)
      FOURWORDINLINE(0x7000, 0xA094, 0x3028, 0x0010);

     /*     = {                                                            */
     /*     0x7000,            /* MOVEQ    #$00,D0        // Input must be 0    */
     /*     0xA094,            /* _ServerDispatch         // Hop to the trap    */
     /*     0x3028,0x0010      /* MOVE.W ioResult(A0),D0  // Move result to D0 because */
     /*     };                                           // File Sharing doesn't.   */

     #ifdef powerc
     /* Call the 68K code from the PowerPC through the Mixed Mode Manager */
     static pascal OSErr mySyncServerDispatch(SCParamBlockPtr PBPtr)
     {
     ProcInfoType myProcInfo;
     OSErr result;
```

```
/* Need an RTS at the end to return ... */
static short code[] = {0x7000, 0xA094, 0x3028, 0x0010, 0x4E75};

    /* Build the procinfo (note use of register based calls) */
    myProcInfo = kRegisterBased
                        | RESULT_SIZE(SIZE_CODE(sizeof(OSErr)))
                        | REGISTER_RESULT_LOCATION(kRegisterD0)
                        | REGISTER_ROUTINE_PARAMETER(1,kRegisterA0,
                                    SIZE_CODE(sizeof(SCParamBlockPtr)));

    result = CallUniversalProc((UniversalProcPtr) code, myProcInfo, (PBPtr));
    return result;
} /* mySyncServerDispatch() */
#endif

void Report_Err_Message(long messageID)
{
unsigned char errorString[256];

    GetIndString((unsigned char *) errorString, LOG_ID_STR, messageID);
    if (errorString[0] == 0)        /* Is there a string present? */
        {
        SysBeep(30);            /* No, give up */
        return;
        } /* end if */
    ParamText(errorString, NIL, NIL, NIL);
    CautionAlert(ERROR_MESS_ID, NIL);

} /* end Report_Err_Message() */

void Report_Error(OSErr errorCode)
{
unsigned char errNumString[8];

    NumToString((long) errorCode, errNumString);
    ParamText(errNumString, NIL, NIL, NIL);
    StopAlert(ERROR_BOX_ID, NIL);
} /* end Report_Error() */

/* Look for File Sharing Extension process in memory. Do search by signature */
/* creator & type rather than by file name, so that code works overseas. */
Boolean Get_FS_Info(void)
{
```

```
        gthisFileSpecPtr = &gthisFileSpec;
        gprocessSN.highLongOfPSN = kNoProcess;
        gprocessSN.lowLongOfPSN = kNoProcess;

        gprocess.processInfoLength = sizeof(ProcessInfoRec);  /* Store size of record */
        gprocess.processName = (unsigned char *) NewPtr(32);  /* Allocate room for the name */
        gprocess.processAppSpec = gthisFileSpecPtr;           /* Direct towards our storage */

        while (GetNextProcess(&gprocessSN) == noErr)          /* Loop until all processes found */
           {
           if (GetProcessInformation(&gprocessSN, &gprocess) == noErr) /* Obtain detailed info */
              {
              if (gprocess.processType == FILE_SHARING_TYPE &&         /* Is the process File */
                  gprocess.processSignature == FILE_SHARING_CREATOR)  /* Sharing Extension? */
                  return TRUE;
              } /* end if */
           } /* end while */

        return FALSE;
        }/* end Get_FS_Info() */

        /* Determine if the volume in question is being shared. If it is, save the File */
        /* Sharing process info so that we can restart it later. */
        Boolean File_Share_On(short volRefNum)
        {
        HParamBlockRec          ioHPB, volHPB;
        GetVolParmsInfoBuffer   volInfoBuffer;

        /* Get volume reference number */
           volHPB.volumeParam.ioCompletion = NIL;  /* No completion routine */
           volHPB.volumeParam.ioNamePtr = NIL;     /* No volume name */
           volHPB.volumeParam.ioVRefNum = volRefNum;
           volHPB.volumeParam.ioVolIndex = 0;      /* 0 = Use only volRefNum to obtain the info */
           if (!PBHGetVInfo(&volHPB, FALSE))
              {
        /* Get volume's characteristics */
              ioHPB.ioParam.ioCompletion = NIL;
              ioHPB.ioParam.ioNamePtr = NIL;
              ioHPB.ioParam.ioVRefNum = volHPB.volumeParam.ioVRefNum; /* from PBHGetVInfo() */
              ioHPB.ioParam.ioBuffer = (char *) &volInfoBuffer;
              ioHPB.ioParam.ioReqCount = sizeof(volInfoBuffer);
              if (!PBHGetVolParms(&ioHPB, FALSE))
                 {
```

```
               if (volInfoBuffer.vMAttrib & PERSONAL_ACCESS_MASK)    /* The disk is shared */
                 {
                 if (Get_FS_Info())              /* Look for the File Sharing Extension */
                    return TRUE;                 /* Got the file info we need to restart sharing */
                 } /* end if */
              } /* end if !PBHGetVolParms */
           } /* end if !PBHGetVInfo */
     return FALSE;
} /* end File_Share_On() */


/* Send a shut down immediately message to the File Sharing Server */
void Stop_File_Sharing(void)
{
DisconnectParam    serverBlock;
SCParamBlockPtr    serverBlockPtr;

   serverBlockPtr = (SCParamBlockPtr) &serverBlock;   /* Point to our message block */
   serverBlock.scCode = SHUT_DOWN;                    /* Server command to shut down */
   serverBlock.scNumMinutes = 0;                      /* Do it immediately */
   serverBlock.scFlags = SEND_MESSAGE;
   serverBlock.scMessagePtr = NIL;

   if (mySyncServerDispatch(serverBlockPtr) == noErr)
      {   /* Let the OS get at the event */
      WaitNextEvent(everyEvent, &gmyEvent, LONG_NAP, NO_CURSOR);
      WaitNextEvent(everyEvent, &gmyEvent, LONG_NAP, NO_CURSOR);
      } /* end if */
   else
      Report_Err_Message(PROBLEM_STOPPING_FS);

} /* end Stop_File_Sharing() */


/* Launch the file that has the File Sharing application in it. The file name used for the */
/* launch was obtained from the process when it's memory, or by searching the start up disk */
void Start_File_Sharing(void)
{
OSErr                 launchErr;
LaunchPBPtr           thisAppPBPtr;
LaunchParamBlockRec   thisAppParams;

   gthisFileSpecPtr = &gthisFileSpec;
   thisAppPBPtr = &thisAppParams;
   thisAppParams.launchBlockID = extendedBlock;    /* Use the new format */
```

```
      thisAppParams.launchEPBLength = extendedBlockLen;
      thisAppParams.launchFileFlags = 0;              /* Don't care about file flags */
      thisAppParams.launchControlFlags = (launchNoFileFlags + launchContinue + launchDontSwitch);
      thisAppParams.launchAppSpec = gthisFileSpecPtr; /* Give it file name grabbed */
                                                      /* by Get_FS_Info() before File */
                                                      /* Sharing was stopped */
      thisAppParams.launchAppParameters = NIL;        /* Send just Open event */

   if ((launchErr = LaunchApplication(thisAppPBPtr)) == noErr)
      WaitNextEvent(everyEvent, &gmyEvent, LONG_NAP, NO_CURSOR);
   else
      Report_Err_Message(PROBLEM_STARTING_FS);


} /* end Start_File_Sharing() */


/* Look for the File Sharing Extension file. User might not have started File Sharing yet, */
/* so we can't grab the name from a process that isn't there. So, we search the boot */
/* disk. */
Boolean Find_File_Sharing(void)
{
HParamBlockRec    searchPB;
FInfo             fileSharingExtInfo, fileSharingMaskInfo;
CInfoPBRec        searchSpec1, searchSpec2;
Point             nilPoint = {0, 0};

/* Set up creator and type for File Sharing Extension */
   fileSharingExtInfo.fdType = FILE_SHARING_TYPE;
   fileSharingExtInfo.fdCreator = FILE_SHARING_CREATOR;
   fileSharingExtInfo.fdFlags = 0;
   fileSharingExtInfo.fdLocation = nilPoint;
   fileSharingExtInfo.fdFldr = 0;

/* Set up masks */
   fileSharingMaskInfo.fdType = (OSType) 0xffffffff;
   fileSharingMaskInfo.fdCreator = (OSType) 0xffffffff;
   fileSharingMaskInfo.fdFlags = 0;
   fileSharingMaskInfo.fdLocation = nilPoint;
   fileSharingMaskInfo.fdFldr = 0;

/* 1st spec block */
   searchSpec1.hFileInfo.ioNamePtr = NIL;                       /* Search by file type, not name
*/
   searchSpec1.hFileInfo.ioFlFndrInfo = fileSharingExtInfo;  /* Type & creator to look for */
```

```
/* 2nd spec block */
   searchSpec2.hFileInfo.ioNamePtr = NIL;
   searchSpec2.hFileInfo.ioFlFndrInfo = fileSharingMaskInfo; /* Mask */

/* Set up search call */
   searchPB.csParam.ioCompletion = NIL;
   searchPB.csParam.ioNamePtr = NIL;                /* No volume name */
   searchPB.csParam.ioVRefNum = gsysVRefNum;        /* Search on startup volume */
   searchPB.csParam.ioMatchPtr = &gthisFileSpec;    /* Search result goes here */
   searchPB.csParam.ioReqMatchCount = 1;            /* Looking for 1 file */
   searchPB.csParam.ioSearchBits = fsSBFlFndrInfo;  /* Search based on file characteristics */
   searchPB.csParam.ioSearchInfo1 = &searchSpec1;
   searchPB.csParam.ioSearchInfo2 = &searchSpec2;
   searchPB.csParam.ioSearchTime = 0;               /* Don't time out */
   searchPB.csParam.ioCatPosition.initialize = 0;   /* Start at the beginning */
   searchPB.csParam.ioOptBuffer = NIL;              /* No search cache required */
   searchPB.csParam.ioOptBufSize = 0;

   if (PBCatSearchSync((CSParamPtr) &searchPB) == noErr)
      return TRUE;
   else
      {
      Report_Err_Message(CANT_LOCATE_FILE);
      return FALSE;
      } /* end else */

} /* end Find_File_Sharing() */

void Toggle_File_Sharing(void)
{
   if (Get_FS_Info())                       /* File Sharing already on (and in memory)? */
      Stop_File_Sharing();                  /* Yes, turn it off */
   else                                     /* No, look for the file */
      {
      if (Find_File_Sharing())              /* Find the File Sharing Extension file */
         Start_File_Sharing();              /* Launch it */
      } /* end else */

} /* end Toggle_File_Sharing() */

/* Build high-level event dispatch table and add our handlers to it. Must use static */
/* declaration so that the dispatch table has file scope. */
```

```
Boolean Init_AE_Events(void)
{
OSErr    err;
short    i;
static AEinstalls HandlersToInstall[] =           /* The 4 required Apple Events */
   {
      {kCoreEventClass, kAEOpenApplication, Core_AE_Open_Handler},
      {kCoreEventClass, kAEOpenDocuments, Core_AE_OpenDoc_Handler},
      {kCoreEventClass, kAEQuitApplication, Core_AE_Quit_Handler},
      {kCoreEventClass, kAEPrintDocuments, Core_AE_Print_Handler},
   };

   for (i = 0; i < LAST_HANDLER; i++)
      { /* Install each handler in application dispatch table, with a routine descriptor */
      err = AEInstallEventHandler(HandlersToInstall[i].theClass,
                                  HandlersToInstall[i].theEvent,
                                  NewAEEventHandlerProc(HandlersToInstall[i].theProc),
                                  0, FALSE);
      if (err)       /* If there was a problem, bail out */
         {
         Report_Err_Message (PROBLEM_WITH_AE_HANDLER);
         return FALSE;
         } /* end if */
      } /* end for */

   return TRUE;
} /* end Init_AE_Events() */


/* High-level open application event. */
pascal OSErr Core_AE_Open_Handler(AppleEvent *messagein, AppleEvent *reply, long refIn)
{
    return noErr;
} /* end Core_AE_Open_Handler() */


/* High-level open document event */
pascal OSErr Core_AE_OpenDoc_Handler(AppleEvent *messagein, AppleEvent *reply, long refIn)
{
long         dummyResult;          /* Dummy variable for delay() */
register short i, j;
Boolean      fileShareWasOn;
AEDesc       volDesc;              /* Container for sent volume names */
OSErr        volErr, highLevelErr;
long         numberOVolumes;       /* Number of volumes dropped onto us */
```

```
AEKeyword       ignoredKeyWord;         /* Bit buckets for high-level event info we don't need */
DescType        ignoredType;
Size            ignoredSize;
FSSpec          volFSS;                 /* Container for volume names as FSSPecs */

   gtheCursor = GetCursor(watchCursor);   /* Change the cursor to indicate we're busy */
   SetCursor(&**gtheCursor);
   fileShareWasOn = FALSE;                    /* Assume File Sharing on */

  if (!(highLevelErr = AEGetParamDesc(messagein, keyDirectObject, typeAEList, &volDesc)))
     {
     if ((highLevelErr = AECountItems(&volDesc, &numberOVolumes)) == noErr) /* How many? */
       {
       for (i = 1; ((i <= numberOVolumes) && (!highLevelErr)); ++i)          /* Process each */
         {
         if (!(highLevelErr = AEGetNthPtr(&volDesc, i, typeFSS, &ignoredKeyWord,
                                    &ignoredType, (char *)&volFSS,
                                    sizeof(volFSS), &ignoredSize)))
           {
           if (volFSS.vRefNum != gsysVRefNum)      /* Chosen volume the boot drive? */
             {
             if (File_Share_On(volFSS.vRefNum))   /* This volume being shared? */
               {
               Stop_File_Sharing();               /* Yes, turn it off, set flag */
               fileShareWasOn = TRUE;
               } /* end if */
             j = 0;                               /* Set retry count */
             while (((volErr = Eject(volFSS.name, volFSS.vRefNum)) != noErr) &&
                  (j < MAX_TRIES))
               {
               WaitNextEvent(everyEvent, &gmyEvent, LONG_NAP, NO_CURSOR);
               Delay(10L, &dummyResult);
               j++;
               } /* end while */
             if (volErr == noErr)                 /* Volume ejected OK? */
               UnmountVol(volFSS.name, volFSS.vRefNum);
             else
               Report_Err_Message(PROBLEM_ON_EJECT);
             } /* end if != gsysVRefNum */
           else
             Report_Err_Message(DONT_EJECT_STARTUP_VOL);
           } /* end if !highLevelErr */
         } /* end for */
```

```
        } /* end if */
     highLevelErr = AEDisposeDesc(&volDesc); /* Release memory copy of the AE parameter
*/
     } /* end if !highLevelErr */

   if (fileShareWasOn)
     Start_File_Sharing();

   if (gdragNDropFlag >= 0)          /* Did user drag & drop onto us? */
     guserDone = TRUE;              /* Yes, stop the application */

   SetCursor(&qd.arrow);            /* Restore the cursor */
   return highLevelErr;            /* Kick back any high-level problems to calling app
*/

} /* end Core_AE_OpenDoc_Handler() */

/* High-level print event */
pascal OSErr Core_AE_Print_Handler(AppleEvent *messagein, AppleEvent *reply, long refIn)
{
   return errAEEventNotHandled;    /* No printing done here, so no print handler */
} /* end Core_AE_Print_Handler() */

/* High-level quit event  */
pascal OSErr Core_AE_Quit_Handler(AppleEvent *messagein, AppleEvent *reply, long refIn)
{
   guserDone = TRUE;               /* Tell main event loop we want to stop */
   return noErr;
} /* Core_AE_Quit_Handler() */

void Do_High_Level(EventRecord *AERecord)
{
   AEProcessAppleEvent(AERecord);
} /* end Do_High_Level() */

/* Do our checks for system-specific characteristics here. You can use
   the Gestalt Manager for this, but it requires System 7. Here, we're
   using the old SysEnvirons() routine to see if we have System 7. For
   SwitchBank, System 7 alone should have everything we need. */
Boolean Check_System(void)
{
SysEnvRec  machineInfo;                 /* Record with machine-specific data */
short      sysVersion;                  /* System version # */
```

```c
short      versionRequested;              /* Version of SysEnvirons() to use */

   sysVersion = SYSTEM_7;
   versionRequested = 2;                  /* MUST set this value if you want valid results */

   if (SysEnvirons(versionRequested, &machineInfo) == noErr)
      sysVersion = machineInfo.systemVersion;
   else
      {
      Report_Err_Message(TROUBLE_WITH_SYS_INFO);
      return FALSE;
      } /* end else */

   if (sysVersion < SYSTEM_7)            /* Running System 7.0? */
      {
      Report_Err_Message (SYSTEM_7_REQUIRED);
      return FALSE;                      /* No. Sorry, can't run without it  */
      } /* end if */

   return TRUE;
} /* end Check_System() */

/* Handle a command thru menu activation. Don't forget to unhighlight the
   selection to indicate the application is done. (Menu is highlighted
   automatically by MenuSelect.) */
Boolean Do_Command (long mResult)
{
unsigned char   accName[255];
short           itemHit;
Boolean         quitApp;
short           refNum;
DialogPtr       theDialog;
short           theItem, theMenu;
GrafPtr         savePort;        /* place to stow current GrafPort when we
➡activate a Desk Accessory (DA) */

   quitApp = FALSE;                /* Assume Quit not activated */
   theMenu = HiWord(mResult);      /* Extract the menu selected */
   theItem = LoWord(mResult);      /* Get the item on the menu  */

   switch (theMenu)
      {
```

```
        case APPLE_MENU:
          if (theItem == ABOUT_BOX)  /* "About..." selected, describe ourself */
            {
            if ((theDialog = GetNewDialog(ABOUT_BOX_ID, NIL, (WindowPtr) IN_FRONT)) != NIL)
              {
              ModalDialog(NIL, &itemHit);
              DisposDialog(theDialog);
              } /* end if != NIL */
            else
              SysBeep(30);
            } /* end if theItem == ABOUT_BOX */
          else                          /* It's a DA */
            {
            GetPort(&savePort);                 /* Save port (in case the DA doesn't) */
            GetMenuItemText(GetMenuHandle(APPLE_MENU), theItem, accName);
            refNum = OpenDeskAcc(accName);    /* Start it */
            SetPort(savePort);                  /* Done, restore the port */
            }
        break; /* end APPLE_MENU case */

        case FILE_MENU:
          switch(theItem)
            {
            case I_QUIT:
              quitApp = TRUE;
            break;
            } /* end switch */
        break; /* end FILE_MENU case */

        case EDIT_MENU:
          SystemEdit(theItem - 1);
        break;

        case SWITCH_MENU:
          Toggle_File_Sharing();
        break;

        default:
        break;
        } /* end switch */

    HiliteMenu(0);        /* Switch off highlighting on the menu just used */
    return quitApp;
```

```
} /* end Do_Command() */

/* The main chunk of code that processes events as they occur. Execution remains in */
/*   this loop until Do_Command returns TRUE, indicating the user wants to quit. In */
/*   most cases, an event should call a subroutine to handle the event, but in this */
/*   example the actions are so simple most code can be placed in-line. */
void Main_Event_Loop(void)
{
Point       where;

    gdragNDropFlag = 1;
    FlushEvents(everyEvent, 0);              /* Clear out left over events */
    guserDone = FALSE;

    do
       {
       if (WaitNextEvent(everyEvent, &gmyEvent, LONG_NAP, NO_CURSOR))
          {                                  /* We have an event... */
          switch(gmyEvent.what)             /* Field each type of event */
             {
             case mouseDown:                 /* In what window, and where?? */
                gwindowCode = FindWindow(gmyEvent.where, &gwhichWindow);
                switch(gwindowCode)
                   {
                   case inSysWindow:        /* It's a Desk Accessory (DA) */
                      SystemClick(&gmyEvent, gwhichWindow);
                   break;
                   case inDrag:             /* Drag the window */
                   break;
                   case inGrow:             /* Grow the window, if size has changed */
                   break;
                   case inContent:          /* Bring window to front if not, and that's all */
                   break;
                   case inMenuBar:          /* In a menu, handle the command */
                      guserDone = Do_Command(MenuSelect(gmyEvent.where));
                   break;
                   } /* end switch gwindowCode */
                break; /* end mouseDown */
             case keyDown:
             case autoKey:                   /* Command key pressed, pass to MenuKey */
                if((gmyEvent.modifiers & cmdKey) != 0)
                   guserDone = Do_Command(MenuKey((char) (gmyEvent.message
```

```
                                        & CHAR_CODE_MASK)));
                    break; /* end key events */
                case updateEvt:                    /* Update the window */
                    gwhichWindow = (WindowPtr) gmyEvent.message;
                    break;
                case diskEvt:                      /* Handle disk insertion event */
                    if (HiWord(gmyEvent.message) != noErr)
                        {
                        DILoad();
                        where.h = INIT_X;
                        where.v = INIT_Y;
                        DIBadMount(where, gmyEvent.message);
                        DIUnload();
                        } /* end if != noErr */
                break; /* end disk event */
                case activateEvt:                  /* Activate event */
                    gwhichWindow = (WindowPtr) gmyEvent.message;
                    break;
                case kHighLevelEvent:              /* Handle Apple Event */
                    Do_High_Level(&gmyEvent);
                break;
                default:
                break;
                } /* end switch gmyEvent.what */
            } /* end if on next event */
        else                                       /* Null event */
            ;                                      /* Do idle or background stuff here */

/* Use this flag to tell Core_AE_OpenDoc_Handler() whether to shut down app when done */
/*      (user dragged file onto app) or not (user left app running). We bump this flag */
/*      down twice, after which point we stop, because more than 2 events indicates the */
/*      app is running */

        if (gdragNDropFlag >= 0)
            gdragNDropFlag--;
        } /* end do */

    while (guserDone == FALSE)
        ;                                          /* Loop until told to stop */
} /* end Main_Event_Loop() */

Boolean Init_Mac(void)
{
```

```
    Handle      theMenuBar;

/* Lunge after all the memory we can get */
    MaxApplZone();

/* Make sure we've got some master pointers */
    MoreMasters();
    MoreMasters();
    MoreMasters();
    MoreMasters();
    MoreMasters();
    MoreMasters();
    MoreMasters();
    MoreMasters();

/* Initialize managers */
    InitGraf(&qd.thePort);
    InitFonts();
    FlushEvents(everyEvent, 0);
    InitWindows();
    InitMenus();
    TEInit();
    InitDialogs(NIL);


    if ((theMenuBar = GetNewMBar(MENU_BAR_ID)) == NIL)      /* Got our menu resources OK? */
       return FALSE;

    SetMenuBar(theMenuBar);                                  /* Add our menus to menu list */
    DisposHandle(theMenuBar);
    AppendResMenu(GetMenuHandle(APPLE_MENU), 'DRVR');       /* Build Apple menu */
    DrawMenuBar();

/* Look for specific features or set up handlers this app needs */
    if (!Check_System())                                    /* Need System 7 */
       return FALSE;

    if (!Init_AE_Events())                                  /* Set up our high-level event handlers */
       return FALSE;

    if (FindFolder(kOnSystemDisk, kSystemFolderType, kDontCreateFolder,
                   &gsysVRefNum, &gSysDirID) != noErr)
```

```
        {
        Report_Err_Message (CANT_FIND_STARTUP_VOL);
        return FALSE;
        } /* end if */

    InitCursor();                              /* Tell user app is ready */
    return TRUE;

} /* end Init_Mac() */

void main(void)
{
    if (Init_Mac())
        Main_Event_Loop();
    else
        SysBeep(30);
} /* end main */
```

SwitchBank.r

```
#include "SysTypes.r"
#include "Types.r"

#define AllItems    0b1111111111111111111111111111111   /* 31 flags */
#define NoItems     0b0000000000000000000000000000000
#define MenuItem1   0b0000000000000000000000000000001
#define MenuItem2   0b0000000000000000000000000000010
#define MenuItem3   0b0000000000000000000000000000100
#define MenuItem4   0b0000000000000000000000000001000

#define MENU_BAR_ID     128             /* Menu bar resource for our menus */
#define APPLE_MENU      128             /* Menu ID for Apple menu */
#define FILE_MENU       129             /* Menu ID for File menu */
#define EDIT_MENU       130             /* Menu ID for Edit menu */
#define SWITCH_MENU     131             /* Menu ID for File Share control */

#define ABOUT_BOX_ID    128             /* Resource IDs for our windows & dialogs */
#define ERROR_BOX_ID    130
#define ERROR_MESS_ID   131

#define APPL_FREF       128             /* Resource IDs for file refs & icons */
#define DISK_FREF       129
```

```
#define SWITCH_ICON      128

/* Version info for the Finder's Get Info box */
resource 'vers' (1, purgeable)
{
   0x01,
   0x10,
   beta,
   0x00,
   verUs,
   "1.1β",
   "1.1β, by Tom Thompson"
};


/* Menu resources */
resource 'MBAR' (MENU_BAR_ID, preload)
{
   { APPLE_MENU, FILE_MENU, EDIT_MENU, SWITCH_MENU };
};

resource 'MENU' (APPLE_MENU, preload)
{
   APPLE_MENU, textMenuProc,
   AllItems & ~MenuItem2,    /* Disable separator line, enable About Box and DAs */
   enabled, apple,
   {
      "About SwitchBank 1.1…",   noicon, nokey, nomark, plain;
      "-",                       noicon, nokey, nomark, plain
   }
};

resource 'MENU' (FILE_MENU, preload)
{
   FILE_MENU, textMenuProc,
   AllItems,
   enabled, "File",
   {
      "Quit",                   noicon, "Q", nomark, plain
   }
};

resource 'MENU' (EDIT_MENU, preload)
{
```

```
   EDIT_MENU, textMenuProc,
   AllItems & ~MenuItem2,        /* Disable separator line */
   enabled, "Edit",
   {
      "Undo",                    noicon, "Z", nomark, plain;
      "-",                       noicon, nokey, nomark, plain;
      "Cut",                     noicon, "X", nomark, plain;
      "Copy",                    noicon, "C", nomark, plain;
      "Paste",                   noicon, "V", nomark, plain
   }
};


resource 'MENU' (SWITCH_MENU, preload)
{
   SWITCH_MENU, textMenuProc,
   AllItems,
   enabled, "Controls",
   {
      "Toggle File Sharing",     noicon, "T", nomark, plain
   }
};


/* Our error messages */
resource 'STR#'(128, purgeable)
{
   {
   /* [1] */   "A problem occurred stopping File Sharing.";
   /* [2] */   "A problem occurred starting File Sharing.";
   /* [3] */   "A problem occurred while ejecting the volume.";
   /* [4] */   "You can't eject the startup volume.";
   /* [5] */   "Couldn't find the startup volume.";
   /* [6] */   "Couldn't get valid system information.";
   /* [7] */   "Couldn't locate the File Sharing Extension file.";
   /* [8] */   "A problem occurred while loading the Apple Event handlers.";
   /* [9] */   "Sorry, SwitchBank requires System 7 or later to run.";
   }
};


/* This ALRT and DITL are used as an About Box */
resource 'DLOG' (ABOUT_BOX_ID, purgeable)
{
   {31, 6, 224, 265},
   altDBoxProc,
```

```
    visible,
    noGoAway,
    0x0,                    /* No refCon */
    ABOUT_BOX_ID,
    ""                      /* No window title */
};

resource 'DITL' (ABOUT_BOX_ID, purgeable)
{
    {
        /* Item 1 */
        {154, 80, 175, 180},    Button { enabled, "OK" },
        /* Item 2 */
        {4, 68, 38, 193},       StaticText { disabled, " SwitchBank 1.1\nby Tom Thompson" },
        /* Item 3 */
        {86, 11, 102, 250},     StaticText { disabled, " Copyright © 1994 Tom Thompson." },
        /* Item 4 */
        {44, 114, 76, 146},     Icon { disabled, 128 },
        /* Item 5 */
        {107, 43, 133, 217},    StaticText { disabled, "Written in Metrowerks C " }
    }
};

/* The ALRT and DITL for the basic error screen */
resource 'ALRT' (ERROR_BOX_ID, purgeable)
{
    {40, 40, 127, 273},
    ERROR_BOX_ID,
    {
        OK, visible, silent,
        OK, visible, silent,
        OK, visible, silent,
        OK, visible, silent
    }
};

resource 'DITL' (ERROR_BOX_ID, purgeable)
{
    {
        { 52, 162, 72, 220 },    Button { enabled, "OK" },
        { 54, 17, 70, 151 },     StaticText { disabled, "I/O error, ID = ^0" }
    }
```

```
   };

   /* Alert and DITL for error message screen */
   resource 'ALRT' (ERROR_MESS_ID, purgeable)
   {
      { 40, 40, 147, 280 },
      ERROR_MESS_ID,
      {
         OK, visible, silent,
         OK, visible, silent,
         OK, visible, silent,
         OK, visible, silent
      }
   };

   resource 'DITL' (ERROR_MESS_ID, purgeable)
   {
      {
         { 73, 168, 93, 226 },        Button { enabled, "OK" },
         { 53, 14, 97, 157 },         StaticText { disabled, "^0" }
      }
   };

   /* File reference resources */
   resource 'FREF' (DISK_FREF)
   {
      'disk',
      1,
      ""
   };


   resource 'FREF' (APPL_FREF)
   {
      'APPL',
      0,
      ""
   };

   /* Bundle resource */
   resource 'BNDL' (128)
   {
```

```
   'SWCH', 0,
   {
   'ICN#', { 0, SWITCH_ICON },                  /* Only 1 icon */
   'FREF', { 0, APPL_FREF, 1, DISK_FREF }       /* Two types of files */
   }
};

/* Signature resource - all 'STR ' resources must be declared before this! */
type 'SWCH' as 'STR ';

resource 'SWCH' (0) {
   "SwitchBank 1.1ß"
};

/* Our icon data */
data 'ICON' (SWITCH_ICON)
{
   $"7FFF FFFE 4000 0002 5C00 003A 55F8 1FAA"
   $"5D08 10BA 4108 1082 4108 1082 4108 1082"
   $"41B8 1D82 4110 0882 4110 0882 4110 0882"
   $"471C 38E2 4514 28A2 4514 28A2 4514 28A2"
   $"471C 38E2 4110 0882 411F F882 4110 0882"
   $"4110 0882 4110 0882 41FF FF82 4004 2002"
   $"4004 2002 4004 2002 4004 2002 5C04 203A"
   $"5404 202A 5C07 E03A 4000 0002 7FFF FFFE"
};

data 'ICN#' (SWITCH_ICON)
{
   $"7FFF FFFE 4000 0002 5C00 003A 55F8 1FAA"
   $"5D08 10BA 4108 1082 4108 1082 4108 1082"
   $"41B8 1D82 4110 0882 4110 0882 4110 0882"
   $"471C 38E2 4514 28A2 4514 28A2 4514 28A2"
   $"471C 38E2 4110 0882 411F F882 4110 0882"
   $"4110 0882 4110 0882 41FF FF82 4004 2002"
   $"4004 2002 4004 2002 4004 2002 5C04 203A"
   $"5404 202A 5C07 E03A 4000 0002 7FFF FFFE"
   $"7FFF FFFE 7FFF FFFE 7FFF FFFE 7FFF FFFE"
   $"7FFF FFFE 7FFF FFFE 7FFF FFFE 7FFF FFFE"
   $"7FFF FFFE 7FFF FFFE 7FFF FFFE 7FFF FFFE"
   $"7FFF FFFE 7FFF FFFE 7FFF FFFE 7FFF FFFE"
```

```
        $"7FFF FFFE 7FFF FFFE 7FFF FFFE 7FFF FFFE"
        $"7FFF FFFE 7FFF FFFE 7FFF FFFE 7FFF FFFE"
        $"7FFF FFFE 7FFF FFFE 7FFF FFFE 7FFF FFFE"
        $"7FFF FFFE 7FFF FFFE 7FFF FFFE 7FFF FFFE"
};

/* SwitchBank's color icon in icl8 format */
data 'icl8' (SWITCH_ICON)
{
    $"00FF FFFF FFFF FFFF FFFF FFFF FFFF FFFF"
    $"FFFF FFFF FFFF FFFF FFFF FFFF FFFF FF00"
    $"00FF 2A2A 2A2A 2A2A 2A2A 2A2A 2A2A 2A2A"
    $"2A2A 2A2A 2A2A 2A2A 2A2A 2A2A 2A2A FF00"
    $"00FF 2AFF FFFF 2A2A 2A2A 2A2A 2A2A 2A2A"
    $"2A2A 2A2A 2A2A 2A2A 2A2A FFFF FF2A FF00"
    $"00FF 2AFF 2AFF 2AFF FFFF FFFF FF2A 2A2A"
    $"2A2A 2AFF FFFF FFFF FF2A FF2A FF2A FF00"
    $"00FF 2AFF FFFF 2AFF F52A F52A FF2A 2A2A"
    $"2A2A 2AFF F52A F52A FF2A FFFF FF2A FF00"
    $"00FF 2A2A 2A2A 2AFF 2A2A 2A2A FF2A 2A2A"
    $"2A2A 2AFF 2A2A 2A2A FF2A 2A2A 2A2A FF00"
    $"00FF 2A2A 2A2A 2AFF 5454 5454 FF2A 2A2A"
    $"2A2A 2AFF 5454 5454 FF2A 2A2A 2A2A FF00"
    $"00FF 2A2A 2A2A 2AFF 7F7F 7F7F FF2A 2A2A"
    $"2A2A 2AFF 7F7F 7F7F FF2A 2A2A 2A2A FF00"
    $"00FF 2A2A 2A2A 2AFF FF7F FFFF FF2A 2A2A"
    $"2A2A 2AFF FFFF 7FFF FF2A 2A2A 2A2A FF00"
    $"00FF 2A2A 2A2A 2AFF 7F7F 7FFF 2A2A 2A2A"
    $"2A2A 2A2A FF7F 7F7F FF2A 2A2A 2A2A FF00"
    $"00FF 2A2A 2A2A 2AFF 5454 7FFF 2A2A 2A2A"
    $"2A2A 2A2A FF54 547F FF2A 2A2A 2A2A FF00"
    $"00FF 2A2A 2A2A 2AFF 2A54 7FFF 2A2A 2A2A"
    $"2A2A 2A2A FF2A 547F FF2A 2A2A 2A2A FF00"
    $"00FF 2A2A 2AFF FFFF 2A54 7FFF FFFF 2A2A"
    $"2A2A FFFF FF2A 547F FFFF FF2A 2A2A FF00"
    $"00FF 2A2A 2AFF F5FF 2A54 7FFF F5FF 2A2A"
    $"2A2A FFF5 FF2A 547F FFF5 FF2A 2A2A FF00"
    $"00FF 2A2A 2AFF 54FF 2A54 7FFF 54FF 2A2A"
    $"2A2A FF54 FF2A 547F FF54 FF2A 2A2A FF00"
    $"00FF 2A2A 2AFF 54FF 2A54 7FFF 54FF 2A2A"
    $"2A2A FF54 FF2A 547F FF54 FF2A 2A2A FF00"
    $"00FF 2A2A 2AFF FFFF 2A54 7FFF FFFF 2A2A"
```

```
    $"2A2A FFFF FF2A 547F FFFF FF2A 2A2A FF00"
    $"00FF 2A2A 2A2A 2AFF 2A54 7FFF 2A2A 2A2A"
    $"2A2A 2A2A FF2A 547F FF2A 2A2A 2A2A FF00"
    $"00FF 2A2A 2A2A 2AFF 2A54 7FFF FFFF FFFF"
    $"FFFF FFFF FF2A 547F FF2A 2A2A 2A2A FF00"
    $"00FF 2A2A 2A2A 2AFF 2A54 7FFF F52A F52A"
    $"F52A F52A FF2A 547F FF2A 2A2A 2A2A FF00"
    $"00FF 2A2A 2A2A 2AFF 2A54 7FFF 5454 5454"
    $"5454 5454 FF2A 547F FF2A 2A2A 2A2A FF00"
    $"00FF 2A2A 2A2A 2AFF 2A54 7FFF 7F7F 7F7F"
    $"7F7F 7F7F FF2A 547F FF2A 2A2A 2A2A FF00"
    $"00FF 2A2A 2A2A 2AFF FFFF FFFF FFFF FFFF"
    $"FFFF FFFF FFFF FFFF FF2A 2A2A 2A2A FF00"
    $"00FF 2A2A 2A2A 2A2A 2A2A 2A2A 2AFF 54F5"
    $"2A7F FF2A 2A2A 2A2A 2A2A 2A2A 2A2A FF00"
    $"00FF 2A2A 2A2A 2A2A 2A2A 2A2A 2AFF 542A"
    $"2A7F FF2A 2A2A 2A2A 2A2A 2A2A 2A2A FF00"
    $"00FF 2A2A 2A2A 2A2A 2A2A 2A2A 2AFF 54F5"
    $"2A7F FF2A 2A2A 2A2A 2A2A 2A2A 2A2A FF00"
    $"00FF 2A2A 2A2A 2A2A 2A2A 2A2A 2AFF 542A"
    $"2A7F FF2A 2A2A 2A2A 2A2A 2A2A 2A2A FF00"
    $"00FF 2AFF FFFF 2A2A 2A2A 2A2A 2AFF 54F5"
    $"2A7F FF2A 2A2A 2A2A 2A2A FFFF FF2A FF00"
    $"00FF 2AFF 2AFF 2A2A 2A2A 2A2A 2AFF 542A"
    $"2A7F FF2A 2A2A 2A2A 2A2A FF2A FF2A FF00"
    $"00FF 2AFF FFFF 2A2A 2A2A 2A2A 2AFF FFFF"
    $"FFFF FF2A 2A2A 2A2A 2A2A FFFF FF2A FF00"
    $"00FF 2A2A 2A2A 2A2A 2A2A 2A2A 2A2A 2A2A"
    $"2A2A 2A2A 2A2A 2A2A 2A2A 2A2A 2A2A FF00"
    $"00FF FFFF FFFF FFFF FFFF FFFF FFFF FFFF"
    $"FFFF FFFF FFFF FFFF FFFF FFFF FFFF FF00"
};

/* SwitchBank's color icon, in cicn format */
data 'cicn' (SWITCH_ICON)
{
    $"0000 0000 8010 0000 0000 0020 0020 0000"
    $"0000 0000 0000 0048 0000 0048 0000 0000"
    $"0004 0001 0004 0000 0000 0000 0000 0000"
    $"0000 0000 0000 0004 0000 0000 0020 0020"
    $"0000 0000 0004 0000 0000 0020 0020 0000"
    $"0000 7FFF FFFE 7FFF FFFE 7FFF FFFE 7FFF"
```

```
$"FFFE 7FFF FFFE 7FFF FFFE 7FFF FFFE 7FFF"
$"FFFE 7FFF FFFE 7FFF FFFE 7FFF FFFE 7FFF"
$"FFFE 7FFF FFFE 7FFF FFFE 7FFF FFFE 7FFF"
$"FFFE 7FFF FFFE 7FFF FFFE 7FFF FFFE 7FFF"
$"FFFE 7FFF FFFE 7FFF FFFE 7FFF FFFE 7FFF"
$"FFFE 7FFF FFFE 7FFF FFFE 7FFF FFFE 7FFF"
$"FFFE 7FFF FFFE 7FFF FFFE 7FFF FFFE 7FFF"
$"FFFE 7FFF FFFE 4000 0002 5C00 003A 55F8"
$"1FAA 5D08 10BA 4108 1082 4108 1082 4108"
$"1082 41B8 1D82 4110 0882 4110 0882 4110"
$"0882 471C 38E2 4514 28A2 4514 28A2 4514"
$"28A2 471C 38E2 4110 0882 411F F882 4110"
$"0882 4110 0882 4110 0882 41FF FF82 4004"
$"2002 4004 2002 4004 2002 4004 2002 5C04"
$"203A 5404 202A 5C07 E03A 4000 0002 7FFF"
$"FFFE 0000 0000 0000 0005 0000 FFFF FFFF"
$"FFFF 0001 CCCC CCCC FFFF 0002 9999 9999"
$"FFFF 0003 6666 6666 CCCC 0004 EEEE EEEE"
$"EEEE 000F 0000 0000 0000 0FFF FFFF FFFF"
$"FFFF FFFF FFFF FFFF FFF0 0F11 1111 1111"
$"1111 1111 1111 1111 11F0 0F1F FF11 1111"
$"1111 1111 1111 11FF F1F0 0F1F 1F1F FFFF"
$"F111 111F FFFF F1F1 F1F0 0F1F FF1F 4141"
$"F111 111F 4141 F1FF F1F0 0F11 111F 1111"
$"F111 111F 1111 F111 11F0 0F11 111F 2222"
$"F111 111F 2222 F111 11F0 0F11 111F 3333"
$"F111 111F 3333 F111 11F0 0F11 111F F3FF"
$"F111 111F FF3F F111 11F0 0F11 111F 333F"
$"1111 1111 F333 F111 11F0 0F11 111F 223F"
$"1111 1111 F223 F111 11F0 0F11 111F 123F"
$"1111 1111 F123 F111 11F0 0F11 1FFF 123F"
$"FF11 11FF F123 FFF1 11F0 0F11 1F4F 123F"
$"4F11 11F4 F123 F4F1 11F0 0F11 1F2F 123F"
$"2F11 11F2 F123 F2F1 11F0 0F11 1F2F 123F"
$"2F11 11F2 F123 F2F1 11F0 0F11 1FFF 123F"
$"FF11 11FF F123 FFF1 11F0 0F11 111F 123F"
$"1111 1111 F123 F111 11F0 0F11 111F 123F"
$"FFFF FFFF F123 F111 11F0 0F11 111F 123F"
$"4141 4141 F123 F111 11F0 0F11 111F 123F"
$"2222 2222 F123 F111 11F0 0F11 111F 123F"
$"3333 3333 F123 F111 11F0 0F11 111F FFFF"
```

```
    $"FFFF FFFF FFFF F111 11F0 0F11 1111 1111"
    $"1F24 13F1 1111 1111 11F0 0F11 1111 1111"
    $"1F21 13F1 1111 1111 11F0 0F11 1111 1111"
    $"1F24 13F1 1111 1111 11F0 0F11 1111 1111"
    $"1F21 13F1 1111 1111 11F0 0F1F FF11 1111"
    $"1F24 13F1 1111 11FF F1F0 0F1F 1F11 1111"
    $"1F21 13F1 1111 11F1 F1F0 0F1F FF11 1111"
    $"1FFF FFF1 1111 11FF F1F0 0F11 1111 1111"
    $"1111 1111 1111 1111 11F0 0FFF FFFF FFFF"
    $"FFFF FFFF FFFF FFFF FFF0"
};

/* The system's color caution alert icon */
data 'cicn' (2)
{
    $"0000 0000 8010 0000 0000 0020 0020 0000"
    $"0000 0000 0000 0048 0000 0048 0000 0000"
    $"0004 0001 0004 0000 0000 0000 0000 0000"
    $"0000 0000 0000 0004 0000 0000 0020 0020"
    $"0000 0000 0004 0000 0000 0020 0020 0000"
    $"0000 0001 8000 0003 C000 0007 E000 0007"
    $"E000 000F F000 000F F000 001F F800 001F"
    $"F800 003F FC00 003F FC00 007F FE00 007F"
    $"FE00 00FF FF00 00FF FF00 01FF FF80 01FF"
    $"FF80 03FF FFC0 03FF FFC0 07FF FFE0 07FF"
    $"FFE0 0FFF FFF0 0FFF FFF0 1FFF FFF8 1FFF"
    $"FFF8 3FFF FFFC 3FFF FFFC 7FFF FFFE 7FFF"
    $"FFFE FFFF FFFF FFFF FFFF FFFF FFFF FFFF"
    $"FFFF 0001 8000 0003 C000 0003 C000 0006"
    $"6000 0006 6000 000C 3000 000C 3000 0018"
    $"1800 0019 9800 0033 CC00 0033 CC00 0063"
    $"C600 0063 C600 00C3 C300 00C3 C300 0183"
    $"C180 0183 C180 0303 C0C0 0303 C0C0 0603"
    $"C060 0601 8060 0C01 8030 0C00 0030 1800"
    $"0018 1801 8018 3003 C00C 3003 C00C 6001"
    $"8006 6000 0006 C000 0003 FFFF FFFF 7FFF"
    $"FFFE 0000 0000 0000 0006 0000 FFFF FFFF"
    $"FFFF 0001 FFFF CCCC 3333 0002 CCCC 9999"
    $"0000 0003 9999 6666 0000 0004 3333 3333"
    $"3333 0005 BBBB BBBB BBBB 000F 0000 0000"
    $"0000 0000 0000 0000 000F F000 0000 0000"
```

```
        $"0000 0000 0000 0000 004F F400 0000 0000"
        $"0000 0000 0000 0000 05FF FF50 0000 0000"
        $"0000 0000 0000 0000 04F3 3F40 0000 0000"
        $"0000 0000 0000 0000 5FF1 1FF5 0000 0000"
        $"0000 0000 0000 0000 4F31 13F4 0000 0000"
        $"0000 0000 0000 0005 FF11 11FF 5000 0000"
        $"0000 0000 0000 0004 F311 113F 4000 0000"
        $"0000 0000 0000 005F F12F F21F F500 0000"
        $"0000 0000 0000 004F 314F F413 F400 0000"
        $"0000 0000 0000 05FF 11FF FF11 FF50 0000"
        $"0000 0000 0000 04F3 11FF FF11 3F40 0000"
        $"0000 0000 0000 5FF1 11FF FF11 1FF5 0000"
        $"0000 0000 0000 4F31 11FF FF11 13F4 0000"
        $"0000 0000 0005 FF11 11FF FF11 11FF 5000"
        $"0000 0000 0004 F311 11FF FF11 113F 4000"
        $"0000 0000 005F F111 11FF FF11 111F F500"
        $"0000 0000 004F 3111 11FF FF11 1113 F400"
        $"0000 0000 05FF 1111 11FF FF11 1111 FF50"
        $"0000 0000 04F3 1111 114F F411 1111 3F40"
        $"0000 0000 5FF1 1111 112F F211 1111 1FF5"
        $"0000 0000 4F31 1111 111F F111 1111 13F4"
        $"0000 0005 FF11 1111 1112 2111 1111 11FF"
        $"5000 0004 F311 1111 1111 1111 1111 113F"
        $"4000 005F F111 1111 112F F211 1111 111F"
        $"F500 004F 3111 1111 11FF FF11 1111 1113"
        $"F400 05FF 1111 1111 11FF FF11 1111 1111"
        $"FF50 04F3 1111 1111 112F F211 1111 1111"
        $"3F40 5FF1 1111 1111 1111 1111 1111 1111"
        $"1FF5 FF31 1111 1111 1111 1111 1111 1111"
        $"13FF FFFF FFFF FFFF FFFF FFFF FFFF FFFF"
        $"FFFF 5FFF FFFF FFFF FFFF FFFF FFFF FFFF"
        $"FFF5"
};
```

Init.h

```
#ifndef __TYPES__
    #include <Types.h>
#endif

#ifndef __MEMORY__
```

```
    #include <Memory.h>
#endif

#ifndef __GESTALTEQU__
    #include <gestaltequ.h>
#endif

#ifndef __FILES__
    #include <Files.h>
#endif

#ifndef __QUICKDRAW__
    #include <QuickDraw.h>
#endif

#ifndef __RESOURCES__
    #include <Resources.h>
#endif

#ifndef __ERRORS__
    #include <Errors.h>
#endif

#ifndef __FRAGLOAD__
    #include <FragLoad.h>
#endif

#ifndef __TEXTUTILS__
    #include <TextUtils.h>
#endif

#ifndef __RESOURCES__
    #include <Resources.h>
#endif

#ifndef __MEMORY__
    #include <Memory.h>
#endif

#ifdef __MWERKS__
    #ifndef powerc
```

```
            #include <A4Stuff.h>
        #endif
    #endif
```

FlipDepth.c

```
/*
    Portions © 1994 Rock Ridge Enterprises. All Rights Reserved.
*/

/*
    This tells MixedMode.h that we want _real_ versions of
    the various RoutineDescriptor functions and not dummy
    stubs.
*/
#define USESROUTINEDESCRIPTORS 1

/*
    This #define is for testing only. Without it, only the
    68k version of our patch is called.
*/
#undef DO_PPC_CODE_ONLY        /* For testing PowerPC version of patch */

#include "Init.h"

#ifndef powerc
    #include <SetUpA4.h>
#endif

/* Headers required by our custom functions */
#include <SysEqu.h>
#include <Events.h>
#include <Windows.h>
#include <Palettes.h>

#define FALSE          false
#define TRUE           true
#define NIL            0L

/*
    Some low memory globals. We'd rather not use these, but they're
    necessary because we'll be operating in a trap that doesn't move memory.
*/
```

```
#define lowMemKeyStroke      (*(KeyMap *) KeyMapLM)[0]
#define lowMemKeyModifiers   (*(KeyMap *) KeyMapLM)[1]

/* Some constants that define the bits we'll see in KeyMap */
#define SHIFT_KEY        1L
#define CAPS_LOCK        2L
#define OPTION_KEY       4L
#define CONTROL_KEY      8L
#define COMMAND_KEY      0x8000L

#define KEY_COMBO        SHIFT_KEY + COMMAND_KEY
#define T_KEYCODE        0x0200L
#define BLACK_WHITE      128                  /* First video mode ID in sResource list */


#define kOldSystemErr    10000

/*===========================
   We take the PowerPC code from the data fork
   and put it into a resource using a utility
   like Resorcer.
===========================*/
#define kPPCRezType      'PPC '
#define kPPCRezID        300

/*===========================
   The 68k code goes in a normal INIT resource.
   Be sure this is set to "system heap/locked".
===========================*/
#define kInitRezType     'INIT'
#define kInitRezID       300

#define kMinSystemVersion (0x0605)

/*===========================
   This is the name of the ppc fragment - for debugging only.
===========================*/
#define kInitName     "\pEricsInit"

/*===========================
```

```
            to save some screen space, we'll use "UPP" instead of "UniversalProcPtr"
============================*/
typedef UniversalProcPtr    UPP;


/*==========================
   PostEvent Information
========================== */
enum
{
   kPostEventInfo = kRegisterBased
       | RESULT_SIZE(SIZE_CODE(sizeof(OSErr)))
       | REGISTER_RESULT_LOCATION(kRegisterD0)
       | REGISTER_ROUTINE_PARAMETER(1,kRegisterA0,SIZE_CODE(sizeof(short)))
       | REGISTER_ROUTINE_PARAMETER(2,kRegisterD0,SIZE_CODE(sizeof(long)))
};


typedef pascal OSErr ( *PostEventFuncPtr ) ( short eventNum, long eventMsg );
#define kPostEventFuncName "\pMyPostEventPPC"


/* Note separate functions */
short MyPostEvent68k( short eventNum, long eventMsg );
OSErr MyPostEventPPC( short eventNum, long eventMsg );


/*==========================
   GetMouse Information
========================== */
enum
{
   kGetMouseInfo = kPascalStackBased
           | STACK_ROUTINE_PARAMETER(1, SIZE_CODE(sizeof(Point)))
};


typedef pascal void ( *GetMouseFuncPtr ) ( Point *mouseLoc );
#define kGetMouseFuncName "\pMyGetMouse"
void MyGetMouse ( Point *mouseLoc );   /* Only one function required */


/* Functions that change screen depth. Works one both platforms. */
void Change_Depth(long newDepth);
long Fetch_Depth(void);


/*==========================
   This structure is shared between the power pc
```

```
    version of the code and the 68k version.

    Both the PowerPC code and the 68k code have a single
    global variable, "gGlobalsPtr". They point to the
    same area of memory.
===========================*/

#ifdef powerc
    #pragma options align=mac68k
#endif

/*
    Note: do not move these fields around!
    The assembly code in PostEvent68kStub()
    depends on their locations. It must be
    compiled with the 68K packing conventions
*/

typedef struct
{
UPP             gOrigPostEvent;    /* Address of original PostEvent trap */
UPP             gOrigGetMouse;     /* Address of original GetMouse trap */
SysEnvRec       gSystemInfo;
Boolean         gRequestFlag;      /* Flag that signals screen depth change */
GDHandle        gOurGDevice;       /* The GDevice of the screen we're working with */
short           gDevRefNum;        /* Driver ref number for video board's slot */
long            gOldScreenDepth;
} MyInitGlobals;

#ifdef powerc
    #pragma options align=reset
#endif

/*==========================
    Global Variables

    -- each side of the code maintains its own pointer to the
       same block of memory.

    -- we reference the globals ptr by name, so these two must be
       changed together.
============================*/
```

```
MyInitGlobals              *gGlobalsPtr;
#define kGlobalsSymName      "\pgGlobalsPtr"


 /*===========================
    An original trap is called differently from PowerPC
    code than from 68k code because CallOSTrapUniversalProc() isn't
    implemented for 68k code.
===========================*/
#ifdef powerc
    #define CallPostEvent(eventNum, eventMsg)
    CallOSTrapUniversalProc( gGlobalsPtr->gOrigPostEvent, kPostEventInfo,
    eventNum, eventMsg )
    #define CallGetMouse(mouseLoc)
    CallUniversalProc( gGlobalsPtr->gOrigGetMouse, kGetMouseInfo, mouseLoc )
#else
    #define CallGetMouse(mouseLoc) (*(GetMouseFuncPtr)gGlobalsPtr->gOrigGetMouse) (mouseLoc);
#endif


/* Custom function to place our patch code in the system heap */
Handle Get1ResourceSys( OSType rezType, short rezID );


/*
    @@@@@@@@@@@@@@  68000 Exclusive Code    @@@@@@@@@@@@@@
*/
#ifndef powerc


/*===========================
    Prototypes for 68k code
===========================*/
OSErr     DoInitForOldMacs( void );
OSErr     DoInitForPPCMacs( void );
OSErr     CreateFatDescriptorSys( void *mac68Code, void *ppcCode,
                                  ProcInfoType procInfo, UPP *result );
OSErr     PatchTrapsForPPCMac( ConnectionID connID );

void      PostEvent68kStub( void );
pascal void GetMouse68kStub ( Point *mouseLoc );


/*===========================
    This is *always* the INIT's entry point. This is
```

```
        the only routine called by system software at startup.

        This requires that the INIT resource be set to
        System Heap/Locked.
============================*/
void main( void )
{
    long      oldA4;
    Handle    initH = nil;           /* Handle to our own INIT resource */
    OSErr     err = noErr;
    long      ginfo;

    /*******************************
        global variable support
        Place proper value for A4 into hole in INIT resource.
    *******************************/
    oldA4 = SetCurrentA4();          /* Get the proper value of A4 into A4 */
    RememberA4();                    /* save into self-modifying code */

    /*******************************
        Allocate our global variables
    *******************************/
    gGlobalsPtr = (MyInitGlobals*) NewPtrSysClear( sizeof(MyInitGlobals) );
    if ( !gGlobalsPtr )
        {
        err = memFullErr;
        goto DONE;
        }

    /*******************************
        Get some basic system information
    *******************************/
    err = SysEnvirons( 1, &gGlobalsPtr->gSystemInfo );
    if ( err )
        goto DONE;

    /*******************************
        Check the system version
    *******************************/
    if ( gGlobalsPtr->gSystemInfo.systemVersion < kMinSystemVersion )
        {
```

```
    err = kOldSystemErr;
    goto DONE;
    }


/*******************************
   Get a handle to our own INIT resource
*******************************/
initH = Get1Resource( kInitRezType, kInitRezID );
if ( !initH )
    {
    err = resNotFound;
    goto DONE;
    }


/*******************************
   See if we're running on a PowerPC
*******************************/
err = Gestalt( gestaltSysArchitecture, &ginfo );


/*******************************
   Patch all the traps and get everything ready.
*******************************/
if ( err || (ginfo == gestalt68k) )
    err = DoInitForOldMacs();
else
    err = DoInitForPPCMacs();

DONE:
if ( err )
    {

    /* Display "bad load" icon here */

    if ( gGlobalsPtr )
        DisposPtr( (Ptr)gGlobalsPtr );
    }
else
    {
    /* Display "good load" icon here */

    gGlobalsPtr->gOldScreenDepth = Fetch_Depth();   /* Get screen depth for later */
```

```c
    /* Make sure the init stays in memory when the INIT file closes */
        DetachResource( initH );
        } /* end else */

    RestoreA4( oldA4 );                                 /* restore previous value of A4 */
} /* end main() */


/*===========================
    DoInitForOldMacs

    Initialization code for non-PowerPC Macs.
==========================*/
OSErr DoInitForOldMacs( void )
{
    /* patch the trap */
    gGlobalsPtr->gOrigPostEvent = NGetTrapAddress( _PostEvent, OSTrap );
    NSetTrapAddress( (UPP)PostEvent68kStub, _PostEvent, OSTrap );
    gGlobalsPtr->gOrigGetMouse = NGetTrapAddress( _GetMouse, ToolTrap );
    NSetTrapAddress( (UPP)GetMouse68kStub, _GetMouse, ToolTrap );

    return noErr;
} /* end DoInitForOldMacs() */


/*===========================
    DoInitForPPCMacs

    Initialization code for powerpc Macs.
==========================*/
OSErr DoInitForPPCMacs( void )
{
    OSErr          err = noErr;
    Handle         ppcCodeH = nil;
    SymClass       theSymClass;
    Ptr            theSymAddr;
    ConnectionID   connID = kNoConnectionID;
    Str255         errName;
    Ptr            mainAddr;

    /*******************************
        load the powerpc version of the code into
        memory. since some of our trap patches may be
        called at interrupt time, don't use disk-based
        versions of the code.
```

```
*******************************/
ppcCodeH = Get1ResourceSys( kPPCRezType, kPPCRezID );
if ( !ppcCodeH )
   return resNotFound;
HLock( ppcCodeH );


/*******************************
   open a connection with the code fragment we just loaded
*******************************/
err = GetMemFragment( *ppcCodeH, GetHandleSize(ppcCodeH), kInitName,
                      kLoadNewCopy, &connID, &mainAddr, errName );
if ( err )
   {
   connID = kNoConnectionID;
   goto DONE;
   }


/*******************************
   find the global variable ptr that the powerpc
   code uses.
*******************************/
err = FindSymbol( connID, kGlobalsSymName, &theSymAddr, &theSymClass );
if ( err )
   goto DONE;


/*******************************
   Modify the powerpc global variable pointer to point
   to the area of memory we've already allocated.
*******************************/
*(MyInitGlobals **)theSymAddr = gGlobalsPtr;
err = PatchTrapsForPPCMac( connID );


/*******************************
   Cleanup
*******************************/
DONE:
if ( err )
   {
      /* Close the code frag mgr connection if we got an error... */
   if ( connID != kNoConnectionID )
      CloseConnection( &connID );
```

```
            /* ...and release the memory we allocated */
        if ( ppcCodeH )
            ReleaseResource( ppcCodeH );
        } /* end if */
    else
        {
            /* No error -> keep the ppc code around when file closes */
        DetachResource( ppcCodeH );
        } /* end else */

    return err;
} /* end DoInitForPPCMacs() */


/*===========================
    PatchTrapsForPPCMac
===========================*/
OSErr PatchTrapsForPPCMac( ConnectionID connID )
{
    Ptr                symAddr;
    SymClass           symType;
    OSErr              err = noErr;
    UniversalProcPtr   upp = nil;

    /*
        Fat Patch _PostEvent
    */
    err = FindSymbol( connID, kPostEventFuncName, &symAddr, &symType );
    if ( err )
        return err;

    err = CreateFatDescriptorSys( PostEvent68kStub, symAddr, kPostEventInfo, &upp );
    if ( err )
        return memFullErr;

    gGlobalsPtr->gOrigPostEvent = NGetTrapAddress( _PostEvent, OSTrap );
    NSetTrapAddress( upp, _PostEvent, OSTrap );

    /*
        Fat Patch _GetMouse
    */
    err = FindSymbol( connID, kGetMouseFuncName, &symAddr, &symType );
    if ( err )
        return err;
```

```
      err = CreateFatDescriptorSys( GetMouse68kStub, symAddr, kGetMouseInfo, &upp );
      if ( err )
         return memFullErr;

      gGlobalsPtr->gOrigGetMouse = NGetTrapAddress( _GetMouse, ToolTrap );
      NSetTrapAddress( upp, _GetMouse, ToolTrap );

      return noErr;
} /* end PatchTrapsForPPCMac() */


/*===========================
   CreateFatDescriptorSys


   Creates a fat routine descriptor in the system heap.
===========================*/
OSErr CreateFatDescriptorSys( void *mac68Code, void *ppcCode, ProcInfoType procInfo, UPP
*result )
{
   THz   oldZone;
   OSErr err = noErr;

   oldZone = GetZone();        /* Save current zone */
   SetZone( SystemZone() );    /* Get us in the system heap */

   #ifndef DO_PPC_CODE_ONLY
   *result = NewFatRoutineDescriptor( mac68Code, ppcCode, procInfo );
   #else
   *result = NewRoutineDescriptor( ppcCode, procInfo, kPowerPCISA ); /* debugging only
*/
   #endif

   SetZone( oldZone );

   return( *result ? noErr : memFullErr );
} /* end CreateFatDescriptorSys() */


/*===========================
   PostEvent68kStub


   This is the 68k version of PostEvent. Because it's a
   register-based trap, we have to use assembly code
```

```
to see what was passed to it. Because the routine
can't move memory (it might get called during an
interrupt), we also have to call a custom 68K
function that doesn't disturb the machine environment.
===========================*/

asm void PostEvent68kStub( void )
{
    // reserve space on stack for "real" PostEvent address
    sub.l      #4, SP

    // save registers (not A0 & D0, though)
    movem.l    A1-A5/D1-D7, -(SP)

    // push A0 & D0 on stack for call to MyPostEvent68k below
    // we must do this before SetUpA4 since it modifies registers
    move.l     D0, -(SP)         // push event message
    move.w     A0, -(SP)         // push event code

    jsr        SetUpA4           // give us global access

    // put address of "real" postevent in place reserved on stack
    // note that it is the first field in the gGlobals structure
    move.l     gGlobalsPtr, A0
    move.l     (A0), 54(SP)

    // call MyPostEvent68k
    // parameters are on the stack already
    // D0.w returns with the new event code
    jsr        MyPostEvent68k

    move.w     D0, A0            // A0.w = event code
    add.l      #2, SP            // clear old event code from stack
    move.l     (SP)+, D0         // restore event message from stack

    // restore registers
    movem.l    (SP)+, A1-A5/D1-D7

    // jump directly to original PostEvent code
    // the address was placed on the stack in the above code
    rts
} /* end PostEvent68kStub() */
```

```
pascal void GetMouse68kStub( Point *mouseLoc )
{
   long  oldA4;

   oldA4 = SetUpA4();
   MyGetMouse ( mouseLoc );
   RestoreA4( oldA4 );
} /* end GetMouse68kStub() */


#endif      /* 68k code */


/*

   @@@@@@@@@@@@@@@  Shared Code    @@@@@@@@@@@@@@@

   This code gets compiled into both 68k and PowerPC object code.
   The 68k code gets called from 68k patches & code.
   The powerpc code gets called from powerpc patches & code.

   If these routines were very large, or called infrequently, we could
   just have a single version that is called by the "other" object code,
   but it's not worth the hassle & context switch.
*/
Handle Get1ResourceSys( OSType rezType, short rezID )
{
   THz         oldZone;
   Handle      h;

   oldZone = GetZone();
   SetZone( SystemZone() );
   h = Get1Resource( rezType, rezID );
   SetZone( oldZone );
   return h;
} /* end Get1ResourceSys() */


/* Our custom GetMouse function. We do our screen stuff here because
   GetMouse is allowed to move memory, and is called frequently.
*/

void MyGetMouse( Point *pt )
{
long  currentDepth;
```

```
    if ( gGlobalsPtr->gRequestFlag )            /* Event is for us ? */
        {
        gGlobalsPtr->gRequestFlag = FALSE;      /* Clear flag or else get called indefinitely */
        currentDepth = Fetch_Depth();
        if ((currentDepth == BLACK_WHITE) && (currentDepth != gGlobalsPtr->gOldScreenDepth))
            Change_Depth(gGlobalsPtr->gOldScreenDepth);
        else
            Change_Depth(BLACK_WHITE);
        } /* end if */

    CallGetMouse( pt );                          /* Hop to original GetMouse() */

} /* end ourGetMouse() */

/*
    Note:
    returns the (possibly modified) event code

    Don't modify the local variables eventNum & eventMsg
        -- they're used by the stub routine and modifying
        -- locals here can have a global effect
*/
short MyPostEvent68k( short eventNum, long eventMsg )
{
short   newEventCode = eventNum;

    if ( (eventNum == keyDown) || (eventNum == autoKey) )
        {
        if ( (lowMemKeyModifiers == KEY_COMBO) && (lowMemKeyStroke == T_KEYCODE) )
            {
            newEventCode = nullEvent;            /* Suppress the event */
            gGlobalsPtr->gRequestFlag = TRUE;
            } /* end if KEY_COMBO && T_KEYCODE */
        } /* end if */

    return newEventCode;
} /* end MyPostEvent68k() */

#ifdef powerc
OSErr MyPostEventPPC( short eventNum, long eventMsg )
{
```

```
OSErr   result;

   if ( (eventNum == keyDown) || (eventNum == autoKey) )
      {
      if ( (lowMemKeyModifiers == KEY_COMBO) && (lowMemKeyStroke == T_KEYCODE) )
         {
         eventNum = nullEvent;              /* Suppress the event */
         gGlobalsPtr->gRequestFlag = TRUE;
         } /* end if KEY_COMBO && T_KEYCODE */
      } /* end if */

   result = CallPostEvent(eventNum, eventMsg);
   return result;
} /* end MyPostEventPPC() */

#endif

/* Get the current screen depth. Also get the GDevice of main screen and its
   device number (to use the driver) */
long Fetch_Depth(void)
{
long     screenDepth;                /* Current bit depth of our screen */
GDHandle thisGDevice;

   thisGDevice = GetMainDevice();                    /* Get GDevice of main screen */
   gGlobalsPtr->gOurGDevice = thisGDevice;           /* Hang onto this gDevice's handle */
   screenDepth = (**thisGDevice).gdMode;             /* Get current video mode */
   gGlobalsPtr->gDevRefNum = (**thisGDevice).gdRefNum;   /* Get screen's device ref. # */
   return screenDepth;

} /* end Fetch_Depth() */


/*
   Change screen depth. New screen depth is resource ID of
   a display mode the video hardware supports.
*/
void Change_Depth(long newDepth)
{
GrafPtr     oldPort;
Rect        ourGDRect;
```

```
RgnHandle    thisScreenBoundary;
GrafPtr      theBigPicture;
WindowPtr    theFrontWindow;

   HideCursor();                     /* Hide pointer since its depth will change */
/* At last we change the screen depth! */
   InitGDevice(gGlobalsPtr->gDevRefNum, newDepth, gGlobalsPtr->gOurGDevice);
   theFrontWindow = FrontWindow();
   ActivatePalette(theFrontWindow);   /* Use active window's color palette */
   AllocCursor();                     /* Draw cursor at new screen depth */
   ShowCursor();                      /* Put it back on-screen */

/* The desktop's still a mess: redraw it */
   thisScreenBoundary = NewRgn();     /* Get a region to hold this screen */
   if (!MemError())                   /* Trouble? */
      {                               /* No */
      ourGDRect = (**gGlobalsPtr->gOurGDevice).gdRect;
      RectRgn(thisScreenBoundary, &ourGDRect);   /* Get boundary of gDevice */
      GetPort(&oldPort);              /* Save current port */
      GetWMgrPort(&theBigPicture);    /* Get Desktop's port */
      SetPort(theBigPicture);         /* Make it the current port */
      DrawMenuBar();
      PaintOne(NIL, thisScreenBoundary);  /* Paint the background */
/* Now the other windows */
      PaintBehind( *(WindowPeek *) WindowList, thisScreenBoundary);
      SetPort(oldPort);
      DisposeRgn(thisScreenBoundary);
      } /* end if !MemError() */
   else
      SysBeep(30);                    /* Couldn't make the region, complain */

} /* end Change_Depth() */
```

Klepto.c

```
#include <Types.h>
#include <QuickDraw.h>
#include <Windows.h>
#include <Fonts.h>
#include <Memory.h>
#include <ToolUtils.h>
#include <StandardFile.h>
```

```c
#include <Errors.h>
#include <Resources.h>

/* Various constants */
#define NIL             0L
#define FALSE           false
#define TRUE            true
#define DEFAULT_VOL     0
#define ONE_FILE_TYPE   1
#define POWER_PC_FRAG   'PPC '              /* PowerPC resource type */
#define FRAG_ID         300                 /* PowerPC resource ID */

void Move_Fork(short input);
void main(void);

void Move_Fork(short input)
{
OSErr       fInputErr;
long        codeFragSize;
Handle      fragBuff;

   fInputErr = GetEOF(input, &codeFragSize);        /* Get file length */
   if ((fragBuff = NewHandle(codeFragSize)) != NIL)   /* Enough data buffer memory? */
      {
      if (!(fInputErr = FSRead(input, &codeFragSize, *fragBuff)))  /* Read in fragment */
         {                                          /* Treat buffer as a resource */
         AddResource(fragBuff, POWER_PC_FRAG, FRAG_ID, NIL);
         if (!ResError())                           /* Trouble? */
            {
            WriteResource(fragBuff);                /* Write frag to resource fork */
            if (ResError())
               SysBeep(30);
            } /* end if !ResError */
         } /* !fInputErr */
      } /* end if != NIL */
   UpdateResFile(CurResFile());                     /* Update file's resource map */
   ReleaseResource(fragBuff);                       /* Free the memory */
} /* end Move_Fork() */

void main(void)
{
unsigned char       fileName[14] = {"\pKlepto.π.rsrc"};
```

```
OSType          fileCreator = {'RSED'}; /* File type and creator for our output file */
OSType          fileType = {'rsrc'};
OSErr           fileError;
short           inFileRefNum, outFileRefNum;
StandardFileReply  inputReply, outputReply;
short           oldVol;
SFTypeList      shlbType = {'shlb'};     /* File type for shared libraries */
CursHandle      theCursor;               /* Current pointer icon */


/* Lunge after all the memory we can get */
   MaxApplZone();

/* Make sure we've got some master pointers */
   MoreMasters();
   MoreMasters();
   MoreMasters();
   MoreMasters();

/* Initialize managers */
   InitGraf(&qd.thePort);
   InitFonts();
   FlushEvents(everyEvent, 0);
   InitWindows();
   InitMenus();
   TEInit();
   InitDialogs(NIL);

/* Open the input file */
   StandardGetFile(NIL, ONE_FILE_TYPE, shlbType, &inputReply);
   if (inputReply.sfGood)
      {
      GetVol (NIL, &oldVol);           /* Save current volume */
      if ((fileError = FSpOpenDF (&inputReply.sfFile, fsCurPerm, &inFileRefNum)) != noErr)
         {
         SysBeep(30);
         return;
         } /* end if error */

/* Open the output file */
      StandardPutFile ("\pSave code fragment in:", fileName, &outputReply);
```

```
            if (outputReply.sfGood)
                {
                SetVol(NIL, outputReply.sfFile.vRefNum); /* Make the destination volume current */
                fileError = FSpCreate(&outputReply.sfFile, fileCreator, fileType, smSystemScript);
                switch(fileError)                        /* Process result from File Manager */
                    {
                    case noErr:
                    break;
                    case dupFNErr:                       /* File already exists, wipe it out */
                        if ((fileError = FSpDelete(&outputReply.sfFile)) == noErr)
                            {
                            if ((fileError = FSpCreate(&outputReply.sfFile, fileCreator,
                                                fileType, smSystemScript)) != noErr)
                                {
                                SysBeep(30);
                                FSClose (inFileRefNum);
                                SetVol(NIL, oldVol);
                                return;
                                } /* end if != noErr */
                            } /* end == noErr */
                        else
                            {
                            SysBeep(30);
                            FSClose (inFileRefNum);
                            SetVol(NIL, oldVol);
                            return;
                            } /* end else */
                    break;  /* end case dupFNErr */
                    default:                             /* Unknown error, try to abort cleanly */
                        SysBeep(30);
                        FSClose (inFileRefNum);          /* Close the input file */
                        SetVol(NIL, oldVol);             /* Restore original volume */
                        return;
                    } /* end switch */

/* Open file's data fork. We do this only to get a file ref number */
        if (!(FSpOpenDF (&outputReply.sfFile, fsCurPerm, &outFileRefNum)))
            {
/* MUST create resource map in resource fork or no resource writing occurs */
            FSpCreateResFile (&outputReply.sfFile, fileCreator, fileType, smSystemScript);
            if (!ResError())
                {
```

```
                FSpOpenResFile (&outputReply.sfFile, fsCurPerm);   /* Open resource fork */
                if (!ResError())
                    {
                    theCursor = GetCursor(watchCursor);            /* Change the cursor */
                    SetCursor(&**theCursor);
                    Move_Fork (inFileRefNum);
                    FSClose (outFileRefNum);
                    SetCursor(&qd.arrow);                          /* Restore the cursor */
                    } /* end if !ResError */
                } /* end if !ResError */
            FlushVol (NIL, outputReply.sfFile.vRefNum);
            } /* end if !FSpOpenDF */
        } /* end if outputReply.sfGood */
    FSClose (inFileRefNum);
    SetVol(NIL, oldVol);                                          /* Restore current volume */
    } /* end if inputReply.sfGood */

} /* end main() */
```

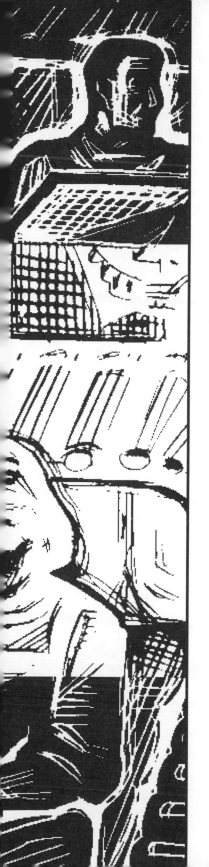

Where to Go for Help and Information

If you run into problems (remember, please don't contact Metrowerks directly for support until after you buy the commercial version of CodeWarrior) or if you just want to link up with other people using Metrowerks CodeWarrior, there are a number of forums on various online services that you can get involved in. To find out what forums are available and where you can find them, Metrowerks has established a system that will automatically send you a complete listing of the forums currently operating, product and order information, and the latest Metrowerks news.

To get this listing, you need to send an E-mail message to the Internet address **news@metrowerks.ca**. Any message will do. You're going to get an automatic response, so don't expect to have a conversation through this address. However, you will gets lots of valuable information.

How to Address Your Request

Even if you don't have direct access to the Internet, you can still send the request through most online services. If you don't know how, limited instructions are provided below. These give you the addressing schemes for Internet messages for some of the major services. If you need additional assistance, refer to a book on the Internet such as Hayden's *Internet Starter Kit for Macintosh*.

AppleLink

To send the request from AppleLink, add `@internet#` to the end of the address provided on the previous page. So send an E-mail message to: `news@metrowerks.ca@internet#`.

CompuServe

To send the request from CompuServe, add `>INTERNET:` to the beginning of the address. Thus, from CompuServe, address your request to: `>INTERNET:news@metrowerks.ca`.

GEnie

From GEnie, add `@inet#` to end of the address, like so: `news@metrowerks.ca@inet#`.

America Online

To send the request from AOL, just use the address `news@metrowerks.ca`.

Delphi

From Delphi you don't need to do anything special. Just use the address `news@metrowerks.ca`.

After You Get the List

After you receive the list, find a suitable forum and get into it. You can bet that there will be a lot of people to talk to and undoubtedly someone will have the same questions that you do. Who knows, you might even be able to answer someone else's questions!

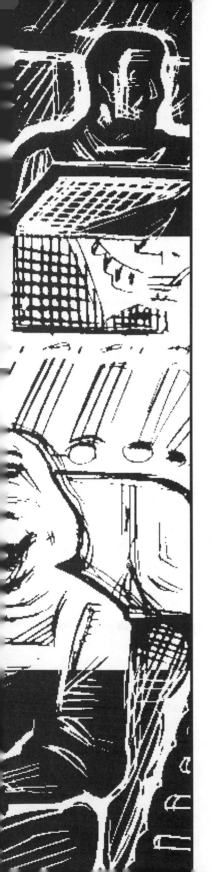

Glossary

A5 world   The area within a 68K application's memory partition that contains the application's global variables and references to functions in other code segments. (*See* Jump table.) All of the objects are referenced as offsets from a base address contained in the A5 register, hence the name.

API   Application Programming Interface. A standard or specification that describes an operating system's services and how to use them. The various Managers implement the Mac API.

Apple Events   An interapplications communications protocol that complies with the Apple Event Interprocess Messaging Protocol (AEIMP). It uses high-level events to communicate with other applications.

AppleScript   A programming language that automates repetitive operations or can control one or more Mac applications in a predefined sequence. It uses Apple Events to direct the applications.

Breakpoint   A software marker in program code that suspends the program's execution and transfers control to a debugger. Used to stop a faulty program's execution in suspect areas so that the code and variables can be examined just prior to a crash.

CISC   Complex Instruction Set Computing. So called because the machine instructions can perform a complicated set of operations. A single CISC instruction might fetch a value from memory, add a value to it, save the value elsewhere, and then index to a new memory location. These instructions achieve a high code density: That is, a small number of instructions can implement a sophisticated algorithm. The down side is that the processor requires a complex instruction decoder to decipher each instruction into its corresponding processor actions. *See also* RISC.

Code fragment   The basic unit of PowerPC executable code on the Power Macintosh. Code fragments can be shared libraries, applications, or stand-alone executable resources. They can be any size, and are usually stored in a file's data fork. The executable code in a Power Mac application is a single code fragment, although the architecture supports multiple sections of code.

Code Fragment Manager   The set of Mac OS routines that manage the loading and use of code fragments. The Process Manager uses the Code Fragment Manager to load a native Power Mac application's code fragment into the memory partition.

Code segment   A unit of 680x0 executable code, stored as a resource of type 'CODE'. Code segments usually have a maximum size of 32K. This is due to the fact that the program code uses only PC-relative instructions, whose offset limit was 32K.

Debugger, high-level   A debugging program that trades robustness for ease of use. It relies on the integrity of the operating system so that it offers a sophisticated interface. It displays the program under test as source code and lets you examine variables by name and in a variety of formats.

Debugger, low-level   A debugging program that uses minimal operating system resources and thus continues to function after a severe program crash. For this same reason, it also has a minimal user interface, although certain debuggers blur this definition by providing high-level debugger features.

DeRez   A MPW tool used to disassemble resources into a textual description that describes the resource. *See also* Rez.

Emulator   A program designed to read, interpret, and faithfully execute the machine code of another processor. The emulator program might be part of an application that mimics the environment and processor of another computer system (such as Insignia Solution's SoftWindows), or part of the operating system (such as the Power Mac's 68LC040 emulator).

Event   An action initiated by either the user or a computer subsystem. These events might be handled by an active application or the operating system. Low-level events are keystrokes, mouse clicks, and disk insertions. High-level events are messages sent between applications to request services.

Event loop   The program loop that's the heart of an event-driven application. The event loop constantly looks for any events sent to the application. The loop determines the type of event it has received and calls the appropriate functions to handle the event.

File fork   A stream of bytes on disk. The Mac's file system recognizes two types of forks in a file: a data fork that contains data created by an application or code fragments, and a resource fork that contains resources. *See also* Resources.

File signature   A pair of four-character codes that uniquely identify the file. The first code, called type, describes the file's contents, such as whether the file contains text data (type 'TEXT') or is an application (type 'APPL'). The creator code identifies the application that created the file (MacWrite Pro, Photoshop, or Excel, for example). The file's signature codes are stored in the desktop database for use by the file system.

IDE   Integrated Development Environment. A program, such as CodeWarrior or THINK C, that incorporates a program editor, compiler, and linker into one application. This enables a fast turnaround time in the development cycle and it also allows the various components to communicate information to one another.

ISA   Instruction Set Architecture. The instruction set and programming model of a processor.

Jump table   A table of addresses that points to functions in different 68K program segments. Each table entry contains either a function address or a trap word that invokes the Segment Loader to load the missing code segment into memory. These entries are referenced off a base address stored in register A5. *See also* A5 world.

Make   Compiling and linking library files to make an application or code resource. Often used as a verb, as in, "Make the SwitchBank application."

Manager   A group of related Mac OS routines, such as the Code Fragment Manager and File Manager.

Microcode   Software within a processor that directs portions of the processor hardware to execute the instruction. Typically found in CISC processors.

Modifier   A key that changes the meaning of other keystrokes when it is held down. The modifier keys are Shift, Control, Option, and Command keys.

MPW   Macintosh Programmers Workshop. A term for Apple's collection of development tools.

Native   A program or code resource, written in PowerPC code, as in a "native" application.

PC relative addressing   A program whose machine instructions make jumps to other portions of the program, relative to the current address in the program counter (PC). This enables the program code to be position-independent. On the 68000 processor, the largest offset possible was 32K.

PEF   Preferred Executable Format. Developed by Apple, this file format stores PowerPC code in a compact form. All code fragments are stored in the PEF layout.

PlainTalk   The voice recognition software and text-to-speech engine used in AV Macs and AV Power Macs.

Procedure   The Pascal equivalent to a C function.

Process   A running application or task.

Project   A CodeWarrior file that encompasses all of the information required to build a program. It contains references to the source files, object files, symbols, and the preferences for various components in the integrated environment.

QuickTime   A collection of routines used to create, control, and display time-dependent data, such as sounds or digital movies.

Rez   A MPW tool used to compile textual descriptions of a resource into a binary format.

RISC   Reduced Instruction Set Computing. A processor/instruction set design that uses simple instructions to achieve high throughput. While each instruction might not accomplish as much as a CISC instruction, a RISC processor's pipelines enable it to process more instructions over a given interval and at a constant rate.

Resource   Data or code stored in a special format. Each resource has a type and ID number that uniquely identifies the resource to the Mac OS. The resource type tells the Resource Manager how to interpret the resource's contents.

Routine   A Toolbox function. The term is used to differentiate between your program functions and those written by Apple to implement the Mac API.

Routine descriptor   A data structure used to identify to the Mixed Mode Manager what ISA the routine is written in and the type of arguments the routine requires.

SANE   Standard Apple Numeric Environment. A hardware-independent library of floating-point math routines.

Segment   *See* Code segment.

Segment Loader   The part of the Mac OS used by the Process Manager to load 68K code segments into a memory partition.

Shared library   A code fragment that exports routine names and data. This makes it capable of being shared among two or more applications. The first application requiring the library's services has the Code Fragment Manager load it into memory. The shared library is removed from memory when it is no longer used by any application.

Stand-alone code   Code loaded and executed in place. Contrast this to application code, where the Process Manager builds an A5 world for the program code (68K application) or the Code Fragment Manager prepares a code fragment for execution (native Power Mac application).

TOC   Table of Contents. The TOC resides in the code fragment's data area and contains pointers to data in an application's own code fragment or to data or functions in other code fragments. Portions of the TOC are set up by the Code Fragment Manager when it prepares a code fragment for execution.

Tool   A program that has little or no interface code. It only operates within the environment provided for it by the MPW shell or ToolServer.

Toolbox   The collection of basic system routines that implements the Mac API. Technically, the Toolbox handles most low-level system services, while other services, such a File I/O and printing, are considered operating system routines. To minimize confusion, both types of routines are grouped under this term.

Transition vector   A data structure used by one code fragment to access a function in another code fragment. The structure consists of one pointer to the target fragment's TOC and a second pointer to a function within the target code fragment.

Trap   A 68K instruction that causes an error condition or exception. The processor automatically responds to this exception by calling a handler written to deal with the problem. Apple uses certain trap values to route a 68K program's execution to the Toolbox routines.

UPP   Universal Procedure Pointer. A data structure that's wrapped around a procedure (function) pointer and describes the target function's ISA, argument passing convention, and the size of each argument.

XCOFF   Extended Common Object File Format. A file format for Macintosh PowerPC binary files. It's an enhancement of a binary file format used by UNIX workstations. This format is prevalent on IBM RS/6000 workstations and is partially supported by the Code Fragment Manager. XCOFF files were used during Power Macintosh development while the operating system was being written using IBM development tools.

Index

Symbols

A

E

F

G

H-I

U-V-W

X-Y-Z

To Order:

Fax to: (419) 281-6883 or call (800) 247-6553

or Mail to: **BookMasters**
1444 U.S. Route 42, RD 11
Mansfield, OH 44903

For Sales info:

Metrowerks Inc.
Attention: Matt Vacaro
Suite 300, 1500 du College
St. Laurent, QC
H4L 5G6 Canada
Voice: (514) 747-5999, ext 301
                    (617) 246-4525
Fax: (514) 747-2822
applelink: saleswerks

Software License

PLEASE READ THIS LICENSE CAREFULLY BEFORE USING THE SOFTWARE.

BY USING THE SOFTWARE, YOU ARE AGREEING TO BE BOUND BY THE TERMS OF THIS LICENSE. IF YOU DO NOT AGREE TO THE TERMS OF THIS LICENSE, PROMPTLY RETURN THE UNUSED SOFTWARE TO THE PLACE WHERE YOU OBTAINED IT AND YOUR MONEY WILL BE REFUNDED.

1. License. The application, demonstration, system, and other software accompanying this License, whether on disk, in read only memory, or on any other media (the "Software"), the related documentation, and fonts are licensed to you by Metrowerks. You own the disk on which the Software and fonts are recorded, but Metrowerks and/or Metrowerks' Licensors retain title to the Software, related documentation, and fonts. This License allows you to use the Software and fonts on a single Apple computer and make one copy of the Software and fonts in machine-readable form for backup purposes only. You must reproduce on such copy the Metrowerks copyright notice and any other proprietary legends that were on the original copy of the Software and fonts. You may also transfer all your license rights in the Software and fonts, the backup copy of the Software and fonts, the related documentation, and a copy of this License to another party, provided the other party reads and agrees to accept the terms and conditions of this License.

2. Restrictions. The Software contains copyrighted material, trade secrets and other proprietary material. In order to protect them, and except as permitted by applicable legislation, you may not decompile, reverse engineer, disassemble or otherwise reduce the Software to a human-perceivable form. You may not modify, network, rent, lease, loan, distribute or create derivative works based upon the Software in whole or in part. You may not electronically transmit the Software from one computer to another or over a network.

3. Termination. This License is effective until terminated. You may terminate this License at any time by destroying the Software, related documentation and fonts and all copies thereof. This License will terminate immediately without notice from Metrowerks if you fail to comply with any provision of this License. Upon termination you must destroy the Software, related documentation and fonts and all copies thereof.

4. Export Law Assurances. You agree and certify that neither the Software nor any other technical data received from Metrowerks, nor the direct product thereof, will be exported outside the United States except as authorized and as permitted by the laws and regulations of the United States. If the Software has been rightfully obtained by you outside of the United States, you agree that you will not re-export the Software nor any other technical data received from Metrowerks, nor the direct product thereof, except as permitted by the laws and regulations of the United States and the laws and regulations of the jurisdiction in which you obtained the Software.

5. Government End Users. If you are acquiring the Software and fonts on behalf of any unit or agency of the United States Government, the following provisions apply. The Government agrees:

(i) if the Software and fonts are supplied to the Department of Defense (DoD), the Software and fonts are classified as "Commercial Computer Software" and the Government is acquiring only "restricted rights" in the Software, its documentation and fonts as that term is defined in Clause 252.227-7013(c)(1) of the DFARS; and

(ii) if the Software and fonts are supplied to any unit or agency of the United States Government other than DoD, the Government's rights in the Software, its documentation and fonts will be as defined in Clause 52.227-19(c)(2) of the FAR or, in the case of NASA, in Clause 18-52.227-86(d) of the NASA Supplement to the FAR.

6. Limited Warranty on Media. Metrowerks warrants the diskettes and/or compact disc on which the Software and fonts are recorded to be free from defects in materials and workmanship under normal use for a period of ninety (90) days from the date of purchase as evidenced by a copy of the receipt. Metrowerks' entire liability and your exclusive remedy will be replacement of the diskettes and/or compact disc not meeting Metrowerks' limited warranty and which is returned to Metrowerks or a Metrowerks authorized representative with a copy of the receipt. Metrowerks will have no responsibility to replace a disk/disc damaged by accident, abuse or misapplication. ANY IMPLIED WARRANTIES ON THE DISKETTES AND/OR COMPACT DISC, INCLUDING THE IMPLIED WARRANTIES OF MERCHANTABILITY AND FITNESS FOR A PARTICULAR PURPOSE, ARE LIMITED IN DURATION TO NINETY (90) DAYS FROM THE DATE OF DELIVERY. THIS WARRANTY GIVES YOU SPECIFIC LEGAL RIGHTS, AND YOU MAY ALSO HAVE OTHER RIGHTS WHICH VARY BY JURISDICTION.

7. Disclaimer of Warranty on Apple Software. You expressly acknowledge and agree that use of the Software and fonts is at your sole risk. The Software, related documentation and fonts are provided "AS IS" and without warranty of any kind and Metrowerks and Metrowerks' Licensor(s) (for the purposes of provisions 7 and 8, Metrowerks and Metrowerks' Licensor(s) shall be collectively referred to as "Metrowerks") EXPRESSLY DISCLAIM ALL WARRANTIES, EXPRESS OR IMPLIED, INCLUDING, BUT NOT LIMITED TO, THE IMPLIED WARRANTIES OF MERCHANTABILITY AND FITNESS FOR A PARTICU-LAR PURPOSE. METROWERKS DOES NOT WARRANT THAT THE FUNCTIONS CON-TAINED IN THE SOFTWARE WILL MEET YOUR REQUIREMENTS, OR THAT THE OPERA-TION OF THE SOFTWARE WILL BE UNINTERRUPTED OR ERROR-FREE, OR THAT DEFECTS IN THE SOFTWARE AND THE FONTS WILL BE CORRECTED. FURTHERMORE, METROWERKS DOES NOT WARRANT OR MAKE ANY REPRESENTATIONS REGARDING THE USE OR THE RESULTS OF THE USE OF THE SOFTWARE AND FONTS OR RELATED DOCUMENTATION IN TERMS OF THEIR CORRECTNESS, ACCURACY, RELIABILITY, OR OTHERWISE. NO ORAL OR WRITTEN INFORMATION OR ADVICE GIVEN BY METROWERKS OR A METROWERKS AUTHORIZED REPRESENTATIVE SHALL CREATE A WARRANTY OR IN ANY WAY INCREASE THE SCOPE OF THIS WARRANTY. SHOULD THE SOFTWARE PROVE DEFECTIVE, YOU (AND NOT METROWERKS OR A METROWERKS AUTHORIZED REPRESENTATIVE) ASSUME THE ENTIRE COST OF ALL NECESSARY

SERVICING, REPAIR OR CORRECTION. SOME JURISDICTIONS DO NOT ALLOW THE EXCLUSION OF IMPLIED WARRANTIES, SO THE ABOVE EXCLUSION MAY NOT APPLY TO YOU.

8. Limitation of Liability. UNDER NO CIRCUMSTANCES INCLUDING NEGLIGENCE, SHALL METROWERKS BE LIABLE FOR ANY INCIDENTAL, SPECIAL OR CONSEQUEN-TIAL DAMAGES THAT RESULT FROM THE USE OR INABILITY TO USE THE SOFTWARE OR RELATED DOCUMENTATION, EVEN IF METROWERKS OR A METROWERKS AUTHO-RIZED REPRESENTATIVE HAS BEEN ADVISED OF THE POSSIBILITY OF SUCH DAM-AGES. SOME JURISDICTIONS DO NOT ALLOW THE LIMITATION OR EXCLUSION OF LIABILITY FOR INCIDENTAL OR CONSEQUENTIAL DAMAGES SO THE ABOVE LIMITA-TION OR EXCLUSION MAY NOT APPLY TO YOU.

In no event shall Metrowerks' total liability to you for all damages, losses, and causes of action (whether in contract, tort (including negligence) or otherwise) exceed the amount paid by you for the Software and fonts.

9. Controlling Law and Severability. This License shall be governed by and construed in accordance with the laws of the United States and the State of California, as applied to agreements entered into and to be performed entirely within California between California residents. If for any reason a court of competent jurisdiction finds any provision of this License, or portion thereof, to be unenforceable, that provision of the License shall be enforced to the maximum extent permissible so as to effect the intent of the parties, and the remainder of this License shall continue in full force and effect.

10. Complete Agreement. This License constitutes the entire agreement between the parties with respect to the use of the Software, the related documentation and fonts, and supersedes all prior or contemporaneous understandings or agreements, written or oral, regarding such subject matter. No amendment to or modification of this License will be binding unless in writing and signed by a duly authorized representative of Metrowerks.

METROWERKS AND METROWERKS' LICENSOR(S), AND THEIR DIRECTORS, OFFICERS, EMPLOYEES OR AGENTS (COLLECTIVELY METROWERKS) MAKE NO WARRANTIES, EXPRESS OR IMPLIED, INCLUDING WITHOUT LIMITATION THE IMPLIED WARRANTIES OF MERCHANTABILITY AND FITNESS FOR A PARTICULAR PURPOSE, REGARDING THE SOFTWARE. METROWERKS DOES NOT WARRANT, GUARANTEE OR MAKE ANY REPRESENTATIONS REGARDING THE USE OR THE RESULTS OF THE USE OF THE SOFTWARE IN TERMS OF ITS CORRECTNESS, ACCURACY, RELIABILITY, CURRENTNESS OR OTHERWISE. THE ENTIRE RISK AS TO THE RESULTS AND PERFORMANCE OF THE SOFTWARE IS ASSUMED BY YOU. THE EXCLUSION OF IMPLIED WARRANTIES IS NOT PERMITTED BY SOME JURISDICTIONS. THE ABOVE EXCLUSION MAY NOT APPLY TO YOU.

IN NO EVENT WILL METROWERKS AND METROWERKS' LICENSOR(S), AND THEIR DIRECTORS, OFFICERS, EMPLOYEES OR AGENTS (COLLECTIVELY METROWERKS) BE LIABLE TO YOU FOR ANY CONSEQUENTIAL, INCIDENTAL OR INDIRECT DAMAGES (INCLUDING DAMAGES FOR LOSS OF BUSINESS PROFITS, BUSINESS INTERRUPTION, LOSS OF BUSINESS INFORMATION, AND THE LIKE) ARISING OUT OF THE USE OR INABILITY TO USE THE SOFTWARE EVEN IF METROWERKS HAS BEEN ADVISED OF THE POSSIBILITY OF SUCH DAMAGES. BECAUSE SOME JURISDICTIONS DO NOT ALLOW THE EXCLUSION OR LIMITATION OF LIABILITY FOR CONSEQUENTIAL OR INCIDENTAL DAMAGES, THE ABOVE LIMITATIONS MAY NOT APPLY TO YOU. Metrowerks liability to you for actual damages from any cause whatsoever, and regardless of the form of the action (whether in contract, tort (including negligence), product liability or otherwise), will be limited to $1.

What You'll Find on the CD

The Power Macintosh Programming Starter Kit CD contains a limited version of Metrowerks CodeWarrior as well as all sample code discussed in the book. This version of Metrowerks CodeWarrior is limited in that it can only be used with the code provided on the CD. Certain commands (such as New Project and Add File...) have been disabled. But, this version retains the functionality of CodeWarrior except for those functions. So, you can use almost all of CodeWarrior's features to learn to program your Power Mac. You can even run it on a 68K Mac as well!

Metrowerks cannot provide technical support for this limited version of CodeWarrior bundled with the "Starter Kit". If you have trouble, see appendix D for where to go for help, but please do not call Metrowerks until you have purchased the fully-functioning version of CodeWarrior.

Using the CD is simple; just pop the disc into your drive and dive in. You probably will want to read chapter 2 first so you can get a good idea of how to use CodeWarrior.